Jehovah
the First Godfather

An Agnostic's View
of the Bible, God and Religion

By
Carlton Morris

Olympus Story House
www.olympusstoryhouse.com

I wish to express my eternal thanks and gratitude to Sue Gilpin and Kathy Johnson for their astute insight, suggestions and hard work without which this manuscript may never have been completed.

DEDICATION

It is dedicated to the seekers of religious truths and to the lost souls who have never been fortunate enough to have found peace in the worship of their god, their faith or their religion. It is for the individual whose prayers have never been answered and it is for those whose faith in their god has never been strong enough to move the mountain now they will be able to understand why.

INTRODUCTION

This book is a critique, a review of the Christian Bible, the Old and New Testament books of the Christian Bible from a new and unique perspective. It is a perspective that will never be heard preached from the pulpit or taught in Sunday school. It is not a contradiction to what has been written. That is man's basic concept of his God', man and religious as it has been taught and believed for the last couple of thousand years. It is a realistic examination of biblical scripture, not from how it has been understood and interpreted by the ancient religious leaders, scholars and theologians but from what is now the factual and understood modern scientific and medical technology.

What was once assumed to be a truth behind the biblical story of Genesis was based on a belief that the story came from a being believed to be a god. Therefore the Genesis story must be true and therefore says exactly what God said means what he meant.

This book does not intend to alter in any way what has been written. It merely offers to the religious disciple a different and unique perspective that more completely explains the scriptures upon which he bases his religious faith and beliefs.

It is a new and different perspective by which a religious disciple is able to not only more fully understand the scriptural message but how that understanding can enhance and benefit their existing reality, their religious belief and reality.

If true what is written and understood from this unique perspective reveals for the first time the true identity of the biblical gods, their purpose on earth and how and why they created man as their slave and servant. It is a perspective supported by scripture and provides a realistic explanation for the existence of the gods of man and his relationship with them. It is a realistic examination of the biblical beginning, the creation of first man and Jewish history.

In every known culture in the world today whether it is civilized or barbaric the people of those cultures believe in, worship, pray and offer up sacrifices to a god or gods of some kind. Those gods may take many different forms, and are known by many different names, but each and every one is a vital part of the everyday life and culture of that community. All religious disciples regardless of their faith are led by religious leaders who are also called by many different names that are recognized and unique to particular religious denomination, faith, cult or sect.

Jewish leaders are called rabbis; Catholics are governed by their priests while Protestant leaders go by the names of pastor and minister. However, almost all religious leaders regardless of the faith are referred to as your Reverent or your Eminence.

In Islam their Holy Men are called Ayatollahs or Imam. The followers Buddha, Confucius, Taoist, witch doctors of Africa they like the shaman and the medicine men of the aborigine are unique to their particular religious faith and rituals. Each of these leaders may be a follower of one or many gods but each serve as holy men and are the intermediaries between their god and their congregations.

These gods and their followers may be good or bad according to the desires of the believers, but they all have one thing in common. Whatever their belief, they have a subconscious belief in, fear of, and a desire to serve and obey their particular god. Whether this need and desire was a part of the original programming of man, or one he has imposed upon himself out of fear, ignorance and tradition is immaterial. The desire is there, it exists and for man it needs to be obeyed.

But exactly what does the average individual really know about the Deity and the religious faith they so fervently serve except for what one learned by attending the devotional services of their faith and what they are taught by their religious leaders? Statically the average individual knows practical nothing about the reality of their god, their faith or how it began.

This book. "Jehovah the First Godfather" has absolutely nothing to do with any religious organization especially the one known as the Jehovah Witnesses. This book cannot and does not speak for all religions. it does however address the beginning of the Jewish and Christian faiths based on the scriptural text of the Torah, the writings of the Old Testament prophets and New Testament apostles.

Jehovah the First Godfather is a critique of the Christian Bible from a new and unique perspective. It is a perspective that will never be preached from the pulpit or heard taught in Sunday school.

This perspective is a biblical revelation that each and every individual must understand from their own spiritual, emotional and religious reality if it is to be of any realistic value to their lives.

Jehovah the First Godfather is a realistic review of the history of the Jewish people and their relationship with their god according to what has been recorded in scripture.

This review has a message for each and every religious disciple regardless of their faith or denomination. It is a message that must be understood by each individual according their beliefs and religious background if the message is to have any meaning for them and their religious beliefs.

This book began as a revelation that generated an obligation that required me to reveal what I believe to be a biblical truth. It is not a truth that has been taught and believed by organized religion for the last four to five thousand years but according to a truth that can be understood and accepted because of the modern medical and scientific miracles of today.

Both the Jewish and Protestant religions base their religious faith and beliefs on their understanding and interpretations of the Torah and the writings found in the Old and New Testament.

These writings are not the stories of man or the human species but of one people, the descendents of two mortal flesh and blood beings identified in religious scripture as the Lord God and his subordinate Yahweh (Jehovah), the God of Abraham. Scripture is the recorded relationship that existed between the descendents of these two individuals.

Because this relationship was not understood by the ancient theologians and in their failure to acknowledge what was recorded in scripture the Lord God and Jehovah became one, the God of Abraham, Isaac, Jacob and the Jewish Nation. Jehovah became the Lord God and the authority responsible not only for the creation of man and the god of organized Jewish and Christian religions but of creation itself.

But what if what man has been taught and led to believe was only a half truth? The creation of man happened because he exists. The gods exist in one form or another because we have records of their exploits and relationships with man. These are some of the truths. What is not a truth is the misunderstood reason for the creation of man and his relationship with his creator. The truth is recorded in scripture but until today has never been understood.

The science of today confirms the biblical description of the beginning of creation and what is believed to have happened in the manner that was recorded by Moses in Genesis over six thousand years ago.

The misunderstanding and interpretation of scripture begins with the creation and purpose of man by an alien species of organic life that was a part of the beginning creation of all that exists. Because of that misunderstanding man has for thousands of years been worshiping his ancestors, mortal beings that he had elevated to the status of gods in confused aftermath created by the biblical flood. Before the flood there were no gods only slaves and their mortal masters.

For the Jewish people their faith is founded on their history and understanding of the Torah and the writings of the Old Testament prophets as they were interpreted by their religious leaders. The Christians also use these writing but to support the New Testament teachings and writings of the apostles It helps them to understand the teachings and interpretations of their believed savior Jesus, the Christ. It is their belief that one cannot know the present or the future without knowing the past.

The Holy or Christian Bible is in reality a small collection of individual writings or books, short stories if you will that were deemed to be holy by the ancient scholars and theologians only because they referred in one way or another to their god and his relationship with the people.

Each book or short story while it was written either by an Old Testament prophet or a New Testament apostle is each concerned with either an individual or some special event that concerned an association of some kind with the biblical god and as such was therefore considered important enough to become holy writ.

Jehovah the First Godfather is just another one of the thousands of books concerning God that have over the generations been put into print. It is not holy writ because I have had no heavenly vision, spoke to no angelic angel, heard no voices and I certainly did not talk with God. I did have a revelation, an insight into scripture that began as a single thought. That thought became the key that helped me to begin to understand the scriptures from a new and unique perspective. It did not happen overnight. It took ten years of biblical study and research before that revelation was able to evolve into a perspective that gave logic and support to the scripture and the story of man and his beginning.

The book of Genesis is a simple story that when understood from a new perspective brings a logical and a realistic understanding of the scriptures. It gives meaning to what has been written by clarifying the purpose of the gods, their reasons for creating man and in explaining the relationship that existed then between God and man then and how that relationship effects man today.

In essence Genesis is the story of the beginning of creation, the steps involved and what was created as seen through the eyes of an alien life form told and recorded by the biblical prophet Moses. That life form was Jehovah the God of Abraham, Isaac, Jacob and Esau.

"Jehovah the First Godfather" is a critique of the Genesis story from a new and unique perspective. It is a perspective that is supported by scripture and brings clarity to what has been written misunderstood and taken out of context for over six thousand years.

This book and perspective began in August of 1988 when on vacation in Canada doing some research trying to find as much information as possible on the existence of aliens and UFO's. I was a member of MENSA and had been asked to participate in a debate as to whether aliens did or did not exist. I agreed. I found what I was looking for, the proof I needed to support my position that both aliens and UFO's were a fact of life and very real in the makeup and history of man. It was the biblical description of the creation of Eve created from the red blood cells of Adam that justifies that belief..

That description was the key that opened Pandora's Box and allowed me to understand for the first time the biblical mystery of the creation of man and his genetic biological relationship with his gods. I now understood why it became necessary for man to understand the how and why of his existence. In that moment all of the pieces of the biblical puzzle began to come together and gave me what I need to justify my belief in the existence of alien gods this was confirmed when they created Eve as a wife and companion to Adam and gave them the laws, customs and traditions that they were to live man became modified subculture of their race and society.

When man was given the laws, culture and traditions It was based on that of our their existence and the beginning of man's culture and civilized society. It was based on that of the highly evolved pieces that I needed to put the puzzle together were right before my eyes. It had all been recorded five thousand years ago.

To understand the Genesis story one must realize and accept that organic life in forms and dimensions beyond our imagination has to exist everywhere within the known universal or man himself would not exist. He does exist because he is a modified form of life cloned from a life form one that already existed, the Living Creature". This is not blasphemy but fact and is clarified in scripture by the biblical description of the creation of both Adam and Eve.

In addition to the Living Creature" are the Seraphim and Cherubim who accompanied and protected the "Living Creature".

Eve was cloned from the red blood cells of Adam who had been cloned from the DNA and blood cells of the Lord God. This understanding of how man began does not change the fact that he was created it only gives us an explanation of how it was accomplished. There was no magic, spiritual or divine power involved only sound medical and scientific principles. We know this to be true because that technology exists today and is being used to modify and enhance more a few forms of existing life on this planet.

My biblical understanding came with the word clone and the description of the creation of Eve. That understanding gave me a unique insight into the differences between what I was taught by the church and what I came to understand about biblical scripture. What I found was what I now believe to be a biblical truth, one that had been hidden from man from his beginning of his creation...

I had in my hand the key to open Pandora's Box and release all of the misunderstood religious contradictions and beliefs that had plagued man throughout his history.

There are no biblical mysteries only misunderstood interpretations and misrepresentations of the facts, events and individuals that made up the Bible and Jewish History.

Jehovah the First Godfather is an attempt to clarify those misunderstandings and interpretations. It is a modern attempt to make things right by understanding the past as it is revealed by the science and medical miracles of today.

To do this it becomes necessary to examine not only what was written and to determine what was not that supports what was.

When Genesis is examined from this perspective it becomes a short narrative of the beginning of creation and the beginning and evolution of organic life beyond earth in forms and dimensions beyond the imagination of man.

According to scripture movable organic life began during the fifth creative time era almost 6 billion years ago, a time when the earth was still young. Life existed and it evolved and in that evolutionary process created many different forms and diverse forms. One of those forms was the Living Creation. It grew, it evolved, gained knowledge and wisdom and one reached for the stars. In their travels they stepped down on many different worlds. Earth was one of those worlds. According to scripture there is evidence that they may have at some time in the past tried to colonize this planet. That attempt evidently failed because all we have today to verify that attempt are some very ancient and unique artifacts,

The Genesis story is a brief explanation of their most recent attempt and that attempt was not to colonize the planet but to mine it. With the creation of Eve they succeeded in doing both.

With the creation of Eve given as a wife came biological reproduction, children, families, laws, customs and traditions. A community guided and governed by an emerging civilized society. Man, a cloned modified subspecies of the gods began a part of their culture.

To justify this concept we can begin with the first question, exactly who were the beings that came to this planet? Why did they come and what did they do when they got here?

If man was created by the spoken word of God as taught and preached by organized religion why would a divine power capable of creating a universe have a discussion concerning the shape and form of a new life form they intended to create? Who was involved in this discussion and to what purpose?

Why was gold, the onyx stone and bdellium considered so important that they are recorded in the beginning of scripture and biblical history?

How was Adam and Eve and first man, biological life forms created outside of the normal biological reproductive process? What were purpose and relationship with the Lord God the power and authority responsible for their creation? Why were special animals created before the creation of Eve and females? Why were laws, regulations and commandments given to the newly created male and female creatures? The answers to these questions are just a few pieces of the puzzle that helps to explain the existence of the gods and their relationship with and religion.

When we begin to answer these questions the misunderstood biblical picture begins to come together. It is a far different picture than the one seen by the religious disciples of the past six thousand years.

Biblical wisdom comes with an understanding of the Genesis story explained without religious mysticism. and the realization that the Bible, the Old and New Testament are first of all the saga of the Jewish people and has basically no relationship to the human species except that the biblical Adam and Eve were only one small aspect of the biblical history of man. The Old and New Testament is a collection of short stories and letters that have nothing to do with mankind but with places, events and unique individuals that were governed and controlled by a belief in a mortal entity that was believed to be a divine god.

The history and saga of the Jewish people began with the Lord God, while he and the other gods of man did come from the stars it was from a planet similar to earth. They were an alien form of organic life that came into existence during the fifth era of creation. That life evolved, gained knowledge and wisdom and reached for the stars. Eventually they came to this planet first as explorers, then as colonists and finally as a mining conglomerate in search of gold, the onyx stone and bdellium.

The Lord God was one of the leader of that mining conglomerate of several companies each led by a Lord God. The word Lord God was nothing more than a title of power and authority. The biblical Lord God and his crew through ignorance and superstitions of the men and society they created eventually became the religious gods of man. They were not divine until they received that status from the survivors of the biblical flood.

The gods came to this planet as a mining conglomerate to mine for gold, the onyx stone and bdellium, a fragrant gum resin considered important by their society.

When the conglomerate made up of several mining companies landed on this planet they separated and each company led by their individual Lord God and his crew proceeded to the mining location that had been assigned to them. Each of these locations were rich in gold and the onyx stone. Each company was led by a leader identified as the Lord God and each company created their own Adam and Eve and the slaves need to mine the gold and process the ore to obtain that gold.

Each company created their group of slaves in their image and after their likeness and did so not out of love but a commercial necessity This slave labor, even though they were cloned modified repodtion of the gods themselves were expendable and would be abandoned when the conglomerate completed their mission and left the earth leaving behind a world of single males This had to be the intent of the miners. This idea is justified because logically there were no females, wives, children or families for the first couple of hundred years. With only male companionship the emotional and biological libido began to take effect on the workers nd their duties. In an attempt to resolve this problem relationships developed among the workers that began to created problems for the gods.

To solve this problem special animals were designed and created. When the failed to satisfy the needs of the slaves and working environment it was decided to change the mining mission to one of colonization. The gods created the biblical Eves as wives and helpmates for both man and the gods. Eve was seduced by one of the gods, became pregnant and gave birth to Cain it was the beginning of biological reproduction, the end of required cloning and the unification of two families the Lord God and Jehovah. Cain was the first born of a god and his descendant. Adam , Eve, Abel and Seth were not.

Jehovah the First Godfather is only concern with one of those companies, the one led by the Lord God of Ethiopia. It was he who was the power and authority responsibly for the creation of the Adam and Eve. Cloned from his DNA they were his flesh and blood kin. They were slaves but also a subspecies of his highly evolved cultured society. Adam was a modified of the Lord God in his image nd after his likeness, logically the Lord God was in the image and after the likeness of his created clone.

Even though Adam was a modified clone of the Lord God created without a father or mother he was created from the DNA of the Lord God which automatically makes him a genetic and biological offspring of the Lord God, his son. When it came time to create a female the medical and scientific staff of the Lord God put Adam sleep, They removed one of his ribs closed the incision closed and took the rib to the laboratory where he medical staff again modified the altered blood of Adam to create a female of the new sub-species of the alien gods. How that was accomplished will be discussed later. For the moment The Lord Gods of each the mining companies now had the beginnings of a new line of descendents. The only one this book is concerned with is the line of descendents of the Lord God that began with Adam Eve and Seth but not Cain who was sired by Samuel the household supervisor of Eve.

Thus began the long road of evolution that took Adam and Eve as the kin and descendents of the lord from slavery before the flood to a rich and powerful nation after it. The broad was made longer by the introduction of religion, misunderstood sacrifices and rituals.

It all started when the company led by biblical Lord God established his camp at the head waters of four great rivers. He planted a garden for food and through the process of genetic engineering by his medical and scientific engineers began to create the slave labor he needed to mine the gold, process the ore and care for and serve the needs of the Lord God and his crew.

While he was organizing and establishing the location of the mines and what need to be accomplished to begin the mining operations his medical and scientific staff had taken his DNA, RNA and chromosomes and were in the process of modified that DNA, RNA and chromosome in order to created a proto type of a new life form suitable to work, and survive on this planet.

When that proto type, Adam was found functional and satisfactory the DNA of his crew became the basic material for the creation of the rest of this new life modified life forms that would now serve and meet the needs of the gods.

The aliens came to this planet as a mining conglomerate to mine for minerals which included gold, the onyx stone *an bdellium.*

They needed labor to work the mine, process the ore and care for the basic needs of the camp. Using their medical and scientific skills they proceed to create this new life form in their image and after their likeness through a process known today as genetic engineering. These clones workers were not created out love as depicted by organized religion but out of commercial necessity.

The alien mining conglomerate consisted of several companies each given the mining rights to specific locations around the planet. The signs and emblems of those companies can be seen from the air and are call the Nazca Lines.

Man and the human species became a new and functioning life form because he was created from the DNA, RNA and chromosomes of a race of organic life that was ancient while th earth was still young.

Man in and the human species are modified clone of that ancient race. This is all a part of the Genesis story that no one ever took time to look at because until recently genetic engineering was beyond the ability of man to understand.

The gods of man may have come a different world but because we carry the same DNA which we receive from them when we were cloned both species can biologically mate and reproduce offspring. Those offspring were known in biblical times as "mighty men of old".

In my youth I was a dedicated disciple and in my search for enlightenment, wisdom and a better and deeper understanding of my faith I asked many questions and received no answers. I now understand why. It was because at that time the answers to my questions and the biblical truth were still hidden behind the misunderstood interpretations of the past.

But I now had the key that I hoped would open Pandora's Box of biblical miracles where I hoped to find the answers too many of the questions that I hope would bring clarity to my religious faith and beliefs.

This key was the beginning of a new perspective and a whole new world of religious deceptions to explore.

When I opened the box it was to a whole new world of gods, man and religion that denied everything I had ever been taught by the church and my religious faith.

This revelation answered almost all of my questions and gave me a completely new understanding of the Genesis story. A story that was straight forward but misunderstood not by what was written but what was not recorded that gave support to what was.

It was a realistic reality that was given to man at the time Jehovah revealed the beginning of creation. This understanding did not come from a divine experience but a revelation that had been a part of my subconscious. This reality had been locked away and passed down to me through all of the past generations of my family. It had been waiting for the right moment, a time when I was ready to accept and understand what I was about to receive.

Christians believe in the infallibility of Holy Bible. That belief is based on their acceptance of their religious faith and the belief that scriptures are the direct words and commands of God. The Jewish people also rely on what they believe to be the Holy Books of the Old Testament as the words of God passed down to them through the prophets.

We will rely on the faith of those words as we begin to decipher the meanings and the reality of the words that most of the various religious denominations of man consider sacred.

The followers of God and the believers of the various faiths fall into three categories: those who believe that every word written in their holy book was inspired by God and that these books and writings say exactly what God means and mean exactly what is said; then there are those who believe that only certain passages of scripture are the exact words of God and that those are the only passages which are not subject to interpretation or debate; finally there are those who believe that while the words may have come from God, they are not absolute. They were given to man to be used for guidance, instruction, interpretation and discussion.

This disparity of beliefs opens up a wide range of possible avenues by which a religious disciple might take to arrive at their particular belief in a god and the manner of worship they believed is best suited to please their god.

It presupposes that the words, interpretations and accuracy of the holy scripture did come from God and that these words, over the eons, have been correctly interpreted so as to give to a disciple the exact thoughts, words and actions of God himself.

I do not believe that they do because the biblical stories, as they are recorded in the Torah and the Christian Holy Bible are only as accurate as the beliefs of the ancient prophets allowed them to be. What has been written in these books is the perception of what the authors believed to be the truth.

We will assume for the sake of discussion that the words written in scripture are truly those from Jehovah and recorded exactly as they were given to Moses and the prophets. It should also be remembered that the possibility exists that those same words, thoughts, commands, ideas and laws said to have come from God, came instead from the priests and prophets themselves. They are the words, thoughts, ideas, commands and laws the writers believed or felt that God wanted them to say or rather what they wanted the people to believe and obey.

The preachers and clergy of today do the very same thing in the name of God. They quote the scriptures and then tell their congregations what they believe to be the will and command of God.

During the time of the Exodus the congregation obeyed the commands of the priests or they died. During the time of the Crusades men, women and children died believing in and obeying the words of God preached from the pulpit. There seems to be little difference between the ancient priests of God and the religious evangelists of today. They interpret for us what they say God is telling them he wants us to believe and obey.

Therefore, I will use the very words of God, his prophets and his priests to expose the servants of God for whom and what they are, scavengers of the human spirit. When I do the reader will learn the truth about religion and the myth of at least one god, Jehovah, the God of the Jews and Christians.

To expose the Jewish and Christian god for what he is, he must first be exposed for what he is not, and that is a divine god.

The book of Genesis is a short synopsis of man's beginning, of how he came into existence and how and why we are associated with the gods. This book, while based on short excerpts concerning specific individuals, certain events with some culture background should give the reader a bit of insight into an aspect of religion never taught or revealed.

It is a condensed version, not of the history of mankind, but of a family related to the gods in a very unique way.

The confusion existing today concerning the writings, meanings, and interpretations of the Torah and Christian Bible has come down to us through the misinterpretations and misunderstandings of those writings by our ancient religious leaders.

The misunderstanding and misinterpretations of scripture are based on fear, ignorance and superstition. That ignorance, fear and superstition became the basis upon which early man generated the belief that created a divine god and the creation of man and the human species as an act of that holy god. The Book of Genesis is the recorded record on which those misunderstanding interpretations are based.

All of my life I have been subjected to the teaching of the Holy Bible in one form or another, as both a Catholic, and as a protestant. It wasn't until I matured and began to study the scripture with the intent on becoming a member of the clergy did I realized that almost everything that I had been taught as a child was base on lies and misunderstandings.

The first lie was, that according to the bible my religious faith at that time was that there was only one true god and was identified in three parts: the father, the son, and the Holy Ghost. I accepted that belief as a part of my faith until the day that I realized that this was an untruth. That day I realized that there were in fact three distinct biblical individuals identified as God. One was the God of Abraham, the Father, Son and Holy Ghost of the New Testament, a subordinate to the Lord God the power and authority responsible for the creation of man and the human species and the one true god the divine power responsible for the creation of al that exists.

That was the day I realized that all what I had been taught about God, the Bible, and religion was either wrong or wrong or a misunderstood truth. I became basically an agnostic in my faith and questioned all that was being taught and believe by the various religious denominations. It would be years later that through my esoteric study I became a Pantheist, someone who believes that God is everywhere and a part go everything. He is not the flesh and blood mortal being that sits on a throne in the religious sanctuaries of modern man.

I will assume that all Jews and Christians disciples are aware of the Book of Genesis not only as the first book of the Torah and the Christian Holy Bible but a short synopsis of creation and the beginning of all things. It is also basically the foundation for the basic religious beliefs of the Jewish, Christian and many other religious denominations.

Genesis describes in simple details the beginning of everything, from the designated creator of the universe to the beginning of life itself. To this creator and to no other belongs the power, the glory and the title of GOD. This entity is the Supreme Being, which has no name, requires no worshipers and has no need for gifts, sacrifices or praise. This is the first of the three major Biblical Gods. There is a fourth, Murdock; the God of Hammurabi who some theologians believe in time became the God of Abraham and the Jewish Nation.

The second biblical god is the Lord God, a member of a race of organic life forms which came into existence along with all of the other life forms that have existed throughout the universe. His race as a form of organic life like the whales, fowl of the air, and beasts of the field, were a natural part of the original evolutionary design processes. This race evolved, gained knowledge and wisdom and one reached for the stars.

In their travels they stepped down on many worlds, this planet was one of them. In time they returned led by the Lord God. He was the power and authority responsible for the creation of man and the human species. Jehovah who is the third major biblical god and is the God of Abraham, Isaac and Jacob and subordinates of the Lord God.

Adam, Eve and the human creations which followed became the next generation of a new and different organic life forms. Man, as a sub-spies of the ancient race to which the Lord God belonged became another element added to the ever expanding universal creation.

The third biblical god is the individual biblical entity identified as Jehovah. He was the God of the Jews, believed father of Isaac, the grandfather of Esau and Jacob and possible the supposed father of Jesus. He was not the universal creator, nor was he the creator of Man. He was not a god, but an alien organic life form and member of the ancient and high civilized culture of the Lord God.

Jehovah was a minor god but assumed the title of Lord God when he was given Jacob as an inheritance and control as senior caretaker of the earthly property of the Lord God.

He became a major god when he convinced the Hebrew people to follow and render to him gifts, sacrifices and worship.

His reign as god began with the actions of the Lord God recorded in Deuteronomy 32:7-9.7:

> Remember the days of old, consider the years of many generations; ask your father, and he will show you; ask your elders and they will tell you. When the Most High gave to the nations their inheritance, when he separated the sons of men, and fixed the bounds of the people according to the number of the sons of God: for the Lord's portion is his people, Jacob his allotted heritage.

According to the above scripture, the highest God was the creator of Man and when he departed the earth he divided his property, the sons of man between the members of his race which were to be left behind. To Yahweh, Jehovah, the God of Abraham, Isaac and Jacob he left Jacob and his descendants as his property. He was now the only minor god who owned property. The rest of mankind still bounded to the Lord God but under the supervision, care and responsibility of the other minor gods.

It should be remembered that no one leaves an inheritance to anyone unless they are about to die or be away for a very long time. The fact the Yahweh received only a part of the inheritance of the Lord God clearly indicates that he was not the creator of man nor was he the one god of the bible. The realization that there was more than one God during the beginning history of man is the beginning of biblical wisdom.

In the beginning there was but one GOD, the power and intellect responsible for the creation of all that exists. Whether this power and intellect was one or a part of many entities it existed before creation began.

When creation did begin it took many forms. One of those forms was movable organic life that evolved gained knowledge and wisdom. And in time began to travel the stars. They came to this planet with a purpose and created a cloned modified version of themselves to fulfill that purpose. When that cloned individual (man) was found suitable it went through a learning process in preparation and required for it to function and fulfill its purpose.

One of the first commands given to him is recorded in Genesis 1:28. 28.

And God blessed them, (a biblical error because at that time there was no them, Eve had not yet been created.) But the biblical intent was there. When she was created it would be the beginning of the human species and the command would become valid. Man, male and female, were to unite, become one flesh be fruitful, multiply and replenish the earth. They were to subdue it, dominate and care for all that existed, the fish of the sea, the fowl of the air, and over every living thing that moves upon the earth.

One does not replenish what has never existed. For man to replenish the earth clearly indicated that a life form, like unto Man had at sometime in the pass existed here on earth. Therefore Adam and Eve as a newly created form of life may not have been the first alien life to inhabit this planet. But it is possible that they were the first of their species.

Biblically Adam and Eve were given many commands all of which are conductive to a highly cultured and civilized society. They were told to marry and reproduce the species. They were taught to care for and domestic sheep and cattle, grow grain ,make bread and care for fruit bearing trees, the tree of the knowledge of good and evil and the tree of life. They were made aware of the terms father, mother, and a few of the laws of a civilized society.

Since these things have no relationship to an entity capable of creating a universe I must assume that they came from a cultured life form similar to that of man.

Who or what was the power required in creating man and the universe? We have been taught to believe that the universe was created by a power or powers we are just now beginning to understand. For the lack of a better understanding religion calls this power GOD. The power behind the creation of man was a lot less sophisticated. Man was created by the use of science and technology. It was medical science, without the benefit of the powers of a god, science that can now duplicate that creative feat. Our doctors are now our gods of science and medicine.

Adam and Eve were created through a process known today as genetic engineering a process known and practiced by the ace of technically advanced beings identified in Scripture as "The Living Creature."

Man is said to have been created in their image and after their likeness. But without a biological father or mother man must have been created in some manner not known or understood by anyone down through the ages.

That has changed and an understanding of how the ancient aliens, the gods of man, created man and our race in their image and after their likeness can now be explained and proven. This proof of how man was created and why completely changes the basis for the religious faiths and beliefs of man.

Man and the human species began as modified clones of an ancient race of liens created by a medical and scientific process known today as genetic engineering.

The ancient gods using their own DNA, RNA, and chromosomes as the basic material modified those DNA, RNA and chromosomes in order to create an organic life form capable of working, surviving and reproducing the species on this particle planet.

It was necessary to modify their DNA because of the differences in their world and the earth. The aliens came from planet with less oxygen, a weaker sun and less gravity. So while man was created in their image and after their likeness mentally and biologically it was his physical structure that had to be altered in a way that allowed first man to be able to work and survive on his planet.

His eyes were reduced in size due to a brighter, his physical structure strengthened because of a denser gravity and his lungs reduced in size because of the increase in the oxygen in the atmosphere. Otherwise biologically man and the gods remained compatible with each other and did mate and reproduce offspring.

Biblical Scripture says that God and man are flesh and blood. The differences, outside of our physical appearances and intellect, concern the length of our lives. While the life span of man was originally intended to be a thousand years or more that expectancy was affected and changed by the advent of the flood. Because of the flood, the makeup of the atmosphere changed. This, along with the changes in his diet this affected the basic metabolism of man. Man changed from a vegetarian to a carnivorous creature. When he did his life span was reduced to approximately one hundred and twenty years.

Another factor which was instrumental in the reduction of the life of man was the lack of medical facilities and assistance which he had received from the gods prior to the flood. Man was on his own when the Lord God turned everything over to his subordinate Jehovah and returned to his home world.

Man was created to live for a thousand years, the apparent life span of the gods. This assumption is substantiated by the statement made by the Lord God, which says that man, with the knowledge of good and evil, and by eating a certain food, the tree of life, could be as a god and live forever.

It therefore stands to reason, that if the gods lived for long periods of time, it was due to their medical expertise and special foods. The gods of man were not an incorporeal being without form or substance, an immortal entity which requires no food or water nor does it ever cease to exist. It cannot die. The Lord God, our creator, can and did die. I refer to Revelation 1:18:

I am he that lives and was dead; and behold, I am alive for evermore, Amen; and have the keys of hell and of death."

This god sounds to me like he is the Lord Jesus an entity who was dead and brought back to life, who has become the living dead that has the keys not to heaven and paradise but to hell and death.

The Lord God told man that if he ate the fruit of a certain tree he would die. Satan, another name for the serpent approached Eve and told her that she would not die if she touched or ate of the tree of good and evil.

The serpent was one of the gods. Why would he want Eve to disobey a commandment of his superior the Lord God? Was he so naive that he believed that the Lord would not find out or was his motive so intense that he did not care?

Gen. 1:4-5: and the serpent said to the woman, you shall not die: for God knows, that in the day that you eat of this tree your eyes shall be opened; and you shall be as the gods, knowing both good and evil.

Adam. Eve and first man were clones a life form created without a biological father and mother. As such they were innocent disposal slaves and servants taught to obey the gods who were their masters.

When Eve was approached by the biblical serpent and given a command and permission to disobey the command was a superior god she was placed in an awkward position. How could she refuse to obey her superior? Which god was she obligated to obey the serpent her immediate superior of the Lord God?

The serpent was enticing Eve to eat of the tree of the knowledge of good and evil because of an ulterior motive he wanted to have sex with her. When told or convinced by Satan to eat of the tree of the knowledge of good and evil she obeyed. When she did she became euphoric. She got high. The chemical in the food which she ate activated her mind, and unlocked her programming.

The tree of the knowledge of good and evil was a narcotic, a relative of coco plant. When Eve chew the plant the chemicals in that plant activated some part of her mind which allowed her to obtain conscious thinking beyond that for which the scientist desired in the creation of man.

When Eve convinced Adam to also try the plant they became unreliable and untrustworthy. They now had independent thought, and even though they were slaves they now presented a danger to the Lord God. He could no longer allow Adam, Eve and the other men access to the garden and the tree. So he barred all men from the garden. Otherwise once the word was out about the effects of the tree everyone would want a sample. All of the men would then obtain independent thought and one day the control of the slaves would become difficult.

So man was put into a situation where he was no longer a danger to the gods and to himself. He was placed outside of the immediate vicinity of the garden, and a protective shield was set in placed around the garden. Man no longer had access to the garden or the tree of the knowledge of good and evil.

The question here is why has the biblical god suddenly afraid of man? It could be that man was physically stronger and automatically gifted with the intelligence of the gods no longer reliable and their function as a work force diminished.

Religion teaches us that the right hand of God is power. This power is exercised through the priesthood and their religious teachings. These teachings, along with the laws of God and the church have put fear and trembling into the hearts, minds and souls of its believers. These fears feed on the hopes and dreams of the lost, destitute and the hopeful. These fears began with the superstitions beliefs of a single family, who became wandering nomads,

In time they parlayed their beliefs and experiences into a worldwide religion. It was a family who became a nation. It is a family which has been able to create a dynasty for themselves and for their descendants. It is the family of the Godfather, Jehovah.

During the time of Adam and Eve and up until the time of Mary and Jesus, the gods interbred with man and produced offspring. This mixed breed of children, are known as the mighty men of old. What made them mighty was the intellect of their fathers and the strength and physical structure of their earth mothers.

Nowhere in the realm of nature is it possible for two difference species to united and produce offspring unless the DNA, Chromosomes and RNA sequences of both species are biologically compatible.

The bible says that Adam and Eve had no father or mother. The scriptures clearly indicate that the Lord God had no magical powers only those of an individual in authority. Therefore some kind of advanced scientific and medical technology must have been used to create man as a modified clone of and in the image of the Lord God.

Man is not a new species of life, a modified clone of an existing one. We are a cloned modified subspecies of an alien race of beings. Adam was the biological son of the Lord God which makes the Lord God and his people our ancestors.

Man had to be created with a heavier and stronger physical structure to withstand the higher gravity stresses he would encounter in his workaholic days. His lungs were smaller because of the higher oxygen content of the atmosphere, his eyes smaller to accommodate a brighter sun and his blood chemistry altered to allow him to adapt to the flora and fauna of his new world.

Once Adam was found to be functioning without difficulty in his environment, other men and special animals were created to help in the work that had to be accomplished. Eve was created as an afterthought when the special animals, created as helpmeets for Adam were found to be incompatible with him. Eve created from the altered DNA and blood cells of Adam and like Adam a modified clone able to biologically mate with both him and the gods to produce offspring.

The alien scientists put Adam to sleep, removed one of his ribs and closed up the incision. The rib was taken to a laboratory where the DNA, RNA and chromosomes were removed from the red blood cells of Adam's rib and through genetic engineering procedures altered that DNA to create a female and suitable mate for Adam. By changing the male "YX" chromosomes pattern of Adam to an "XX" chromosome pattern the aliens created a female.

Adam, Eve and the human species exist today for one reason, the gods wanted and needed gold, the onyx stones and earth minerals for universal trading. These could be found on earth. To obtain these items a work force was required.

The gods had three options bring that force with them at great expense from their world, from another world or create their own on arrival on earth. The first two were abandoned because of time, space and replacement labor cost. The creation of a labor force on was selected as the preferred solution. Then it became a question as to what species of life would best fill their needs? But again why did the gods need a labor force?

Adam and Eve to be created, and why did the Gods come to this planet in the first place?

Biblically the answer is simple if one reads and understands the words and meaning of the scriptures outside of the religious mysticism which surrounds religious text. The gods came to this planet mine for minerals. In order to that they needed a work force of individuals which could be specially trained to become skilled workers. Workers who could and would be abandoned when the mining was completed and the gods returned to their home world. The descriptive location of the "Garden of Eden", the minerals mentioned and the different tasks given to first man attest to this hypothesis.

In the meantime the gods needed food, shelter, and slaves who would obey their every command. Adam, Eve and the rest of early man were created as slaves in order to serve that purpose. Like animals, they were naked, slept in the open, and ate grass, herbs and fruit. They raised the food served at the God's table. Man herded the sheep and cattle, killed and cooked the meat which was served to the gods. The remembrance of this servitude condition remains with man today. It was the foundation upon which he bases his bloody sacrificial rituals.

As man scattered across the face of the earth, different cultures began to modify their ideas of the old gods, create new ones and establish new and different religions. Men of insight and greed and having a desire for power began to prey upon the superstitious fears of the people. They became the priests who built the temples and established the sacrificial rituals which controlled the multitude through fear and ignorance. They became rich and lived off of the gifts and wealth brought into the temples.

The Hebrew the descendants of Jacob, were in this condition serving the priests and the many gods of Egypt. When Jehovah, a name recognized by the people as the god worshiped by their ancestors Abraham, Isaac and Jacob, decided to become a god with a temple, priests, and servants he decided to try and get the Hebrews to become those servants and his followers. The Hebrew was a community without a leader. Pharaoh was their god. Moses, who became a prophet of Jehovah, convinced the people that life would be better serving their own god rather than those of Egypt. He convinced them that Jehovah was better and stronger than Pharaoh and the gods of Egypt. Whether the people believed Moses or not, after the plagues of Egypt brought on by the so called wrath of the Hebrew God, the Hebrews followed Moses into the desert out of fear for their lives from the anger of the Pharaoh and the Egyptian people. Once in the wilderness, they were unable to return to Egypt. It was then that they came under the complete control of Jehovah and Moses. What they did to control the people on Jehovah's road to becoming a god, is recorded in the writings of the Jewish faith and the books of the Christian Holy Bible.

Both Moses and Jehovah killed people both as individuals and by the thousands, depending on their mood at the moment. It is not record as to how many people suffered and died as a result of the plagues placed upon the Egyptian people who had committed no wrong. Pharaoh's army drowned in the midst of the Red Sea and Moses and the Levis' killed thousands of their own people when Moses found the people celebrating a golden calf. God himself is recorded as destroying Korah, his family and the families of Dathan, Abiran and their followers. And according to scripture God even allowed his son to die without assistance.

Like a Godfather of today, Jehovah controlled the people by fear and intimidation. He demanded and received protection monies, gifts and sacrifices. Disobedience to his laws resulted in death.

Today the Mafia, works upon the same principle. Because of the similarly between the two organization, I find "Jehovah the First Godfather" to be a very appropriate title.

So, if the god of biblical scripture is not a god, but a godfather, why does Man worship him and others like him? Does Mankind really need a God? The animals, birds, fish, insects and all manner of life, eat, sleep, procreate and survive as a species. They do this by their own instincts. They worship no god, offer up no sacrifices, attend no temples of worship, belong to no denomination and yet they survive.

We worship the gods out of habit. We offer up gifts and sacrifices out of misunderstanding. And we fear what we do not understand. We have been taught that the gods are all powerful. We owe them our love and our obedience. This is not true. Man does not need the gods. The gods needs man. Without our worship, gifts, sacrifices and rituals, the gods would cease to exist except in memory, myths and legends.

The immortality of the gods extends only to the next generation of believers. When there are no more followers, the temples of the gods will crumble, their priest will fade into oblivion and the immorality of those particular gods will cease to exist. The fact that any god ever existed can be found only in the mind of Man, perpetuated his belief in his own myths and legends. There is only one GOD. It is the universal creator. It needs no gifts, sacrifices, temples or adoration of man. It is sufficient unto itself. It is man and man alone who have created the gods he now worships through his religion.

"Jehovah, the First Godfather" is a hypothesis as to how, when and why these ideas came to become a part of the heritage of man and the human species.

There was a time, a few years ago, when I would have considered the term "Jehovah, the First Godfather," blasphemy. This was before I came to the realization that we humans believed that our creator and the creator of the universe were one and the same entity. We are wrong. Our creator did come from the stars, but he was flesh and blood. He was a living creature and not immortal. In our belief that our creation was the result of the universal creation we began to worship this creature as our God. But our god, as a god, exists only in our imagination. The Jews and the Christian call that god Jehovah. He is not now, nor has he ever been a divine being.

According to the Torah and the Christian Bible, while he is worshipped as a god, he was not the creator of man. He was a heavenly being only in the fact that he came to this planet as a member of a race of being from another world. Therefore, he did come from the stars. He was a member of a race of beings old long before the time of man.

Our creation was the by-product of a need by that ancient race. We were created as a sub-species, a subservient race. As a result of the process used in the creation of man, we became a distant relative to the race of beings which created us, and the ones which we now worship as our gods.

They are our ancestors. It is only because of our ignorance, misunderstanding of history, legends and written records that we have made them into gods. We are physically, mentally, emotionally and biologically similar to the gods we worship. We are capable of physically uniting with each other and reproducing a species. The differences between our races lie in the mental and physical abilities of the races. The offspring of the gods, men like Jesus, Buddha, Zoroaster, Alexandra the Great, Muhammad, and Sampson, have by their intellect, strength and wisdom and examples have shown us our rightful potential.

Of course some of these men were born to greatness while others with others it was thrust upon them.

Jesus of Nazareth was such a man. It is said that he was a god born to an earth woman. He became a messiah, a healer and the savior of man. He was a man believed to have been born with wisdom and power, a man who derived that power from his father also a god. He was said to have communicated with angels and heavenly hosts and raised the dead to life. No one seems to neither believe nor care that his wisdom and power might have come from education, study and training. He was not just a poor humble carpenter's son but the rightful heir to the throne of Israel. Mary his mother was a direct descent of the Maccabeus. Jesus as her first son became heir apparent as ruler and high priest of Israel. This is the main reason that Herod, a descendant outside of the line of David, became obsessed with the death of Jesus, his rival for the throne.

Jesus and the other great men of history, said to be the result of the cohabitation between the gods and earth women are a common theme found in almost all cultures, religious writings and legends. In all of these cultures, there are found many references to the mighty men of old, children of the gods and women. All of these religions have one other thing in common they all theorize that the beginning of mankind began with the creation of a male and a female by a heavenly power, a power that came from the stars.

In the Jewish and Christian community mankind began with a male and female which we called Adam and Eve. They are believed to have been the first humans ever created. They were the beginning of our species. We have been taught and we believed that they were created by the divine power of a being which we call God. Because we were not able to understand how this creation came about, we attribute it to the power of God, and surrounded it with an aura of heavenly mystique.

The gods created living beings out of apparently nothing. To bring into life a male and female, outside of the normal realm of biological concepts, was something beyond the comprehension of even the most learned of ancient men. Only a god was capable of achieving such a feat. This belief in the power of a god continued down through the ages until this day. Only recently has it become known that the power of creation has been taken away from the gods and given to men.

The creation of new life is taking place every day in scientific laboratories around the world. This new type of created life is in most cases an exact duplicate of the original life form and is a clone. These newly created life forms are the results of modern day miracles. They are accomplished through the process of manipulating the genes of the DNA of a living cell. This manipulation of the genetic structure of the cells is capable of not only reproducing an identical life form but is also capable of producing enhanced or altered new creations. The basic materials used in this new and exciting process are the red blood cells in the bone marrow of the living host. New life can be created without a father and a mother outside of the normal reproductive processes of a species. Adam was cloned from the DNA taken from the blood cells of God. Eve was cloned from the DNA taken from the red blood cells taken from the bone marrow of Adam's rib.

It does not take a great leap of faith to realize that the biblical story of the creation of Adam and Eve is a simple explanation of the process of cloning. I realized the enormity and the significant impact such a procedure holds for the organized religions of the world. This medical miracle completely changes not only the concept of the creation of man, but the whole basis and foundation of religions everywhere.

The creation of man was not a divine act of God but the result of efforts made by scientists and medical personnel of a highly advanced civilized society. The biblical description of the creation of Eve bears witness to the idea of cloning. Adam, created without a father and a mother would, logically, also has been a clone. We were created out of a test tube. God was not a divine being but an authority over men of science. Without divinity, he was not a god.

If the gods worshipped by man are not gods, then there is no validity to the religions which serve them. Without gods or religion there is no need for the priests, who serve those gods, or for the disciples who offer up to them their worship, gifts and sacrifices. Gods exist in our minds as a part of our legends, culture, and traditions. They are kept alive only by the beliefs of each successive generation. Without belief in their divinity the gods fade into oblivion.

Today, I challenge the divinity of two of the biblical gods, our creator and the god of the Jews and Christians. I question the validity of any religion based on the belief that they are divine entities. I query the sanctity of the individuals which serve them. I do not do this out of malice but out of a firm belief in what I now believe to be the true beginning of man, his reason for existence, and the relationship that exists between him and his creator.

I challenge the traditions of organized religion, not as a member of the Society of Educated Theologians, but as an uneducated layman. I do this from a unique position, one which I call a new perspective. Biblical scriptures, ancient artifacts, medical science and the findings of archaeological expeditions, bear out almost every assumption which

I have made in outlining this new way of looking at and analyzing biblical scripture.

This new perspective begins with an understanding of the process of cloning and the realization that the description of the creation of Eve found in Gen. 2:22, are similar in all aspects except time. Adam is put to sleep and one of his ribs is removed. From the DNA of the blood cells found in that rib a new creation, woman, is made. From an understanding of the description of this creation it is fairly easy to assume that Adam and Eve were cloned individuals. They were the result of a medical and scientific marvel. This marvel is being duplicated in medical laboratories around the world today.

What is not understood by the religious layman today is that the creation of mankind through the marvel of genetic engineering came not from Jehovah, the god worshipped by the Jewish and Christian but by the authority of the Lord God. Jehovah was, like Satan, subservient to the Lord God. He put on the robe of divine power when the Israelites accepted him as their leader. He became a god after he had established the priesthood, formed a religion and obtained dedicated followers. Without all of the above, the priests, temples, rituals, gifts, sacrifices, and disciples, he was merely a name with no power or authority.

When he was accepted by the Israelites as a god, he obtained the power and authority he needed to become a god. He ordained Aaron and the tribe of Levi as his priests to serve him. He established the laws and rituals which became their religion. And through the power of his priests, laws, rituals, and sacrifices, he became their God. It was the abuse of his power and the authority given to him by the Israelite people that justifies and entitles him to be called the First Godfather.

He did not rule with love and respect, but through fear, greed, bloodshed, and death. Our fear of God begins at birth. Our parents, afraid of our premature death and damnation, take us before a priest who gives us a name and christens us in the name of the father, son and Holy Ghost. That fear is instilled in us by our parents and reinforced by religion throughout our lives. There we are taught that to be separated from God at any time during our lives and at the time of our death leads us to the fires of hell and eternal torment. Therefore, out of fear of eternal torment, we renew the pledge of our fathers and renew our membership in the temples of religion.

As a child I was christened into the Roman Catholic faith. The sign of the cross, the name of the father, the son and the Holy Ghost was placed upon my forehead. When I received this mark of God, I was given a name by which he would know me. I became a member of the church congregation, a servant of God, and because I had received my name under the sign of the cross my God would always know me.

As I grew to manhood, I learned what a servant of God was supposed to know. I learned to talk to my god through prayer. Then there came a time, when for many years we did not communicate. It was not until my middle years, after I had retired from active military service did I began to realize that I was not going to live forever. It was in the fear of eternal damnation that caused me to seriously renew my religious studies and my association with God, the church, and organized religion.

As I became more and more active in church related activities I began to realize the impact that greed and corruption had on the normal every day operations of the church. The more I saw of its' ugly head the more I realized that greed had always been a vital part of religious society.

The Hebrew under their God Jehovah were captive slaves with nothing but promises of freedom, land, riches and power but only if they obeyed and accepted Jehovah as their God.

Today in modern religion the greed and corruption of religious denominations are satisfied by T.V. Evangelists, tax deductable donations and promises of rewards in heaven. As always where greed and corruption of power are present so too can be found bloodshed, death, mutation and ostracized disciples struggling to survive in their religious horror. A prime example of this can be found in the struggle between the Protestants and Catholics of Ireland and the Jews and Moslems of Lebanon.

Knowing all of this I continued in my belief in the goodness and holy benevolence of God until an unrelated incident occurred which drastically changed my life and my beliefs.

In 1973 I became aware of Mensa, a worldwide organization of individuals with IQ's at or above 98% of the average public. Out of curiosity more than anything else I became a member. The group openly encouraged questioning life, seeking answers and finding truths. As a result of the interaction within this intellectual environment, I accidentally stumbled upon what I can only describe as a unique insight into the Bible, God and religion. It could only have come from the one true universal GOD. This insight led me to understand God, religion, the Bible and the creation of man from an entirely new perspective.

It began with a simple idea that idea was that man was first created by cloning. (Gen. 2:22.) He was a non-entity, a slave, no more or less than the animals with which he lived and worked. These two ideas became the foundation upon which I have built my hypothesis. They are also the key which began to unlock the spiritual mysteries of the Bible. It was a simple idea, but it allowed my entry into the unknown. It set into motion the hypothesis upon which this book is based, and it completely changes my belief in God and religion. From this perspective came the hypothesis which I have outlined in this book.

As a layman I had many questions, but very few answers concerning God, religion and salvation. Once I realized that my idea concerning the creation and condition of Adam and Eve was feasible, I applied that idea to the scriptures. It gave me a new way of looking at the Bible and creation. I began to study the Bible from this new perspective. Answers began to materialize. They completely altered my religious beliefs. It did not change my belief in a Supreme Being, only who that Supreme Being really is.

As I studied the scripture again I realized that the Supreme Being, GOD, was not the creator of man nor was it the god of the Jews. It was an entity entirely separate from the gods of the Bible and the creator of man. The biblical gods of man were all mortal flesh and blood alien life forms that were ancient when the earth was still young. The most amazing thing of all is that they are for all practical purposes our ancestors.

The biblical being which I had worshipped as a child was not GOD, the creator of the universe. He was not even the creator of Man.

He was the leader and God of the family of Jacob, the Hebrews and the Israelites. These were the only people who considered him a god.

In my study of scripture I realized that there are in fact three separate and distinct individuals which have been known by the title of God. The word God becomes a term used today to denote any supreme religious authority. The first biblical GOD is the Almighty, the supreme ruler and creator of the universe. The other two are identified by many names. The most common according to biblical scripture are the Lord God, the Highest God, and his subordinate Jehovah the God of Abraham, Isaac and Jacob.

The Lord God was the authority responsible for the creation of man. He was also identified by Melchizedek, king and high priest of Salem, as the Highest God. In order for the Lord God to be considered the Highest God there would have to be lesser beings that were also considered gods by the people under their control. These lesser individuals paid homage to and were under the control of the Highest God. Jehovah the God of Abraham, Isaac, and Jacob was one of those lesser gods. All three are called God but, regardless of the title, they should not be confused with each other.

The biblical gods, the Lord God, Jehovah and Satan, required food, drink, clothing, and shelter. They walked, talked, had regrets, bouts of depression and knew anger, lust and greed. They were flesh and blood beings who could die. They were from the same race of beings. They had a culture and a civilized society. They followed and obeyed laws, had a language, were industrious, and they were aware of war, conflict, good and evil.

The GOD which is believed to be the creator of all that exists is omnipotent, an incorporeal being which exists throughout the width, depth and breadth of the universe.

For the incorporeal Almighty, these needs and concepts of man do not exist. For hat power and intellect all that was, is, and will be. Everything cause and effect and all work in harmony, one with the other. There is no conflict. The concepts of good and evil are those of the gods and man and do not exist for the Almighty.

The biblical Lord God, Jehovah and Satan were not gods. They were a different life form, who came to be worshipped as gods through the ignorance and misunderstandings of man. Because our fathers believed these entities to be gods so do we. But, not everything that man has believed is true.

Not long ago scientist believed that the atom was the smallest complete particle to be found in nature. Today we now know that this is not true. It too is made of particles, which are themselves made of even smaller units of matter. Therefore, we can only assume that whatever we choose to believe about anything may only be a partial truth, based on the factual evidence available to us at the time. This applies to all of our religious scripture.

Religious writings are entertaining. They cover the gambit from the divine to the ridiculous. But for the most part they appear to be suggestive, amplified by innuendos and filled with fabrications which contain very few elements of truth.

The Jewish Torah and the Christian Bible based on the Torah is writings which form a very important part of our culture and our heritage. As a written record, they give us some insight into the beginning of God, man and civilization. How much is truth and how much is conjecture must be decided by each individual.

Although religious writings are somewhat obscure in their presentation, a lot can be ascertained by reading between the lines and by understanding what the scriptures do not say. How much of the scripture is the truth and how much is fiction is debatable. I will, for the sake of this book, assume that everything written within the pages of the Torah and the Holy Bible to be the truth.

This being said, I have no intentions of questioning the words of these religious writings. I will however question the interpretations which have, over the last few thousand years, been attached to those writings.

I also have no intention of attempting to ascertain the origin of GOD the Almighty. That understanding is beyond the scope of man. I am concerned only with the origin of the biblical gods who the creator of man might have been and the process by which man was created. I am concerned about religion: how it began, what was its purpose then and what is its purpose now.

Once the reader is made aware of the fallacies which exist between what they have been taught by their religious denominations and what their religious writings actually say, they lives will begin to take on a new and different meaning. The guilt of sin, affecting so many religious disciples of today will disappear. They will begin to lead healthier more trouble free lives. They will find peace of mind and a balanced harmony of mind, body and spirit which can only bring about a better more enlightened society.

I believe that the Bible is nothing more than a highly entertaining saga which concerns itself not with mankind but with one family of individuals. It is not the divinely inspired word of God but of the individuals under his control. Therefore, I no longer feel that what I have written is blasphemy. I also believe that I am in no way going to spend my eternity in the hellfire of damnation. I am no longer concerned about my religious salvation or where I shall spend my eternity. I am and always will be afraid of death because of what I shall leave behind in this world that I know and enjoy. I am in no hurry to find out if there is a paradise beyond the grave the hereafter can take care of itself.

I like the way that the biblical prophet Micah put it. Micah 4:4-5. But they shall sit every man under his vine and under his fig-tree and none shall make them afraid. For all people will walk very one in the name of his god and we will walk in the name of the Lord our God forever and ever."

Joshua said basically the same thing to the congregation when he was about to die:

Joshua 24:15: "And if it seem evil unto you to serve the Lord, choose you this day whom ye will serve, whether the gods which your fathers served that were on the other side of the flood, or the gods of the Amorites in whose land ye dwell: but as for me and my house we will serve the Lord."

Micah, a prophet of God, does not seem to believe in hell and neither does Joshua, the great leader of the Jews. Both individual believed that a man has a choice as to which god he cares to serve. It is only fear and the rigid teachings of religion which makes the worship of Jehovah mandatory if one believes in him and wishes to enjoy a life in the hereafter.

I have asked myself many times why the Hebrew congregation, living within the very presence of God during the Exodus, wandering together under his command in the wilderness and having first hand experiences with him, would ever consider serving any other god. Why would it be considered evil to serve him if he were the loving God portrayed by modern religion and who were the other gods served by their fore fathers on the other side of the flood. Evidently it was not Jehovah.

Man has come to believe in a life after death. This idea probably came from earlier times when first man saw individuals who were hurt, dying or thought to be dead going into the medical facility of the gods and come out healed and alive. Early man saw individuals, thought to be dead, place into a chamber and later arose from that chamber alive again. This misunderstanding of life and death has lead to the embalming procedures, coffins, burial ceremonies and the religious beliefs of today. Even if there is a life after death, which I do not believe, I can always rely on the parable of the prodigal son and recall the time that I was christened, given a name by which Jehovah would know me, and henceforth believe that I am protected by his power. Or am I?

Baptism marked me as a dedicated and faithful servant to God. In return, he became my savior, my protector and salvation in this life and the one to come. I was marked upon my forehead. But, when I read the book of Revelation I find another reference to the mark upon my forehead. In Revelation it is the mark of the beast. So who do I serve? Am I the servant of the God Jehovah or the servant of the Beast, the God Satan?

Revelation 13:13-18: "And he does great wonders so that he makes fire come down from heaven on the earth in the sight of men. 14. And deceives them that dwell on the earth by the means of these miracles which he had power to do in the sight of the beast; saying to them that dwell on the earth, that they should make an image to the beast, which had the wound by a sword, and did live. 15. And he had power to give life unto the image of the beast, that the image of the beast should both speak, and cause that as many as would not worship the image of the beast should be killed. 16. And he caused all, both small and great, rich and poor, free and bond, to receive a mark in their right hand, or in their foreheads; 17. And that no man might buy or sell, save he that had the mark, or the name of the beast, or the number of the beast. 18. Here is wisdom. Let him that hath understanding count the number of the beast: for it is the number of man; and his number is six hundred threescore and six."

Who do I serve? Who do the believers in the Jewish and Christian faiths serve? Are the priests, the servants of God, or are they the minions of Satan?

Perhaps we should reread the scriptures to find out.

Ezekiel 9:4-6: "And the Lord said unto him, Go through the midst of the city, through the midst of Jerusalem, and set a mark upon the foreheads of the men that sigh and that cry for all the abominations that be done in the midst thereof. 5. and to the others he said in mine hearing, Go ye after him through the city, and smite; let not your eye spare, neither have ye pity: 6. Slay utterly old and young, both maids, and little children, and women: but come not near any man upon whom is the mark; and begin at my sanctuary. Then they began at the ancient men which were before the house."

Both Jehovah and the Beast, require a man to bear his mark upon his forehead. How am I to know to which God I belong? It seems that I am protected no matter which path I chose to follow.

All my life I have been taught that the Christian God was a God of Love. He was also a fearful God, omnipotent, the power and controller of all things. As I grew older I found the opposite to be true. If there is a god of love, it is not Jehovah. Such a god can only be found in the teachings of the priest and dedicated uninformed disciples. It certainly cannot be found in scripture.

The Lord God was a benevolent ruler. Nowhere is it recorded that he killed, mutilated, destroyed or severely disciplined any man before the time of the Flood. It is recorded that man exists today because of the efforts of the Lord God. Jehovah, on the other hand was a bloody, vindictive tyrant, who ruled with an iron will and killed without mercy.

Gen. 19:24, Gen. 38:7, Gen. 38:10, Lev. 10:2, Num. 26:10, Num. 31:9-11 are but a very few examples of the leadership of Jehovah. Not only did he kill the Egyptians but his own people. Any disobedience by anyone to his commands was justification for their death. Moses and Aaron, dedicated disciples that they were, also suffered from his wrath. I have no recorded instance where Jehovah ever forgave anyone their trespasses, an indication of his hard and cruel rule over the Jewish nation.

In order to better understand the biblical gods I studied the beliefs and practices of other faiths. There are many differences in the approach of different faiths to their worship of their particular god, and his religion. Many denominations professed to worship the same God and claimed to use the same scriptural text. Their interpretations of that text and their methods of worship are very different. One example of this difference can be found in the religious practices of the Snake Cult. This is a group who use poisonous serpents as a test of their faith in God. If and when they are bitten by the snakes, they believe that if their faith is strong enough they will be healed by the power of God. Should they die of those bites it was believed due to their lacked of faith in the ability of God to heal and make them whole. I question this practice and the many different interpretations of the scriptures that are practiced by many religious denominations.

Until recently I had very few answers to my many biblical questions. They were questions that the ministers and servants of God were unable to answer. I was told to have faith and the answers, if it was the will of God, would be made known to me in his own time.

They were right. The answers did come but they were not from any minister, church organization or religious scholar. They came from my own sub-conscious and were completely alien to the religious concepts and beliefs I had accepted all my life as biblical truth. They shook the very foundation of my beliefs.

I lay awake at night wrestling with these new ideas trying to find flaws in their logic. The more I tried, the more convinced I became in the truth of what these new ideas were trying to tell me.

Whether my thoughts brought me to the brink of blasphemy and condemnation to the fires of hell is debatable. Even in my fear I could not stop the answers from coming or stop new questions and revolutionary new ideas from forming.

As the answers to each new idea came, I waited for the wrath of God to descend upon me. At night I lay in fear believing that at any moment I might burst into flames to be consumed by his fire. According to what I had previously been taught and believed, these revolutionary thoughts which now filled my mind had already condemned my soul to damnation and the everlasting torment of the fire of hell.

When I did not die nor begin to suffer the trials and tribulations of Job, I began to take heart and to follow the dictates of the power that was now influencing my thoughts and action. I did not believe that these radical new ideas were coming from Jehovah nor did I believe that Satan was involved. To me they were merely opposite sides of the same coin. So I reasoned that there must be a power greater than the two. As such I had no choice but to write down the thoughts and the ideas given to me by that power. Apparently I did what I was supposed to do because my life has been more bountiful than I had ever imaged. I have been blessed.

I realized that with this book and its revolutionary new ideas, I am sowing the seeds of religious discontent. I have no idea as to what kind of harvest these seeds will produce. I leave that to the reader, history, and posterity. I only know that with the completion of this book, I have accomplished what I believed I was destined and ordained to do. No matter what the consequences and what others may think or say, I am satisfied with what I have done.

I am well pleased and found some small satisfaction in the following scripture.

Ecclesiastes 3:22. "Wherefore I perceive that there is nothing better, than that a man should rejoice in his own works; for that is his portion: for who shall bring him to see what shall be after him."

The history of mankind is a history of work and labour, both of gods and man.

It began with a simple statement found in Genesis 1:26-27. *And God said, Let us make man in our image, after our likeness: and let them have dominion over the fish of the sea, and the fowl of the air, and over the cattle, and over all the earth, and over every creeping thing that creeps upon the earth. So God created man in his own image, in the image of God created he him; male and female created he them.* In Genesis 2:18-22.The Lord God said, *It is not good that the man should be alone: I will make a help meet for him. And out of the ground the Lord God formed every beast of the field, and every fowl of the air, and brought them unto Adam to see what he would call them; and whatsoever Adam called every living creature, that was the name thereof. And Adam gave names to all cattle, and to the fowl of the air, and to every beast of the field: but for Adam there was not found a help meet for him. And the Lord God caused a deep sleep to fall upon Adam and as he slept; the medical personal of the Lord God removed one of his ribs and closed up the incision. The rib from Adam containing the modified DNA of the Lord God taken to his lab where the modified DNA of Adam was used to clone a female as a mate and when complete and functional was taken to Adam. The human species began with the command of the Lord God for them to become one flesh and reproduce the new sub species of life.*

These are simple statements. There was no divine power mentioned or indicated. Yet, when these statements were made to a group of primitive people who were controlled by awe, fear and superstition, they represented the statements and power of a god. How much truth is there in the above statements? If there is truth, what is not being said?

In Gen 1:26 Man is created in the image and likeness of God. He is to have dominions over all life, indicating that life already exists. In Gen. 2:19 God creates the beasts of the field and fowl of the air and brings them to Adam to be named.

Did life exist before Adam? If so, who was the creator? Were there different time periods for the creation of animals and fowl? If so who was their creator? This should be explained and understood if one is to understand the scripture in its proper context.

Primitives were and still are awed by the power of nature. Even today modern man respects the power of a storm. He trembles in fear as lightning flashes across the sky and the roar of thunder vibrates the very foundations of the earth upon which he stands. Men and women, in fear, still hide from the dark shadows of the night. In fear, we clothed ourselves in superstitions beliefs and rituals. Each individual believes in their own way that their superstitions beliefs and religious rituals will somehow protect them from those things which they cannot see, feel, touch, or understand. To them natural phenomenon like earthquakes, floods, volcanic eruptions and wind storms are an outward manifestations of the anger and the wrath of God.

To the uneducated people of early history, the biblical story of the creation of Adam and Eve would have been a divine mystery. Only a being of infinite power and wisdom like a God would have the ability to create new life.

Today we are more enlightened. We do not all tremble when we see lightning flash across the sky. We do not all fear the roar of thunder, or the natural phenomenon of nature. But no matter how educated and worldly we like to believe ourselves to be, we still hide in fear from the shadows of the night. This fear is not the fear of God, but of Satan, the devil, the bogeyman, and the things which go bump in the night. It is the fear of these things which we cannot see and have no power to control which have placed into the power of our gods. These are all things which man, at one time or another considered evil. There is no evil in the realm of nature only in the mind of man.

If there is such a thing as evil it existed long before the advent of man. If it exists at all, it is merely a concept generated by the laws and regulations of a civilized cultured society. This concept simply stated means that what is in the best interests of a society is good and what is not in their best interest is evil. There is no such thing as good and evil in the universe. This is the concept of the gods and of man not of GOD the universal creator.

In nature, i.e. the universe and GOD, everything works in harmony with each other, neither good nor bad. Sin, on the other hand, is the transgression of a religious or biblical law. In the case of Eve it was the command never to touch the tree of god and evil. When she did she sinned.

Any action or thought considered contrary to, or in the best interest of God and the church denomination or congregation is considered evil. Dancing, for instance, while a part of the religious ceremonies of some congregations is frown upon and considered a sin against the beliefs of the Baptist denomination.

Why? Because it takes one's mind away from the main purpose of religion and service to God. Even though the two words sin and evil are worlds apart in their meanings they have come to be synonymous with each other. When Eve disobeyed the command of the Lord God not to touch the tree of knowledge she committed a sin, a trespass or violation of a religious law of God. There was no evil involved in the act itself. As a result of her act of disobedience she became untrustworthy and aware of certain things which the gods considered evil. When she ate the fruit of that particular tree it gave her the understanding of what the gods considered the differences between good and evil. Since good and evil is a concept of the gods and existed before man the concept of sin and evil are gifts of the gods. As such each individual must decide for themselves, in the light of their background, culture and/or heritage as to which is which. Today almost all cultures consider slavery of humans as an evil practice. In biblical times slavery was accepted as a normal part of everyday life. So much so that the God Jehovah, in a fit of rage did on several occasions sold his own people into that condition.

The Israelites along with every culture of their day, and in accordance with the laws and edicts of their God Jehovah stole, capture, killed, sold and kept slaves of their own.

Contrary to religious beliefs and teachings The Lord God and the God Jehovah were not against slavery. When man was first created he was created as a slave therefore no laws were necessary. After the flood slavery among the survivors became an accepted fact. When Jehovah took control of the Hebrews after they left Egypt he again reinforced this condition on them by giving them strict laws on concerning their conduct towards slavery. The Jewish prefer the term bondsmen. But anyone who buys is the master and anyone who is brought is a slaves.

Numbers. 31:9,17-18. *And the children of Israel took all the women of Midian captives, and their little ones, and took the spoils of all their captives, and all their flocks, and all their goods Now therefore kill every male among the little ones, and kill every woman that hath known man by lying with him. But all the women-children, that have not known a man by lying with him, keep alive for yourself.*

Adam and Eve were slaves and property. They were naked individuals who ate, slept and worked alongside the animals created as their helpmates. They were slaves because that was the position they were created into. They knew nothing of freedom. They knew only to obey the power which had created them. To them their creation was no miracle. It was accepted as a fact of their condition. Their creation became an after-the-fact miracle based on assumptions and ignorance of the individuals which later wrote the biblical stories which achieved divine status.

The biblical account, describing the creation of Eve, does not strike me as a heavenly miracle, but merely a modern hospital operation. Adam was anaesthetized by God, or one of his medical personnel. While he was under the drugs he was operated on. Medical personnel removed one of his ribs, and the incision closed. The rib was then taken to a laboratory where scientists removed the DNA from the red blood cells of the bone marrow. The DNA from those cells was altered, recombined and used as the basic genetic material for the creation of a new type of life. From the cells of Adam, Eve, was created. She was born without a father or a mother. Like Adam, she was created out of a test tube. Today this creative procedure is a medical and scientific process known as cloning.

Eve came into being as an altered copy of Adam. She was not a true clone because a true clone would have been a duplicate of the original. But her creation was through the cloning processes. She became an altered form of Adam, a female, a compatible form of life necessary for the new species, mankind (human), to be able to reproduce itself.

This was accomplished by recombining the chromosomes, and RNA of the DNA, found in the blood cells of Adam. Once a male and a female had been successfully created, and proved capable of conceiving and bearing children, the cloning process was no longer required.

The birth of Cain proved that the new species that of Adam and Eve, was able to biologically reproduce offspring. The species could survive.

Using the successfully altered red bloods cells of Eve, other women were cloned or created from her DNA. Her cells required no further alterations. This made the process of creating women as mates for the existing male workers of that time a lot simpler. They too were like Adam produced through the cloning process.

Recently a scientist claimed that he had produced a computer program which traced the DNA of all women back to one woman. That woman was Eve or her counterpart. His theory was disputed because there is something unique about certain women who disproves his theory and indicates that there was more than one woman created at the time of Adam. There is another factor in the equation which could make his theory valid. That factor, simply stated, is that there was more than one Eve, more than one Adam and more than one Eden. This would account for the various blood types among men and women. This can be explained through scripture, artefacts, medicine, and archaeology.

If each of these various women were created using the DNA of the particular Adam belonging to a particular group, how was the original Adam of each group created and who furnished the DNA for their beginning? It is a simple question and it has a simple answer.

The genetic material used for the creation of the biblical Adam came from the blood cells of the Lord God. This is not beyond the realm of possibilities if one believes in the truth of the words of the translated Torah.

If the words of the Torah are the truly inspired and divine words of God himself then Adam is, by biological heritage, a son of God. This idea is believed to have some merit in Jewish history.

Luke 3:38: *Which was the son of Enos which was the son of Seth, which was the son of Adam, which was the son of God" While the lineage of Jesus does not change an understanding from this new perspective does change its understanding.*

Cain was the first born of a new subspecies. Biblical he has two possible fathers, the serpent who seduced Eve in the garden and Adam. Both eliminate Cain as the beginning of the human species. Eve gave birth to Cain. There are two possible fathers, the serpent who seduced Eve in the garden and Adam. Biblically there has always been a question as to that father might.

If Cain was sired by the serpent he becomes a hybrid, half alien god and half human, a bastard child with no worth just another slave. If on the other hand Adam was the father of Cain and was a clone of the Lord God than Adam is also the Lord. Cain then fathered by Adam in essence is also the son of the Lord God through genetic DNA and explains why he was not punished at the death of Abel.

This lineage strongly supports the Jewish idea that they are the chosen people of God. Not because he freed them from Egyptian but from biological DNA. If the Bible and history are correct, then their blood line goes directly back to God and the alien travellers who created man.

While the slave labour created after Adam were cloned by the same genetic process the DNA material used in their creation came from the blood cells of the crew members of the Lord God. Today those crew members are called angels, messengers and known as the minor gods and nothing like the beings that we call angels today.

Even though it was the DNA of the Lord God that was used to create the first human it had to be modified, altered in order for man to be specifically adapted to this planet's environment. The blood cells had to be medically modified because of the differences between the physical, biological, and chemical structures of the two different life forms and the sun, environment and atmospheric conditions involved planets: this planet and the home world of the gods.

Once Adam was found to be completely acclimatized to his environment, his cells became the basic materials for the creation of Eve. Mankind began as a cloned and altered sub-species of the living creatures, our gods.

There was no magic or divine power involved in our creation. We were created out of sound medical and scientific principles and techniques. Our creation as a species was not out of godly love, but one of material and industrial necessity. We were created as slaves to do the will and bidding of our masters who became our biblical gods.

Out of the ignorance, fear, superstition and misunderstandings of oral traditions, a god, a religion, priesthood and a way of life was born. Mankind is not the chosen beloved of God and religion is not our way to salvation, but a path which we have been using in ignorance and stupidity to return to the condition of human bondage from which we were once freed.

Today, the most underlying principle of all religion is to return man, of his own volition, to that condition of human bondage from which there will be no reprieve. Once man has accepted his servitude to a god there is no escape. The church, led by the disciples of God, strive to recruit as many of the human race as possible into the armies of two opposing forces, the forces of good and evil. The difference between the two depends upon one's point of view.

At some time in the future these opposing forces will do battle for the possession of the earth, the soul of man and the complete rule and dominance of all.

It must be noted that the terms good and evil are misnomers. They are words which describe concepts. They can also be applied to the methods used by the different forces of God and Satan, good and evil, to recruit and maintain control over their individual disciples. In reality, there is little or no difference between the methods used by these two opposing forces over the years and certainly no difference in their ultimate goals.

The good guys of God are every bit as vicious as the minions of Satan. Only honesty and the reality of these opposing beliefs and practices appear to favour the camp of Satan rather than that of God. At least Satanic Cults are honest in their belief and ritual sacrifices. It is highly conceivable their satanic rituals were copied from the practices and rituals given to the Israelites by Jehovah himself.

Jehovah gave the people a procedure for killing, preparing and cooking the food he and his men required. He called it a sacrifice because it was a part of the worship service to him. Man made it symbolic in their efforts to please him.

Jehovah began his rule as a god with death and destruction. Throughout his leadership he exercised his authority by continued demands of blood, destruction, pain, torture and torment. His influence was so ingrained into the psyche of the Israelites that it has become a part of their history and their everyday lives. His leadership and doctrine of blood, death, and mass destruction, is believed by many to be projected into the future. There he will supervise the destruction of all things in order that all evil be eliminated and a new and better world will be established. The only problem with this scenario is that the new empire, the new holy city of Jerusalem, will be here on earth and very much like the one which existed a few thousand years ago. Instead of eliminating evil, evil will be a part of man's everyday existence. Man will once again be a slave subject to the will and whims of a dictator god.

The book of Revelation describing the end of evil man is a look at the horror and cruelty of Jehovah. He is not a god of love, but of hate, wrath and vengeance. Is he a noble loving god or is he the beast? If he is not Satan, the beast, where is the difference between his actions as God and those of Satan?

I believe that there is a third power, a power greater than Jehovah and Satan. That power is the Most High God, the creator of Man. It is that power which I believe now guides my thoughts and actions, not through a conscious level but through the sub-conscious.

I do not believe in a heaven or a hell and I certainly do not want to assist anyone who intends to make my life, such as it is, into one or the other.

Rev. 21:2: *And I John saw the holy city, the New Jerusalem, coming down from God out of heaven, prepared as a bride adorned for her husband. And I heard a great voice out of heaven, saying, Behold, the tabernacle of God is with men, and he will dwell with them, and they shall be his people, and God himself shall be with them, and be their God.*

Rev. 22:14-15: *Blessed are they that do his commandments that they may have the right to the tree of life, and may enter in through the gates into the city. For without are dogs, and sorcerers, and whoremongers, and murderers, and idolaters, and whosoever loves and makes a lie."*

Who shall have the right to live in this new city of God?

According to scripture, it will be the slaves and servants who are willing to bow down, worship and serve this new god. Paradise is not to be found in heaven but here on earth. Those individuals who refused to submit themselves to the services of a self proclaimed god and his entourage will be the free thinkers and independents. They will reside outside of the city. They shall be the ones who will be free to pursue and enjoy their lives as best they can in a world which has been destroyed and laid waste by the fight between the gods.

The new kingdom of God is to be here on earth. It will be a physical kingdom not some spiritual paradise in some far distant corner of the galaxy. Entry to this new kingdom will be restricted to individuals who have voluntarily made slaves of themselves in the name of their God Jehovah. They will be allowed to enter, dwell there and serve him. Since the Bible clearly says that all other survivors of the war between the gods will reside outside of the cities it must be fairly event to the thinking man that there is to be no hell, fire and damnation because the earth itself will be that hell.

If the war between the gods and the destruction of the earth, as it is depicted in Revelation, is to come true then the earth will be devastated. It will be covered with radiation contamination. The water will be contaminated; there will be little or no plant and animal growth for many years after the war. Those forced to live outside of the cities will be forced to suffer starvation, thirst and pain without medical help. This could the living hell of Revelation. If one considers this as a possibility then they must also consider that the following must also be true. The cities of God in such an environment will have to be in enclosed domed, protected and self efficient environmental units.

Long ago the gods came to this planet. When they did they created us as slaves not out of love but commercial and industrial necessity. Even though mankind has found an abundance of evidence to support other and older life forms we refuse to accept their existence. Taught by our religious leaders that we were create as the noblest creatures within the kingdom of GOD, created out of love, we believe that we are unique. Reinforced by religious teachings we have come to believe that this is true. Until recently we have refuse to accept the fact that other life may exist outside of our world. We do not wish to acknowledge that there may be other species within our realm of the universe superior to ourselves.

Moses himself, in recording for the Hebrews, the story of the universal creation and of man, gave us written evidence as to the existence of a superior race of beings beyond man. It has been mans misunderstanding of those writings which has led to his confusion as to who and what the gods are.

Moses, a Hebrew, was instructed by Jehovah one of those gods responsible for the creation of man. He told Moses of this creation in simple terms that uneducated people could understand. Along with the creation story Moses also received a short synopsis of the history not of mankind but a particular family of individuals directly related to the gods. That family began with Adam, his son Seth and his descendants through the time of Jacob and his twelve sons. As a member of the tribe of Levi, one of the sons of Jacob, Moses was a part of that heritage even though his linage has never been recorded.

According to scripture Moses was personally instructed by Jehovah. He received from Jehovah, to be given to the Hebrews, the laws, rituals, commands and customs of his race and culture he deemed appropriate. Jehovah, in giving the Hebrews those laws, rituals, commands and customs established their rights as a people. They became a part of and a subculture of the race from which Jehovah originated. Those rights and obligations established a religion, constituted a form of government and became a way of life for the Hebrews. How the Hebrews dealt with those laws and customs has also established certain traditions which have been passed down to modern man in the form of prophetic writings called the Torah and the Christians Holy Bible. These written passages handed down to us as the perfect words of God have been interpreted and misunderstood by man from their inception.

The Genesis story, told to Moses by Jehovah, begins with the statement that GOD during the creation of the universe created life, in all of its diverse forms and dimensions as a part of the original creative process. Therefore, if GOD, the universal creator, created life as a part of that process, it must exist throughout the universe. If one believes in the words of the Torah and the Holy Bible this becomes a foregone conclusion. I believe it is safe to assume from our observations of the diversity of life on this planet that such diversity exists. One has only to look at the various life forms found in the sea, in the air, on and under the ground of both plant and animals in order to believe that life could and must also exist through the universe wherever there are suitable circumstances.

A couple of those forms are mentioned in the Torah. They are the "Living Creature", the Seraphim and the Cherubim. These life forms, created in a time before man, along with the whales, birds, grass, herbs, cattle and beasts of the field are a part of the universal creation by GOD. The living creature is the term used by Jehovah to identify his own race of people. What is not mentioned by biblical scholars is the origin of the Cherubim and Seraphim. One is described as the protectors of God and the other as the guardians of the Garden of Eden. They certainly were not created nor did they originate on this planet. Therefore, they must have been created and existed somewhere else. If so, then there is life beyond the stars. Because we ignorant savages have not seen or met them does not mean that they cannot and did not exist.

The races of the gods, who were the living creatures and who were protected by immortal creatures were our creators and ancestors. Once we were created they became our masters. Man served the whims of the gods. After the flood, the gods were no longer physically walked, talked and associated with man. But man still remembered his place and his service to them. This was amply demonstrated by Noah, his family, and the feast they prepared and held in honour of God after the flood. The flood is believed to have destroyed most of the people on earth. Since there were so few individuals to govern and control after the flood the gods ceased to be physically present among us. Man in his desire to continue to serve built temples and ordained priests to be available to serve the gods at any time should they decide to return to earth and take their place again among men. When the gods failed to return they were made into spirits of divine origin and the congregations continued to serve them in their temples with rituals and bloody sacrifices.

At some time during the creative processes of the universe a race of beings, as a distinct life form came into existence.   Whether they began as a one cell amoeba to evolve from a simple cell into a higher life form is immaterial. They existed. During the process of their evolution, they obtained a reasoning ability. With a reasoning ability they became a thinking and intelligent race of individual beings. How they evolved and how long it took for that evolution to take place is not our concern. They existed. They were life forms no different than the whales, birds, beasts of the field and all of the other forms of life which have evolved from a simpler state of being into a race or species of life, capable of adapting and surviving down through the millennium of time. As intelligent beings, they grew in knowledge and wisdom. They developed a civilized, cultured society and like man today they reached for the stars. As they travelled the cosmos they left their mark on the worlds which they passed or stepped upon.

The planets or worlds, which they found capable of supporting their species, they tried to colonize. Earth was one of those worlds. Some of their colonies, scattered among the stars, may have survived and have themselves become travellers of space. From the evidence Archaeologists have been able to uncover indicates that the original attempt to colonize this planet failed. For whatever the reasons, that initial attempt did not survive as a civilized society.

There are several things which the Archaeologists have found which they believe support the idea of a colonizing attempt by an advance race of intelligent beings.

There is a tribe of natives called the Uros who live on islands made of reeds on Lake Titicaca. It may well be that these islands were their answer to the flood. It was to them what the ark was to Noah. It saved them from the flood which struck South America. Their legends say that they are unlike other men. As a people, they lived before the white man was created. They are different. Their ancestors came from the stars while the earth was still in darkness. At that time their blood was black and not red as present day man. If their legends are true and most legends do have some element

Are the Uros the descendants of an ancient alien attempt to colonize the earth and have over the millennia evolved into their present physical state due to the earth's environment, their diet and their culture?

It is highly possible that the original colony, like man during the time of Noah, suffered some kind of cataclysmic event which destroyed their civilization. The few remaining members of their race, concerned only with survival, digressed into their primordial beginning. The Uros may be the exception. Their part of the world may have been fortunate enough not to have been subjected to the complete effects of a massive asteroid impact, similar to the one which occurred during the time of Noah.

At the creation of Adam and Eve, (Gen.1:27), God gave them a very unique command. This command is found in Gen. 1:28. They are given a very specific command. They were told to be fruitful, multiply and replenish the earth. One does not replenish something which has never existed. Because of this particular it can be assumed that Adam, Eve and the rest of mankind created in the beginning of our era were not the first intelligent life to exist upon this planet. The gods in creating man were aware of the life which existed before man. The command given to Adam and Eve by the Lord God lends credence to the legend of the Uros, and tends to validate the finds of the archaeologists.

To multiply and replenish the earth was secondary to the primary purpose for which man was created and that was to serve them and mine for minerals they came to this planet to obtain.

The commands which were later given to man by the gods were the laws and principles by which he was expected to live. They were for his conduct and social behaviour which clearly indicated that the Lord God and his entourage were from a highly advanced civilized society.

When the alien expedition first landed on this planet, it was in an area that was rich in minerals, gold, bdellium and the onyx-stone. This was the reason they came to this planet and the reason that this is mentioned in the first few chapters of Genesis. It establishes their purpose on earth, the reason for the creation of man and the human species. Genesis is not only the story of our beginning but of their version of universal creation and their place in it.

When the alien came to earth it was as a conglomerate of mining engineers, medical and scientific personal. When they arrived the various companies making up the conglomerate separated from the mother ship and proceeded to the area of earth where they had exclusive mining rights.

The Lord God and his entourage, assuming he was the leader and ultimate authority was assigned to the land of Ethiopia, an area extremely rich in gold, bdellium and the onyx stone. (Genesis 2:10-14).

There they selected an area where water was plentiful to aid in the mining, planted a garden for food and began creating the slaves needed to obtain the minerals.

Based on scripture, science and medical practices there must have been a trial and testing period as the gods and their scientific and medical personnel searched for a suitable solution as to what type of worker was required. Scriptures states that the created being most suited was one in their image and after their likeness. The basic material for achieving this goal was through a process known today as genetic engineering or cloning where the DNA, RNA and chromosomes of the aliens was modified, altered to allow the newly created clone the best opportunity to work and survive on this planet.

During the creative process there were evidently many failures and monsters before a successful unit was found that met the needs of the minors. Because of the work involved in maintaining a camp for miners, mining and processing the ore it is possible that the aliens in creating first man created them in three sizes, large, the biblical 9 ft giants, small, the pygmies of Africa for work in the mine and a medium size or normal size man that tended to the needs of the camp, serve the gods and processed the ore.

The giants carried the heavy loads, the pygmies worked the small close spaces within the mines and normal man cared for the garden, the camp and served the needs of the aliens.

As other men were created according to the needs of the camp it was found that the mining was so successful that work became too difficult for man alone. It was soon decided that it was necessary to create an entirely new and special group of animals to help man in his labour. The bible speaks of them as helpmeets. When Adam and these helpmeets were found to be incompatible it was then that a decision was made to create a female. Eve was that female created as an afterthought to be a mate for Adam and together become the foundation of a new subspecies of universal life.

This is a simple story but it suggests many things.

First, the garden was a source of food necessary to supplement the rations brought by the alien gods to earth. The fact that they planted a garden suggests that it supplied them with the fresh vegetables and fruit depleted during their journey to earth. It ensured them that suitable nourishment of a kind acceptable to their taste and biological system would be available to them during their stay on earth. The fact that man was allowed to eat only vegetation and that it was from the same garden clearly suggests that the food and the physical bodies of the gods and man are the similar.

Man was a slave, a tenant farmer made to tend the garden, to serve and wait on the gods. The Bible says that he was made from the dust of the ground, and into his nostrils was breathed the breath of life. When he came alive he became a living soul. (Gen. 2:7).

Isn't the following merely a different way of saying the same thing?

Dust, which is made of the elements of the earth was the basic material used to create a man. The blood cells of the body are composed of those elements. So if one were to use the blood cells of the body then one was also using the dust of the earth to create a man.

What is the breath of life except the electrical spark which flows through our neuron network, furnishing the power to our nervous system, which allows the conversion of matter into electrical, chemical and mechanical energy?

Man is a machine operating on a battery. If there is a break in any one of his circuits that prevents the electrical current from completing the circuit, he stops operating. We take him to a doctor who checks him out, find and repairs the break in the circuit and man functions again. The break heals forming a scar which does not allow the current to flow as smoothly as it did before the break. Man can still function but not as well as he did before the break. His heart (man's generator), furnishes the current. As long as it runs there is life. When it stops, life stops. The brain monitors, and regulates the entire process.

Scientists and medical technicians in modern medicine have taken the blood cells of animals and man (the dust of the earth), and created new life. Electricity activates the new life. Today we call this process cloning. Before cloning the dust of man and the breath of life were found in the egg and sperm of man. The friction necessary to create the sperm also gave it the breath of life. Before the sperm acquired the spark of life it was simple organic material capable of being used as the body dictated. Today through the cloning procedures man has created man.

In the past we have worshipped the gods because they alone possessed the power of creation. What we have never understood is that we have always been gods because we too create life. Every time a child is born we have duplicated their feat of creation. Our method of creating new life has been the process of natural childbirth but the end results was always the same. The differences between natural child birth and the cloning process is that the results of one is random and the other predictable.

The gods cloned Adam and Eve. They were made to order. The gods used their own blood cells to create Adam, and they used the blood cells of Adam to create Eve.

Adam was created to design specifications similar but different from the gods. Had he been cloned as an exact duplicate of the gods it would have created problems in his adaptation to the environment. There would have been problems in the work which had to be accomplished, in identity, prestige and discipline. If the gods and man were identical in appearances how could the gods tell the differences between themselves and their slaves?

Physically man was made stronger than the gods because of the difficult labour tasks he had to perform, the heavier earth gravity, and the higher oxygen content of the atmosphere. These differences required a change in both body chemistry and physical structure. The chemical change was required for the higher oxygen atmosphere that resulted in a blood chemistry which appeared to be red instead of black when exposed to the atmosphere. The physical structure of man varied according to the tasks he was assigned to do.

Adam was a test model. When he proved successful others were created in his likeness, not in the likeness of the gods. He was taught to speak and was taught the necessary skills required to care for garden, feed and care for specific kinds of animals and in the beginning how to mine for minerals. At the death and expulsion of Cain the biblical story changes and man, now that Eve was a part in the new order is given another child to continue the genetic line of the Lord God through Adam. A second genetic is begun through Cain as the believed child of Eve and the Serpent. From Cain came the industrial society of man. As he was learning how to build a city that would house the aliens, his family and descendants were being taught the skills required to build that society. Industry now had a beginning that flourished until the time of the biblical flood. This is scripture.

While Adam was trained as a gardener, the other workers created after him were trained for different and more specific tasks. Scripture mentions a few of the more common ones. They were shown how to raise grain, herd sheep, and build cities, work in metals, weave cloth, make and play musical instruments and wait on and serve the gods. These were the tasks meant to make life a little easier and as enjoyable as life could be for the aliens away from home on a strange planet.

The reason the aliens were on this planet in the first place was not to create man but to mine the minerals found here. But, in order to do that they needed labourers. This was the reason they required slaves and this was the real reason that man was created. This is not mentioned but implied in scripture text by the location of Eden and the work and skills performed by the sons of Cain in:

Genesis 4: 20-22: *And Adah bare Jabal: he was the father of such as dwell in tents, and of such as have cattle. And his brother's name was Jubal: he was the father of all such as handle the harp and organ. And Zillah, she also bare Tubal-cain, an instructor of every artificer in brass and iron: and the sister of Tubal-cain was Naamah.*

The Garden of Eden was in a land where there was gold, bdellium and the onyx-stone. Tubal-cain was an instructor in brass and iron. Brass is an alloy made of zinc and copper. In order to obtain this product, it is necessary to find the ore, mine it, take it to a smelter, where the ore is processed and the raw material is obtained. From there the raw materials are sent to a facility where they are combined in order to produce brass.

This example of the skills, knowledge and information given to first man could only have come from individuals educated in a civilized, cultured society. The gods passed down to man some of their culture, tradition and laws, but also many of their industrial skills and knowledge.

They taught man to build cities (Gen. 4:17), mine ore, make alloys of metal,(Gen. 4:22), plant gardens, (Gen. 2:8), grow wheat for bread(Gen. 3:19), breed and herd animals (Gen. 4:2), weave cloth (Gen. 4:20), make and play musical instruments (Gen. 4:21).

Food was required to feed both the slaves and the gods. Certain seasonal foods were not always available. The gods improvised. The slaves ate the food of the animals, herb bearing seed, and fruit. The gods ate what they obtained from the garden, along with meat from the herds of sheep and cattle. Man   slept outside in the elements. The aliens slept in the cities constructed by Cain and his fellow craftsmen.

To ease the pain and suffering and to be able the people to endure the elements the gods supplemented their diet with coca leaves. The dried leaves of this plant was and is used today by people of the Andes in their religious festivals and according to legend is believed to have been given to them as a gift from their god.

These leaves are a stimulant and act as a local anaesthesia. When chewed, it eases the pangs of hunger, relieves stress, and enables one to endure physical extremes of heat and cold. It is also believe that these leaves are similar to the leaves and fruit of the tree of good and evil, a fruit that helped the gods endure their long journey through and why they were so protective of the tree in the garden.

During the time man was serving the gods he was also being taught the values and the foundation of their civilized society. Those values were first passed down to Adam, reinforced by the laws of Hammurabi to the Sumerians and later given to the Hebrews by Jehovah and Moses. Since then those laws and commandments, amplified, modified and extended have become known as the value and rights of man. Once known as the laws of Moses they are now known as "human rights" and "civil liberties."

First man was taught to grow food, make thread, weave cloth and fabricate clothes and shelter. He was instructed in how to make and play musical instruments, how to serve and entertain the gods. He was taught to mine, smelt ore and how to make things of iron and brass. He was taught how to survive.

The idea that the aliens came to this planet in search of minerals can be substantiated by the biblical description of the landing location and the Garden of Eden.

Gen.2:10-14. *And a river went out of Eden to water the garden: and from thence it was parted, and became into four heads. The name of the first is Pison: that is it which compasseth the whole land of Havilah, where there is gold; and the gold of the land is good: there is bedellium and the onyx-stone. And the name of the second river is Gihon: the same is it that compasseth the whole land of Ethiopia. And the name of the third river is Hiddekel: that is it which goeth toward the east of Assyria. And the fourth river is Euphrates.*

The second chapter of Genesis clearly indicates that the biblical gods were concerned with gold and semi-precious stones. This concern of the gods clearly justifies the Genesis description for the types of occupations taught to early man at the time of his creation. Men were instructed in and became the fathers of agriculture, animal husbandry, music, construction, mining and the smelter of ore. These are industrial occupations, not religious, or part of a god serving agenda.

Throughout the ages people of all races and nationalities have been duped into believing in the holiness of the gods and the necessity of religions. Neither a belief in a god, faith or religion adds any significant meaning to the lives of a believer. It does however maintain them in a condition of servitude while providing them with a scapegoat to blame for their misfortune and personal failures. A god is also the power that is thanked for all of the blessings achieved through their individual hard work and efforts'

If the scriptural text recorded in the Book of Genetics describing the creation of Adam and Eve is valid, then the first humans began, not a dust from the earth but as clones of a highly evolved race of flesh and blood mortal beings.

The creation of man based on that assumption takes on an entirely different meaning. In that context the Old and New Testament lose all of its religious significance. It changes from a book of Holy rite to a saga of separate but loosely connected narratives that while they profess moral and political ideals, are still just collections of events, relationships, individual exploits, and a relationship between a people and a being which they made, worshipped and believe, to be a God.

The Bible is no longer a book of holy writ but a saga of power and control. The role of the biblical God changes from that of a holy deity, to that of a leader, a ruler or king. The differences between the rule of Jehovah and the kings, queens and emperors which have controlled man from his beginning were only different in the methods they used get and keep that control.

Jehovah ruled and controlled the Hebrews or Israelites through spiritual, mental and the mortal fear of death perpetuated by priests and a set of religious laws and rituals. Other rulers controlled their subjects through the fear of death, slavery and physical force.

Like most of the kings and rulers of man down through the ages Jehovah ruled by what is known today as the "Divine right of Kings", a right given to them by their god. Jehovah had this right because it was given to him by the Lord God in Deuteronomy 32;9. This right is usually passed down from one generation to the next. For Jehovah there was no next generation. While he is still the God and ruler of the Jewish nation his right to rule has been delegated to the priests and the descendents of the kings and high priest who from Adam through the line of David to the time of Herod.

When one combines the rule of Jehovah, the techniques and miracles of modern medicine with the cryptic passages of the Bible, those passages can and do reveal a bible with an entirely different point of view than the one usually taught by the Jewish and Christian religions.

The Bible read and understood from this new perspective becomes a story of a tribal history passed down from one generation to next. It is a story of how the children of one family became a rich and powerful nation. The Bible is a collection of short stories which clearly indicate how the beliefs, actions and reactions which were directly related to their religious beliefs, customs and laws helped them to become a very rich and powerful people. They became the nation they are today not because they believe in a god, but because they believed in themselves. Their belief in their god only helped to unite them in mind, body, spirit and efforts as the people evolved from a group of wandering tribes to become what they are today, a very strong and powerful nation.

The Hebrews became a nation when the family of Jacob, the twelve tribes, banded together under the leadership of Jehovah and Moses. Out of their fear of Moses and the wrath of their god the families began to act in unison one with the other. Following the dictates of Moses they organized a religion complete with a temple, priests, laws, rituals and began the religious customs which exists today. Out of their religion came their state, their nation. They became a people unto themselves. The fact that they worshipped and followed the edicts of a particular god was their way of expressing their power. It made them strong. One of their laws or edits was male circumcision. This is the mutilation of a particular part of the male genitalia. It is a practice demanded by Jehovah and goes back to the time of Abraham. The mutilation of one's body, and the blood and sacrificial edicts of God, conditioned the people of the congregation to torture, robbery, mutilation, slavery and death. It moulded them into one people.

The Jewish people believed that, as a people, their race began with Adam, the very first man. Their records, legends and myths record his as the son of God. Therefore as his descendants they were and are a very special people.

Luke 3:38. *This was the son of Enos, which was the son of Seth, which was the son of Adam, which was the son of God,*

They base their assumption on the scriptural passages of Genesis and the genealogy found in their legends and sacred writings.

Genesis is a book of the beginning. It is a synopsis of creation and all that dwells within it. It describes the foundation of sin and the destruction of the relationship which first existed between God and man. They believed that because one man sinned all of mankind automatically fell from grace. As such, when the Lord God became angry with us, a thousand years after the sinful act of Adam and Eve, he decides to destroy us along with all of the life on this planet. Before the destruction of man the Lord God decides to allow a few humans and animals to survive. He instructs them in the construction of an ark, a vessel of survival. This is rubbish.

Again the fact that mankind still exists is laid to the grace, love and benevolence of a great, kind and loving god. This too is rubbish. The Lord God instructed and assisted Noah and his family in the construction of the ark and the saving of the animals so that he would have a nucleus from which he could rebuild mankind after the advent of a flood he was unable to prevent.

Not only Noah and his family but many other individuals also survived the flood. As these people began to multiply and spread across the land, as a result of their experience during the time of the flood they began live closer together. They began to form individual communities. With the knowledge and wisdom taught to them by the gods before the flood they began to build a structure called "The Tower of Babel". Was this building supposes to reach the heavens and the gods or was it a place of safety where man would be able to go should another flood occur.

The Lord God and his entourage were again afraid of what man would be able to accomplish if left to his own devices. To prevent this from happening he ordered that the people around the tower be separated and relocated in isolated places around the globe. This explanation offers us a reason why man can be found even in the remotest corners of the earth and certain words of their various languages not only sound alike but carry the same meanings. Each group left to their own way developed their own particular types of speech. These have become what we recognize as the many different languages and dialects found around the world today.

The Bible is reasonably clear in giving us an explanation for the survival of man, his sometimes isolated location and both the differences and similarity in the languages of man.

We are even given some idea as to who created the universe, man and how and why religion came into existence. The Bible is in some ways limited in what it has to say about this and many other things but the same passages, read from a new and different perspective, can give one almost as much information from between the lines and from them. That is one of the purposes of this book, to read between the lines.

Unless one attempts to find out the true and complete meanings of what the scriptures say the Bible will continue to remain a mystery. The gods of man will remain forever deities and the religions of man, sponsored by the priest, rabbis and protestant clergy will continue to grow, to flourish and bilk man of his spirit and his material possessions.

As long as man continues to believe in gods and religion the longer he will delude himself and the generations to follow   in perpetuating the most gigantic hoax ever played on man by man. This hoax is the belief in the sanctuaries of gods which do not exist except in the minds of religious believers.

In the beginning when the Lord God first created man there were no temples, priests, worshippers or sacrificial rites. Man served the gods as slaves on a day to day basis. All of the above, the temples, priest and sacrificial rites came later. It was after the flood and the story of the burnt offerings of Noah which help to lead man into the confused misunderstandings of his original association with the gods. This confusion has further been misunderstood during the millenniums which have passed by mans misinterpretation of certain passages of scripture. The idea of worship, service and sacrifice had its foundation in the following verse of scripture. This verse along with all of the stories of the beginning was handed down from generation to generation as a part of the history and legends of the Hebrews before they were finally written down.

Gen. 4:26: *And to Seth to him also there was born a son; and he called his name Enos: then began man to call upon the name of the Lord."*

In the beginning when man first serves the Lord God and his crew they began to have problems amongst themselves and the different guilds and groups. God was called upon to settle these disputes. Calling upon the name of god had absolutely nothing to do with sacrifices and worship.

As man multiplied, conflict occurred between various individuals, groups and between the gods and man himself. These problems became so intense that it caused the Lord God to make the following statement:

Gen. 6:5-7: *And God saw that the wickedness of man was great in the earth, and that every imagination of the thoughts of his heart was only evil continually. And it grieved the Lord in his heart that he had made Man. He said, I will destroy and remove from the earth both the man and the beasts that I have made along with the creeping thing, and the fowls of the air; for it grieves me that I have made them.*

Only man was considered evil, yet he was created pure. If man was evil it was because he learned it from the gods. The author of Genesis indicated that the Lord God wanted to destroy all life on the planet because of his failure and lack of leadership. It was not ma that was evil but the acts of the gods copied by man that created the problem.

The evil which existed in the hearts of men, the conditions which existed between early man, and the lesser gods and the real reason which caused the Lord God to make such a statement had nothing to do with the evils of man but of the gods. It had everything to do with the crew of the Lord God, the half breed children, the lesser gods called the mighty men of old, and the common man. These conditions will be discussed and explained in the chapter which discusses the Sons of God.

The Lord God had a problem. It was one which he considered and one for which he had no solution. The resolution to the above problem can be said to have been solved by the advent of the flood.

Did the Lord God cause the flood? Did he annihilate all life except what was aboard the ark as claimed by the Bible? Or did he, unable to prevent the flood, use the ark in an attempt to salvage some remnant of life on the planet?

A flood did occur but was it caused by the wrath of God or by the impact of a giant asteroid? Evidence exists which clearly indicated that such an asteroid hit the earth in the Caribbean Sea at about the same time as the flood is recorded to have occurred.

Newsweek Nov. 23, 1992, in an article by Sharon Begley, entitled "The Science of Doom"

Quote: City size: Asteroids or comets larger than three miles across, like Swift-Tuttle, hit every 10 to 30 million years. According to one calculation if it was the dinosaur comet, thought to have been about six miles across-hit in the Gulf of Mexico. It would have created a tidal wave three miles high. Nine hundred miles away, the mammoth wall of water would still be 1,500 feet high. Such an asteroid landing in the Gulf of Mexico would cause floods in Kansas City. The impact would make the entire continent of South America to burst into flame, block out the sunlight and make agriculture impossible. Humans might go the way of the triobites."

An asteroid the size of the Swift-Tuttle did hit the earth and is believed to have created the giant crater found in the Caribbean Sea just north of the Yucatan Peninsula.

The flood changed the course of the biblical history. From the beginning of history mankind began and existed as a saga of one family of individuals. It was a story, a general description of the relationship which existed between the Lord God and the descendants of Seth, not Adam. After the flood the biblical story takes on a mythical aura of a forgiving God, who in his benevolence, saves one family of men along with certain kinds of animals from total annihilation.

In the belief that all men except Noah and his family perished in the flood, the Biblical history again focuses its narrow beam from Noah to one man Abraham and again to only one of his sons, Isaac. Isaac was a bit player and of little importance except for his son Jacob.

From the time of Jacob the Bible becomes a history of the various members of his family, their trials, tribulation, joy and sorrow as they deal with Jehovah, their God, his prophets, themselves and their neighbours.

From Abraham came Ishmael and Isaac. Like Cain, the son of Adam, Ishmael, the first son of Abraham and Esau, the first son of

Isaac, are forgotten men of history and not deemed worthy enough, except in passing, to be a part of Jewish history. Why?

Could it be that according to at least one legend the father of Cain was Samael (Serpent), that Ishmael was born to a slave and that Esau was not as beautiful as Jacob in the eyes of Jehovah?

Before Abraham, the gods known to Noah and his sons were not gods but the masters which came to be called gods. After the flood the Lord God, his crew, Noah and his family, had a barbeque to celebrate their survival. The Bible called this feast an offering to God:

Gen. 8:20-21. *"And Noah built an altar unto the Lord, and took of every clean beast, and of every clean fowl, and offered burnt-offerings on the altar and the Lord smelled a sweet savour; and the Lord said in his heart, I will not again curse the ground any more for man's sake; for the imagination of man's heart is evil from his youth: neither will I again smite any more everything living, as I have done."*

If Noah wished to make a sacrifice, an offering unto the Lord as a sacrificial token of thanks, it would not have been necessary for him to kill and burn one of every clean animals and fowl on board the ark. Nor would God have said in his heart, or out loud, that he enjoyed the smell of the burning flesh. From this celebration until the time of Abraham, the sons and descendants of Noah establish their own gods and worship as they felt the need. It is believed that they came to worship the names of the masters served by their fathers before the flood. Man still feared what he did not understand, and in remembrance of his salvation from the flood, continued to offer up sacrifices in the names of the individual's beings he came to understand as gods. The pleas, worship and sacrifices of man were made by him in his pleas for help, guidance and protection.

As time passed, the stories of the flood, along with the salvation of Noah and the feast, became a part of the history and culture of the descendants of Noah and his family. Bloody sacrifices, religious rituals, priests, holy men and shamans began to appear as among the various tribes and nations of people a result of their belief and understanding of the event. The flood and mans survival became a part of mans history and his heritage.

The feast of Noah, believed to have been a religious sacrificial offering to God for saving man from death became a part of mans worship and in the belief that in his time of need and trouble call upon his God for help.

The priest saw to it that temples were built not only to honour the gods but that man would have a meeting place where he could go to in order to give thanks, offer sacrifice and worship his god. The temples became the gathering place for the wealth of the gods. They housed the wealth, gifts and sacrifices to the gods which the priest, holy men and shaman proclaimed were due and necessary to appease them.

The religious orders, with their magnificent temples, like all things new, were bright and shining examples the noblest ideals of man. They still are, but then, as it is now, those ideas have been were used by the temples guardians and the religious leaders to further their own greed and lust for power.

Religious organizations, controlled by men of power, greed and ambition, were formed to give to the people what was believed that they wanted. Sometimes it was for rain during a drought. Other times it might have been for good crops, fair weather, a safe shelter or freedom from sickness and disease. In answer to the pleas of the people the religious leaders dispensed the wishes and wisdom of God.

Since no layman was considered worthy enough to approach God no one did. So there was no way that the people could know the will of God except through the teachings of the religious leaders of their faith. So in reality the wishes and wisdom of God was the wishes, wisdom and the desires of the priest and holy men who ran the temples and controlled the religious order.

Each community created, pursue and worshipped a god that best suited the desires of the local community in whatever manner best pleased the general population. They might have worshipped one or many gods. It made no difference as long as they had a god they felt they knew could listened to, be blessed by and in their time of need protected by it they were happy. Jehovah was one of those gods. He is identified by several names including Baal.

It was almost three hundred years after the flood before Jehovah becomes the entity known as the God of Abraham. Abraham believed him to be a god and passed that belief down to his sons Ishmael and Isaac. Because of the paths taken by these two sons the beliefs of Abraham split into two of the world's great religions, Islam and Judaism. From Judaism came a third great religion. It is called Christianity.

Ishmael, the oldest son of Abraham and the rightful heir of Abraham, took his beliefs to a place called Mecca. There Allah, "The God" blesses him and his descendants with a mighty empire. In time a prophet called Muhammad, or Mohammed brings their faith and beliefs into a total submission to God in their Holy Book, The Koran.

Isaac, the second son, the one which becomes the heir of Abraham passed his beliefs down to his first two sons Esau and Jacob. Again it is the second son and not the first who inherits the rights and privileges of Abraham. Jacob stole that right from his older brother by subterfuge. At sometime during his travels to avoid the wrath of his brother Esau, Jacob meets Jehovah, the God of his father and of Abraham. Deuteronomy Chapter 32 describes that relationship. Jehovah loved Jacob until he became fat, lazy, insolent, and disrespectful. Because of this disrespect Jehovah cast Jacob aside and placed a curse upon him and his descendants. That curse began in Egypt and was fulfilled in the wilderness of Sinai.

Abraham was a nomad. As he led his herds across the land to feed, he must have encountered many people who followed different and varied religious customs in their worship of the many gods. Their methods and the ways in which they worshipped may well have been entirely different from the ones he had been taught at home as he was growing up. Regardless of what he originally believed he had to have been affected by those varied customs which altered his original faith in the gods. This idea is substantiated by his willingness to butcher his son Isaac as a human sacrifice.

Sometime during his travels he encountered Jehovah, a being who convince Abraham that he was a god. Abraham, an uneducated nomad shepherd believed and accepts him as the one and only God and began to serve, worship and sacrifice to him.

For this service Jehovah gave Abraham advice and suggestions. Abraham in following those suggestions left the home of his father and began to wander the land of Syria and Canaan. Soon there was drought and famine in the land. It seems that the only help he is able to get from his god is the suggestion that he takes his flocks and travel into Egypt. This he does. There, in order to survive he allows his wife to become the consort of a king.

Today there may exist a hatred between the Egyptians and the Jewish nation for a multitude of reasons, but if history is correct, there would be no Jewish nation or many of the other nations in existence today if it had not been for the generosity of Egypt in allowing it to become a sanctuary, a haven for the drought stricken inhabitants of the desert lands.

During the time of Abraham the being which Abraham knew, the being that walked, talked and ate with him, the being who had to walk to Sodom and Gomorrah in order to verify the rumours of corruption, who bargain with Abraham was worshipped by Abraham as the God.

During this relationship a covenant, an agreement, was established between them.

Gen. 12:1-3: *"Now the Lord had said unto Abram, Get thee out of thy country, and from thy kindred, and from thy father's house, unto a land that I will show thee: And I will make of thee a great nation, and I will bless thee, and make thy name great; and thou shall be a blessing: And I will bless them that bless thee, and curse him that curses thee: and in thee shall all the families of the earth be blessed."*

Abraham did become the father of two great nations, the Jewish nation and the nation of Islam. He also made another covenant with Abraham, one which the Jewish people refuse to recognize:

Gen. 15:18: *In that same day the Lord made a covenant with Abram, saying, to thy seed have I given this land, from the river of Egypt unto the great river Euphrates.*

Who are the seed of Abraham? Who are those entitled to that land of Canaan?

They are the descendants of: Ishmael, Isaac, Zimran, Jokshan, Medan, Midian, Ishbak, and Shuah.

Ishmael became the father of the Arabic nations. This promise came true. Isaac, believed to have been the son of Abraham and Sarah, became the father of the Jewish nation. But what if Isaac was the son of Jehovah and Sarah and not Abraham would he still be the promised heir of Abraham, the one from his loins?

The rest of the seed of Abraham have been forgotten. They were never allowed to become a part of the history of Abraham. So the agreement between Jehovah and Abraham becomes the prelude to the beginning of the real Biblical saga. It was not the story of the sons of Abraham, or of their children. It is the story of one man, Jacob, his relationship with Jehovah, and the curses place on him by the anger of Jehovah. The result of those curses on his descendants, his twelve sons, and the twelve tribes of Israel, are the stories which became a part of the Torah, the Jewish religion and the history of the Jewish nation.

From the Torah came the Christian's Holy Bible. It, like the Torah, is merely a collection of short stories, essays in which the author relates to the reader the dialogue, thoughts, actions, past events, future occurrences, and directs the reader to the conclusion desired by the author.

Moses in writing Genesis, thousands of years after it had happened, is somehow able to relate the very thoughts of God, his actions and his personal conversations with beings like himself, and his servants, retold for our benefit.

Two excellent examples are the discussions between the Lord God, Adam and Eve, and the wager between God and Satan concerning Job, a perfect and upright servant of Jehovah.

A few of the thoughts of God to which the biblical writer was somehow privy to are:

Gen. 1:3: *"And God said, let there be light and there was light."* (Thought)

Gen. 1:26: *"And God said, let us make man in our image, after our likeness: and let them have dominion over the fish of the sea, and over the fowl of the air, and over the cattle, and over all the earth, and over every creeping thing that creeps upon the earth."* (Dialogue)

Gen. 2:7: *"And the Lord God formed man of the dust of the ground, (the elements) and breathed into his nostrils the breath of life, and man became a living soul."* (Action)

Gen. 3:8. *"And they heard the voice of the Lord God walking in the garden in the cool of the day: and Adam and his wife hid themselves from the presence of the Lord God amongst the trees of the garden."* *(Habits of God)-(Actions of man)*.

Job 1:6: *"Now there was a day when the sons of God came to present themselves before the Lord, and Satan came also among them."* *(Visitors)*.

Gen. 7:21: *"And the Lord smelled a sweet saviour; and the Lord said in his heart, I will not again curse the ground any more for man's sake; for the imagination of man's heart is evil from his youth: neither will I again smite any more everything living, as I have done."* *(Assumptions)*

Other than some of the locations specified in the Bible and a record of some of the events which are recorded there, the Bible is nothing more than a saga with special characters, special events and dialogue which makes those individuals and events interesting. Most of the events which are believed to have been the miracles of God can easily be explained by modern technology, either scientific, medical or the result of natural phenomena.

However, whether the scriptures of the Torah and the Bible are fact or fiction is really immaterial. They have had a direct influence on the world and the history of mankind for the last few thousand years and must therefore be evaluated from that perspective.

However good the intentions of the Torah and the Bible might have been, they are both pieces of literature which have been used by religion to contribute to the slavery, misery, death, and destruction of millions of believers. The misuse, misinterpretation, and false teachings of religion and man have made priests and rabbi's vampires of humanity.

The teaching of the Torah and the Bible are not without redeeming grace. One of the most important is that they seems to teach us that mankind, with or without a god, is a bloodthirsty, greedy, lustful race without a consciousness. This is not the fault of man rather it is his gift from the gods. According to the Bible these traits, if they are not the traits of all of the gods are at least the traits of one god, Jehovah.

As the reader follows the review of the biblical passages within this book this statement will become abundantly clear.

Some religious orders have led individuals to believe that all men are all equal in the sight of God and the law. This a fallacy, preached by religious organization in order to gain converts and to control congregations. It used this belief to play upon the guilt and compassion of humanity in order to make the church a stronger, richer and more powerful organization.

We do not look alike, think alike, or have the same mental and physical abilities. We do not approach problems the same way, and we certainly do not come from the same social, religious and ethical backgrounds. In today's society we are not even conceived or born in the same way. How can anyone claim with authority that we are equal? To say that we are all equal in the sight of God is to deny his own words of separation. To Jehovah men are different from women. Jews are better than Gentiles. And individuals born without blemish are superior to those born or who obtain disfigurement and deformities in this life. If there is one thing which does make us equals it is the breath of life and the fact that we shall all die and return to the elements of the earth. In that we are all a part of the universe and we are all equal.

Our individual differences are the one thing which binds us together and should make us stronger as a race. It is the single most important trait which has allowed mankind to survive and flourish. Without our differences we would be nothing more than robots, clones and duplicates, reciting and mimicking all that we see and do.

It is unfortunate that everyone is not able to share in all of the joys and material things of life in the same or to the same degree but each of us has been given a uniqueness not shared by any other. That uniqueness forces each of us to use our abilities in different ways and to different degrees. How much and how far we are able to go in our efforts is the measure of our success or failure. This determines our position in life.

Just as nature has ordained that no two snowflakes are ever to be the same so it was with man before science and medicine dictated otherwise. In the natural order of all things in the known universe there is no one exactly like another. Our uniqueness adds beauty and excitement to the world around us. We are each given a limited number of opportunities in this life. What we make of those opportunities is our measure as a man.

Some men have used their opportunities to control and to impose their beliefs and ideals upon their fellow countrymen. They believed that the acts they committed were for the good of their fellow countrymen and ultimately the whole of mankind.

Great men have led their people to great wars in the name of God and King. But of all the men women and children who have suffered and died nothing has ever really changed the condition of mankind in general.

Is it any wonder that people in general and religious disciplines in particular have never found true peace and harmony in studying the Bible, religious text or in the worship of any god?

It is difficult to comprehend the blessing that are suppose to come to everyone by following the commandments of self denial, suffering and want in order to be more acceptable to a being who is never satisfied.

The sun shines on the rich and poor alike. Each man received his own reward by his own efforts. When life is over, we all perish and no man leaves with anything more than he had when he came. What one accumulates on this earth is merely to make one's stay more acceptable, pleasing and enjoyable.

No one was more aware of this than Jehovah, the God of the Jews.

He ate on gold plates. Sat on gold chairs and was surrounded with furs and beautiful tapestries.

Abraham was also aware of this. Didn't he allow his wife to bed other men in order to save his own life? His morals at the time would be considered offensive today. But during those days many customs were allowed which would not be condoned today. His morals he passed down to his children and his grandchildren. Deception or guile may well have been considered an admirable trait to someone who had to live by their wits. Today such men are called con men, thieves and crooks.

Abraham deceived Pharaoh and is rewarded. Jacob, his grandson deceived his father-in-law and he too is rewarded. They were both blessed with much material wealth. Abraham had his given to him because of the efforts of his wife. Jacob, with the help of his sons killed and stole for his.

The one thing which custom decreed a man must have in order to be truly great was children. With all of his wealth this was the one thing he lacked. He needed children. He was childless. Sarah, his wife, was not able to conceive and he waited for the promise of heirs, to be fulfilled.

In time, when Abraham was a very old man he does have a son by going into the handmaiden of his wife Sarah. The name of his first born was Ishmael. Through him came the nation of Islam. Abraham was the biological father of Ishmael, but was he the biological father of Isaac? If he was not then he was not the father of the nation of Israel.

We are told that Sarah was the mother of Isaac but who was his father? Was it Abraham or the god Jehovah?

Nothing much is said of the sons of Abraham except that they existed. It is Jacob the son of Isaac and grandson of Abraham which has become the main focus of scripture.

Esau, the grandson of Abraham, twin of Jacob, is only important to the history of Israel because Herod, a descendant, sat on the throne of Israel right before the time of Jesus. He was not a descendant ruler through the line of David but was appointed ruler and king of Israel by Rome authority.

The conflict which existed between the descendants of the two sides of the family of Abraham, Ishmael and Isaac and the family of Isaac, Esau and Jacob, was a continuation of the conflict between family members since the time of Cain and Abel. Cain killed Abel. Noah cursed his grandson Canaan. Ishmael was forced out of his inheritance by his younger half brother Isaac and Jacob robbed his older brother Esau of his birthright. As a result two distinct societies have come into being.

Jacob, like his grandfather Abraham, spent time with Jehovah. They were friends of a sort. Jehovah was said to love Jacob, until he became fat, lazy and sarcastic. Jacob shared his experiences with his children. In this way they came to know Jehovah by name. Whether they believed he was a god is uncertain.

It has never been recorded as to who the Hebrews worshipped while they were in Egypt. It is not know if they ever worshipped Jehovah.

It was not until 400 years after the death of Jacob did the name of Jehovah reappear in the history of the Hebrews. They recognized his name, not as Jehovah but "I Am." Their respect for the name of the God of Abraham, Isaac and Jacob, was no greater than that shown to any ruler, man of wealth or power.

Jacob was taught by his mother to lie, cheat and steal. These marvellous attributes, he passed on to his children. The children learned their lessons well. Scripture relates incidence after incidence where the children of Jacob followed in the footsteps of their patriarch Jacob.

Jacob stole from his brother, cheated his father-in-law, and ridiculed Jehovah, so too did his sons to him. They sold their brother into slavery, lied to their father, and through lies and deceit murdered all of the men of a city. They stole the wealth, burned the city, captured and sold into slavery the women and children of that city.

In a time of drought, the family of Jacob like the family of his grandfather before him found it necessary to journey into Egypt to find food, water and shelter in order that they might survive.

In Egypt they found life to be good and plentiful. They were given their own land and began to multiply. Protected by Joseph, the right hand of Pharaoh and the brother which they had sold into slavery, the family of Jacob lived very well.

Joseph had overcome his condition of slavery, and had become a favourite of Pharaoh. He was great in the land. He controlled the food and supplies of Pharaoh. During the times of droughts and other circumstances, his power was magnified. After Joseph died the clan of Jacob, now called the Hebrews, ere no longer to enjoy the favours of Pharaoh. Force to live according to their own merits, abilities and efforts their freedom as outsiders slowly diminished and they eventually came under bondage to Pharaoh.

For almost four hundred years the Hebrews lived in Egypt without the help and assistance of their god Jehovah.

Why did Jehovah, after allowing his people the Hebrews to suffer almost four hundred years in bondage did he decide it was time to intervene?

Jehovah decided to become a god like all of his compatriots. They had land temples, priests, and worshippers. They received gifts and were offered sacrifices. Jehovah had nothing.

He decided that the Hebrew would make great servants. Physicals conditions were right and he could use the results of a predicted natural phenomenon, the eruption of the volcano on the isle of Crete to his advantage. If he were able to free the Hebrews from the control and power of Pharaoh he would be able to obtain the worshippers he needed to make himself a god with a name feared and respected among his peers. He would train and lead the Hebrews in a battle of conquest. Under his rule and control they would obtain land, establish a priesthood, laws and rituals. He would demand certain gifts, sacrificed and a temple according to his own design. He would become the greatest of the gods by destroying the temple of the other gods and by elimination their worshippers. Without temples, priest and worshippers the names of the other gods would disappear. He would teach his sons and daughters to corrupt his grandson Jacob and of making fun of him.

Once under his yoke the Hebrews served him and not Pharaoh. They became his slaves and servants. He exercised the right of the inheritance given to him by the Lord God.

Before Abraham accepted Jehovah as his god Jehovah was a no-body. He had nothing that he could lay claim to with one exception: there are some theologians that believe he may have been the God Murdock, the God of Hammurabi and one of the gods worshipped by Abraham.

Besides Abraham and his sons he had no worshippers, no one offered up sacrifices, brought him gifts, gave him praise, honour and glory. He had no priest to serve him, no temples, altars laws, or religious rituals as did the other gods. If he was to gain the respect he felt he deserved than he needed all of these things. When he decided that it was time to become a god worthy of recognition he put his pride aside and again made himself known to the Hebrews, the descendant of Jacob, his grandson.

He selected them as his congregation and servants for a number of reasons. His name was still a part of their oral tradition. They were already in bondage and knew how to serve. They were also destitute and were most vulnerable to bribes and suggestions. Moses, a Hebrew and a member of the household of Pharaoh was selected as his spokesperson.

Moses was an educated man. As a member of the nobility he has training in many fields. He also had access to Pharaoh himself. Moses was well adapted to plead the case of Jehovah before Pharaoh.

The Hebrew people during their 400 year stay in Egypt had over the years placed themselves into bondage to Pharaoh and were now considered his property.

Originally it was not Jehovah's intention to free the Hebrews from that condition he merely wanted them to worship and offer up sacrifices to him. He was willing to let Pharaoh have the headache of administration. To do this he only requested that Pharaoh allow the Hebrews permission to journey three days into the wilderness, a thirty mile trek where they could offer to him their worship, sacrifices and praise. Moses was chosen by Jehovah as his spokesperson the new leader of the Hebrew people who at that time hah none.

Why did God want the Hebrews to travel for three days into the hot desert wilderness just to worship him? There was a reason and it was a part of Jehovah's plan to become god of worth. At the end of that three day walk was an old abandon calf temple, one of many found in and around the land of Goshen. It was the temple and would be Jehovah's first once he was able to gain control as a god with disciples.

This did not happen because while Pharaoh agreed to let the people go to worship Moses wanted to take their herds of cattle with them. This Pharaoh could not allow. This rejection led to the ten plagues of Egypt.

As a result of the plagues Pharaoh agreed to let the people go glad to get them out of Egypt.

When the Hebrews finally camped upon or near Mt. Sinai at the site of an old abandon calf temple they had Aaron fashion a golden calf for them to worship and give thanks for their deliverance from Egypt.

They had barely started to worship the calf instead of Jehovah the God of their forefathers when Moses returned from the mountain.

When he saw their iniquity he became so angry that he ordered the Levites to go throughout the camp and slaughter everyone who had participated in the ceremony. Only the Levi involved in the slaughter were exempt.

Archaeologists believe they have found this particular mountain and the ruins of a temple believed to have been that of a calf cult. It is a reasonable explanation as to why Aaron and the people built and began to worship the golden calf so soon after their departure from Egypt. This worship was for the Hebrew an old tradition they were used to, Jehovah was still just a name from the past that had no religious meaning to them as a god worthy of worship.

When Moses first approached Pharaoh for permission to allow the Hebrews to leave his immediate control and wander into the wilderness to worship their god Pharaoh refused. It became necessary for Jehovah to devise some rather means other than words to gain what he wanted. He found those means in the natural physical phenomenon which often occur as an after affect of a volcanic eruption.

The time line of history are not always accurate but at the same time as the Exodus occurred so too did the eruption of the volcano on the Isle of Create. This eruption destroyed the Minoan civilization. The after effects of this eruption were felt in Egypt. These natural affects are what have been passed down to us as the plagues of Egypt, the wrath of a mighty god.

The natural phenomenon created by this eruption, were used by Jehovah, to give the Egyptians and the Hebrews the illusion of his power as a god.

Jehovah used the opportunity of this natural occurrence to create the impression that the plagues of Egypt were a result of his power alone. The belief, instilled in the minds of the people, and the death of so many Egyptians, caused by the last plague, resulted in freedom for the Hebrews.

Pharaoh finally agreed to let the Hebrews follow Moses into the wilderness, but only to sacrifice.

Exodus 10:24: *"And Pharaoh called unto Moses, and said, Go ye, serve the Lord: only let your flocks and your herds be stayed: let your little one also go with you."*

That was not good enough for Moses. Moses wanted it all.

Exodus 10: 25-27: *"And Moses said, Thou must give us also sacrifices, and burnt-offerings that we may sacrifice unto the Lord our God. Our cattle also shall go with us so that there shall not be a hoof left behind. For these we must take to serve the Lord our God because we do not know what we must serve the Lord, until we get there."*

Pharaoh was willing to let the people go and worship their god, provided they left behind their livestock. This was his assurance that the people would return. Moses wanted more, and demanded that Pharaoh allow the people to take their herds as sacrifices and burnt offerings. Both he and Pharaoh knew that the whole herd would not be sacrificed. Why was it necessary it take the complete herd unless the Hebrews had no intention of coming back to Pharaoh's control?

The Bible says that the Lord harden's Pharaoh's heart. It was not the Lord that hardened Pharaoh Heart but the demands of Moses telling Pharaoh what he must do. No one commanded Pharaoh, much less a Hebrew Slave.

When the last plague, death to all of the first born, was placed upon the Egyptians, death came to the entire nation as promised.

Pharaoh called Moses and Aaron, relented and gave them permission to leave the land of Egypt. He did not give them permission to rob his people. The Hebrews did that on their own once they were given permission from Moses who said it came from their new god.

The Hebrew people began their new life of freedom as thieves. Not satisfied with leaving Egypt they took advantage of the death and misery of the Egyptian people to borrowed (steal) from them their jewels, silver, gold and raiment. This was in addition to those things they would require in their travels once they were out of Egypt and into the desert wilderness. Given permission by Jehovah and Moses the Hebrews looted as much of the wealth of Egypt as they could safely carry with them on their journey to what they believed was the promised land of Canaan.

Exodus 12;35-36: *"And the children of Israel did according to the word of Moses: and they borrowed of the Egyptians jewels of silver, and jewels of gold, and raiment. 36. And the Lord gave the people favour in the sight of the Egyptians, so that they lend unto them such things as they required: and they spoiled the Egyptians."*

When Pharaoh discovered what the Hebrews had done to his people he sent his army to intercept and return them to his control for justice and punishment.

While trying to cross a shallow area of the Red Sea the army of Pharaoh was caught by a flash flood in the flat dry washes of the tributaries which flowed between the Mediterranean and Red Sea and was destroyed. The Hebrews escaped   the wrath of Pharaoh only to find themselves at the mercy of Jehovah and Moses. Alone in the desert with no place to go, they trade their bondage to Pharaoh for the slavery, servitude and bondage of their new God, Jehovah.

The Exodus began a new era in the history of the Jewish nation. Twelve families united under one rule, serving with one god, united in purpose became the foundation of a new nation, the nation of Israel.

The scriptures are a condensed synopsis of the trials, tribulations, successes and failures of this particular group of people as they made their way through the pages of history.

Jehovah gave the people one god to worship instead of many. He gave them a religion, controlled by a priesthood, rituals, laws and commandments. He gave them a beginning and a history. He gave them a culture, and through that culture and history, a reason to believe that they are the chosen people of God.

They are his chosen, but how does the history they believe in, and the reality of the scriptures relate one to the other?

It might be said that their history began with their understanding of the following statement, they believe came from their god.

Genesis 1:26, *God said "Let us make man in our image, after our likeness."*

This particular phrase indicates, first and foremost, that the writer identifies the speaker as God. The word is identification, a title and does not imply divine power, wisdom or deity. These are all attributes given to that title by man himself. Prior to this statement there had evidently been some discussion among a group of individuals concerning the making of a creature they identify as man. It was purposed by the individual called God that the man is made in their image after their likeness. Evidently the purpose of the man dictated his form. The indication here is that other forms of life were considered but the design of man which best suited the purposes of the makers was a design after their own structure and with a physical resemblance.

Man was created to live, work and survive on this particular planet. In adapting his anatomy to that purpose the form of God, who or whatever his race or origin happened to be, was considered to be the best for the tasks that lay ahead. Second and just as important for us to remember is that in the makeup of man was made in the image of the being identified as God. Therefore, if something is made in the image or likeness of anything there is a resemblance. If something is made in the image of something, then not only do these objects resemble each other, but they are alike as well.

Since man is flesh and blood we must by logic assume that the individuals we call the gods were too. This assumption is verified by scripture.

Gen. 6:3. *"And the Lord said my spirit shall not always strive with man, for that he also is flesh: yet his days shall be hundred and twenty years."*

If we are images of and we resemble the gods who are flesh and blood by the process of logic, either we are both gods and we are not.

The Bible does not tell us that God and man was biologically compatible but the fact that the sons of God had intercourse with human women and children were produced is I believe a very clear indication that this was fact.

Jewish legend says that Cain was the son of Eve and Samuel, a god. Jehovah had intercourse with Mary and Jesus is said to have been the result. Then there was the mating between Jehovah and Sarah who produced Isaac, Menorah and an angel sired Samson and John the Baptist was sired by an angel and his barren mother Elizabeth.

Nowhere in nature are two different species able to united and procreated unless they are biologically compatible. Their DNA must be the same. The sons of God, which is another way of saying his staff and his crew, the lesser gods, went in unto the daughters of men and fathered children as a result of those sexual unions.

Genesis 6:2: *"the sons of God saw that the daughters of men were fair and they took all that they chose and made wives of them all."*

Gen. 6:4: *"There were giants in the earth in those days; and also after that, when the sons of God came in unto the daughters of men, and they bore children to them: the same became mighty men, which were of old, men of renown."*

What made the half breed children of man and the god's men of renown? Were giants or because they had the mental abilities of the fathers and the physical strength statue of mortal man?

This is very significant in understanding who God, the creator of man, was. It shows that he and his crew were members of a highly advanced civilized society. They were aware of male/female relationships. They knew of, need and enjoyed sex. Sexual relationships were not evident in the creation of Adam because there were no women available. Adam could not reproduce children until Eve was created. God tried to create mates for Adam and the other male workers by creating special animals to help them in their labours. Because the DNA of these newly created animals was different, not biological compatible their union with man could not produce offspring.

First man had a biological need to reproduce. It was an inherent part of his emotional and physical makeup inherited from the gods who also suffered from this condition. Until females were created to satisfy those that human need it is possible that the need was satisfied by use of the animals and between men themselves.

Gen. 2:18-20: *And the Lord God said, It is not good that a man should be alone: I will make a help meet for him. And out of the ground the Lord God formed every beast of the field, and every fowl of the air, and brought them unto Adam to see what he would call them: and whatsoever Adam called every living creature that was the name thereof. Adam gave names to all of the cattle, the fowl of the air, and to every beast of the field but for him there was no was no help meet.*

Because these new animals were specially created they differed from the animals created as a part of the original universal design. They were therefore created differently. They too were cloned from genetic DNA in a process similar to Adam and Eve and similar to the numerous animals created or cloned in our medical and scientific laboratories today.

In the original creation, the one by GOD we have the following:

Gen. 1:24: *"And God said, let the earth bring forth the living creature after his kind, cattle, and creeping thing, and beast of the earth after his kind: and it was so."*

For Adam, Eve and the rest of the first created men we have the following.

Gen. 1:26. *"And God said, Let us make man in our image, after our likeness: and let them have dominion over the fish of the sea, and over the fowl of the air, and over the cattle, and over all the earth, and over every creeping thing that crept upon the earth."*

This is a different creative God than the GOD which created the universal. This is the separation of the two biblical gods which the misunderstanding of man and religious leaders have combine into the one single entity worshipped by many religious denominations.

Eve was also a new creature. Like Adam and the special animals of the Lord God she too was cloned. She was created in a laboratory by medical personnel and scientists who modified the DNA taken from the cells of Adam. As the result of the modification of the genetic cell structure of Adam the physical structure and biologically makeup of Eve was changed. She was made a female. As such she became a wife and a producer of children. Those children born to her and the other earth women who were created for the male workers were able to produce the replacements slaves of the gods which died of old age, accidents and disease. The new earth women were also used by the sons of God as a means of satisfying their sexual desires.

Adam, and early man, created in the image of God as flesh and blood beings and biological compatible with the gods had to have come from the same basic genetic material which made up the Lord God and his crew. The creation of Adam, Eve and the others, including those special animals created to assist Adam, could only have resulted from some medical or scientific technology which closely resembles the cloning procedures of today.

Just as Eve was cloned from the cells of Adam so too was Adam was cloned from the cells of God.

Man was created by modifying the cell structure of the Living Creatures. The cells of God were manipulation by science. From the alterations made to genetic cell structure of God came the basis makeup of Adam.

What were the necessary modifications required?

First the genetic makeup of God had to be altered in order to allow Adam to be biologically and physically adaptable to the environment of this planet. That adaption included but was not limited to his physical structure, his biological and chemical makeup as well. Once Adam, as a new modified creature in the likeness of the gods was found to be in harmony with his surroundings other male workers were created each with a particular modification to suit his particular job description. When the other created individuals were found to compatible with the earth and their new surroundings the gods knew that Eve cloned from the cells of Adam would also be able to function without any difficulties.

Man was not created by magic nor spiritual mysticism. He was made in a laboratory, by highly skilled surgeons, using advanced technology, and scientific equipment.

Adam was merely the first of many men to be created in this manner by the gods. From the blood cells of the crew, are they called angels, messengers or whatever, the gods created the other men who lived in the time of Adam? They became the workers which served the gods, tilled the fields, herded the cattle, build the cities, wove the cloth, created shelters for the gods, work the mines, smelted the ore, made and learned to play the musical instruments which entertained and pleased the gods.

Man was a slave, created to work and serve the needs and desires of the gods.

As each individual worker was created, their genetic makeup was modified by genetic engineering in order to endow each individual with specific skills, traits and abilities. The initial workers, with their unique skills, became the leaders who established the different trades and/or crafts groups required by a vibrant society. Each group was an organization within itself, accountable only to its immediate supervisor. Those supervisors were the crewman or angels of God, from which the group members themselves were cloned. These supervisors later became some of the other gods later identified and worshipped by man.

The children born to the first created men and women and those from the gods and earth women became the foundation of the human race. They were created by natural biological processes.

When children were born to the supervisors, the sons of god, and the women they called wives, these children were called the mighty men of old. As half breed gods, they began to act as supervisors, by the authority of their fathers. This was the beginning of the idea of a ruler, ruling by the will of God. It was also the beginning of what we call today the blue blooded aristocracy.

If we believe the legends of the Uros, the blood of the gods was black. The blood of man was red. When the two different types of blood were mixed by the interbreeding between the god and women not only were different type of blood produced but this mixed blood gave the appearance of having a blue tint. Therefore, if an individual was pricked the colour of their blood would identify who they were, black blood, god, red blood man, blue blood, half breed.

When man demonstrated his ability to adapt and surviving in his new environment, a woman was cloned. She was called Eve. From her genetic structure other women were made. The other women became the wives of the workers already in existence. Created as helpers to the men, they also became reproductive individuals. Human reproduction reduces the need for the cloning process. It also increased the working population faster than the machines.

All of this will be explained in greater detail as the scriptures are critiqued. That critique will also clearly show why there is no foundation for the belief in a god nor is there any justification for a religion to worship and serve a god that does not exist.

This is a new perspective on God, man and religion which I believe will change the way that modern man looks at God. It should clarify who and what is God, and establish Man's place in the natural order of things. By these relationships I hope to remove the guilt of sins carried by so many religious disciples, sins created by false and misleading religious concepts. If guilt, created by false beliefs, can be removed, peace of mind is sure to follow.

Before man there was one and only one true God. As the name implies, it was the ultimate authority to which man has given that title. It was the enigma, the creative power and the force, believed to have existed, and within the vast regions of space, before time and the universe were first created.

What that power was, or is, we do not know. In order for us to identify it as the creator of the universe and in a way that is recognizable by everyone man gave that enigma a name. He called it GOD.

That name was also used by the society of the living creature to represent its ultimate authority except that the word Lord was added. This completely changed the meaning of the word GOD. It changed from the ultimate authority to "a person who has dominion over others, as a feudal superior.

The word lord in biblical references then separates the words GOD and God into two separate entities. GOD then becomes the ultimate authority of the universe and the Lord God the superior over members of his race and of man, by whose authority they were created.

At the moment of our creation our ultimate authority was the Lord God who later was worshipped by Melchizedek, priest and king of Salem, as the Most High God.

As the ultimate authority among men it is only appropriate that he called himself by that same name.

The universal god is the force and power believed to have been responsible for the creation of the universe and all that exists within. This creation which goes far beyond our abilities to comprehend is a creation so vast that it makes the universe, galaxies, nebulae, and stars beyond calculation.

It is the ego and stupidity of man, which has helped to convince him that the universal creator, that power beyond calculation, forsook the cosmos, the vast regions of space beyond calculation in order to come to this planet and create, love and reside with Man.

While there appears to be no factual evidence to support such a claim, indirectly this statement could be considered true but only in a second hand way.

There is every indication in scripture, that during the creative processes, many diverse forms and types of life came out of the original creative beginning. I believe that it was one of those different life forms that eventually came to this planet and created man in their image.

As the universe was undergoing its creative expansion, a part of that expansion was the beginning of organic life. This is recorded as having taken place before the formation of the solar systems. As such, organic life, in whatever its shape or form, exists not on a particular planet, but throughout the galaxies.

Organic life began when certain elements, accidentally or by design combined in a specific way. Life in it's' struggle to survive and to adapt to its' environment began to evolve into all manner of life forms. Some became plants others animals, fowl, creatures of the seas, bacteria, viruses and forms of life that we are as yet unaware. Each life form in its own way, in its own environment, adapted, evolved and began the perpetuation of its species. These life forms all conformed, in one way or the other, to the laws and principles by which all life exists. These are the laws of GOD, which when broken lead to death. Since it is believed that the laws and the principles of GOD exist throughout the universe it stands to reason that so too does life.

Until we travel the stars we have no way of knowing if the above statement is fact or fiction. What we do know is that at least three of those life forms, distinct from all the others, are mentioned in religious scripture. Those life forms are "The Living Creature", Cherubim and Seraphim.

The term "Living Creature" is the name use by Jehovah to identify his race of people. He gave that name to Moses when he was relating to Moses the history of the Hebrew people.

Since the Cherubim and Seraphim served the Lord God, the living creature, both in the beginning of Biblical scripture and are said to be present at the end time then it can be said with certainty, that they are immortal.

We now have in existence before man, three distinct and different life forms. Since the scriptures are clear in that the Cherubim are the guardians of the Lord God than it is possible that God is the Living Creature. If so than it cannot be the GOD of Creation, an entity which does not need protection.

From the beginning of scripture there are mentioned three distinct beings called God or identified by that title. There is GOD, the creator of the universe, the Most High God, the creator of Man, and last but not least there is Jehovah, the God of the Hebrew, Israelite and Jewish people. Along with Jehovah, there have been other minor gods, worshipped by man, and given many different names according to the language of the people.

I am concerned only with the three gods which form the foundation of the Jewish and Christian faith. The god of the bible is not one god but three distinct and separate individuals. This is one of the biblical mysteries which I came to understand after I began to study the bible from my new perspective.

During the time when the action, reaction and interaction of all matter within the universe began establishing its place in the natural order of things, the laws governing those relationships became a part of the universal continuum. In accordance with biblical scripture, organic life began to evolve in accordance with those laws. A few of the more familiar laws are those which deal with biology, chemistry, physics, gravity and magnetism.

Modern man is only now beginning to understand some of the more complex applications of those laws. Each day he finds that he has just now began to touch the surface of the knowledge which he does not comprehend. The universal laws are the unchangeable laws of God. The biblical laws given to man by the Lord God are changeable. They are the laws which govern relationships, society and human behaviour. They are the laws which maintain a stable relationship, and are laws of civilized conduct. These laws, given by the Lord God and by Jehovah have become a part of the societies established by individual's peoples in order that they might live and survive in peace and harmony with each other.

Soon after the Lord god had created man he began to instruct man in the laws of his society. They were given to man in order that he become a part and learn to function in the civilized culture of the society to which the Lord God belonged.

Understanding the laws which were first given to Adam, Eve and early man help us to obtain a rather clear insight into the civilization of our gods.

Like man the gods were an individual and distinct form of life. They had movement, intelligence and the ability to reproduce their own species.

If they are identified as a unique individual life form within the universal families of life then we have a unique individual species capable of movement and reproduction which becomes a part of all life from the micro to the macro. Included in these groups we must includes not only the animals, sea creatures, flying life forms, bacteria, microbes, germs and all organisms capable of movement and reproduction living outside of our normal domain.

There are life forms which are able to live and survive in the acid of our stomachs, Viruses which can survive in vacuums and those who can survive in boiling water. These are only a few of the diverse forms of life which have been discovered within recent history. But what of all the possible forms of life which may exist within the universe which we have yet to discover? Do we say they cannot and do not exist because we cannot see, hear or feel their existence.

The scriptures mention a creature called a Cherubim, the guardian of the garden and one of the protectors of the Lord God. It was a creature capable of flight. It also appeared to have been a combination of several different life forms, part human and part animal.

The question one might ask at this point is whether this particular creature was a genetic creation of the Lord God and his people or was it an individual species, beings that were under the control of the Lord God and his people? It is really unimportant except to clearly demonstrate that life exists beyond our limited vision, knowledge and understanding. Whatever the Cherubim and the seraphim might have been at the time of the beginning of man scriptures indicate that they are to be standing before the Lord God at the time of mans demise. They are therefore immortal beings no less than the Lord God. That is assuming that the Lord God and his people are immortal.

To the best of our knowledge and in accordance with the scriptures the natural order of creation began with the particles of matter which made of the atom. From the atom came light and energy that began to organize those atoms into a formation of energy which became the waves of the electromagnetic spectrum which determines the degree of heat and cold that all matter must conform.

The scriptures say that before there were the stars, which furnish the heat, light and energy that were required for organic life as we know it to exist and survive such a form already existed. It was a form of organic life capable of reproduction without the heat from the stars but from the energy of the spectrum alone. This must be a kind of organic life which we know absolutely nothing about and it must exist everywhere.

Genesis 1:11-14: *And GOD said, Let the earth bring forth grass, the herb yielding seed, and the fruit-tree yielding fruit after his kind, whose seed is in itself, upon the earth: and it was so. And the earth brought forth grass, and the herb yielding seed after his kind, and the tree yielding fruit, whose seed was in itself after his kind: and GOD saw that it was good. And the evening and the morning were the third day And GOD said, Let there be lights in the firmament of the heavens, to divide the day from the night; and let them be for signs, and for seasons, and for days, and years."*

This organic life was more than primitive algae. It may have started with algae but by the time of Jehovah and man it had advanced into what Jehovah described as grasses, herb yielding seed and fruit trees who's seed was in itself. This type of organic life was evidently types of plants which may have been completely alien to anything existing on earth. For these plants existed before there were suns or stars to furnish the necessary energy needed for their growth.

Genesis 1:24-31 is the recorded beginning of animal life not on or in a specific place but everywhere within the known creation of the universal GOD, whoever or whatever that might be. It was organic life and specifically mentions the Living Creature as one of those life forms, along with cattle, creeping things and other beasts of the earth. I find it significant that in verse, verse 25, the Living Creature is not mentioned, while the rest of the verse is a repeat of verse 24.

It his instruction to Moses Jehovah used the terms fruit trees and cattle. These are terms which relate to certain conditions of a society. The term cattle refer to animal domestication, and fruit trees to cultivation which existed before man was created. This must be so if the Lord god came to this planet and planted a garden.

If cultivation and the herding of animals existed before man, it had to be a part of an existing civilized society. Such references used by Jehovah, indicate that he was not a spiritual deity but a member of that cultured group. The word God, used in the title of the Lord God and by Jehovah referred not to GOD the creator but to the individuals within the society of the living creatures who was the ultimate authority within a given community.

I believe it is at this point in scripture, based upon how it was written, that the word GOD, the creator of the universe became synonymous the individuals, the Lord God and the God Jehovah.

GOD the creator is omnipotent. The Lord God and Jehovah are not. They required food clothing and shelter.

Cain grew the grain which was made into flour and bread. Abel herded sheep which furnished the gods with meat for the table and wool which was woven into cloth and clothes for the gods.

When Abel brought the firstlings of his flock as an offering to the table of the Lord God we are not told who domesticated those sheep nor from where they were obtained. They were already domesticated when Abel was assigned the task of watching over them. We can therefore rightly assume that they were a product of the culture and civilization of God.

The sheep and cattle, herded by man must have been a source of meat for the table of God. It could not have been for man because he had not been given permission to eat meat or to wear clothes. He was naked. He ate greens, fruit, herbs and nuts. He ate, worked and slept in the open with the animals. He was not permitted to eat meat so why was he required herd and care for animals that had no purpose for man?

The sheep were valuable to the gods for other reasons than meat. Their wool was used to make the threads that were used to weave the cloth and made into the clothes that covered the gods. When Adam and Eve were forbidden access to the garden they too began to wear clothes. Each received a suit of the clothes biblically called "coats of skin".

When the gods created man, they gave to him a legacy, a part of their history and their culture. They also gave to him a kinship with themselves.

The scientists and technicians of the Lord God had at their disposal, as our doctors do today the DNA of many life forms along with a list of genetic traits, skills and specifications. This gave to them the abilities to create any kind of life form they desired from their genetic shopping list. An excellent example of this might be the beasts of our legends, the centaur, chimera, sphinx and gargoyles. They may well have been the result of cloning experiments by the gods but I believe they were the animals especially created for specific tasks those animals created as helpmeets for Adam. Today those special animals live only in the memories and legends passed down to us from the time before the flood.

The "Living Creature," existed. Mankind is the modified image of that life form. Biologically the gods of man are an altered image of us regardless of how radical that form might be. Biologically we are the same.

Jehovah told Moses that to look upon his face was to face death.

Exodus 33:20. *And he said, You cannot see my face: for no man see me, and live.*

Was Jehovah so ugly that his face was like the Medusa? Perhaps that is why man came to believed that the aliens were gods and came in many different forms.

Moses was permitted a view of the rear end of Jehovah but not his face. All of which indicates that Jehovah walked and talked among men and he had a physical structure recognizable by man.

As a species, the gods evolved, grew in wisdom, knowledge, science and technology. As their technology expanded so too did their curiosity. They began to reach for the stars. As they travelled the far reaches of space, they left their mark on all of the planets upon which they stepped. In time they came to this planet, the one we call earth. That was approximately 15,000,000 years ago, a time estimate based upon the impression of several boot print found in several parts of the world. One at least was found in sandstone, which solidified about that time. I believe that these prints were made by the aliens, the living creatures at a time I believe might be considered as their colonization period, a time of seeding and exploration. This planet was one of those seeded not only with a segment of their race, but with those animals and plants beneficial to their growth and survival. It is unfortunate that during the intervening millennia this planet suffered one of its many heavenly catastrophes, a collision with another celestial mass.

That collision not only destroyed most of the life on the planet but was the beginning reversal of a proud and advanced culture. Eventually the gods returned to this planet. When they did, it was to find that the colonists had reverted to their primordial state. They were little more than animals, individuals living day by day, interested only in self survival.

The legend of the Uros of Bolivia, tend to verify, to some extent, the above hypothesis. Their legends state that their ancestors originally came from the stars. This was a time long before the creation of man. They believe this because their legends state that they are not like other men. Are they the remnants of a failed colony or were they a part of the crew of God who were left behind to tend the planet when the Lord God and his entourage returned?

Had the original colonists been successful in populating the earth, it would not have been necessary for the aliens to create man when they returned. Nor would it have been necessary for God to issue a commandment to man, that he multiply and replenish the earth.

Gen. 1:28: *"And God blessed them, and God said unto them, Be fruitful, and multiply, and replenish the earth, and subdue it: and have dominion over the fish of the sea, and over the fowl of the air, and over every living thing that moves upon the earth."*

The legends of the Uros, the star knowledge of the Dogon tribe of Africa and the above command are strong indicators that tend to verify the colonization theory.

Scientists continue to search for what they call the missing link. This is a creature which is believed to have been the connecting species between ape and man.

There are no missing links. There are apes, there are the descendants of the colonists from the home world of the Living Creatures and there is man. There is a common bond between all three. It has been determined that each of the above species contain basically the same genetic structure and biological makeup. Only the DNA pattern is slightly different. Man, the Uros, and the gods were and are biologically compatible. Man and the ape are not. If the gods were able to impregnate the daughters of men, they would not be able to do so with apes. However, they could have impregnated female apes with the fertilized eggs of their species, and the apes could have carried those eggs to birth. But at birth the individuals, born from the apes, raised by the apes would still belong to the species from which the sperm and egg originated. This procedure would still have required a mother and a father something which Adam and Eve did not have.

Man is a separate entity. He is a cousin and blood kin to the gods, but he is not one of those gods. What man is not is a hybrid, the result of intercourse between space aliens and apes. Man is also not the result of an alien operation where alien intelligence was implanted into the mind of an ape. If either of the above scenario were true it would still have required aliens with highly skilled medical and scientific personnel to accomplish the medical procedure. The speculation that either of the above events took place is a condition that is not acceptable by any religious or scientific community.

If one adheres strictly to the scriptural text, rather than the individual interpretations of the world's most renown scholars, one would realize that life exists throughout the universe, not just on this planet. The gods were one of those life forms and the human species is another, a sub-culture of that alien race.

When they decided to return to earth it was as a mining expedition to obtain its minerals. Much planning had to be done and many decisions had to be made. Such a venture, requiring many logistical factors, had to be considered. Some of those factors might have been how large was the expedition to be? What kind and type of equipments was going to be needed? How many individuals would be necessary to accomplish the job? What was the estimated requirement for food and water for the journey? Were there any intermediate stops along the way were diminished supplies might be replaced or new material obtained? Upon arrival at their destination what type of plants and animals could they expect to find? How much reliability could they place in the information gathered by their explorers? Could the plants of this planet be used for food? What type of atmosphere would the planet most likely have? Would special breathing apparatuses be required? How long was the growing seasons? Could a garden be planet and relied upon for sustenance? What kind of facilities would be necessary to house the expeditionary force? Would they be able to live on board their ships or were outside shelters going to be required? Where and how were they going to obtain the workers to do the actual labour of mining the minerals? What kind of an environment would they encounter? What special tools, technical support, equipment and materials was it necessary for them to transport to the planet, and what materials would they be able to use upon their arrival?

Most of the above logistical problems were minor compared to the problem of labour. Were there workers available from planets already under their control? If so, would they be able to survive the long journey through space? If they did, would they be able to adapt and survive on the new planet? Would they be able to eat the food available, breath the air and last long enough to be worth the effort? How would replacements be made for those who died of old age, sickness and accidental death? How long would worker replacement time be? For a journey which could have taken anywhere from ten to a thousand years, a lot of work days would be lost. How were the slave workers to be housed, how were they to be fed, and what would happen to those workers when the miners closed shop and returned to their home world?

There was one more rather important question. It was the one which had to do with training and discipline. Would any worker from any of their dominated worlds be intelligent, trainable and disciplined?

It would be the job of the workers from where ever he was obtained to work the mines, process the ores and smelt the ore in order to obtain the minerals desired. It was decided that the workers had to be capable of reproduction in order to replace those which would die by accidents, old age, and disease. To meet these requirements there were three alternatives.

First: The aliens knew of the colonizing attempt eons ago. Would it be possible to obtain a labour force from the colonists? I would assume that the aliens believed, based on pasted experience, that the colonists, so long abandoned by the home world would not be receptive to what they would consider an alien invasion of their planet, especially one in which their resources would be taken away. This possibility was considered unreliable and therefore out of the question.

The next possibility was to find, capture, train and transport suitable life forms from their home world to an alien environment and hope that they would be able to adapt, survive and be productive once they arrived on this planet. This created many more perplexing problems than it solved.

That left the aliens with the one solution they felt would best solve this particular problem. They would wait until they arrived on the planet, evaluated the situation and then decide what type of life force they felt would best meet their needs. Whatever the life force it would be one created from the DNA, RNA and chromosomes stored in their data bank of existing life forms found throughout the galaxies. Their DNA would be used as the basic material needed to clone through genetic engineering the slave labour needed to meet the needs of the mining conglomerate.

When the mining conglomerate reach the planet and determined what life form they felt best suited their needs it was decided to create their new slave force in their image and after their likeness.

To obtain the best DNA for the prototype the leaders of the various companies that made up the mining conglomerate decided to use their own DNA.

How many monsters were created in the cloning process before Adam was found to be a successful and satisfactory prototype is unknown. But the creative process was a success and was used to create the labour force needed by the alien gods to begin their mining operations.

While Adam was a modified clone of the Lord God the rest of the create workers were modified clones of their immediate superiors. These supervisors are the individuals that became the minor gods of man after the flood.

As space travellers it is highly likely that the space ship of the conglomerate had on board a very advance medical hospital and laboratory. In the date banks of that laboratory they would have carried samples of the basic genetic materials, the DNA, of all of the life forms they encountered in their travels. It would be from this storage vault that the Lord God obtained the necessary DNA to clone thereby creating the special animals that he would one day create as a help meet for Adam and workers.

From this shopping list they were able to select the most advantageous genetic material necessary to populate any plane and create whatever life form they deemed to be the most appropriate to that planet. The doctors were able to implant into their new creations whatever special traits and characteristics required for those forms to adapt, survive and function successfully in their new environment. The problems of transportation, food, replacements and adaptability would all be taken care of.

Since the aliens, as we all do, carried within themselves the DNA, the basic building materials, for cloning themselves, they could create their own workers. All they required were the special incubation machines necessary for the procedures to take place. I would suppose that on each and every planet that was mined for its minerals, the procedure was pretty much the same.

On each planet, probably the only differences might have been the design and the image of the workers. Their design would have depended upon the type of mining desired and the environment of that particular planet. On this planet the gods decided that the most desirable design was to create the workers in their own image.

Through the process of genetic engineering, a work force of cloned slaves was created. Such a possibility is not so unbelievable when one understands that the very same thing is being accomplished in the scientific and medical laboratories around the world today.

Many different species of life, including man, have already been genetically created and duplicated in the laboratory. In Japan they are experimenting with artificial blood and are working on a human incubation machine which will act in the same capacity as a human mother.

In the future it will be possible for the fertilized egg of any species to be placed in this incubation machine. There the egg will be nourished until it is ready for birth. During the incubation period, if the egg is human than the fetus while it is being developed can be taught and programmed through sound implant vibration to its' subconscious.

Before the human egg is placed in the incubation machine the egg will be genetically altered with specific traits and characteristics desired by the parents before the egg is placed in the embryonic fluid. The child will be educated and born without parents, disease or birth defects a perfect creation, the twenty first century Adam and Eve.

Our scientists today are able to create new life outside of the normal and natural biological processes of birth, are they not to be considered gods?

They have restored the breath of life to bodies which have stopped breathing. They have replaced human hearts, started ones which have stopped, replaced lungs, kidneys, and operated on our brains. Do they not have the power of life and death over us? Where is the differences between them and our creators, the ones we call gods.

When I considered the following: the legends of the Uros, the footprints in solidified sandstone, a nest of baby dinosaurs destroyed by blasts of radiation, the underground cities, the stone skeleton with ten sets of ribs, the Nazca lines and the words of the Most High God I cannot but help but realized that the gods are not divine entities only flesh and blood beings.

Once I understood and believed in the idea of cloning, substantiated by the biblical story of the creation of Adam and Eve it was easy to begin to believe that God, religion and salvation was a myth created by man through ignorance and misunderstanding. As I began to study the Bible from this new idea the questions led to answers which led to more questions and more answers. As I began to understand the biblical writings a little better I also began to see how the thoughts and ideas of others fit into the picture. The writings of Erich Von Daniken are an excellent example of what I mean.

To quote Erich Von Daniken from his book "The Gold of the Gods", "The Uros who live on reed islands in Lake Titicaca, Bolivia, claim that their people are older than that of the Incas, indeed that they already existed before To Ti Tu, the father of heaven, who created the white men. The Uros swear black and blue that they were not men, for they had black blood and were alive when the earth still lay in darkness. We are not as other men, for we came from another planet. The few Uros who are still alive avoid any contact with the rest of the world. Proudly and stubbornly they defend their otherness as the heritage they brought with them from another planet."

If the legends of the Uros are true, are they the last of the original colonists or is it possible that they might be the remnants of the alien expeditionary force left behind after the flood. Were their reed islands the ark that kept them afloat and alive when flood is supposed to have covered the earth?

Man when he was created was genetically adapted to the high oxygen atmosphere of this planet. His body chemistry was altered. He was created specifically to survive and to adapt to the food, air and environment of earth.

The biblical scripture indicates that the basic cloning material used for the creation of the first man, Adam, came from the blood cells of God, the leader of the expedition. The building materials for the men which followed Adam came from the cells of the crew of God.

The hospital ship, as a part of the expedition, had on board all of the necessary laboratory equipment and medical expertise required to accomplish this vital part of their expeditionary procedures.

The cloning process was not limited to man. Animals were also produced. These animals had special characteristics which gave them the ability to work with and assist man. They were separate from the domesticated animals used for food and other essentials. The domesticated animals were used for meat, the hides for leather, milk for drink, and various assorted other material used in clothing and shelter. The special animals, those created to help man, are the ones identified in Gen. 2:18-20. Among those special creations might easily have been the Sphinx, the Centaur and the Minotaur.

The Sphinx, with its powerful wings, flew the ore to the smelting site. The Minotaur worked the mines, and the Centaur, with its powerful legs, pulled the ore carts from the mines. All of these animals were genetically mutated creatures used for a specific purpose. Because of their human characteristics they were intelligent, easily trained, and were endowed with the strength and special features of the animals incorporated within their makeup. It was these special animals that man was found to be incompatible with.

In one sense of the word man was not a new and different species but a genetically altered form of an existing race. In another sense, he was different. While his foundation was based on the alien race, he was special. He was specifically created to exist in the atmosphere, and the biological environment of earth. He was given the skills, traits and training to become what he was created to be, a trained, docile, obedient and faithful slave. A servant, if you will, to the race of beings, who were his master, the title of which was Lord, Master or God. In time it was man himself that eventually changed the word of God, a title of authority, to mean a being worthy of worship, a divine heavenly being.

The owner/slave relationship which existed between the Lord God and man changed after the time of the flood. It was at that time that the gods, our owners, ceased to take any vital interest in our welfare. Man, reminiscent of his earlier condition when he had physically served the gods, relied upon them for guidance, protection and stability. This was especially true following the flood disaster. It was this need of man and his capacity to service the gods that eventually took on the form of worship, prayers and sacrifices.

The memory of preparing and serving food to the gods became the sacrificial rituals, which have been practised by most societies down through the ages.

The confusion which exists in the mind of man over both the name of God, and which god created what, came about through the misunderstanding of the definition of the word God. It really began with the simplified story of the creation, told to Moses by one of the beings involved with the creation of man. That individual was the being identified in the Bible as "I am that I am." This was a being who wanted to become a god, a being that the Israelites, freed from Egyptian bondage, began to follow, to worship and later to call the Lord God Jehovah.

The following is a critique of that misunderstanding. It is also a review of the religious beliefs and practices of the religious community. It is a consolidation of the many different ideas that focus on the biblical god, religion and the priesthood which carry out the supposed will and commands of that god.

This collection of ideas, questions and answers are put forth in order to give to the reader an explanation for many of the religious enigmas so often associated with God and religion. Its primary purpose is to help the reader to determine for them whether there are in fact gods and whether they are real or merely figments of man's imagination.

To my knowledge these ideas are not those expressed by any organized religious group, author or community. In that sense I believe that they are uniquely mine.

To a religious disciple this book would be considered controversial and blasphemous. That is to be expected. Any idea which remotely proposes that any religious faith is without merit and that their god or gods, especially the Jewish and Christian God is not what their congregations believe them to be, would fall into this category.

While the Bible itself clearly indicates that Jehovah was not the creator of man nor was he the creator of the universe, it seems that it is considered blasphemous for me to say so.

Jehovah was the God of the Jews, the Most High God or Lord God was the authority behind the creation of man. They were two totally and distinctly different individuals. The Most High God served by Melchizedek was apparently an understanding and tolerant individual. On the other hand, Jehovah appears to have been a bloodthirsty, aggressive and highly emotional one.

They were both life forms similar to and competing with man for what they both considered the necessities of life. Those necessities included, but were not limited to wealth, power and pleasure.

Therefore any religion based on the belief that the gods of the Bible were divine beings, capable of offering paradise and salvation to a soul, are based on assumptions and statements not supported by facts or evidence.

If there is one and only one true God and his worship is based upon the infallible words of his book, the Holy Bible, why is there so great a chasm between the beliefs and practices of the various denominations claiming to be the true and only way back to redemption, God and salvation?

In my search for what I considered the truth, I asked many questions of the clergy of a few of the various denominations. I was given many different answers. The most frequent answer, especially to one the clergy could not answer, was that God would answer my questions in his own time. Until then, I was to have faith what I had been taught was his will.

I accepted these explanations because the clergy had no more of an answer to my questions than I did. I resigned myself to forever be denied this forbidden knowledge.

One day my answers begin to come, not from the religious community, but from my own sub-conscious. Those answers became the foundation upon which this book, my new perspective on God, man and religion, is based.

It is a new perspective. It is not based on ideology but upon the words of the Bible, correlated with science, archaeology, palaeontology, unexplained phenomena, medical and modern technology.

It all began with a single question. Was the creation of Eve the result of a cloning procedure? The answer was yes. It was so simple after that to reread the Bible and to find that the story and information contained within had a new and completely different meaning. If Eve was created as a clone then what about Adam who also had no mother or father? A whole new world of information began to come together to form a new hypothesis. This new hypothesis was verified by biblical scripture. As one thought led to another, and one answer to another answer, the thoughts, questions and the answers began to multiply until they became a flood, like a torrent of water gradually breaking through a crack in a dam. As soon as I had found the answer to one question, another would take its place. Soon the crack in the dam became so wide and the torrent so strong, the dam broke. The flood of questions and answers which followed washed away all my previous religious beliefs and convictions. I was washed clean of my old god, his religion and the clergy which serves him. What I had left, was a belief in a new GOD, a force of intelligence who created and controlled the logic, action, reaction and interaction of the universal forces. My new GOD is omnipotent. He has no need for servants, gifts, sacrifices or worship. Therefore I had no need to worship any god nor was there any need for a religion. When man was created he was complete within himself. If there is a true GOD it dwells within each of us. If we break a bone or injure ourselves our bodies heals themselves. Doctors and medical personal only help the process to do a better job.

During an injury the body takes material substances, food, air and water, absorbs it, and changes it into a form and substance which it uses for mechanical, electrical and chemical energy. From this transformation of the elements repair materials are generated transported to the injury and the injury begins to heal itself. This procedure has manifested itself throughout the long history of man without doctors or medicine.

I live and I breathe. I am in essence a living fusion reactor, a self contained entity. If there is a breakdown anywhere my system, and an infection occurs, antibodies and repair mechanisms immediately respond to correct the flaw. Where in all of this marvellous creation does a spiritual or mythical god help or aid me in any way in my existence? With this reality before me I found that I had arrived at the foundation of an entirely new and different perspective concerning God, man, and religion.

The idea for this book began with an article on the cloning of living organisms, a process where duplicate or modified life forms are created not through the normal process of natural birth but through scientific technology.

I became interested in cloning and alternative birth procedures because my wife's association with Dr. Webster, a member of the team of doctors who were responsible for the first test tube baby. The article stated that scientist involved in alternate methods of reproducing a species had found that the richest material for this new procedure, they call cloning, was found to be the DNA of the blood cells found in bone marrow. For some reason I cannot explain the biblical story of the creation of Eve came to mind. I began comparing the new cloning procedure of modern science with the biblical story of Eve and the two procedures were close as that it seemed to me to be one and the same. Both stories seem to support each other. With this in mind I began to look at the Bible in a very different light.

If Eve was created in a laboratory by scientist what does this make the Lord God? If there is no divine power involved in man's creation how sacred is the Bible and the stories it contained? If the description of Eve's creation is true then is there any mystery to the Bible? Is it in reality a very straight forward account of the creation of man, who his creator was, how they came to create man and a general description of the history of man through the eyes of the Jewish people?

These questions were so intriguing that I began to reread the Bible, not as an uninformed layman, but as a serious student.

I began with the assumption that if the scriptural text describing the creation of Eve was true, then so were the rest of the biblical passages. The bible than became for me a literal path which led me to the conclusions I have written in this book.

No matter how religious or devoted a person might be to the god of their faith, there is no way that they can consider the scriptural description of the removal of Adam's rib in any other way, then that of a modern day hospital operation.

Genesis 2:21-22: *"And the Lord God caused a deep sleep to fall upon Adam, and he slept; and he took one of his ribs, and closed up the flesh instead thereof: And the rib, which the Lord God had taken from man, made he a woman, and brought her unto the man."*

From that rib the genetic scientists, in the company of the Lord God, removed the DNA from the marrow of that rib. This was the basic material used for the creation of Eve. The DNA, RNA and the chromosomes of those cells were modified from that of a man to that of a female.

A male has an "XY" chromosome pattern and a woman an "XX" pattern. Some individuals have been found to have an "XYX" and some an "YXY" chromosome makeup. These individuals are known as hermaphrodites. In animals it is those which have both male and female gametes. In man and higher vertebrate it is those who have both male and female reproductive organs. Which sex becomes the more dominate one depends on the order of the chromosomes.

Eve was created through and by the science and technology of the Lord God and his crew. She was cloned from the cells of Adam and Adam and his fellow men were cloned from the cells of the Lord God and his crew, individuals which have been called messengers, angels, and in the beginning were called gods.

With this beginning in mind, we now have a whole new way of analyzing the Bible, understanding God, the role of mankind and of religion.

Today we understand and accept cloning as a modern medical breakthrough. Through this modern miracle new life can be created outside of the normal processes of natural birth. New species can be created by modifying the DNA material. Exact duplicates can be created and medical defaults correct. Traits can be enhanced and each new life can be given genetic capabilities never thought possible before. We now have the capability to order to specifications modified and enhanced versions of ourselves. We can now create new life in a laboratory. We can now created supermen, a new species an enhanced copy of that exists outside of the natural biological processes. New life can, was, and is now being created without a father and mother. We no longer needed to combine the sperm and egg of a species in order to procreate our or any species. If we have this technology today how much greater was that of the aliens beings who travelled the stars and created us?

Adam, made to order, to certain specifications, was put to sleep, (anesthetized), one of his ribs removed, and the incision closed. From that rib, Eve was created, also to specification. This scriptural text along with the article on cloning became the key idea which removed the mystery surrounding the creation of man, the identity of the Lord God and the eventual formation of the Jewish nation and their religion.

Once I understood the manner by which man was created, and who his creator was, the mystical mystery of the Bible began to disappear. I began to understand the story of the Bible and the story it had to tell. I had unlocked and opened the door to the mysteries of the Bible. It was a door which I can never close.

Eve was a clone, created or made from the basic material taken from Adam. How was Adam made? Was he a clone? If so who was his host being?

The Bible indicates that it was the Lord God.

Gen. 1:27. *"So God created man in his own image, in the image of God created he him; male and female created he them."*

In the genealogy of Jesus it states:

Luke 3:38: *"This was the son of Enos, which was the son of Seth, which was the son of Adam, which was the son of God."*

If Adam was the son of God, he came from God. There was no mother so how else could Adam be of God in the image of God unless it is by creating him out of the material of God himself. Therefore man is from God and is himself God. Whatever that particular word happens to mean. To me it is simply a title given to one in a position of authority, as was the Lord God during the time when man was crested. It has been man himself who has attached power, glory and divine meaning to the word. Man is, flesh and blood made in the image of

God. As such God ceases to be a spirit but also becomes a flesh and blood individual.

Genesis 6:3: *"And the Lord said my spirit shall not always strive with man, for that he also is flesh: yet his days shall be an hundred and twenty years."*

Except for those who lived before the flood, and the people of a small country called Georgia, when has man achieved this long a life?

Today with modern medicine, organ transplants, cell regeneration, and cloning, man now has the potential of reaching this goal.

God and those beings that came with him to this planet, with the exception of the Seraphim or Cherubim, were flesh and blood individuals. They lived and they died. Who were they and where did they come from? Who created them, and if they were not created than from what did they evolved?

Some of these questions we can answer. The others will have to remain a mystery until we again meet our makers.

The word clone is a recent term. Used by the medical and scientific communities to describe a process which duplicates, modifies or reproduces new life outside of the normal biological reproductive process? A clone is a scientifically, genetically created new life created from the blueprint of life found in the DNA of the particular species to be created.

In the creation of new life the DNA can be genetically altered by chromosome and RNA manipulation to be a copy of the original, a modified version, or a new creation all together.

Adam was an altered form of God. Eve was a manipulated form of Adam. Both created in a laboratory and both images of God. But who was God? Why did he cause man to be created? What purpose is served by religion and finally, what is the relationship which existed between them?

I found the answers to all of my questions in the scripture. With the answers came knowledge but with that knowledge did I also find wisdom? Evidently not because in writing this new theory and biblical perspective of God, man and religion I am questioning over six thousand years of biblical and religious teachings and beliefs. Whether this unique perspective is every accepted by man it is a perspective that had to be explained. Only time and circumstances will determine whether the sharing of my ideas and beliefs to be considered as wisdom or folly. But, unless they are shared, they are meaningless and will be lost in obscurity.

What I have written is not something I had been taught. I never went into a trance, experience any revelation by God or feel that I am being instructed or controlled by a power greater than myself. What I believe is what logic dictates from the words, facts and records available to me.

With the world bordering on global annihilation, ethic cleansing and religious persecution I feel that what I have written is somehow important.

In looking back across my life I somehow feel that it has all been leading me step by step to this particular point in time. I feel that I really had no choice but to write what I feel I had been led to believe was a biblical truth.

Ecclesiastes 3:18-22: *I said in mine heart concerning the estate of the sons of men, that God might manifest them, and that they might see that they to are beasts. For that which befalleth the sons of men befalleth beasts; even one thing befalleth them: as the one dieth, so dieth the other; yea, they have all one breath; so that a man hath no per-eminence above a beast: for all is vanity. All go unto one place; all are of the dust, and all turn to dust again. Who knoweth the spirit of man that goeth upward, and the spirit of the beast that goeth downward to the earth. Wherefore I perceive that there is nothing better, that a man should rejoice in his own works; for that is his portion: for who shall bring him to see what shall be after him?*

I do not know how or why I received the ideas which triggered the enclosed responses. I can only assume that this knowledge is universal carried somewhere within our sub-conscious. Stored within our DNA and been passed down to us from the beginning, one generation to the next. Somehow I was able to get passed the lock the mental *flaming sword which turned every way, to keep the way of the tree of life.* and somehow activated my genetic code where all of the memories of all of the generations of my ancestors was stored waiting to be unlocked at the right time in history. It will be a time when each of us will become a part of and receive an understanding of all that made us the unique individuals that we have become. It will be at the moment when the mental block, place in the mind of man in Eden, will be removed. Once again man will be able to have access to his total memory. He will know his ancestors, not in a heavenly kingdom but in an enlightened mental state of mind.

This book challenges the fundamental principles which form the foundation of all existing religions. Until now the idea that mankind was created by a holy and divine, omnipotent being, was not based on fact but religious conjecture. I offer a new foundation for a realistic belief one base on written records, evidence and fact.

"Jehovah, The First Godfather", is not a look at the mythical god of religion, but rather a look at the reality of the biblical one. It is a look at his cruelty, his uncertainty, his obsession with wealth, power, control, barbarism and death. It is a partial review of his supposed thoughts, words, and deeds. The Bible is a written testimony to the greed, horror and bloodshed of his leadership.

It is a realistic look at the supposed biblical miracles, analysed in the light of modern science and technology. It is an agnostic's explanation for and of the words, thoughts, action and meaning of the biblical god as they are expressed in biblical scripture. It is a look at both the heart and soul of God and Man.

We must assume that the events, words, thoughts, deeds and commands of God as they are written the Bible, fact or fiction, to be the true convictions of the authors. They recorded not only what they believed were the exact thoughts, ideas, and commands of God, but also his intent. Theologians must also believe this, or the books that make up the Bible would not be considered as some of the world's most sacred text.

The Jewish and Christian communities take the words of the Torah and the Bible to be the infallible words of God. Therefore, to take those same words and explain those from an entirely different perspective should not be considered blasphemy, even though it changes completely the religious impact of the Bible, God and religion.

Libraries are filled with books about God, gods, devils, aliens, UFOs' unexplained artefacts, unusual drawings, and strange markings. They were all written by authors who believed what they wrote to be true. In addition to these writings there is a substantial and convincing pool of evidence suggesting, that at some time during the last few million years, an advanced race of beings walked this planet. We do not know who they were but we do know that they left behind enough evidence to show that they existed.

According to Erich Von Daniken in his book "The Gold of the Gods", tunnels have been found in Central America believed to be manmade and extend for many miles. Located in Central America approximately 750 feet below the surface, these tunnels are estimated to be thousands of miles in length. They have right angles, glazed side walls, and evenly spaced air shafts, each with a specified circular dimension. One of these tunnels contained a large vaulted chamber. Within the chamber were found metal sheets which contain writings of unknown origin, a table and chairs moulded out of an unknown material and a skeleton coated in gold dust.

One of the more remarkable finds was a humanoid like skeleton, carved from stone, having what appear to be ten pairs of ribs all anatomically accurate.

These particular artefacts', along with the boot prints found in sandstone, estimated to have solidified around 15,000,000 years ago, a ceramic spark plug like object discovered buried deep underground in a pocket of coal, the tunnels, underground cities, iron columns that never rust, ancient symbols and legends, amplified by religious text make it possible to believe that they are all connected in one way or another to alien beings. All of these objects, facts in evidence, individually and collectively lead to and support the hypothesis that life existed on this planet long before man came into existence.

The tunnels with glazed sidewalls, right angle, air shafts, table, chairs and records on material of an unknown are a strong indication that they are the result of a mining expedition.

The underground cities may have housed the workers from the mines. The iron columns which never rust, might possibility have been part of a communications system. The signs and symbols might well be the result of individual cultures, abandon by the gods, trying to hold on to, or to recall the gods to their presence.

The tunnels found in Ecuador, are believed to reach from Ecuador all the way to Peru. The large vaulted room measured "153 by 164 yards. (Von Daniken's The Gold of the Gods). Within this room was found, a table with seven chairs, made of an unknown material, and a library of very thin metal plaques. The metals sheets, only millimetres thick, are stamped or printed with writings we cannot as yet identify. I believe that the writings were the tabulations of the mining information. Von Daniken believed that they may possibly be a history of mankind. If this were a mining location then the tablets belong to them. If on the other hand the tunnels and the vaulted room were an underground city similar to others which have been found throughout the world then the sheets of metal may well be some of the records left by the original alien colonists, a record of that civilization.

If these rooms are in fact a part of a lost civilization there is one explanation which may lend credence to this theory and reinforce the legends of the Uros people.

At some time in the past, a few million years ago, an attempt was made by an alien life form to colonize this planet. During that colonization attempt the colonists became aware of some kind of a heavenly event which was about to occur which would have an impact on everyone living on the planet surface. In order to survive this event, they built underground cities until the danger was pasted. At that time they returned to the surface and resumed their normal lives.

In any event, we are back to the existence of alien colonists existing before the time of man, a culture and a civilization of a highly advanced race of beings.

When one brings together the above unexplained mysteries of the region, the unexplained Nazca Lines, self contained lighted spheres, electric generating apparatuses and ceramic materials, all made long before man appears capable of such engineering accomplishments, and connect them to the biblical scripture a clear picture begin to appear. This picture makes the possibility of an advanced race of beings existing on this planet before modern man almost a certainty. That civilization died out. It was now time to replace it with another more suitable to the planet environment.

Genesis 1:28: *"And God blessed them, and God said unto them, Be fruitful, and multiply, and replenish the earth, and subdue it: and have dominion over the fish of the sea, and over the fowl of the air, and over every living thing that moveth upon the earth."*

One does not replenish what has never existed. When man was told to replenish the earth it was a clear indication that some kind of related life form had existed before him.

Man was the replacement. He was told to be fruitful and multiple. How could he do this without a female of the species? Eve was not created until the animals especially created to help were found incompatible. Yet religions and their leaders would have us believe that the original sin of Adam and Eve was sex and an awareness of their nakedness. This is not true. The sin of Adam and Eve was their disobedience to a lawful command of the Lord God and had nothing in the world to do with being naked or with sex.

What we know today is that the technology of man is slowly approaching that of the Gods. We have ventured into space. We are about to begin our exploration of the stars. In the future man will be the traveller, the explorer, and the one who will step down on distant planets. There he will leave his footprint in the sands of time.

Man has landed on the moon, sent instruments to Mars, Venus and the far reaches of the galaxy. Where and when will he take that next step that will carry him to the stars is something we do not know but .when he does will he be ready for what he may find?

Modern technology has reached a point where science is now able to duplicate or at least understand many of the so called miracles of the Bible. We have developed self contained chemicals of light, only we have not advanced to the point where, like the alien units, they are self perpetuating. We have specialty metals that will take lifetimes to rust and we now have electric generators and high heat ceramics. We can create life from life. We no longer need to rely on natural birth as a means for the perpetuation of our or any species.

Many of the biblical gods like miracles came to be understood as man advanced into the industrial revolution. When it was found possible to fertilize an egg of one species in a test tube and successfully place that egg inside the reproductive organs of another species and a natural birth was able to take place, man had taken another step towards his evolution as a species. The fertilized egg from one female, no matter what the species, carried to term in the womb of another species is known as a birth from a surrogate mother. Individuals created and born through this procedure first became known to us as test tubes babies. The first baby known to be born this way was Louise Brown, born in Britain in 1978. In 1988 surrogate mother Mary Beth Whitehead of New Jersey made the headlines when she refused to relinquish her daughter. (Time Magazine Nov. 8, 1993)

After test tube babies were found to have no natural abnormalities, the next step was to find out if the fertilized egg of one species could be carried in the womb of a surrogate mother. This too was found to be successful. The final step came when it was found to be possible to create a new life without the use of sperm and eggs, but from the DNA helix. This process known as cloning was highly successful and placed for the first time, in the realm of the gods. Man like the gods could produce a new species of life by using the DNA cells of another species.

Man no longer needs the egg and sperm of a species to reproduce the species. It can now be done in a laboratory by qualified scientist and medical personnel. They can now create new life designed and modified to exacting specifications by the process of cloning. In our society our scientists and technicians through science and modern medicine have become the gods of tomorrow.

Somewhere back in time another race of beings reached and exceeded our level of expertise. They created man just as we are now creating sheep, cattle and monkeys. These animals serve our needs and purposes. Man served the needs and purposes of the gods. When they created us we meant no more to them than our animals mean to us. We were property which they used as they saw fit. Some will say that they loved us. This may be true in a way. I do not believe that their love for us was any different than the love we show for our pets and animals.

The gods came from a cultured and a civilized society. This we can assume from the descriptions of the laws that were given to us, from the training they gave to early man and from the words they used to inform man of their desires. From this we are made aware of many of their customs, their culture and their society.

Other than what we are told in the Bible, and the evidence of their existence found in primitive drawings, what do we really know about them?

If we assume that the stone skeleton with ten pairs of ribs carved out of stone and found in the tunnels of Ecuador was that of the Living Creature, our god and our creator, then we can also make the following assumptions.

If the Living Creatures were beings who had ten sets of ribs, great technical skills and the ability to travel the stars, it brings into focus a number of other things based on logic and what appears to be factual evidence.

Those ten sets of ribs suggest that the planet from which the aliens came was low in oxygen and or atmospheric pressure. Such an environment would require that any life form living in such an environment be equipped with a very large lung capacity in order to survive. With extra large lungs there would also exists the necessity to protect those lungs. This would account for the extra set of ribs. Their atmosphere, low in oxygen, would have created a blood chemistry of a darker hue than the red blood of man caused by the higher oxygen atmosphere of this planet. The low oxygenated darker hued blood of the aliens would give anyone looking at their blood the impression that their blood was black. This assumption correlates with the legends of the Uros of Central America, who say that this was the original colour of their blood, and that of their ancestors.

The images of aliens reported to have been seen by many modern day individuals all indicate that the aliens have large dark eyes and long slender limbs.

The large dark eyes indicated a planet with a dim or fading light. Their long slender limbs would be the result of a planet with a low gravity. There strength and muscle mass would not be as important as it is here on earth.

When the gods came to this planet and decided to create man to serve their needs they took the DNA of their species and modified that DNA to suit the atmosphere and the environment of this new world.

When man was cloned, his DNA, chromosomes, RNA biological and chemical makeup were altered so that the deficiencies of the gods would not affect man in his new environment.

The modification of man was the alteration of the chemistry of the alien black blood so that man would be more adaptable to the high oxygen content of his environment. This change gives the blood of man the appearance of being red. His physical structure, bone and muscle mass were enhanced to allow for increased gravity, and his eyes reduced in size to accommodate the brighter sunlight of our sun.

Most of the religious disciples, aware of my theory, flatly refuse to believe that man was created by another living life force. To them we were created by an omnipotent incorporeal being they call God. They refuse to believe otherwise.

Modern medicine and scientific technology has cloned and created new life, new species, and duplicated life that already exists. Religious disciples and society as a whole are aware that life has already been created in a test tube. Scientists have cloned in addition to monkeys, sheep, cattle and a host of other creatures including man and they still refuse to accept this reality. (I refer to the November 1993 issue of Time Magazine.)

The above article was a successful creation of a cloned life, one which we know about. What we do not know about and what scares the be-jesus out of most people are the accidents and the unusual creations which have and will probably occurred during these experiments. When we begin to tamper with life there is no way of telling what monsters we may in time unleash. These are the experiments and the results that we shall never hear or learn about?

Did the gods also experience some of these failed experiments? The memory of man is made up of many legends of monsters and grotesque gargoyles. Many such figures adorn some of our most beautiful temple to God. They are found on the fringes of our cathedrals and act as the guardians of the sanctuary?

I realized that man is afraid of what he does not understand but why should the idea that he was created as a clone to the gods is so difficult to accept and understand? Does it really make any difference how we were created? We are who we are and where we are, not by the power of some magical or mythical being, but through our own efforts. Whether we evolved from prehistoric slime, created by other living beings or by a spiritual and divine force does not change our existence. We are still who we are and no amount of speculation as to how we began will change what we are. What should be of a greater significance to us is that we were first created as slaves and we have overcome that condition. We have gained our freedom from the gods.

Are our egos so fragile that we must believe we are supreme in the universe in order to survive? We cannot change our beginning with wishful thinking but we can control our future.

What does all of this mean to us today?

It means that if there are no gods, there is no need for the religions set up to worship beings which do not exist. Basically religion is a man made Conn thriving on the superstitious fears and beliefs in powers that man as yet been unable to understand. A god and a religion offer man away by which he can justify his failure and his misfortune.

There is no need for religion and there is no need for the clergy, the servants to gods which do not exist.

I shudder when I think of all of the deaths and the amount of bloodshed throughout history by the thousands upon thousands of men, women and children, who were murdered, mutilated, or tortured because of someone's religious beliefs. These individuals suffered because of the ignorance and superstitious beliefs of those in power. It is a shame that in our enlightened world today that ignorance and superstition still exists.

There is no god to fight over, no god to care who does what to whom and there is certainly no god looking down on man with a plan for his salvation. Gods are and always have been the figments of mans' imagination, passed down to him by the beliefs and superstitions of his ignorant forefathers. Their beliefs and superstitions were fostered and strengthen by their belief in witchcraft and the sorcery of the dark ages.

There were beings which created us and in their eyes we were property but just because they created us do not make them gods. To the Jewish God Jehovah the Hebrew was property. They served and obeyed him. In, under and because of the circumstances with which he ruled, he considered himself to be a god. He demanded blood sacrifices, rituals, gifts and servitude. What is not understood by the layman is that those sacrifices were prepared in a certain way and served to him in a manner which he specified. His servants, the Jewish priests, prepared, cooked and served Jehovah his meals, morning and night.

Ex. 25:8. *And let them make me a sanctuary; that I may well among them.*"

Ex. 25:22. *And there I will meet with thee, and I will commune with thee from above the mercy-seat, from between the two Cherubim which are upon the ark of the testimony, of all things which I will give thee in commandment unto the children of Israel.*

Ex. 25:29. *And thou shall make the dishes thereof, and spoons thereof, and covers thereof, and bowls thereof, to cover withal: of pure gold shall thou make them.*"

Ex.29:38-45. *Now this is what you will offer on the alter; two lambs of the first year day by day continually. The one lamb you shall offer in the morning; and the other lamb you shall offer in the evening And with the one lamb a tenth-deal of flour mingled with the forth part of an him of beaten oil: and the forth part of an hin of wine for a drink-offering. And the lamb that you shall in the evening shall you will do according to the meat-offering of the morning, and according to the drink- offering thereof, for a sweet savour, an offering made by fire unto the Lord. This shall be a continual burnt-offering throughout your generations at the door of the tabernacle of the congregation before the Lord: where I will meet you to speak unto thee. And there I will meet the children of Israel; and the tabernacle shall be sanctified by my glory. And I will sanctify the tabernacle of the congregation, and the alter and I will sanctify also both Aaron and his sons, to minister to me in the priest's office and I will dwell among the children of Israel, and I will be their God.*

Judges 2:14. *And the anger of the Lord was hot against Israel and he delivered them into the hands of spoilers that spoiled them. He sold them into the hands of their enemies round about so that they could no longer stand before their enemies."*

Only someone who owns property has the right to sell that property. Jehovah owned the Israelites and when they displeased him he sold them in order to appease his anger.

Today many of the servants of God still believed that they are the property of God. They are willing to endure whatever kind of life that their dedication and their religious leaders dictate. This dedication and self sacrifice extends even into the realm of slavery.

This book was written with the hope that the thoughts contained within will bring some light into the dark catacombs of the human mind. Hopefully these thoughts will help remove the chains which bind the soul and allow the spirit to be free to enjoy the wonders of the world as it was meant to be. With the mind free of guilt and religious fetters perhaps the reader will find what I have found, a peace which brings harmony and understanding to one's life and soul.

Disagreement with my opinions and assumptions will not alter the religious facts and evidence of history. Disagreements will not change nor delete the medical breakthroughs which have taken place today, nor will they alter the thoughts, actions, words and statements made by the biblical God and recorded in the Bible.

Those biblical words of the Lord God and those of Jehovah are the statements, thoughts and actions believed by the Jewish and Christian people to be the unalterable words of their God. They were preserved, collected, passed down and presented to modern man as their guide for living and dying. This collection of words, thoughts and actions called "The Holy Book of God", are believed by Jewish and Christian disciples to be the truth.

I also believe my book to be the truth howbeit a different one. It is not for the religious believer but for those who seek the truth and ask the hard questions. It is for those who would move the mountain. It is for mankind, if not for his salvation, then for his peace of mind. It will not change the mind of the true religious believer, but it should enlighten the mind of those who do not understand God, and his religions. It is not for those who choose to live in ignorance. That is their cross to bear.

My insight into scripture, limited as it might be, was not something taught to me by the church. Therefore I must assume that it was given to me, by some higher force, for a reason I have yet to understand.

Whether my thoughts were inspired by some power greater than my sub consciousness is debatable. I must believe that whatever the force which initiated the process which began this book was activated within me for the eventual good of my fellow man.

When the idea first came to me that the man was made by living breathing creatures, who were not gods, I was petrified. I lay away nights afraid to venture to far into this new and terrifying unknown territory. I fully expected the fires of hell or the wrath of God to descend upon me and to suffer the torment of the damned for my blasphemy. When the fires did not come, and no torment entered my life, I found myself looking deeper into my new understanding of scripture. The deeper I went the greater my understanding and the more at peace I felt with myself. I felt a harmony and understanding which I have never experienced before. I found a kind of peace, harmony and understanding outside of religion that I never knew inside of it.

May my thoughts and ideas help the reader to find theirs?

In order to understand the God of the Jewish nation and of the Jewish and Christian religions, one must first realize that the god of the Jews was not the god of mankind. He was the God of Abraham, Isaac, Jacob and his descendants. Jehovah was a God in name only to the descendants of Jacob. It was only after these descendants were led out Egypt at great personal lost to themselves do they begin to accept the laws, priesthood, religion and Jehovah as their God.

It was out of the fear of death, hunger, thirst and weariness that the people accepted the heavy hand of Jehovah. He became a god and was accepted as one as soon as he had crushed any and all resistance to his rule from the minds of the people. After the deaths of thousands of their family members and those of their neighbours the Israelites became humble servants. As Egyptians bond servants or slaves they were docile sheep, led by Jehovah and Moses. Their servitude under the guidance of Moses and Jehovah gave them purpose. Under the hardships they faced and endured along the way to the Promised Land under the rule of the tyrant Jehovah, they became strong. They learned to endure, to survive and to eventually overcome every condition of hardship to become the nation they are today, a strong and proud people and vibrant people. They became a strong and proud people not out of love and reverence for Jehovah but out of fear.

Once one understands the rule of Jehovah, the motivation for his actions and the fact that there was never any love neither given nor received between him and the Jewish people we can begin to understand the scriptures. It was not the actions of Jehovah which gave deity and mystery to his name, but the reverence and fanatical belief of his prophets. Once this is understood, the shroud of mystery and superstition which surrounds and protects God, religion and the clergy will be removed. Once the shroud is removed, the power of a mystical god and many of his so called miracles disappear.

Without the heavenly power believed to have cause the so called biblical miracles, Jehovah ceases to be a god and is recognized for who and what he really was: a flesh and blood, mortal being, who, by his acts, thoughts and deeds, earned for himself the title of, " the first Godfather".

Theologians believe that Moses wrote genesis, the first book of the Bible. In the authorized King James Version edition Genesis is identified as "The First Book of Moses called Genesis". Moses is also given credit for the next four books, Exodus, Leviticus, Numbers and Deuteronomy.

No one knows for certain how extensive the education of Moses might have been. Was he educated enough to write these books or did he delegated this responsibility to others? Where did Moses obtain the information he recorded in these books? Were they a part of written history or did he receive them from someone who was knowledgeable of such events?

If the biblical story is based upon fact and Moses was raised in the court of Pharaoh it can be assumed that he was well taught and that his education was extensive. Among his many studies would have been the gods and religions of Egypt. From these studies he would have received some idea as to the beginning of man but from the perspective of the Egyptians priests. The beginning scriptures indicated a greater understanding of the universe, man, and his beginning than could possibly be known by the priests of his day. It must therefore be assumed that the knowledge of the beginning of creation had to come from some other source. The only person who could have knows and passed this knowledge on to Moses was Jehovah. But does having the knowledge of man's beginning which differs from the stories found in Egyptian myth necessarily make Jehovah a God? It does not but it does indicate knowledge of creation that man could not and did not know until the modern era of scientific exploration.

Was Jehovah a heavenly being? He did come from the stars. Was he immortal? Maybe, but he was according to scripture one of the sons of God left behind to monitor the earth? Any one of these scenarios is a possible explanation for his existence and his reason for being on the planet. What we do know is that he was not a spirit but a flesh and blood being. As such he can die. If he can die he is not immortal and if he is not immortal than he is not a god.

It must be assumed that the information Moses received concerning the beginning of man came from Jehovah when he and Moses were on the mountain called the mountain of God.

Jehovah, in explaining the beginning what he knew of the beginning of creation, of life and of man was straight forward in his explanations. Later biblical confusion concerning those creations resulted from mans' misunderstanding of what Jehovah told Moses and what Moses wrote down for future generations to read and to try and understand.

It seems that over the years, in the telling and retelling of our beginning, different writers place their emphasis on different aspects of our creation. These different stories, called the priestly versions, were finally combined into one story which incorporated the many different priestly versions. As a result confusion and misunderstanding became a part of religious scripture.

I feel certain that those who wrote the scriptures believed that what they were recording were the words thoughts and will of their god. This belief in the truth and reality of the scriptures is a belief that has been passed from one generations to the next each believing in the teachings and authenticity of the Bible. They all believed because they had nothing but faith upon which to base their beliefs.

Ignorant of scripture, religious congregations have, down through the ages, followed dedicated, but often illiterate and misguided leaders. Because they were ignorant of scripture those individuals who followed such misguided messiahs came to believe in and accept the explanations of scripture by those messiahs as the undisputed word of God. In time their teachings have become church doctrine and sectarian dogma.

Today we are better educated. We are more aware of the scripture and through the advent of television, the various aspects of different religions and we are able to get a look at goals of the clergy which serve them.

I do not present a new religion. What I offer is a new foundation upon which the layman can re-evaluate the biblical stories, the religion which came out of the Exodus, the God Jehovah and the relationship which existed between him and the Hebrew nation.

True it is an agnostics' point of view but a view that clearly focuses on God, the bible and religion. It is not clouded by passed teachings and is based solely upon the same scriptural text as that which is taught by the clergy to their denominations.

I would like to start with a few simple questions.
1. Who, or what, is a god?
2. Is there more than one? If so, how many and who are they?
3. Was the Creative God of the universe, the creator of man?
4. Was the creator of man the same as the god of the Jewish people? Are they one and the same entity?
5. Did the Jewish religion begin with Adam or with the Hebrews at the time of the Exodus?
6. was religion necessary or was it the result of the control and rule of the Jewish god?

7. What is the relationship which exists between God and man?

8. How has man benefited if any from that relationship?

These are logical questions and each will be answered, not necessarily to the satisfaction of the religious community, but logically, using biblical scripture, correlated and supported by modern medicine, technology and scientific facts.

The Christian and Jewish communities believe that there is one, and only one, true God. That God is the one which they call Jehovah. The scriptures clearly disagree with this assumption. There are, in fact, three major beings in the Bible and each bears the title of God.

Webster describes God as "(in polytheistic religions) a being to whom worship is ascribed // an image of such a deity // an idolized person or thing, money is his god. God (in monotheistic religions) the Supreme Being, seen as the omnipotent creator and ruler of the universe..."

In one instance we are talking about a god that might be anything or anyone, in the next we are referring to the one and only true GOD which is the universal creator.

When most people mention the word god it is with the understanding that they are talking about one god which created all things, the universe, man and the one to whom the Jews and Christians worship.

This is the beginning of mans' misunderstanding. There is the one true GOD whoever or whatever that might be but that power is not the biblical gods, but the omnipotent creator of the universe an entity we believe to an incorporeal immortal being. Religion teaches us that it existed in the emptiness of space before the beginning of time. It is an existence beyond our ability to understand and it is the GOD believed to be responsible for the creation of the universe and all that it contains. It is not only immortal, but it created and controls, the motion of the stars, planets and all that exists within the confines of the universe itself. Through the laws which it established, it maintains universal stability. That stability governs the action, reaction and interaction of all its creative aspects. These laws are believed to extend in uniformity beyond areas which mankind has yet to imagine. This is GOD, an entity, which we cannot identify except by what we can determine with our senses and our intellect. It is the Supreme Being. It is omnipotent.

The gods of the bible, man and religion, we can identify. In almost every culture there are written documents containing statements of their existence, their actions, their laws and their ideas. They are given many names, and sometimes many faces, but they are all flesh and blood beings who co-habit with man, united and bear children from these unions. They live in our myths and legends. In some cultures they are still respected and worshipped as gods. In other culture they are believed to be merely figments of the past and of mans imagination.

This is not true, because at some time in the history of that culture those gods did in fact exist.

The Biblical gods fall within this category. There was the Lord God or the Most High God, I Am that I Am also called Yahweh, Jehovah, Elohim, Baal, Moloch, and Satan or Lucifer.

In the first chapter of the book of Genesis, there are, in reality, two separate entities identified as GOD. The first is the universal creator, an incorporeal entity, a spirit and an immortal. The second is the Lord God, a flesh and blood individual by whose authority man was created. It was the Lord God which strived, walked and talked with man in the cool of the evening. He was the authority worshipped or honoured as the Most High God by "Melchizedek, high priest and king of Salem."

Mans' confusion began when he first united these two entities into the same being. This is the union of the two gods which religious scholars have overlooked and have assumed that the word GOD in verse 24, chapter 1 had the same meaning as the word God in verse 25. I ch.1:24 God said and it happened.

Genesis 1:24: *"And God said, Let the earth bring forth the living creature after his kind, cattle, and creeping thing, and beast of the earth after his kind: and it was so."*

This is the creation of life as it evolved through evolution. Since earth, according to scripture, refers to land masses everywhere in the universe, this means that life has evolved beyond this planet in areas, and in forms, which we not begin to image.

In Gen. 1:25 we have a different god. This god does not create by thought he makes the things he wishes to exist. The one difference between the two gods is the term or method of their creations.

The living creatures, indications of more than one god in Gen. 1:26 declare their a desire to make man in their own image rather then in the image of other beings in existence.

The word god carried with it the meaning that the word is used to describe someone in supreme authority. In Genesis 1:24 it is GOD the supreme authority of the universe. In Genesis 1:25 it is the title of the supreme authority of the living creatures.

The idea that organic life in many forms exist beyond this planet can be substantiated Genesis 1:11-12.

Genesis 1:11-12: "*And God said, Let the earth bring forth grass, and herb yielding seed, and the fruit-tree yielding fruit after his kind, whose seed is in itself, upon the earth: and it was so.12. And the earth brought forth grass, and herb yielding seed after his kind, and the tree yielding fruit, whose seed was in itself, after his kind: and God saw that it was good.*

I should not have to point out that the formation of organic life began or occurred during the evening and morning of the third day of the universal evolution. The suns and planets did not come into existence, according to scripture until the evening and the morning of the fourth time continuum. So the term earth does not refer to this planet alone but to the solidified combined masses of elements found throughout the universe.

In order for the God which was responsible for the creation of man to be considered and called the Most High God, there must have been lesser gods which were subservient to him.

The title of the Lord God was given to the highest authority on earth at the time of the creation of man. That individual walked, talked and did strive with man before the flood. After the flood he was identified as the Most High God. Is he also the God of the Jews and by association with the Jewish faith the god of the Christian? The answer is no if one believes in biblical scripture.

The god of the Jews and Christians is, "I am that I Am", the God of Abraham, Isaac and Jacob. He is the entity who came to be called Jehovah.

Who was he, this god of the Jews?

Deuteronomy 32 tells us that he was an underling, a subservient individual under the authority of the Lord god. He was an individual who received, from the Most High God, as an inheritance, Jacob and his descendants. He became their god and they became the Jewish Nation.

This book is concerned with his deity and that of the Lord God. A review of scripture proves that their deity as immortal gods did not exist. If it can be shown that Jehovah was not a deity, a god, then the holiness of the Lord God, Jesus and the other biblical gods lose their religious significance.

Did the Lord God, Jehovah and the other gods come from the heavens is not in dispute. They were for all practical purposes heavenly creatures but divine entities they were not.

The original supervisors of the mining conglomerate who were left behind as caretakers of the earth became the gods of man after the flood. It was man and not these supervisors who elevated their status from earth masters to divine gods. Jehovah was the last to obtain this status. This did not occur until he created that status for himself.

In a comparison with the rest of the world's great religions it might be said that he is the last of the great gods of history. He did not appear as a god worthy of note until the time of Abraham. And if it had not been for Abraham who first identified him as a God by his worship and sacrifices he may never have existed.

It was not until after the time of the Exodus that the name of Jehovah went beyond the descendants of Jacob and become known as the god of a particular people.

The Hebrew families of Jacob called Israelites and later the Jews, came to accept Jehovah as their god, not out of love and reverence, but out of fear, and continuous indoctrination.

He was a destructive god. His acts of retribution, fits of anger, his inhuman brutality against his own servants as well as those who opposed him resulted in bloodshed, death, and total submission. Disobedience of any kind against one of his laws or commandment could and usually did result in the death of the transgressor. Under the rule of their new god the Israelites lived in fear of death. Sometimes it was from hunger, thirst, plague, or the desert. But most of all they feared the sudden wrath of Jehovah. They became a submissive congregation out of the need to survive. They were controlled and governed by the laws of a religion and a government ruled and controlled by the priests, who operated under the laws of Moses, who claimed that those laws came from their God.

Jesus believed to be the son of a god, was considered by his followers who are called Christians was deemed worthy of worship. If he was the son of Jehovah and Mary, he was part alien and part human. As such how could he be an immortal god?

The following passages will help explain why I believe that Jehovah is not the one and only biblical God, he is not the Universal Creator, nor was he responsible for the creation of man. He was an underling, a sub-servant to the Most High God, the Lord God.

Joshua 24:2-6: *"And Joshua said unto all the people, Thus said the Lord God of Israel, (not of man but of Israel) your fathers dwelt on the other side of the flood in old time, even Terah, the father of Abraham, and the father of Nachor: and they served other gods And I took your father Abraham from the other side of the flood, and led him throughout all the land of Canaan, and multiplied his seed, and gave him Isaac. And I gave unto Isaac, Jacob and Esau: and I gave unto Esau Mount Seir, to possess it; but Jacob and his children went down into Egypt. I sent Moses also and Aaron and I plagued Egypt according to that which I did among them: and afterward I brought you out. 6. And I brought your fathers out of Egypt: and you came to the sea; and the Egyptians pursued after your fathers with chariots and horsemen unto the Red Sea."*

Joshua 24:13: *"And I have given you a land for which ye did not labour, and cities which ye built not, and ye dwell in them; of the vineyards and olive-yards which ye planted not do you eat."*

Joshua 24:15: *"And if it seem evil unto you to serve the Lord, choose you this day whom ye will serve, whether the gods which your fathers served, that were on the other side of the flood, or the gods of the Amorites in whose land ye dwell: but as for me and my house, we will serve the Lord."*

There are questions to ask here. If there was one and only one god at the time of the creation of man, and there were gods before the flood, who were the other gods served by Abraham, his father, and the fathers of the congregation?

Before the flood there was the Highest God. In order for him to be in this position it was necessary for minor gods to exist, gods which were subservient to him.

God is known by many names. In the English translation of the Bible he is first called The Lord God by Adam. During the time of Abraham he was call the Most High God by Melchizedek, king and High Priest of Salem. After the Exodus he was called Elohim by the Jewish congregation and he identified himself as, "I Am that I am. He has also been called Yahweh these names all refer to a title.

The Zondervan Compact Bible Dictionary defines the Biblical god in this way as YHWH. The "Tetragrammaton," the four consonants, standing for the ancient Hebrew name for God commonly referred to as "Jehovah", or "Yahweh". YHWH was considered too sacred to pronounce so 'adonai (my Lord) was substituted in reading. When eventually a vowel system was invented, since the Hebrews had forgotten how to pronounce YHWH, they substituted the vowels for adonai, making "Jehovah," a form first attested at the beginning of the 12th century A.D."

Elohim is according to the Zondervan Bible Dictionary, the most frequent Hebrew word for God (over 2,500 times in the OT). It is plural in form, but singular in construction (used with a singular verb or adjective). When applied to the one true God, the plural is due to the Hebrew idiom of a plural of magnitude of majesty (Gen. 1:1, etc.).When used of heathen gods (Exod. 18:11, 20:3; Gen. 35:2; Josh. 24:20, etc.) or of angels (Ps. 8:5; 97:7; Job 1:6, etc.) or Judges (Exod. 21:6; I Sam.2:25, etc.) as representatives of God, Elohim is plural in sense as well as form. It means either "be strong," or "be in front," suiting the power and pre-eminence of God. Jesus is quoted as using a form of the name from the cross (Matt. 27:46, Eli; Mark 15:34, Eloi.

There was "Baali, (my lord, my master) the common name for all local gods, as well as "Jehovah." Hosea demands that this degradation cease and that Jehovah be no longer called "my Baal," but "Ishi" (my husband) (Hos.2:16). The Israelites later abandoned the use of "Baal" (lord, possessor, husband) for "Jehovah."

The word Baal appears in the OT with a variety of meanings: "master" or "owner" Exod. 21:28, 34; Judg. 19:22), "husband", Exod. 21:3 and II Sam. 11:26). Usually however it refers to the farm god of the Phoenicians and Canaanites and was responsible for the crops, flocks and fecund farm families.

Each locality had its own Baal. The Baalim were worshipped on high places with lascivious rites, self-torture, and human sacrifice. Alters to Baal were built in Palestine; Jezebel in Israel and Athaliah in Judah championed Baal worship (I Kings 16:31, 32; II Chron. 17:3). 3. Descendent of Reuben (I Chron. 5:5). 4. Benjamite (I Chron. 8:30). 5. In composition it is often the name of a man and not of Baal, e.g. Baal-Hainan (I Chron. 1:49).

Hosea was one of the Old Testament prophets and one that Jehovah commanded to demand that the people refrain from calling him Baali, and henceforth refer to him as Ishi, a term which means "my husband". Evidently Jehovah no longer want to be called God, ruler or Creator, but "Ishi which means my husband. (Hosea 2:16)

"Jehovah, is the English rendering of the Hebrew tetragram Yhwh, one of the names of God (Exod. 17:15. Its original pronunciation is unknown. The Jews took seriously the third commandment " Thou shall not take the name of the Lord thy God in vain; for the Lord will not hold him guiltless that takes his name in vain" (Exod. 20:7) and so, to keep from speaking the holy name carelessly, around 300 B.C. they decided not to pronounce it at all; but whenever in reading, they came to it, they spoke the word adhonai which means "Lord." This usage was used until the sacred name was changed to "Kurios" i.e. Lord.

Consequently in the KJV, the word Lord occurs instead of Jehovah, whereas in ASV the name "Jehovah" is rendered When the vowel points were added to the Hebrew consonantal text, the Massoretes (Jewish scribes) inserted into the Hebrew consonantal text the vowels for adhonai. The sacred name is derived from the verb "to be," and so implies that God is eternal ("Before Abraham was, I AM") and that He is the Absolute, i.e. the Uncaused One. The name "Jehovah" belongs especially to Him when He is dealing with His own, while "God" is used more when dealing with the Gentiles. See for instance II Chronicles 18:31 where "Jehoshaphat cried out and Jehovah helped him; and God moved them to depart from him.

There are ten combinations of the word "Jehovah" in the O.T. Besides the five with which succeeding articles deal, there are Jehovah-ropheka, Jehovah that healeth thee" Exod. 15:26 Jehovah-meqaddeshkem, "Jehovah who sanctified you' Exod. 31:13 Jehovah-tsabaoth, "Jehovah of hosts" I Sam. 1; 3 Jehovah-elyon, "Jehovah Most High" Ps. 7:17 and Jehovah-roi, "Jehovah, my Shepherd" Ps. 23:1

Where is the reference to Jehovah as my God? Which was he, god, ruler, king, guardian or the resident overseer of man by direction of the Lord or The Most High God?

The above definitions refer to the many names by which the Jewish and Christian Gods were identified. Nowhere are they ever referred to as the God or gods of creation. Only the Lord God is mentioned as the authority and power responsible for the creation of man. It was the misunderstanding or misinterpretation of scripture by the early religious leaders and theologians that gave Jehovah credit for the achievements of the Lord God. This has all been an assumption on the part of the religious disciples who follow the Jewish and Christian faiths.

Jehovah, is the title of the being to which the religious followers of the Jewish faith offer their prayers and sacrifices. Jesus, his son, called the Christ, is worshipped as the intercessor of the Christians. Neither makes references to the Universal Creator, the true GOD, nor do they mention the creator of man. Therefore, there are at least three different beings identified in the Bible by the title of God.

They are GOD the universal creator, the Lord God the authority responsible for the creation of man, and Jehovah, the biblical god of the Hebrews.

GOD, the creative power of the universal we know cannot be identified except by his handiwork, the earth, nature and the universe.

The biblical gods we can identify from the general information found in written scripture and the other holy writings, myths and legends that have been handed down to from the past.

From these writings we have their various titles, some of their deeds, laws, thoughts, actions and the religious ceremonies which honoured them. They also give us some idea as to who and what they were.

With so many gods to choose from it is no wonder that early man became confused. Let's see if we can place a face to the title and the name.

There is an old saying that is very appropriate at this time. It goes something like this: if it looks like a duck, walks like a duck and quacks like a duck, there is a very good chance that it is a duck. By the same token if it looks like a god, acts like a god, walks and talks like a god then there is a very good chance that it is a god.

Was Jehovah a god? Did he walk, talk and act like a god but how does one know what a god is supposed to look like, act like, talk or walk like a god? That can only be determined by each individual as to what makes up the reality of their god.

I contend that he did not. What he did look, act and talk like, is a present day Godfather, a statement I do not make lightly.

In order to establish a basis for such a statement I wish to first define the biblical gods and what they were supposed to have accomplished.

Gen. 1:1 says: *"In the beginning God created the heavens and the earth."*

Here the word God refers to the power and authority believe responsible for the creation of the universe and the laws and principles that govern and control the action, reaction and interaction of all that exist.

Biblical scholars, theologian and the clergy all seem to believe and agree that this is the same power and authority that one ay came to this planet and created man an organic life form in its image and after its likeness. They apparently see no distinct separation between the two.

Perhaps in presenting a new theory and an extremely unique perspective I can help clarify the distinction and the confusion that surrounds the biblical gods of man.

In Gen. 1:24 God said: *"let the earth bring forth the Living Creature after his kind."*

The Living creature was the race to which Jehovah belonged. They were an advanced form of organic life which evolved somewhere in the universe at sometime before the advent of man. The Dogon believe that they came from a planet near the star we call Sirius.

The Zondervan Compact Bible Dictionary identifies the living creatures as:

The "Living Creatures, mentioned in Ezekiel 1:5-22, 3:13, 10:15-20 and Revelation 1:4:6-9 (KJV as beasts) are apparently identified with the Cherubim.

The Zondervan Compact Bible Dictionary also identifies the living creature as: "Creatures, Living, a symbolical figure presented first in Ezekiel's vision Ezek. 1:5-22 and again in Revelation 4:6-9, 5:6, 8, 11; 6:1, 3, 5-7. In Ezekiel's vision there are four living creatures. They had the general appearance of a man, but each had four faces and four wings, and the feet of an ox. Under their wings they had human hands. The front face was that of a man; to the right and left of this were the faces of a lion, and of an ox, and in the back was the face of an eagle. Fire gleamed from their midst. Later they are called "cherubim." The living creature in Revelation are somewhat modified from those in Ezekiel's vision."

Of course they are different. The creatures standing before the throne of the Lord God are identified as Seraphim, which means burning ones, or celestial beings.

Genesis 1-24 disagrees with the assumption that these beings are the living creature but a unique form of life. The Living Creature was a life form entirely different from that of the beasts. If the cherubim were beasts than the living creature was not. If it was not a beast what was it? It was a form of life or created entity that was created or designed as the guardians and protector of the Lord God.

If the Seraphim were the protectors of God and God needed protection who or what did he need protection from? If he was is the creator of all things, than he controlled all things, and therefore has no fear of anything which he had created. But this was not so with the

Lord God who created man, a creature he feared and unsure as to what that creature might do.

If the Cherubim and Seraphim were not the living creatures they were unique. According to scripture there were only four of them. They did come from the heavens with the Lord God as his protectors. Were they organic life or created devices? Either way they are an indication that life and intelligence exist somewhere beyond this planet. They may be immortal either as a life form or a mechanical device because they are mention in Revelation as standing before God in the last days.

Were they a part of the original creation, a part of the beginning or did they evolve in some other way? Is it possible that they, like man, were created for the specific purpose of protecting God? Is it also possible that they are immortal because they are robotic machines created by the science and technology of the gods themselves?

They existed before man. Revelation indicates that they are immortal because we are told in Revelations that they will be standing before God at the end of the world as we know it to be. If one analyzes the description of the Cherubim it is easy to believe that they are a composite of many different life forms, a combination of the most advantageous traits of each species. As such I believe that if they are not robots than they are the result of genetic engineering by the scientists of the race of Living creatures.

"GOD" says and it was so. In Gen. 1:25 "God" made and saw that it was good. It should be noted that the "Living Creature" in verse 24 is not made along with the other life forms noted in verse 25. It is at this point in the story of the creation where the name of GOD the universal creator and the word God, a tile of supreme authority, used by the Living Creature, become one and the same.

Today the words king, ruler, emperor, pharaoh and president, all represent our idea of authority. In the society of Jehovah and his race of people the word God was used to indicate their highest authority. This is one of the words which have become a part of our language and a part of the heritage given to us by our creator.

If the life span of Cherubim covers countless generations, and they serve a species older than themselves, which we call God, it is also likely that the species that they serve is the Living Creature. If these two species are recorded in the Bible, how many other different and diverse forms of life could there have been down through the ages which have never been recorded? How many may still exist somewhere in the universe?

To connect all of these questions into a manner which gives us a plausible explanation for our existence and reliance upon a god we must rely on the Biblical Scriptures.

The beginning scriptures are believed to have been written by Moses, a prophet of Jehovah. In order for him to have become aware of the creative beginning he must have been instructed by someone who knew and had knowledge of the events. The only one capable of knowing and instructing Moses in this matter was Jehovah. As a heavenly being and space traveller, he would have known of such things. This would have been knowledge passed down to him through his culture, his travels, his education, knowledge of the universe, and the legends of his ancestors.

If one assumes that the scriptures say exactly what they mean and mean exactly what they say, then the following possibilities exist.

A couple of million years ago an expeditionary or colonizing force, of a race of beings, identified by Jehovah as, "the Living Creatures" came to this planet. What they expected to find or do we do not know. What we do know is that the very first command given to man after his creation was for him to be fruitful, multiply and replenish the earth. In order to replenish the earth there had to have been something which had once existed here but was now extinct.

Ancient artefacts, pictures, and legends lead us to believe that at sometime during the periods of the dinosaurs an ancient race of beings did existed on this planet. It is also possible to believe that they were virtually destroyed by a cataclysm event which destroyed them along with the dinosaurs.

There is factual evidence found throughout the world which supports the idea that a cultured society existed before the advent of man. That society may have been the result of a colonization attempt by the living creature a few million years ago. As a result of a global catastrophe, all but a few of those life forms perished.

From scientific findings, an evaluation of the magnetic alignment of the atoms found in various minerals around the world, it has been determined that the mantel of the globe has shifted at least three times in the planet's history.

This mantel shift helps to explain why tropical animals and green vegetation has been found frozen in the ice of what is now called the tundra. These tropical animals with green vegetation still in their mouths were frozen solid almost instantly. To create this type of rapid freezing, the earth's mantle would have had to rotate so fast that these animals were frozen solid before they could swallow their food. Only the impact of an asteroid of massive proportions hitting the earth's mantle a glancing blow could have create such an event. This sudden rotation of the mantel around the molten core would also account for the realignment of the mineral atoms. This shift would also have destroyed almost all life living on the planet surface.

There is another theory, science fiction of course, but it does lend credence to the legends of flying carpets and would give us some explanation for the steel columns found around the world which do not rust.

At sometime in the past, a few million years ago a colony of the living creature came to this planet and established a colony. As space travellers the colonists would have achieved a very high level of technical, scientific and medical expertise. If various colonies were establish around the globe they would have established a system of transportation. This would be a vital link in their economical structure and social welfare.

Suppose for the sake of argument that their transportation system operated on magnetic waves paths which used the magnetic flux of the earth as their primary power source. This would account for the legends of flying carpets. It would lends credence to the legends of the lost continents of Atlantis and Mu and give us an explanations for the steel columns which have never rusted down through the ages. Again let us assume that they had constructed giant power transmitters erected at the north and south poles. With the power furnished by these towers the poles even the poles enjoyed a tropical environment. This is not out of the range of possibilities because tropical plants and animals did exist there. If we elect to believe this scenario than we must rule out the shift in the earth's mantle. This we cannot do because of the scientific proof that the shift did occur. It is possible that both occurred.

Somehow these transmission towers shorted out. When they did the following would have occurred. There would be an instant freeze at both poles. Gigantic wind storms would have uproot trees tore them apart and hurled them, like spears, in all direction. The animals found in the tundra had such stakes driven through their bodies while the green food was still in their mouths. They were frozen in an instant. Electrical and mechanical engineers have experienced this same phenomenon when a generator shorts out. The technology to use the power generated by magnetic waves is being tested and used today. One day our society may be able to cross the planet by using the magnetic flux of the earth.

In the past an expeditionary force of the Living Creature led by the Lord God came to this planet to mine for minerals. The biblical description of their landing site, the location of what is called the "Garden of Eden" and the descriptions of the jobs given to early man substantiate this assumption.

The biblical Garden of Eden was located in Ethiopia. There too is where the mystical mines of Solomon are said to be located. It is a land where there is gold, the onyx-stone and bdellium. (Gen. 2-12)

The garden of biblical legend was not the only landing site of the alien miners. Some of the other landing sites and mining location found around the world can be identified by the signs and symbols of the companies which occupied that particular area. Their company identification symbols were what we call today, the Nazca Lines.

For the purposes of this book the only location that is of interest is the one mentioned in the Book of Genesis, the site of the Lord God and the Garden of Eden. From this group came Adam, Eve, Noah, Abraham, Jacob and the beginning of both the Jewish nation and their religion. It was to this group of alien miners that the Lord God controlled and to which the God Jehovah belonged. This was the mining group which settled in Africa, the land of Ethiopia.

All men did not originate from this particular group of individuals as taught by the Jewish and Christian religion. Each group of alien miners created and developed their particular group of workers based on the DNA makeup of their own particular interest. Each group created their own particular Adam and Eve according to the specifications required for their individual groups to survive in the environment of their location. This variation accounts for the diverse outward physical differences found in the various people around the world. On what is called the Sunken Wall in the temple of Tiahuanaco, located on a plateau 13,000 feet above sea level, can be found facial carvings of individual races made in prehistoric times. This wall is pictured in fig.4 of their book "In Search of Ancient Mysteries" by Alan and Sally Landsburg.

If we assume that the nationalities found in and around Africa descended from a created Adam and Eve and the Garden of Eden than we, mankind, began as dark skinned individuals, slaves to the gods? We were first created black? This was mans' adaptive protection from the hot Equatorial sun.

The location of the Garden of Eden suggests this as a definite possibility.

Genesis 2:8-13: *"And the Lord God planted a garden eastward in Eden; and there he put the man whom he had formed. 9. And out of the ground made the Lord God to grow every tree that is pleasant to the sight, and good for food; the tree of life also in the midst of the garden, and the tree of knowledge of good and evil 10. And a river went out of Eden to water the garden: and from thence it was parted, and became into four heads. The name of the first is Pison: that is it which compasseth the whole land of Havilah, where there is gold; and the gold of that land is good: there is bdellium and the onyx stone.13. And the name of the second river is Gihon: the same is it that compasseth the whole land of Ethiopia."*

Here the gods planted a garden.

To obtain the gold, bdellium and onyx stones required a labour force which the gods did not have. So, they used their medical and technical expertise to create one.

This decision was not made out of love or benevolence, but out of commercial necessity.

During the discussions between the Lord God and his subordinates as to what would be the most advantageous form of the new creation, based upon their expected function, it was decided that the creation of the new creatures be made in the image of themselves.

Gen. 1:26: *"And God said, Let us make man in our image an after our likeness."*

Once Man had been formed or created a relationship was established between him and his creator. It was a relationship between a master and a slave. It was not one between a god and his beloved creation. Our belief that such a condition existed is due primarily to our ego, our misunderstanding and misinterpretation of the scripture as recorded and translated in the King James Version of the Bible. Our ego refuses to allow us to believe that we are anything less than the noblest of Gods' treasures.

In the beginning there existed one type of relationship between man and God. It was a physical one reinforced by day by day affairs.

After the flood the Lord God and his supervisors had no need for the daily contact with man. The mines had either been flood, or destroyed by earthquakes. There was really nothing to supervise. Man was then allowed to go his way and to survive as best he knew how. But man, so longed controlled by the gods was lost without someone to guide and control his every day existence.

Independence was a giant step for man to take. Previously he had relied on the gods to tell him the what, when, where, how of those things desired by the gods. Today we call individuals under that condition institutionalized. It is commonly found among criminals who have been locked behind bars for long periods of time.

It was at the time of Noah that the more dominate individuals of a social group began to take advantage of this emotional need of man. They took control, became leaders, established religion, began sacrificial rites and organized society in a manner that catered to this ingrained trait of man. These individuals realizing the power of the fears and superstitions of man prey upon those fears and superstition in order to become rich and powerful.

Man in passing down his remembrance of his past services to a master made that master a god. God was changed from a physical being to a spiritual entity.

Through fear and ignorance, man continues to place himself under the yoke of powers he considers greater than himself. Today the control of man is exercised by what is called government, a society, which is itself controlled by two distinct organizations, the church and organized crime.

Both religion and organized crime are operated and controlled by powerful men that exercised control over their followers.

In religion these powerful men are called Pope, Cardinal or Bishop. For organized crime, the society of the brotherhood, the Mafia, they are called the Godfather or the Don.

In religion, Jehovah was the Godfather of the Jews. He set the pattern, the rules and the guidelines by which the other organizations pattern themselves.

When the Most High God, gave the order to create man, it was with specific instructions as to the kind of individual he was to be. He was to be a male, capable of working and surviving in the elements of the planet earth. His genetic makeup, his DNA, and his blood chemistry, was to be coded so that he would be able to adapt to this planet's food sources, atmosphere and environment. He was to have the power of speech, an intellect which allowed him to learn and adapt to changing conditions and situations, and finally he was to be able to reproductive his own species.

There may have been many trial and error monsters created by the alien scientists before and acceptable prototype worker that met their specifications was achieved. That man was the biblical Adam. When completed and found to be functional he was a naked being who lived with, worked and ate alongside the animals. Created or cloned from the DNA of the Lord God he was intelligent. He had the mental capacity of his surrogate father and the modified physical form best suited to survive in its new environment.

His first duty was to care for a garden, a task for which he knew nothing but he was taught and he learned. He must have learned well because it pleased the Lord God during his evening strolls though the garden.

Like the animals he lived and worked with first man was created as a vegetarian. He subsisted on herbs, seeds, fruit, and vegetables. He was a slave, a piece of property who belonged to the Lord God, the expedition commander. Adam and the first men and women who were first created were one thing more than slave's workers and property. Even though they were created through the process of cloning they were a new species of life, modified, adapted and created in order to replenish the earth.

This new species of man learned their jobs and earned their daily bread. But they were unable to reproduce as a new species because woman had not yet been created. In the due process of time the gods determined that man could use some help in his labours. To assist him in his endeavours, the scientists of God created other life forms, animals with specific traits, abilities and functions, whose sole purpose was to become helpmeet for man.

When it became apparent to the Lord God that men, as cloned individuals, were incompatible with the newly created animals, a female was created from the cells of Adam himself. All three, the men, the animals (specific ones only) and the women who were later created as helpmeets for the men were all genetically created beings.

We may not like the idea that mankind began in a laboratory test tube, created by the science and technology of an advance race of beings, but I find the idea far superior to the one which suggests that we evolved from the slime of the earth.

At the time of mans beginning the relationship which existed between him and the Lord God was no different than the one which existed between the plantation owners of the Old South and their slaves. Such relationships can be found to have existed throughout history between kings, emperors, pharaohs and their subjects.

Rulers, like the Lord God, exercised the power of life and death over their subjects. Most of the time it was not a power exercised without a great deal of thought.

In the beginning slaves were few and were therefore extremely valuable pieces of property. They were far too valuable to destroy lightly. As man reproduced and multiplied, slaves remained an important source of wealth and power, but their value decreased as their numbers increased.

Death as a result of harsh discipline during the time of the Lord God may have occurred but it is not recorded in scripture.

Before the flood, there is no mention of the Lord God ever abusing his authority either as a property owner or as the commander of the earth expeditionary force. Except for the death of Abel, which was an accident, there is no recorded mention of any death other than the patriarchs which died of old age. No one was executed as a punishment for disobedience.

There had to have been some form of discipline administered by God and his supervisors or the scriptures would not state that man began to call upon the Lord God for a redress of grievances.

Adam and Eve, as a result of their disobedience to a specific command, were forbidden access to the garden. Cain was marked, placed under the protection of God and sent from his presence as punishment for the accidental death of Abel. Other than these isolated incidents, the Lord God appears to have been a tolerant owner. His care and assistance to Noah and his family before the flood, supports such a supposition.

The flood changed everything. It was not the work of an angry god but the result of a natural disaster. The planet was struck by a giant asteroid. The resulting collision triggered the events specified in the bible as the work of God.

The Lord God as the supreme leader for the earth task force had to be one of the first individuals to be notified when it was learned by his scientist that the earth was in danger of being struck by an extremely large celestial mass. Once this heavenly mass entered the solar system and was noticed by the scientist they began to track its trajectory. When it was determined that the path of this new mass, a giant asteroid was on a collision course with earth and it could not be diverted, the Lord God was informed. He immediately issued orders that his supervisors and the people begin to make preparations for survive the impact. He had to know that with a direct hit of such a mass travelling at the speeds normally associated with celestial bodies that most if not all of life in the area of the impact would be destroyed. As the two masses, earth and the asteroid, drew closer together natural weather patterns would change, earthquakes would occur and volcanoes would erupt killing and destroying most of the life on the planet. He also knew that he did not have the time to do much more than save a nucleus of life from which the planet could be repopulated should they survive the impact.

He had approximately two years in which to do what had to be done. We can only guess at this time frame because we do not know the speed at which the asteroid was travelling. But, our scientist's today estimate that this is the approximately time that it would take for a large asteroid, travelling at the normal speed of space masses, to reach the earth once it entered our solar system.

Noah and his family were evidently one of the families which came under the direct supervision of God himself. They evidently pleased him and as his faithful and immediate servants they were selected to be the core the nucleus for the new beginning of human life.

In order to save as many of the species of life as possible the gods began to make necessary arrangements.

While a boat, identified as the ark, was being built to certain specifications the other slaves of Gods assisted in its construction. Lumber had to be cut, shaped and hauled to the construction site. Scaffolds were built and cranes erected. During the construction of the ark animals pens were built, animals gathered, food raised, harvested and stored while the waterproofing pitch or tar was found, gathered and transported to the ark building site.

The ark was to house all of the animals, birds, reptiles and insects considered by the Lord God as those worth saving. Provisions were made for food storage bins, water containers and a residence facility for the family of Noah.

There is no way we can know how many individuals were involved in the construction of the ark. Nor do we know how many if any were involved with gathering the animals, growing and harvesting the wood, finding, shaping and hauling the building timbers. Our religious leader, at least those that I have I known like to believe that all of this was accomplished by eight people, Noah, his three sons and their wives with the help of God. This I believe is only a half truth. Without the help of God, his and the other slaves in the vicinity of the construction site none of this could have taken place.

The help of God and the saving of Noah, his family and the animals was not some spiritual miracle but the result of back breaking physical labour.

While the supervisors of God were using their spaceships as transportation gathered the animals, the pitch and the timbers, his slaves grew, harvested and stored the grain. They helped to build the animals pens and they helped Noah to erect the ark. The only thing they were not allowed to do was to go aboard the boat when the rains began to fall.

Movies have portrayed Noah and his family as the butt of the neighbourhood joke. Everyone laughed at the crazy old man and his nutty family for building a boat in the middle of dry land. As a result of the ark story religious disciples are led to believe that only Noah, his family and the animals on board the ark were saved from the flood. This is not according to scripture but the teachings of misguided individuals. There were many individuals and animals which survived the flood, one only has to read the bible, history and study the world around them to learn this for themselves.

The Biblical description of the construction of the ark makes it impossible to believe that eight people, Noah and his family, could have accomplished this gigantic task alone.

There was the required timber to cut, shape and carry to the boat. There was tar or pitch to gather, and containers to be built to hold the pitch. There were special implements created for the construction. There was scaffolding to be erected, and hoists constructed for raising the timbers and holding them into place until they were secured. Once the timbers were in place and secured to the superstructure, the whole boat had to be covered with pitch inside and out in order to make it waterproof and to protect the occupants from the elemental forces of nature that were to come.

Animal pens had to be constructed, animals gathered, watered and fed while the construction of the boat was underway. There was food to grow, harvest and store, enough to feed both man and beast for the duration of the upcoming event. After the ark was completed Noah, his family, and the selected animals went aboard. It is said that the Lord God himself shut and sealed the door or ramp to the ark, pitched the outside seams and made the ark waterproof. All of the above acts indicate a kind, caring and benevolent owner.

Genesis 7:15-16: *"And they went into the ark, two and two of all flesh, where in is the breath of life. And they that went in went in male and female of all flesh, as God had commanded him: and the Lord shut him in."*

God and his crew had no reason to fear the impending disaster because they would be safely housed in their spaceship high above the planet and away from all danger.

Shortly before the impact the following events occurred. As the two giant masses drew closer together the magnetic attraction between the two masses created gigantic tidal waves began to hits the coastal areas. Weather patterns changed. Cyclonic winds were generated around the globe and rainfall became continuous. The rivers began to overflow and flooding was everywhere. Earthquakes created eruptions, poisonous gasses contaminated the atmosphere and most but not all of the life on the planet was destroyed.

Before the flood there are no times recorded as times of trials and tribulations for man even though God is recorded as having said that man was evil and wicked and it repented the Lord that he had made man.

Genesis 6:5-6: *"And God saw that the wickedness of man was great in the earth, and that every imagination of the thoughts of his heart was only evil continually. And it repented the Lord that he had made man on the earth, and it grieved him at his heart. What is not said is that if there*

After the flood it was different. During the time of Abraham the scriptures begin to relate incident after incident of death, violence and bloodshed attributed not to Satan nor to just any god, but to Yahweh, the one god, the God Jehovah, the God of the Jews.

For some time after the flood the Lord God remained on the planet to supervise, as best he could the reconstruction of the planet. At that time he was still the controlling authority, the Highest God. When he decided to leave the planet he left one of his subordinate in charge. This is the entity that is identified by the Hebrews as their Lord God Jehovah.

How he came to power and what he did with that power is recorded in the Bible. It is that record and that history that will be discussed and explained as to how and why he earned the title and became "The First Godfather". It is his words, thoughts and actions, and those of the religion, founded to worship and serve him, which give me the right to compare him with The Godfathers of organized crime today.

The scriptures are not clear as to when power was transferred from the Most High God to Jehovah, but it was evidently not a spur of the moment decision. The following passage, made before the flood, indicates that it is to happen sometime in the future.

The Lord God, the authority responsible for the creation of man was a flesh and blood being who worked and did strive with early man. He walked and talked in the garden. He could feel the heat of the day. He ministered to the people and in time they began to call upon his name for the redress of their grievances. He was a man of the people. But he knew that it would all come to an end sometime in the future. It would be at that time when he would be required to return to his home world. When he did he would leave behind a personal representative, who, along with a staff of his people, would govern the earth in his place.

The scriptures do not actually say that God left the earth to return to his home world. We assume that this happened because it is recorded in the Bible, that before he left, he divided his property among those he intended to leave behind. He gave to the gods, who were his crew, their inheritance. One does not leave an inheritance to ones' self.

If the Most High God and Jehovah were one and the same individual god as believed by most religions, then who gave, and who received the inheritance described in the following passages?

Deuteronomy 32:8-10: *"When the Lord God who was the Most High God divided to the nations(the supervisors he was going to leave behind as caretakers) he separated the sons of Adam and set the bounds of the people according to the number of the children of Israel, those who struggled with him). For the Lord Jehovah his portion of the people was his grandson Jacob and his descendants who became the lot of his inheritance. He found him in a desert land, and in the waste howling wilderness; he led him about, he instructed him, he kept him as the apple of his eye."*

At this time there were no children of Israel as such and the word Israel referred to those who did strive with God in the beginning.

No property owner, heir or ruler divides his property or leaves behind an inheritance to anyone unless they are going to die or be away from the area of their property for a very long period of time. In which case the property is either given outright or is placed in the care of stewards who are to carry out the will of the owner. In the biblical case of the Lord God he did not die but departed the earth. When he did he delegated to the other gods, the members of his crew which he intended to leave behind a responsibility to care for the planet and his property.

Religion teaches us that the Lord God and his subordinated the other gods are immortal. As an immortal they could not die. If they did life would return and begin again in a never-ending cycle of life and death.

We must assume that when he stated that his spirit would not always strive with man, that he had other intentions one was to eventually return to his home world. This he did in Deuteronomy 32.

He left the earth with the intent of returning sometime in the future. That intent is recorded in Revelation. It will be at that time that Jehovah and the other gods will be required to account for their stewardship of the planet. It will also be at that time when Jehovah and the other gods will rebel and will do battle with the returning Lord God or a representative of the Lord God from their home world.

The Lord God was aware of the interracial relationships which existed between Jehovah, his crew and man. He also knew that at some point in time, the life span of man, originally a thousand years, was going to diminish from that thousand years to approximately one hundred and twenty years.

When created, man was able to live that thousand years because he had access to special foods, alien medical facilities, scientific technology and the expertise of the alien gods. After the Lord God departed the planet these service were no longer available to man. His years began to diminish. The changes in the atmosphere, flora and fauna of the earth which occurred as a result of the asteroid impact and the flood accelerated the process in the reduction of man's life span. This accelerated was due primarily to the changes which occurred not only in the atmosphere and the environment but with the food supply affected by the collision between the earth and a giant asteroid, an impact which resulted in the biblical flood.

As the giant a steroid approached the earth many changes began to take place here on earth. The gravitational attraction between the two bodies resulted in earthquakes, tidal waves, changes in weather patterns and volcanic eruptions. These eruptions fill the atmosphere with gases, toxic fumes and altered the composition of the air which man needed to breathe and live.

Along with the above events came the flood, said to have destroyed all life on this planet except for those life forms protected within the ark, and the creatures of the sea.

The flood waters carried salt and debris inland to change the composition of the soil and the plants which were necessary for the health of man.

After the flood the Lord God, as the apparent reigning authority of mining conglomerate completed his assessed of the damages done to the planet and the mines by the asteroid impact. He found that almost all life on the surface of the planet had reduced to a very few isolated survivors. His mines were flooded or collapsed, his miners were dead and the primary interest of those who were still alive was personal survival.

When the evaluation of the destruction was completed, it was determined that the damage was too extensive to be economical feasible to renew and rebuild so all mining operations were abandoned. A staff from the crew of the Lord God was selected and placed in charge of overseeing the reconstruction of the earth and to monitor the progress of mankind.

From Jewish scripture we are given to believe that the person who was placed in charge of this governing body was the individual who later came to be called Jehovah.

The Lord God divided the survivors of the flood among his caretakers, placed Jehovah in charge and gave him the title and authority of Lord God. To enhance that authority he was given a piece of property his grandson Jacob and his descendents. They were his people and his inheritance.

After his affairs were in order he, the conglomerate and what remained of his crews departed the earth. The Book of Revelation predicts that some day he will return to this planet and require an accounting for the stewardship of Jehovah and those who had been left behind.

At first Jehovah may have been nothing more than an administrator because the only inherence he received was the care and responsibility of Jacob. He was not a supervisor and had no leadership experiences. In a review of his rule during the time he led the Israelites through the desert we can understand why he was not given the rule, control and responsibility of any group of individuals. He had no experience in leading or governing humans.

He was given the care and responsibility of Jacob because of his sexual relationship with Sarah and the birth of Isaac. He also must have had other relationships with the women of earth because he had sons and daughters under his care.

When he was placed in charge by the Lord God he automatically assumed the title of Lord or God. But he was not referred to as the Lord God but rather as I AM.

When the spaceships of Lord God departed the earth the alien medical facilities, their hospitals, went with him. The medical facilities left behind are what we would call clinics.

The hospital facilities aboard the spaceships are the ones which early man remembered as the chambers which healed the sick, patched up the wounded and brought dead men back to life. During the time of early man these facilities represented the power of the gods. A person went through the doors sick, wounded or thought dead and returned alive. It was then that man came too believed in the power of God to restore life and was the beginning of man's belief in reincarnation.

Before Jehovah was place in charge, the Lord God made a couple of other assignments. He divided the people according to their status as the supervisors of the people who had been under their control. In reality they were the earth family of those supervisors because it had been their DNA that had been used to create them.

These crewmen became in time the other gods who were served and later worshipped by the individuals which formed their particular groups. These groups were the guilds, ones of which Cain was force to join when he had to leave the presence of God.

To use modern terminology, Cain was transferred from a farming unit into a construction group. There, instead of farming, he was taught a different trade. He learned how to build cities. There were other trade groups. There were the weavers, music groups, herders, miners, smelters and workers in metal. Each of these groups was controlled by individual members of Gods crew. They were the supervisors who came to be worshipped as gods to those people placed under their command. It is because of these supervisors, the other gods that the Lord God came to be called the "Most High" God.

When the he departed the earth Jehovah was given the authority to speak as God. He became the overseer to which the other gods reported. What Jehovah was not given were subjects of his own. He had no one to worship and serve him. His only servant appears to have been Abraham, Isaac and Jacob. Why then was Jacob the only inheritance given to Jehovah.

At sometime during his early years Jehovah and Abraham became acquainted and Jehovah became a friend and a god to Abraham. From that friendship a bond was formed between them. Abraham came to believe in and passed on to his sons that Jehovah was a god to be praised, honoured and worshipped. They in turn passed those beliefs down to their children and their children's children.

An analysis of scripture gives us an indication, which is not necessarily proof, as to why Jacob was the only inheritance given to Jehovah by the Most High.

Jehovah did not receive any people as his immediate responsibility because he was an administrator, as a minor member of the Lord Gods staff. He had little or no supervisory experience except for the household servants. So why was he put in charge and given Jacob as his inheritance?

He was a paper pusher. It was his job to keep the records and he was given Jacob as an inheritance because Jacob was his grandson. This gave him and his ego a bit of a rush because even though his job and position of authority was symbolic it gave him a position of honour. He was the Lord God the official representative of the planet, a little man in a big position.

Why was he specifically given Jacob and his descendants as his property, the lot of his inheritance?

This is pure conjecture, but, I believe that it is supported by the scripture in found in Genesis. 18:9-14 and Genesis 21:1-4. He mated with Sarah and reproduced offspring. He had a biological family rather than a genetic one.

I take these passages to refer to a custom said to be prevalent at the time. It was the custom of offering one's wife to an honoured guest as the measure of one's hospitality. Abraham offers Jehovah Sarah. Sarah conceived in her old age and born a son, Isaac. He was not the son of Abraham and Sarah but of Jehovah and Sarah, just as in later years Jesus was to be the son of Mary and Jehovah rather than Mary and Joseph. Because these two sons were born to the first wife and were the first sons, they became heirs to the name and property of the espoused father. Therefore Jehovah having cohabited with earthly women was deemed by the Lord God to be unworthy to return to his home world. He was left behind as an administrator and was given his grandson Jacob and his descendants as his inheritance and his responsibility.

Other than the meetings, dialogue and events which occurred between Abraham and Jacob and until the time of the Exodus Jehovah does not appear to have had any servants nor did he seem to be involved with man in any way, but he does appear to have been in charge of the alien organization left on earth. (Job 1:6.)

Job 1:6: *"Now there was a day when the sons of God came to present themselves before the Lord, and Satan came also among them."*

It can be assumed from the above passage that Jehovah now born the title of Lord and was in charge. As the resident governor of earth he was the authority to whom the sons of Gods, the minor gods, reported.

Satan was also one of the minor gods and based on the story of Job was in a kind of friendly rivalry with Jehovah.

Job 1:1: *"There was a man in the land of Uz, whose name was Job; and that man was perfect and upright, and one that feared God, and eschewed evil."*

By the words of God himself Job was a perfect and upright man. He worked hard and was blessed with sons, daughters, servants and much property. He was considered as the greatest of all men in the east. Job 1:3.

When Jehovah and Satan met, Jehovah began to brag about Job and about how faithful and upright he was how much he feared God and hate evil. Satan questioned the faith of Job and posed a challenged to Jehovah.

Job 1:11: *"But put forth your hand now, and touch all that he has and he will curse thee to your face."*

Jehovah did not have the guts to do this so he gave Satan the power to do with Job as he desired to test him as he willed. Jehovah was willing to let Job suffer the torments of Satan just so his ego could be satisfied. The only thing that Satan was not allowed to do was to kill Job.

Both Job and Moses, faithful and obedient servants, were punished and chastised by their god to satisfy his ego and his image before the other gods.

The way Jehovah dealt with Moses and Jobs, both dedicated servants, are excellent examples of his lack of personal responsibility and leadership qualities. There are many mores misguided, administrative blunders, not just these two which gives us the right to question the right of religion to call Jehovah a loving, caring and benevolent god and father.

His wrath, ignited by the blasphemy of Jacob and the ridicule of the other gods, coupled with his enormous ego, created paranoia in his rule and leadership of the Hebrew people. His anger, his jealously of the other gods and his desire to prove himself above them, led to the atrocities he commanded his people to committed time and again against mankind in his name.

Jealous of the attention paid to his subordinates, the other gods, Jehovah decided and desired to be treated, worshipped and served as the other god under his control. His subordinates had temples, servants, worshippers and sacrifices. He had nothing but authority, and that in name only.

At first he appeared to have accepted his role as Lord, and was satisfied with his association as friend, guide and benefactor to Abraham. He furthered that friendship with Jacob when he took Jacob under his wing, so to speak, and allowed Jacob to become a part of his life. Jacob travelled to the high paces, ate the best of everything and became a part of his family.

Deuteronomy 32:9-10: *"For the Lord's portion is his people; Jacob is the lot of his inheritance. He found him in a desert land, and in the waste howling wilderness; he led him about, he instructed him, he kept him as the apple of his eye."*

Deuteronomy 32:15-20: *"But Jeshurun waxed fat, and kicked: thou art waxen fat, thou art grown thick, thou art covered with fatness; then he forsook God which made him, and lightly esteemed the Rock of his salvation They provoked him to jealously with strange gods, with abominations provoked they him to anger. They sacrificed unto devils, not to God; to gods whom they knew not, to new gods that came newly up, whom your father's feared not. Of the Rock that begat thee thou art unmindful, and hast forgotten God that formed thee. And when the Lord saw it, he abhorred them, because of the provoking of his sons, and of his daughters. And he said I will hide my face from them; I will see what their end shall be: for they are a very forward generation, children in whom is no faith."*

How does anyone read the above passages and still say with any degree of certainty that Jehovah was a god. He was a flesh and blood being. He had children, and like the parents of today had problems with them. They rebelled against his authority. They had no faith in their own father why should we? Jacob, while a stranger to the household of Jehovah, was nevertheless a part of that family. As a grandson of Jehovah he was welcomed. When he became fat, lazy and began to side with the sons and daughters of Jehovah, to make fun of his sire and his protector, he incurred the wrath of his grandfather. He was kicked out of the household and a curse was placed upon him and his descendants. In essence he was cut out of the will of Jehovah, his grandfather. Any future relationships between Jacob, his descendants and God would be based on a relationship of hate and vengeance.

Jehovah, just like the fathers of today tired of having suffered insults and insolence from Jacob and his children kicked Jacob out of his house. But before he did he placed on him, a curse which extended to his descendants in Egypt, the wilderness, the march to Canaan. For many of the Jewish Nation that curse still exists.

Just as mankind suffers from the disobedient act of Eve they suffer from the actions of Jacob, both disrespectful against a god.

In time the descendants of Jacob united under the rule and yoke of Jehovah became the Jewish nation. Are they a blessed people, or a nation still under the curse of Jacob?

Abraham was a friend to God but Jacob was more than a friend he was the love of Jehovah, the apple of his eye. As long as he was respectful, he enjoyed the advantages of Jehovah's generosity. But, with good food and easy living, he grew fat, lazy and insolent. He began to spurned the affections of his grandfather. He took sides with his uncles and aunts who were the sons and daughters of Jehovah and the other gods. He began to ridicule his grandfather before the other gods, sacrificing to devils and with abominations which anger his God. When he began to give his attentions to the other gods who were basically subordinates of his grandfather Jehovah he betrayed a trust and turned his grandfather Jehovah into a vengeful God.

He was cast aside. He was no longer allowed in the presence of Jehovah, his grandfather and it was then that Jacob brought down on himself and all of the generations of Jews to come, the curses of their God. Those curses, placed upon Jacob almost four thousand years ago, still affects his descendants and all who call themselves "the chosen people of God."

Baal, Molech and Lucifer were a couple of the subordinate gods recorded in scriptures. While they reported to Jehovah, they were independent individuals. They had their own temples, servants, territory and people. These were all outside of the jurisdiction of Jehovah. Throwing this up to Jehovah's face may well have been the straw which broke his back and triggered his anger. Humiliated by Jacob, a human, in front of his family and peers, changed a benevolent God into a mean, evil and vengeful one.

Because of the words and actions of Jacob, Jehovah became a jealous, vindictive and vengeful god. He places a curse on Jacob which he carried out before, during and after the Exodus. He swore revenge against the other gods and he used the descendants of Jacob as the weapons needed to destroy them and their temples.

Once Jehovah decided to become a god there were a few things he had to accomplish in order for this to come to pass. First: he needed to find a people who would be willing to follow him, to worship and sacrifice to him. Second: He needed to establish priesthood, a group of individuals dedicated to his service. Third: He needed a place where the people could come and give him the praise, honour and glory he deserved, he needed a temple. And last but not least He needed a land that he could call his own. The Hebrew bondservants in Egypt, the descendants of Jacob, were the perfect choice.

They were use to being slaves. They had suffered greatly under the yoke of Pharaoh for many years. They were large in number and his name was a part of their oral history. They were a group of individual with a very high family tradition and cohesiveness, and they were survivors. They would make excellent servants. They were capable of enduring the waste of the desert and they could be trained to become a formidable weapon of war. With this weapon Jehovah intended and in fact did destroyed the temples, and the congregations of the other gods on his way to the land of Canaan.

When the Israelites were completely under his control Moose was given the order to assemble every male over the age of twenty. These men were to begin training as fighting men. This was the beginning of the army of Jehovah. He started with six hundred and three thousand, five hundred and fifty men above the age of twenty. This was an army greater than most of the civilized countries in the world today. This army trained, marched and endured the desert hardships for forty years. They were hard, disciplined survivors used to the riggers and warfare of the desert.

When the Hebrews came out of Egypt Jehovah obtained his congregation. When they began to offer up sacrifices according to his specifications, he established priesthood to administration those sacrifices to him but he needed two more things in order to be considered a god worthy of respect. He needed a temple and a land which he could claim as his own. At the time of the Exodus the only land through which he could lead his new congregation without risking a fight was the desert of the Sinai, open desert, a land which nobody wanted. Without a permanent land he could not build his temple. The people could not be made to honour and sacrifice to a god without a place of abode so he did the next best thing, he had the people build a portable temple called a sanctuary. This sanctuary was located in the middle of the camp of the Israelites, equally accessible to all of the tribes. There he met and spoke with the people.]

Exodus 25:8: *"And let them make me a sanctuary; that I may dwell among them."*

Once this was achieved he began to organize his army. He specified how they were to be selected, how they were to be located, controlled, under whose command and under what guidelines they were to fight.

Genesis 13:17-20: *"And Moses sent them to spy out the land way southward, and to go up into the mountain: And see the land, what it is; and the people that dwell therein, whether they be strong or weak, few or many; And what the land is that they dwell in, whether it be good or bad; and what cities they be that they dwell in, whether in tents, or in strong holds; And what the land is, whether it be fat or lean, whether there be wood therein, or not. And be ye of good courage, and bring of the fruit of the land. Now the time was the time of the first ripe grapes."*

The Israelite thought to destroy the people and conquer the land. But fear of the people who inhabited the land caused the congregation to falter and it angered their god. For their lack of faith it is said that he refused to allow them to enter into the land of Canaan, the land he had promised to Abraham. Instead they wandered for forty years, until all of the men of the Exodus were dead. The Israelites did not enter Canaan because they were cowards and not ready or able to conquer the people who occupied the land. Jehovah did not want to make an attempt to obtain Canaan with ill trained troops, fail and be ridiculed by the other gods. Besides if he made an attempt to occupy Canaan and failed he would lose his congregation. They would become the slaves of the Canaanites and the worshippers of the other gods.

For forty years the Israelites trained for war. In that time they had minor skirmishes with small tribes and small nations. Gradually their faith in their ability to wage war increased. In time they became an army capable of waging war on all of the nations which stood in their way to Canaan. They became a people capable of and willing to destroy the temples and worshippers of the other gods, gods who were now declared as idols of the heathens.

1 Chronicles 16:26: *"For all the gods of the people are idols: but the Lord made the heaven."*

It was the intentions of Jehovah to annihilating any memory of these other gods by the elimination of their temples and worshippers. If there are no worshippers than the memory of the people and the gods they worshipped would vanish from the memory of man.

Exodus 17:14-16: *"And the Lord said unto Moses, Write this for a memorial in a book, and rehearse it in the ears of Joshua: for I will utterly put out the remembrance of Amalek from under heaven because I sworn that I will have war with the Amalek from generation to generation."*

If the reader is a descendant of the Amalek nation they were and will be forever an enemy of God. Therefore, they will never be allowed to enter into the kingdom of heaven, a paradise which many religion teach will exist in the end time. Because Jehovah declared that he will "utterly put out the remembrance of the Amalek from under heaven", and that he will be at war against them from one generation to the next generation, he cannot be a god with all power. He lied. The name of the Amalek is still with us and will never be erased from the mind of man as long as there is the Torah, the Christian Bible and a religion which worships Jehovah as the lord God, creator of man and the universe.

Jehovah and the gods of the above books were aliens. Their likeness as gods can be found in the legends and myths of the countless generations of man which have existed since his beginning.

After the flood mankind was no longer a vital part of the economic welfare of the gods who no longer walked, talked or took an interest in man. It is possible that the gods did have priests and servants who waited on them, fed, clothed, cared for them and satisfied their needs and desires. But as far as man was concerned their existence became mystical and spiritual rather than physical. The more they were absence from the everyday affairs of men the greater their deity and mystical powers appear to become.

Each of the alien gods was, at one time, a supervisor of a particular group of people. As such they were each given the title of God. They became symbolically the mythical rulers and kings. They were someone or something worthy of worship. That term still applies today.

An example of their control and authority over man can be applied illustrated by the passages of scripture found in the Book of Job.

As an ex-military person, I find the following verbal exchange between the Lord God and Satan, in the following passages, somewhat reminiscent of staff meetings I attended while in the military service.

A challenge was issued by God to Satan concerning a most devoted servant, a man called Job. God was so sure of the loyalty of Job, that he gave Satan the right to punish and to test Job in any way which Satan deem proper short of killing him. Satan accepted the challenge.

Job, a faithful, loyal and devoted servant was made to suffer the most of his family, his property and his dignity in order to cater to the ego of God.

My senior officers often made similar statements, made bets and exchanged challenges to each other. The loser paid for the drinks at the bar. They were simple bets generated to bring out the best in the men under the individual commands. It was a professional rivalry designed to bring out the best is each unit. Did such a rivalry exist between God and Satan? It must have because Job paid a tremendous price in order for God to win his bet.

Job became a pawn in the chess game of power and egos. He was a perfect and upright man. He served his God faithfully and yet this loyal and faithful servant was given to Satan, so that Satan might test him. Because of that test Job was given to suffer unendurable torment. He lost his children, servants, and flocks of sheep, camels, and his livestock. He himself was inflicted with boils from his head to his feet.

If God allowed Job, a perfect and upright man, a faithful servant, to be manipulated by Satan as an ego wager, what might he be willing to do to the rest of us poor sinners, who are far less righteous?

As men began to spread throughout the known world, they retained in their memory, the customs and legends of their servitude to a god. As a result, they began to create different ways in which they believed their sacrifices, rituals, worship and offerings might best attract the attention of their God, whoever or whatever it might have been at the time. Forgotten were the memories of their past conditions of slavery and servitude.

The gods were the overseers of the land. They were the rich landowners who were believed capable of controlling man, crop production, and the balance of nature. Jehovah was one of those individuals. They were all, including Jehovah, called by names with similar meanings which meant lord, husband or possessor.

After the flood the gods no longer made personal appearances or associated with man. There was no reason to. The mines and camps were destroyed and man had no need of supervision. He was on his own.

Man, in fear and ignorance turned to his earthly superiors for guidance. These superiors became the holy men, the shaman and intermediary between man and God. These shaman in order to please the people and to enhance their own political powers began to created elaborate rituals, rules and laws and ceremonies they beleved my please the gods and entice them to return to man The more elaborate the rituals and the more debased the sacrifices rituals, the more powerful the rituals and customs became. During the time of Abraham, the sacrifice of children, virgins and human was an accepted practice not only in Ur the land of Abraham but in many other cultures around the world.

The sons of Jacob and their descendants lived in Egypt for over four hundred years. During that time they came to know and probably followed many of these unusual religious customs. They evidently knew of and approved of the calf cult, because it was this cult that they turned to as soon as Moses was out of their presence.

Exodus 32:4. And he received them at their hand, and fashioned it with a graving tool, after he had made it a molten calf: and they said, These be thy gods, O Israel which brought thee up out of the land of Egypt."

The Hebrews had been conditioned to follow any leader who was a priest and or disciple of a god. Jehovah, in his desire to become a god, used that condition, and his technical expertise to obtain for himself a following of servants. He began his quest with Moses and his brother Aaron. They became his spokespersons. Next he used his knowledge of nature and of natural events to create a fear in the population, of both the Egyptians and Hebrews. These were the plagues of Egypt.

Out of fear and frustration the Egyptians petitioned Pharaoh to allow the Hebrews to leave Egypt. The Hebrews afraid of what Pharaoh might do to them as a result of all of the death and devastation suffered by the Egyptians, caused by Moses and Aaron in the name of the Lord God, and followed Moses into the wilderness. Once they were in the desert and under the control of Jehovah it allowed him to place the people in a situation whereby they had no choice but to follow him where ever he chose to lead them. The Hebrews could not return to Egypt without facing the anger of Pharaoh and the possibility of death. Once in the desert the Hebrews had no choice but to follow Moses and Jehovah. The people had no land and no wealth except for what they stole from the Egyptians. They were outcasts, a people who were not acceptable by anyone. There were two main reasons for this. The first and foremost was the fear and retaliation of Pharaoh should anyone give aid, shelter and comfort to them and the second was memory of the despicable acts of Jacob and his sons at Hamor.

Therefore it was by fear, death, hunger, thirst, and bribery did Moses and God obtain control over the Hebrew people. But it took them forty years to do it. During that time, out of fear, hunger, thirst and abandonment, they agreed to accept Jehovah as their God and leader.

Once accepted as a god Jehovah began to give the congregation his laws, and the commandants by which they were to live. They were given two choices, obey and live or suffer the penalties of plagues, slavery and or death.

To serve him and to carry out his commandments, he selected the tribe of Levi as his immediate servants. They became his priests. As a part of his new religion he prescribed certain rituals, specified particular blood sacrifices, and issued orders as to how the sacrificial animals were to be killed, prepared, cooked and offered up to him. He demanded to be fed on plates made of gold, to sit on a chair and served on a table also made of gold. (Exodus 25)

When the Hebrews agreed to abide by and follow all of these commands, they became obedient servants and worshippers. With a congregation of worshippers, a priesthood to lead them, sacrifices and gifts offered up to him, Jehovah was at last a god worthy to be respected. He was still not a god of worth. He still lacked a temple and a land he and his people could call their own.

For forty years Moses under the direction of Jehovah led the Hebrews, now called the Israelites, around and through the desert wilderness of the Sinai desert. The people were governing by Moses and a select group of individuals who acted as his representatives. They were the judges. They settle the civil disputes and squabbles which arose between the members of the congregation. Any problem which was in conflict with the laws of God or which dealt with religion was taken before Moses.

The judges subdivided their authority to include commanders who controlled lower commanders who were themselves leaders of a select group of the congregation. This type of organization was a prelude to what has become the basic organizational structure of every governmental and military structure around the world.

Once this organization was in place, controlled by Moses and the priest the men of the congregation began to train and be taught the ways of war. Moses having been trained by the best military commanders in Egypt became an excellent leader. Joshua, his protégé, did what Moses was not able to do. He destroyed the inhabitants of Canaan as he marched into and conquered the Promised Land.

For forty years the fighting abilities of the congregation was tested in minor skirmishes with the people they met in their travels. The Israelites learned and improved their fighting skills. As their skills improved so too did their strength, battle knowledge and confidence.

After forty years the Israelites were strong enough to invade and conquer the land of Canaan, a land Jehovah wanted to call his own.

In order for them to conquer the land it also became necessary for them on orders of Jehovah to utterly destroyed or enslave the inhabitants of the land.

When this was accomplished to some degree the land of Canaan, long promised to Abraham, as the Land of God and Israel became a partial reality. The Israelites never completely conquered the whole land of Canaan.

Joshua 13:1: *"Now Joshua was old and stricken in years; and the Lord said unto him, Thou art old and stricken in years, and there remained yet very much land to be possessed."*

In so the land they conquered they did do one thing, they destroyed the enemies of Jehovah, the temples of the other gods who had mocked him, and the people who worshipped those gods. The land, religion and other he was not able to destroy became a thorn in his side. Many of the members of the congregation found the religion of the other gods preferable to that of the Israelite nation. This resulted in the death of many innocent people. This may have been one of the reasons why Israelites never completely conquering Canaan.

Joshua 16:12: *"Yet the children of Manasseh could not drive out the inhabitants of those cities; but the Canaanites would dwell in that land."*

The Israelites did conquer most of the land, and Jehovah and the Israelites finally had a land of their own but it was not due to their god but of the efforts, blood, sweat, tears and sacrifices endured by the Israelite congregation. Jehovah became the God he wanted to be. He had worshippers, a temple and now received gifts, sacrifices, honour and renown. But did he really have respect? He did finally see the fulfilment of the promise he had made to Abraham eons ago that his descendants would one day live in the land of Canaan.

With the annihilation of the altars of the other gods Jehovah believed that he would have no further competition. His congregation was forbidden to worship or to offer up sacrifices to any god other than himself under the penalty of death.

The Jewish people are justly proud of their history and heritage achieved by their faith in their god and his leadership. But exactly what is that history and what is their heritage?

If we start with Abraham, the first recorded disciple of Jehovah and his leadership, we have the following:

Abraham, the patriarch of the Jewish nation left his home and family to become a wandering nomad. In a time of drought he was forced to travel to Egypt in order to survive. There, out of fear for his life, he allowed his wife to become a prostitute, the consort of a king. From the humiliation and degradation of Sarah Abraham became rich and powerful.

When Sarah was unable to have a child by Abraham she allowed Abraham to sleep with her handmaiden. That union produced a son, Ishmael. This was the first born son of Abraham and he and his descendants should have been the rightful heirs of the land of Canaan. This did not happen because the descendants of Isaac as the son of Sarah and Jehovah were more rightfully the heir apparent.

God visited Sarah and she produced a son, Isaac for Abraham. This is an occurrence which appears to have been repeated many times in Jewish history. The last recoded incident was the visit of an angel who is believed to have mated with Mary and produced Jesus, the Christ child.

On what are recorded in scripture as the command of God, Abraham is to have taken Isaac to a certain mountain where he was to offer him up to God as a living sacrifice. Abraham is said to have complied with this command. Only after God was satisfied that Abraham was really going to kill Isaac in order to please him did another sacrificial offering present itself to Abraham?

This god, who was willing to have his own son sacrificed to appease his ego, is the same god who completed destroyed Sodom and Gomorrah because they Gomorrah worshipped other gods and were deemed wicked and beyond redemption.

While the inhabitants of Sodom and Gomorrah were said to be sexually decadent, it was never recorded that they were as brutal, barbaric and inhuman bloody as the Israelites were later to become under the rule of Jehovah.

The blood sacrifices demanded by Jehovah began with the contract between He and Abraham found in:

Genesis 15:9-10, 15:18: *"And he said unto him, Take me a heifer of three years old, and a she-goat of three years old, and a ram of three years old, and a turtle-dove, and a young pigeon 10. And he took unto him all these, and divided them in the midst, and laid each piece one against another: but the birds divided he not.18. In that same day the Lord made a covenant with Abram, saying, unto thy seed have I given this land, from the river of Egypt unto the great river, the river Euphrates?"*

That contract was later amplified by the mutilation and blood ritual of circumcision upon every Israelite male. It seems that the ritual was abandoned while the Hebrews wandered through the wilderness. Circumcision of all Israelite males was revised just prior to entering Canaan.

Joshua 5:2-3. *At that time the Lord said unto Joshua, Make the sharp knives, and circumcise again the children of Israel the second time And Joshua made him sharp knives, and circumcised the children of Israel at the hill of the foreskins.*

Before the Israelites went into battle they were command by God that they killed every living thing animal and human on their way to glory. Later they had compassion for the animals and saved them for the wealth they represented. Only the people were destroyed. As the army matured Jehovah became less vindictive and only the men and women who had known man were slaughtered. The innocent girls and young boys were captured and were either kept as slaves or sold into slavery. The animals, the wealth of the cities and that brought in by the slave trade were added to the coffers and treasure chests of God, the priest, the tribe of Levi and the congregation.

As a result of their conquests the Israelite people became a very rich and powerful nation. The inhabitants of the land they conquered were either slaughter or made into bond-servants to serve the Israelite congregation. A relationship which I believe many of the Jewish people still believe exists today between themselves and the other races which occupy what believe to be their land.

The battle of Jericho is an excellent example of the mentality of the Israelites in their war of conquest, under on and by the laws and commands of Jehovah. Because the people of Jericho refused to surrender to the God Jehovah and the invading army of Joshua, when the walls of Jericho crumbled, Joshua and his army slaughtered every single living thing in the city except for one harlot, a woman by the name Rahab. By the order of God, all was destroyed. No man was to keep even a souvenir. All the silver, gold, and vessels of brass and iron had to be turned into the priest for consecration and the treasury of the Lord. In return for these treasures the Israelites burned the city and killed every living thing within its walls including the oxen, sheep and ass.

Joshua 6:24: *"And the burnt the city with fire, and all that was therein: only the silver, and gold, and the vessels of brass and of iron, they put into the treasury of the house of the Lord."*

One of the men, a man named Achan of the tribe of Jude, took and kept an exceptionally beautiful garment, some gold and a few pieces of silver. Because of this it was said that the anger of the Lord was kindled against the children of Israel.

This trespass by one man was responsible for the entire congregation to be held responsible for his actions.

How was this determined?

Joshua led a battle against an inferior force and was defeated. As a result of that defeat he prayed to God and was told that someone, in one of the families, had kept an accursed thing from the previous battle, one which they had won.

Only by finding and killing the perpetrator, and removing the accursed thing from the presence of the congregation, could the congregation regain their status and again win battles with the help of their Lord. Joshua 7:2-26.

Achan was accused of theft. He admitted taking and keeping a Babylonish garment, two hundred shekels of silver, and a fifty shekels weight of gold. (Joshua 7:19-21.) For his transgression, the entire congregation took Achan, his sons, daughters, oxen, asses, sheep, his tent, the souvenirs and all that he had into the valley of Achor. There the congregation stoned him, his family and all of the live stock which belonged to him. Not satisfied with just stoning Achor and his family to death, the congregation set them on fire and burned to death those who had only been wounded. This actioned ensured that no one would be left alive and every bit of material wealth would be destroyed.

This was the justice of the Israelite god, death to the innocent as well as the guilty.

After the death of Achor the Israelites attacked the people of Ai a second time. This time they were successful. The city was burned and every inhabitant, twelve thousand men, women and children were slaughtered. The cattle and spoils of the city the Israelites were able to keep as a reward for their efforts. Joshua 8:27-28.

It did not take long for the word spread throughout the land that Joshua and his army, like a plague of locusts, was destroying everything and everyone in their path. Five kings, fearing that individually they would be destroyed by the Israelites, gathered their forces together to protect their land and to try and defeat the Israelites.

Joshua destroyed the five kings, all of their men and their cities. By the commandment of God, Joshua and the Israelites completely destroyed the cities of Makkedah, Libnah, Gezer, Lachish, Eglon, Hebron, Debir, and every man, women and child which dwelled within.

Joshua 10:40: *"So Joshua smote all the country of the hills, and of the south, and of the vale, and of the springs, and all their kings: he left none remaining, but utterly destroyed all that breathed, as the Lord God of Israel commanded."*

To maintain absolute control over his army and his subjects, Jehovah established his own religion. He organized a priesthood, specified rituals, demanded sacrifices and gifts. This was the beginning of the dynasty of God and the Jewish religion. The priests enforcement the laws of Jehovah, collected his revenue, and saw to it that all who failed to obey his and their commands, said to have come from God, died or were severely punished. While it was unlawful for the members of the congregation to cheat, steal or use their power unlawfully this did not seem to apply to the priests themselves. Technically the priest did not steal as much as they took what they wanted when they wanted it without permission by the power of their office through fear and intimidation.

The following biblical example of priestly conduct is highly indicative of the behaviour of our modern day mafia, and their neighbourhood protection gangs.

Eli was a judge and high priest of Israel but his sons were said to be worthless and use their position to obtain what they wanted when they wanted it. Any because the people lived in fear of God and sin, the priest were able to do as they pleased.

1 Samuel 2:12-17: *"Now the sons of Eli were sons of Belial; (meaning worthless, wickedness or lawlessness.); they knew not the Lord. 13. And the priest's custom with the people was, that, when any man offered sacrificed, the priest's servant came, while the flesh was in seething, with a flesh-hook of three teeth in his hand; And he struck it into the pan, or kettle, or caldron or pot; all that the flesh-hook brought up the priest took for himself. So they did in Shiloh unto all the Israelites that came thither. And also before they burnet the fat, the priest's servant came, and said to the man that sacrificed, Give flesh to roast for the priest; for he will not have sodden flesh of thee, but raw. And if any man said unto him, Let them not fail to burn the fat presently, and then take as much as thy soul desires; then he would answer him, Nay; but thou shall give it me now: and if not, I will take it by force. Wherefore the sin of the young men was very great before the Lord: for men abhorred the offering of the Lord."*

Was there really any difference between the acts of the priest in the above passages and the actions of protection criminals today? Whether it is called an offering, a donation or extortion the result is the same. A man is made to pay some kind of extortion fee to a select group of individuals in order to exist and to do business in peace.

Today some of us might call such an organization a criminal activity, others the government while others consider religion to fall within the above guidelines. We all, in one way or another, have to pay a price to some organization in offer for us to survive in today's modern society. In biblical times there was only one organization, it was called religion. It represented both God and the state. Today religion still exacts its toll. But now we fear the tax man more than we do the retributions of a god.

The dynasty of the Jewish and Christian God is and has been since its conception, a rule of violence, bloodshed, and sufferings for all who have fallen under its yoke. This steadfast adherence to the principles laid down by Moses and God, followed by the Jewish people accomplished one thing, it moulded the people into a single minded force. This force united the people; they banded together, began to assist each other, strengthen and supported themselves, their families and their community. This one single trait has enabled them to survive intolerances, injustice, pain, torment and attempts of ethnic cleansing.

In their efforts to survive the people realized that wealth was power. The more wealth they were able to accumulate the safer they would become. As the Jewish congregation were evolving into a nation they became exceedingly wealthy from their plunder. So too did the Levi tribe of the priesthood, a priesthood which became so powerful that they have become bankers to the nations of the world.

The religion of the Jewish people is almost four thousand years ago yet in all of that time nothing has really changed except the names, faces and places.

Modern religions, while advocating the most admirable traits of man are still producing the same basic blood vendettas of their predecessors. The Jews kill Moslems, and Moslems kill the heathens who do not believe in and worship Allah. The Catholic and Protestants kill each other just for the right to walk down a certain street. Congregations spurred on by the hated beliefs of their leaders and the differences between their denominations faiths have created hatred and strife in every walk of life in almost every country in the world.

The servants and religious leaders of God regardless of the faith or denomination are nothing more than high pressure super salesmen selling a promise of a future salvation for the materialistic wealth of the present. That wealth in the form of monies, property, time and services collected by these salesmen do not go to God but into the pockets of the servants and the organizations to which they belong.

The salesmen preying on the fears of the people are selling a type of protection insurance called salvation. This mystical protection does not seem to be any more valid than the Mafia insurance protection sold to the Sicilian immigrants in this country at the turn of the century.

The Italian immigrants, as did immigrants from every country in Europe, came to this country in search of a new and better life. They settled in the neighbourhood's where their fellow countrymen resided. They could not speak the language, they were filled with a fear of the unknown, a new country, a new way of life, ethic tradition, and a need to feed and protect their families. Because they were new, unable to fully understand the laws and customs of their new land many times they were taken advantage of by viscous and unscrupulous individuals and organizations. The one thing that almost every immigrant had in common was their religious belief in God. Their religions were diversified. Some were Catholic, Jews, Lutherans, or some form of the Protestant faith.

They all shared a need for some kind of protection from the forces of evil they encountered here. The Italians and the Irish did something about their situation. They formed neighborhood protective associations. The Italian or Sicilian organization later developed into what has been called the Mafia or the Cosa Nostra.

For a while the immigrants were protected. Their neighborhood organizations were the ones on which they could rely to help protect their interests. They had some idea of what they were getting for the monies they were paying out. For the church it was and is different.

To this day no one has ever been able to validate the claims of the church that man at his death will meet God and be called accountable for his sins. As a protection against this possibility parishioners donate time and money in the belief that there will be a hereafter, an accounting and a salvation. The donations made to the church are payments, insurance protection against the afterlife. The church is selling insurance today for the promise of a life in the hereafter. No one can ever verify that the promises of church have the power or will ever be able to honour the policies they sell to their congregations by their salesmen. The promises of a heavenly kingdom and a paradise is not recorded in the Old Testament. Such a place while promised by the Christian faith is completely contradicted in Revelation. The teaching of a salvation after death as it is preached is a religious Conn created by man through fear, faith, hope, and a misinterpretation of scripture.

Nowhere in the Old Testament is there a promise of salvation. There is no guarantee of anything. What everyone appears to be basing their hopes and dreams on is a statement made by a man named Jesus who is reported to have said:

John 14:2: "*In my Father's house are many mansions: if it was not so I would have told you. I go to prepare a place for you.*"

Moses, Aaron and Job are excellent examples of what one can expect from the God of the Jews. They served him faithfully as best as man is capable of Doing. Moses served for over forty years and what did he receive as his reward for his years of loyal and faithful service? While he was still strong, he was killed by God himself and buried in an unmarked grave such to keep him from going into the land of Canaan. Couldn't he have just commanded Moses to stay behind and expect that command to be carried out?

Deuteronomy 34:5-7: "*So Moses the servant of the Lord died there in the land of Moah, according to the word of the Lord. And he buried him in a valley in the land of Moah, over against Beth-peir: but no man knoweth of his sepulchre unto this day And Moses was an hundred and twenty years old when he died: his eye was not dim, nor his natural force abated. 8. And the children of Israel wept for Moses in the plains of Moab thirty days: so the days of weeping and mourning for Moses were ended.*"

This was the reward of Moses. For the disciples of today and tomorrow, is this what one can expected from God after years of faithful and devoted service, death and an unknown, unmarked grave?

Jehovah, in his efforts to become a god, bribed the people with promises. He bargained with Pharaoh, Moses and the Hebrew people like a fishwife at an open market. If the Hebrew people agreed to follow and served him, he would be to them a god. He would protect them, give them land, wealth, power, freedom from disease and slavery. How many of these promises did he ever keep? The land they had to fight and die for. Their wealth came from the efforts of the people they conquered or enslaved. Their power over others was the fear instilled in their enemies by the ruthlessness of their army, their lack of compassion and their willingness to destroy everything and everyone in the path. In essence the Jewish people have never, except for short times in their history, been free in spirit, from diseases or slavery. If there was ever a time when the promises of their god came true it was an illusion.

Exodus 6:6-8: *"Wherefore say unto the children of Israel, I am the Lord, and I will bring you out from under the burdens of the Egyptians, and I will rid you out of their bondage, and I will redeem you with a stretched out arm, and with great judgements: 7. And I will take you to me for a people, and I will be to you a God: and ye shall know that I am the Lord your God, which brought you out from under the burdens of the Egyptians. 8. And I will bring you in unto the land, concerning that which I did swear to give it to Abraham, to Isaac, and to Jacob; and I will give it you for an heritage: I am the Lord."*

They have finally obtained a land of their own, but it is one for which they had to fight and die for. Today, as in the time of Joshua, it is one which they share with those who were and are still their enemies.

Except for very brief periods in their history, the Jewish people, whether they called themselves Hebrews, Israelites, or Jews, have never been truly free. They have always been is bondage of one kind or another, if not to a conquering people, then to their religion and their own history. As for the promise made by their God to keep them free of sickness and disease, this has never occurred.

Ex. 23:25. *And ye shall serve the Lord your God, and he shall bless thy bread, and thy water; and I will take sickness away from the midst of thee."*

Whenever the Israelites failed as a congregation, in whatever they attempted, they believed their failure was a punishment imposed upon them by an angry god. He was angry because the people failed, in some way, to abide by his wishes. Whenever they were successful, they believed it was because God was please with their behaviour and their success was the result of his blessings.

Contrary to the teaching of the church, the promised land of Canaan was not given to the Israelite people by God. He said that they could claim this land because he had promised it to Abraham. Base on the belief that he was God and that he had the right to claim and give the land to whomever he chose they took the land as their own.

They obtained the land and they occupied it for a while, but god never gave it to them. The land of Canaan was obtained by the blood of the Israelite soldiers and the death, rape and pillage of the people they conquered. The Israelites fought and died for every foot of their promised holy land. God did not give them anything except a belief in what they could do. With his permission to kill, enslave and loot, without sin, guilt, or remorse, the Israelites marched undaunted into Canaan.

The wealth and power that was to be a part of their legacy was, for the most part, whatever they were able to steal and capture from the people they conquered.

The peace that was to go with that conquest was like everything else promised by Jehovah, only temporary.

Slavery takes many forms of servitude, including the time when the scriptures say that God, himself, sold them into slavery.

Lev. 25:55: *"For unto me the children of Israel are servants, they are my servants whom I brought forth out of the land of Egypt: I am the Lord your God."*

Judges 2:14. And the anger of the Lord was hot against Israel and he delivered them into the hands of spoilers that spoiled them and he sold them into the hands of their enemies round about so that they could not any longer stand before their enemies.

It was the New Testament writers, as a result of their association with Jesus, which first proposed the hope of a heavenly kingdom, and a paradise beyond this life. Even this promise is bogged down with stipulations.

The idea that once man dies he will live again, and in a place described as a mansion, surrounded with joy, love and all that a man can desire, supports religion, and gains converts. It is the greed and desire of man to always have more than he can ever need or want which created in man a need to follow the teachings of their religious leaders in the first place.

Today, you place your bet with the religion of your choice. You hope that when you die there will be some kind of afterlife complete with bountiful rewards and eternal happiness. If there is, you are betting a very real material existence in this life against a spiritual one that cannot be verified.

Most religious believers, not knowing the origins of, nor truly understanding the words of the Bible, do not realize that, according to the Bible, if life does exist beyond the grave, it will be quite similar to the one they are now living.

The greed of Man, his terror of what he has come to believe or the fires of hell, and fearful of the unknown, has used this fear as the foundation upon he bases his relationship with God.

If one displeases God in any way they can expect to be punished. If one obeys, one expects to be rewarded or blessed with wealth, land, riches and power, both on earth and in the life to come.

The church organization, like the Mafia organization, is founded on fear, intimidation and greed. Both controlled by powerful men, who are so close in similarity and tactics that to examine one is to see the other.

The Catholic Church is an organization ruled by the Pope, Bishops and Cardinals. Other major church organizations, Protestants, Methodist and Presbyterians, are also based upon basically the same structured order of hierarchy. The names and titles are different, but the positions and responsibilities are similar.

The brotherhood or crime organizations are controlled by Godfathers, Dons and Lieutenants. If you obey the commands of the church fathers you are said to be in favour with God and his heavenly hosts. As such, you can expect his blessing to pour forth from heaven. You believe that you will experience peace, joy and fulfilment. You expect these blessings as long as you show God your love and respect. This is demonstrated by in how you live your life, related to the other members of the community and by how much money you place in the offering plate on Sunday mornings.

One considers themselves blessed by the tithes they contribute, the commandments they try to obey and the service and time donated to the church and the congregation. Failure to do any or all of the above, in the eyes of the congregation, can subject the believer to be ostracized from that congregation. To be ostracized is to no longer be considered by the congregation as worthy enough to stand in the presence or sight of God. Unless repentance for transgressions is sought and received, the believer is taught to expect to see the fires of hell and to endure the torment of the Lord Satan for the rest of eternity.

If one is a member of the criminal brotherhood, they are expected to do the same thing expected of the religious disciple. They are expected to show honour and respect to the Godfather. They are expected to pay their tithes and donate their time and talent to the furthering of the aims and goals of the organization. If one should fail, they can expect to see the fires of hells a lot sooner than they had anticipated. They suffered for their transgressions in the here and now.

Jehovah was the first, the original "Godfather". The angels were the original family lieutenants or dons, the priests were the brotherhood that carried out the wishes of the dons, and the congregations were the membership of the order.

Jehovah was the heavenly Godfather. To obey him was to be rewarded with permission to rob, kill, enslave and, as a nation, do whatever the congregation wanted once it was approved by God through his intermediary the priests. To anger or disobey him was to die, suffer plagues, defeat in battle and slavery.

It is written that Aaron and Moses, faithful and obedient servants to God in all that he asked, were destroyed by him when they were no longer of any use to him. Job was a perfect, faithful and upright man..

At the whim of a god he and his family were destroyed to settle a bet made between two egotistical individuals of power.

While Job lost his family and all of his earthly possessions taken away and made to suffer physical, emotional, mental and emotional he continued to keep his faith and belief in his god. While his earthly wealth he had no one to leave it to but the church and priests of god. They won and he lost.

This holy loving and benevolent Godfather gloried in blood. He required blood sacrifices for everything. They were required for giving thanks for blessings received, to atone for failures, and to make amends for mistakes made. What is not often realized is that all of these blood sacrifices were in one way or another, meat for the table of the priests who served this bloody god.

The earthly Godfather also commands and to him is paid tribute. To obey him is likewise to be given permission to rob, kill, buy and sell slaves (prostitutes), and take whatever a man is capable of getting and enjoying in this life.

To obey and to serve God means to obey and serve the church. To be under his protection is to have his permission to obtained riches, land, and to enjoy to the fullest, the pleasures of life regardless of how they are obtained. The only stipulation is the same laws imposed on the Jewish people by the laws of Jehovah, a tithe of ten (10%), a percentage of everything gained or obtained is to be given as thanks and tribute to the Godfathers for their benevolent protection.

To fail or to disobey their commands or to contribute to the coffers of the organizations, what the organization consider to be a fair share of all that one possesses is to suffer physical torment. This could be lost or broken limbs, beatings, family losses, poverty, and even death.

Sacrifices are made to the godfather with one's blood, the blood of one's family, or the blood of one's victims.

Both the priests and the brotherhood demand tithes of gold and silver, donations of money, time, talent, and even one's life if it is considered to be in the best interest of the organizations.

There are differences between the organizations of the heavenly and earthly godfathers. One caters to a man's soul, his emotional and spiritual being while the other to his conscious and physical needs. One is called good and the other evil. Which is which, depends upon an individual's point of view.

Jehovah Biblical Godfather	Human Godfather
Heavenly/Spiritual (Biblical References Only)	**Earthly/Physical** (Editorial References Only)
A. Power of Life and Death	
Supreme Law Demands Absolute Obedience	Supreme Law Demands Absolute Obedience
Assisted by Beings Called Angels	Assisted by Family Called Dons
Orders Issued by Priests, Rabbis, Ministers	Orders Issued by Brotherhood
Commands Enforced by Church Clergy	Commands Enforced by Family Lieutenants
B. Maintain Control by:	
Fear of Death/Punishment	Fear of Death/Punishment
Greed, Promises of Riches	Greed, Promises of Riches
Protection From Enemies	Protection from law
Blessings (permission)	Blessings (permission)
Good life	Good life
C. Power and Wealth Obtained by:	
Murder	Murder
Conquest	Conquest
Exploitation/People	Exploitation/People
Thievery	Thievery

Wealth/Power Maintained by the Following:	
Discipline Contributions	Discipline Contributions
Tax Evasion Commercial Investments	Tax Evasion Commercial Investments
New Memberships	New Memberships
New Churches/Congregations	New Businesses
Legal Manipulations Political Lobbies	Legal Manipulations Political Lobbies

Today both families, advance their wealth, power and position through legalized business ventures. Both organizations, while trying to maintain and improve their standings in the community by acceptable and legitimate business practices, still maintain firm control over their organizations by instilling and maintaining a fear of the consequences should anyone fail to abide by the rules.

A wayward disciple is quickly and severely admonished as an example to any other who might think of leaving the membership.

Wayward spiritual disciples are subjected to the fear of pain, suffering and eternal damnation. They may be forever banned from heaven and the presence of God. They may burn forever in the lake of everlasting fire.

Disobedient disciples of the Mafia brotherhood are subject to pain, loss of wealth and even death. This punishment and termination can, in some cases extend to relatives and loved ones.

Jehovah and his priest used the fear of death and punishment, along with vivid examples, to control the Israelite before the time of Jesus. That fear still exists today.

During the ministry of After Jesus his apostles used what they called the Holy Ghost or Holy Spirit to keep their congregations in line. Both congregations of disciples of those Jehovah and of Jesus were taught to fear their god by stern examples of death, poverty and torment.

In the New Testament, there is the story of Ananias and Sapphira, a husband and wife, who were converts to the teachings of Jesus. They were disciples of what was later to become the new Christian church. They were, like all of the new members, told to go and sell all that they had and to bring the proceeds to the church. Those proceeds, the apostles, as leaders of the new church, would take, control and distribute to the members of the church congregation, according to the needs of the congregation as the apostles deem necessary. We are led to believe that all of the members of this new church complied with the wishes of the apostles except Ananias and Sapphira. When they had sold a certain possession, they kept back a portion of that sale for themselves. The rest, they laid at the feet of the apostles. For failing to give all that they had obtained for the sale of that possession they fell down dead, killed by the Holy Ghost. (Acts 5:1-10.)

It was at this moment that the fear of death entered into the tabernacle of the new Christian Church.

Acts 5:11: *"And great fear came upon all the church and upon as many as heard these things."*

There are many instances in the old testaments where the children of Israel are admonished by their God. He gave them very vivid examples to fear his wrath and to abide by his laws and commandments. One example is found in Numbers 11:1.

Numbers 11:1. *"And when the people complained it displeased the Lord: and when the Lord heard it his anger was kindled; and the fire of the Lord burnt among the congregation and consumed them that were even in the uttermost parts of the camp."*

Just as the death of Ananias and Sapphira had its effect on the congregation of new Christian converts so too did the death of a warrior and his family effect the congregation of the Old Testament Israelites.

Joshua chapter 7 is the story of a warrior, who, during one of the battles against the enemies of God, failed to turn into the priest all of the loot he had found during a battle. This angered God and as a result of this transgression, the warrior, his family, all of their livestock and material possessions were destroyed on the orders of God.

The family and lived stock were stoned to death and everything material possession the family had owned was thrown over the dead bodies and all was burnt to ashes. This was an example of the love, benevolence and forgiveness of the Holy God of the Israelite nation.

After reading the modern day stories of the Mafia organizations, one might ask them self if there really is any differences between the acts of the heavenly Godfather and those of the earthly one? If there is I fail to see it.

Today, both families have included legitimate interests in the accumulation and control of their wealth. Their wealth and influence touch every aspect of our lives and our business communities.

I have read somewhere that one of the most profitable enterprises for one branch of the Baptist denomination is their stock shares in the liqueur industry. The Catholic Church is said to own, among other things, the Bank of America in California.

For the Jewish nation they are in essence following the dictates of their God, and in accordance with biblical scripture they have become bankers to the world.

For the Jewish nation, control of the people began with God and Moses. Through death, plagues, intimidation and superstition, their acts instilled fear in the Egyptians and in the Hebrew people. This fear was amplified and carried on by the priest's of God long after the Exodus was completed. That fear still exists today.

God commanded on the penalty of death that the people obey his commands as they were given to them by his priests and servants. The people were to give to them according to the demands set by God and Moses. It was to be a portion of all they possessed. This custom was amplified by Peter, the Apostle, in the New Testament.

For the New Testament disciples there was an additional sacrificial obligation. They were required to present a portion of all of their profits to the apostles to be distributed among the members of the new Christian congregation not according to the labours of the recipient, but according to the decisions determined by the apostles to be in the best interest of the New Church.

It is what I call the Cain and Abel syndrome. Those who work the hardest and accumulate the most, must feed and care for those who do not. In other words take fro the rich and give to the poor.

Cain laboured diligently in his field while Abel lay around watching his sheep graze. Cain was admonished for his offerings of grain and vegetables said to be unacceptable to the Lord God while Abel was praised for offerings his fattest lamb made so on the grain in the field of Cain.

In the church organizations around the world those who work the hardest and produce the most are expected to feed, clothe, care for and share the results of their of their labours with those who do not.

Since only priests and apostles are said to be able to talk with God, there is no way that the orders of the priests or apostles can be disputed by the congregations. To question their acts or decisions is to risk reprisals by God himself. During the time of Moses, that meant death. An excellent example of this can be found in Numbers 16:1-40.

Down through the ages in communities outside of the Jewish people those individuals who appeared to be the least productive person within a congregation was many times given the task of taking care of the religious obligations of the local congregation. For organized religions these obligations were handled by individuals trained in the rituals and tradition of the local fait. These were the priest, rabbi or minister. They do the least amount of physical labour and yet they reap the greatest benefits. It has always been so since God and Moses first established the priesthood, an organization dedicated to enforcing the laws of God, obtaining, protecting and controlling the wealth given to him by the people.

It is a wealth that God does not use himself, but is used by the clergy to meet whatever needs they feel are or would be in accordance with the wishes of God. Without controls, this wealth becomes the means by which the priests continue to control and manipulate the people.

In the Old Testament, when God walked among the Israelite nation, any disobedience to his wishes, which were the wishes of Moses and the priests, was quickly used as an opportunity to again demonstrate the power and might of God and his priesthood.

Take for example the man who picked up sticks on the Sabbath. By the order of God he was stoned to death by the entire congregation.

The enforcers of his punishment were Aaron and the tribe of Levi. They were the descendants of Levi, one of the sons of Jacob, who is said of him and his brother Simeon that *"instruments of cruelty are in their habitation."* Gen. 49:5.

This one tribe formed a dynasty which began to absorb the wealth of nations by claiming to serve a God who was, in reality, an alien life form. Today the clergy of this assumed God continues to feast on the blood, sweat, toil and tears of their congregations.

Congregation and individuals still give the priests, and clergy offerings and wealth according to the decree of God given to them by those same priests and clergy.

In the beginning those who disobeyed were put to death, suffered disease or were reduced to poverty. Job, who was described by God as a perfect and upright man, suffered at the whim of God. He lost his family, all his material possessions, and suffered great physical torment. Even though he had obeyed God in all things, God allowed Satan the right to do everything he desired to Job except kill him.

The congregation of the Israelites were told by Moses and the priests that those who died or suffered were being punished by God because they had disobeyed his commands. The people listened, feared and obeyed.

They lived in the time of the Exodus. They saw the power of God, demonstrated many times through Moses. They saw the pain, suffering and death of the Egyptians, suffered in the wilderness torment which resulted from what was believed to be a failure to obey the decrees of God. In the shadow of that fear the people obeyed the dictates of Moses and the priests. Today they still do.

They gave their offerings to God and the priests.

Those offerings included but were not limited to: food, wealth, slaves, women, land, and a percentage of everything they owned or controlled. These things were given to the priests for the use and benefit of God.

It is strange that a god who is believed to be able to create all things and has everything including the whole universe, within his control, would demand, from those who had so little, blood sacrifices, gold, silver, fine raiment, fine wine, special foods and fragrances. When he did not receive these things, the people suffered.

In the Jewish communities the fear of God has been passed down from generation to generation. The recorded memories of defeats, slavery and trials under the yokes of their oppressors are ever kept alive in the minds of the people. These memories are reinforced time after time by repetitious reminders of their bondage condition by their religious leaders and prophets.

When the Hebrews people began to follow God and Moses, they replace one type of bondage for another. From Egyptian bondage, they went into religious slavery.

When Jehovah took command of the Hebrew people, which he did by promises and bribery, he placed them back into the original condition of mankind at the time of Adam and Eve. They were once again slaves and servants, waiting and serving a god.

The Ten Commandments and the rest of modern Jewish religious edits were given to the Hebrew people alone. These laws and commandments were never given to the Gentiles; therefore they really do not apply to those outside of the Jewish faith. To disobey any of the laws and commandments of the Old Testament can only be considered a sin by the Jewish people and those who faithfully follow that religion.

Sin is by definition a transgression of a religious edict, which is in effect a law or commandment of a particular god. Sin is not necessarily evil. It is but an act contrary to what the gods considered to be in their best interest. An act committed outside of religious edicts may be considered evil by civil and moral law but because it is evil does not mean that the act is necessarily a sin.

Evil existed before sin and is a product of the gods. Evil is a concept. It is any act which is contrary to the good or best interest of God and man. Sin on the other hand is a transgression, a violation or disobedience to one of the laws of a god or his church.

The idea that certain acts are both sin and evil comes to us as Gentile from the writings and teaching of Jesus and his apostles. When one accepts these doctrines they also accept the responsibilities found in the laws, commandments and guidance of the Old Testament.

The Gentiles, by accepting the Hebrew faith or the Christian doctrine, derived from that faith, have once again placed themselves right back where they were before the time of the flood, slaves and servants to an alien being, the Living Creature, our creator and our ancestor.

The concepts of the Bible and the Jewish religion were given to the people as a guide by whom the Jewish people could live, work and survive in harmony with each other. Those laws were harsh and the penalties severe. But combined with their faith in God and his power the Hebrews became a nation. As the degree of their faith increased so too did their servitude. Following the edits of the Bible and a blind faith in God, mankind has of its own volition, justified a return to a total submission to a god. He has become a slave again.

Jehovah and Satan are raising an army which, according to Revelation, will be used to fight the last battle, the Battle of Armageddon.

Religious leaders in the past have gone to great lengths to ensure that their followers believe that this last great battle will be between the Lord God and Satan, the Lord of good and the epitome of evil.

This is far from the truth. This is not what Revelation has to say. Out of fear and ignorance religious leaders have only told their congregations a half truth, a half truth based upon their understanding and interpretation of Revelation. There will be a great battle and it will be between the gods, but it will have nothing to do with the human concepts of good and evil. It will be for power and control.

This battle will not be fought between the forces of good and evil as supposed by religion but between the forces of Jehovah and Satan against the forces of the Most High God, our creator. This battle will take place when the Lord God returns to this planet and Jehovah and Satan will be called upon to account for their stewardship. It is at that time that Jehovah and Satan will rebel and the War of Armageddon will begin.

The Lord God our creator is the force that will be subdued by the force of Jehovah and Satan and put into the bottomless pit for a thousand years. He is the one that, when released, will raise an army *"the number of whom is as the sand of the sea."* (Rev. 20:8).

This army, the one that will be gathered by the so called beast, will be an army of those individuals who have lived through the thousand years of peace predicted by the writer of Revelation. If mankind will have a thousand years of peace why would there be those "as the sands of the sea", who would be willing to fight and overthrow this regime which will have created a paradise? Could it be that the thousand years of peace, under the rule of the God Jehovah and his son Jesus, will not be all that it is supposed to be?

The Most High God, the Lord God, our creator, was not the first Godfather. He laid down the laws which were to be obeyed, not only by Man, but also by his own crew. They were the laws and customs which he brought with him from his home world. As the owner of first man, he expected them to obey his every wish. When they disobeyed, they were punished. The punishment of Adam, Eve and Cain are examples of his rule and control.

Their punishment was not severe because first of all because they were a very valuable piece of property. Second, they were innocent individuals who did not realize the consequences of disobedience. For Cain, the killing and death of Abel was an accident. It was not done out of malice. Cain had never seen a dead human and had no concept of death.

Adam and Eve were told not to touch or to eat the fruit of a certain tree. They must have been curious as to why they were forbidden to touch or eat this particular fruit when they had been given permission eat everything else in the garden including the fruit of the tree of life.

They were good and faithful servants taught to listen and to obey the gods. They would not of their own accord touch this tree or ate its fruit if they had not been given permission by another one of the gods. He told them it was alright and encouraged Eve to sample its fruit.

Who was the God and why did he entice Eve to disobey?

The Torah and the Christian Bible say that the god who enticed Eve to disobey the Lord God was called the Serpent or Satan. His reasoning had something to do with the overthrown of the Lord God.

Hebrew Myths: The Book of Genesis, by Robert Graves and Raphael Patai, published by Greenwich House in 1983 gives us a very different view of the relationship which existed between Eve and the Serpent.

It is their contention that it was Samael, disguised as the Serpent who persuaded Eve to touch and eat of the forbidden tree. He had sexual relations with her and the result of that relationship was Cain. Cain would then be the first of the might men of old, half man and half god.

Who was Samael that Eve should obey him?

The following is quoted from Hebrew Myths: The Book of Genesis, pp 85 paragraph 2. According to some accounts, Samael never lay with Eve before Adam had done so. God at first intended Samael to rule the world, but the sight of Adam and Eve coupling, naked and unashamed, made him jealous. He swore: I will destroy Adam, marry Eve, and truly rule.' Having waited until Adam had lain with Eve and fallen asleep, he took Adam's place. Eve yielded to him, and conceived Cain.

When Eve looked at the angelically face of Cain she knew that Adam was not his father and in her innocence, exclaimed: 'I have gotten a man-child from Yahweh.

I believe that what is recorded in Genesis 3:1-13 is a logical description of serpent enticing Eve to sample the fruit from the tree of the knowledge of good and evil. If she does she will become high loose her inhibitions and allow Samael to mate with her.

The forbidden tree was some kind of narcotic plant similar to the coco found in Central and South America. The gods used the effects of this tree to help them endure their long journeys through space.

When Eve sampled the fruit or chewed the leaves she experienced a euphoric reaction which assisted Samael in his seduction. She got high. She was happy she had Adam join her. They lost their innocence because now that their mind had expanded from the effects of the drug and they became aware of themselves. In their euphoric condition they tried to play gods by using fig leaves not to cover their nakedness but to imitate the gods who wore clothes. When they began to come down from heir high and realized what they had they tried to hide from the Lord when he took his evening stroll through the garden.

The Lord God was angry with them for this disobedience. But it appears that he was much more afraid of what the consequences of this act might be. To prevent another occurrence and further disobedience, the Lord God refused Adam and Eve further access to the garden and to the tree. Samael he punished another way.

What was so important about the tree of the knowledge of good and evil that once touched and eaten by man it put fear into the heart and mind of God?

Because Adam and Eve disobeyed the command of the Lord God not to touch the tree they were kicked out and forbidden from ever coming into the garden gain. A protection barrior was placed around the garden and Cerubim were assigned to protect the gate. Were Adam and Eve denied access to the garden because they disobeyed a command of God or was it to ensure that neither they or any other slave would have access to the tree?

It is logical to assume that both of the above reasons are justification for the action of God but it is one which will be discussed when I talk about Adam, Eve and the Garden of Eden.

In the beginning the relationship that existed between God and Man was benevolent. Men and women were valuable pieces of property and as such were treated, card for and protected. This slave relationship was not unlike the one that existed in the Old South prior to the war between the North and the South and that which existed for a few thousand years between the masters and slaves of conquered nations.

While the Lords and Masters of kingdoms and territories their servants while referred to as serfs and peasants they were in reality salves.

It was also similar to the relationship which existed between the people of a certain Sicilian community and the Mafia organization when it was first formed in the early 19th century.

The Mafia was originally a group of individuals, who gathered together to protect their families and local community from unjust laws and unwanted influences of those in power. As their power and influence as an organization grew, corruption replace honesty and integrity. It was then that the corruption and greed became a part of their daily operation. In charge of each organizational unit or area was a Godfather. He was considered to be the ultimate authority in all things. His word was absolute, his wishes commandments.

The first Godfather was not that of religion or the church but of the Jewish and Christian faiths. It was Jehovah, the God of the Israelites and Moses was the instrument by which he was able to place the most binding conditions upon the people who became his servants and who made him into a God. His word was absolute, his desires, according to the priests were his wishes, laws and commandments. Just as the Pope, Bishops, Cardinals, and priests are the messengers of God, so are the Dons, Lieutenants and disciples of the Mafia the messengers of the Godfather.

The Jewish faith, created and established by Jehovah and Moses, laid down the laws, the conditions and the commandments under which the Israelites, the servants to God, were to exist. These laws and commandments were not called the laws of god but of Moses. That title still exists today. To disobey any of the laws of Moses was to be punished not by Moses, but by the hand of God. Punishment for any disobedience could be anything from sickness, plagues, poverty and slavery to death.

Jehovah established his authority as the Godfather of the Jewish nation by demonstrating, his power, ability, and willingness to kill his servants individually or in wholesale numbers for any minor infraction of his commandments.

The type of disobedience had nothing to do with the severity of punishment melted out for an offense. The paranoia of Jehovah ranged from the calm deliberate murder of an individual, to the explosive, eruptive fits of anger which killed thousands.

He killed Nadab and Abihu, two of his priests, by devouring them with fire because they offended his senses. They offered a strange fire before him. Genesis 10:9 indicates that they were killed because they were drunk. Evidently they dared to drink the wine that was meant to be served to him alone.

Er, the firstborn of Judah was killed simply because he was wicked in the sight of Jehovah. And Onan, his brother, God killed because Onan refused to impregnate the wife of Er, the man whom God had killed. (Genesis 38:7-10.)

Exodus 22:24. *"And my wrath shall wax hot, and I will kill you with the sword, and your wives shall be widows, and your children fatherless."*

Deuteronomy 32:39-42: *"See now that I, even I, am he, and there is no god with me: I kill, and I make alive; I wound and I heal: neither is there any that can deliver out of my hand. For I lift up my hand to heaven, and say, I live forever. If I whet my glittering sword, and mine hand take hold on judgement; I will render vengeance to mine enemies, and will reward them that hate me. I will make mine arrows drunk with blood, and my sword shall devour flesh; and that with the blood of the slain and of the captives from the beginning of revenge upon the enemy."*

When the Israelites accepted Jehovah as their leader and god, they freely entered into a contract in which they agreed to his conditions. This they did by following Moses into the wilderness. It was the price they agreed to pay in return for (1) freedom from Egyptian bondage and (2) the promises of protection, land and wealth.

Since that time, every catastrophe endured by the Israelite, or Jewish nation has been blamed in some degree upon their lack of obedience to God's commandments or by a lapse in the degree of their faith in his power and protection.

Over the centuries the Jewish people have bemoan their conditions. I was once told by a Jewish neighbour, when we were discussing religion, that many times the Jewish people have wished that their God did not love them so much. If he did not perhaps they would not have suffered as they have down through the ages.

The Israelites were slaves in Egypt. This was a condition they placed upon themselves and had nothing to do with a god of any kind but a need to survive as a people.

In olden times the wealth of a land was owned and controlled by its ruler. For the Hebrews living in Egypt, the land belonged to Pharaoh. In times of drought and famine the people were allowed to purchase food and water from Pharaoh. If the purchaser had no money they were allowed to place themselves into servitude for that food and water. A person accepted into bondage until payment could be made could be the head of the household or one of the family members. Whenever the debt was paid in full the bondage was lifted. This bondage was for all practical purposes, a temporary condition. When retribution was made to Pharaoh the bondage was lifted and the indebted individual or family was free of their debt.

For the Hebrews their condition of bondage evidently remained in effect over such a long period of time that their debt was considered unplayable. Their condition of servitude changed from bondservants to that of a slave with no hope of a reprieve. This condition became their way of life.

When Jehovah decided that he wanted to become a god, with priests, temples, servants and sacrifices, he elected the Hebrews as the people most likely to accept him as their god and leader. They were a perfect choice.

By making the people his servants he would be fulfilling the obligation placed upon him by the Lord God in Deuteronomy 32:8-9)

The knowledge of his existence was a part of the Hebrew oral tradition. It had been handed down to them from the time of Abraham. They were aware of this god through the stories told to them by their ancestor Jacob. During their long stay in Egypt, and in order to survive, they had been conditioned to serve and obey many gods. One more god more or less meant nothing to them. They had nothing and therefore had nothing to lose by following "I AM THAT I AM," the god of Moses.

The Hebrew would be the excellent servants. All Jehovah had to do was get them out of Egypt and under his control. Since he had no land or kingdom to take them to, temple, religion or priesthood for them to follow, he really had nothing with which he could bargain, except a promise to free the people of their bondage and to lead them to Canaan a land flowing with milk and honey. This was the same land that had been so barren that it forth Jacob and his sons to flee to Egypt four hundred years before.

If and when Jehovah was able to free the people he had to lead them somewhere and the only place where there were no gods, temples, priests and obstacles to his plan was the Sinai Desert. There he would be able to gain control of the people, establish his priesthood, sacrificial rituals, laws and commandments.

Once he was sure that he was in absolute control over the Hebrews, and was assured of their ability to survive and fight at his command then he would lead them to the promised land of Canaan. That was to be their land, but only as long they were willing to fight for it. Able to defend it and able to defeat and destroy the nations which had occupied the territory for over four hundred years.

The Hebrew was slaves. Moses brought them out of Egypt. Their ancestors had been slaves to the Lord God before the flood, and Jehovah demanded that the Hebrew, once in his service, go back into that condition and remain so in his service.

During the journey from Egypt to Canaan the Hebrews learned, the hard way, what could be expected from their new God? If they dared question or balk at his commands they suffered and died by both the hand of God and Moses. Isaiah 6:1-11 explains the condition of the Israelites beautifully. *In the year that King Uzziah died I saw also the Lord sitting upon a throne, high and lifted up, and his train filled the temple Above it stood the Seraphim: each one had six wings; with twain he covered his face, and with twain he covered his feet, and with twain he did fly. And one cried unto another, and said, Holy, Holy, Holy, is the Lord of Hosts: The whole earth is full of his glory. And the posts of the door moved at the voice of him that cried, and the house was filled with smoke. Then said I, woe is me: for I am undone: because I am a man of unclean lips, and I dwell in the midst of a people of unclean lips; for mine eyes have seen the king, the Lord of Hosts. Then flew one of the Seraphim unto me, having a live coal in his hand, which he had taken with the tongs from off the alter: 7.And he laid it upon my mouth, and said, Lo, this hath touched thy lips; and thine iniquity is taken away, and thy sin purged. Also I heard the voice of the Lord, saying, whom shall I send, and who will go for us? Then said I, Here am I, send me. And he said, go, and tell this people, hear ye indeed, but understand not, and see ye indeed but perceive not. Make the heart of this people fat, and make their ears heavy, and shut their eyes; lest they see with their eyes, and hear with their ears, and understand with their heart, and convert, and be healed. Then said I, Lord, how long? And he answered, until the cities be wasted without inhabitant, and the houses without man, and the land be utterly desolate.*

This were the words of the God of the Hebrews, a prediction of the end time recorded in the Book of Revelation, This is the time when the earth and all that is within shall be destroyed, Until then make the people to understand that they are to hear my voice and obey my commands. They are never to question me. They may hear of my acts of cruelty, my retribution and the results of my wrath, but they are not to believe. They are to shut their eyes at my atrocities. They are to know who and what I am. I am God. I can do no wrong and I answer to no one. As my disciples you must make sure that the people do not see, do not hear and do not understand with their hearts what I say and do and turn away from me and be healed. For how long Lord and he said for as long as it takes for me to gain complete power and control over them.

Were my lips touched by the hot coals of God? Have all of my sins been forgiven? Probably not because I am in direct disobedience to those commands. I have an obligation that I believe came from a higher power that in all honesty do not know who or what, only that it exists. That obligation is to reveal to man his true beginning, where he came from and where he is going if he does not annihilate himself first.

The following is the reality of Jehovah, the first Godfather. This is about his priesthood, and the congregation of disciples, who, by using his laws and his doctrines, seek to enslave and control the common man.

The control of the Hebrews started with the following command given to Moses on the mountain:

Exodus 3:11-12: *"And Moses said unto God, Who am I, that I should go forth unto Pharaoh, and that I should bring forth the children of Israel out of Egypt? 12. And he said. Certainly I will be with thee that have sent thee. When thou hast brought forth the people out of Egypt, ye shall serve God upon this mountain."*

Exodus 5:3: *"And they said The God of the Hebrews hath met with us: let us go, we pray thee, three days journey into the desert, and sacrifice unto the Lord our God; lest he fall upon us with pestilence, or with the sword."*

Jehovah was not interested in freeing the Hebrew slaves from the yoke of Pharaoh. He was only interested in obtaining slaves to worship, sacrifices, offer up gifts to him. .

He also needed an army to defeat his enemies and in order to do this he had to get the Hebrews, his future subjects, out of Egypt and away from the direct influence of Pharaoh and the Egyptian people.

He had to take the Hebrews into the desert In order to get them away from the other gods and form Pharaoh. Otherwise it would not have been necessary for the people to journey into the desert just to worship and offer up sacrifices. They could just as easily have done that from their homes in Egypt.

Why was Moses instructed to take them to a particular mountain for this worship?

In recent years an abandon temple has been located on what was believed to have been the mountain referred to by Jehovah. This temple appears to have belonged to the calf cult of Egypt. Perhaps that is the reason that the Hebrews demanded and accepted the golden calf as their god when they had reached that mountain.

Was the mountain the abode of God? Is God not everywhere, at all times and in all places, as the Christians believe? Why worship upon that particular mountain unless a temple was there?

If the Biblical God Jehovah was the creator of Man and is the God of the universe, why does the following scripture contradict that belief?

Exodus 4:22-23: *"And thou shall say unto Pharaoh, thus said the Lord, Israel is my son, even my first born. And I say unto thee, Let my son go, that he serve me: and if thou refuse to let him go, behold, I will slay thy son, even thy firstborn."*

Was Jacob or Israel the firstborn son of Jehovah? If so then Jehovah is starting his own dynasty, which means that he was not the original creator of Adam and Eve. Were he that god then Adam by blood or Cain by natural birth would have been the firstborn son.

Once the Hebrews departed Egypt and began to follow Jehovah their name was changed. They began to call themselves the Israelites. This term means they strive with God and survive. This word was first used in the Bible in reference to Jacob and his wrestling match with Jehovah. But it could easily mean all of the individuals from the time of Adam to the Exodus who worked with God. They would have been the first born of God, not Jacob and the Hebrew nation.

Why were Jacob and his descendants selected by Jehovah as his first born? Could it have been that Jacob was a blood relative to Jehovah and the fight between him and Jacob merely a test of strength between Jacob and himself? Or is it possible that Jacob was much more to Jehovah?

Why did Jacob go from the fair haired boy of God to the object of his unforgiving wrath?

According to scripture, Jacob and his descendants, the Jewish Nation, are not the objects of God's love but rather the subjects of his wrath. The following passages are an explanation as to how this all came about.

When Jacob was found wandering in the desert, Jehovah took him in. Jacob became the apple of his eye and began living with his grandfather and his family. It was the best of times until Jacob became fat, lazy and corrupt. He began to spurn the affections of his grandfather and joined the family, his aunts, uncles and their friends in making fun of Jehovah, a god without power, temples and servants. In time the anger of Jehovah became so great that he kicked Jacob out of the house and family.

Jacob and his descendants became cursed for that action. For every curse placed upon Jacob, the Hebrew people suffered. They are still suffering today.

Deuteronomy 32:6-9: *"Do ye thus requite the Lord? O foolish people and unwise? Is not he thy father that hath bought thee? Hath he not made thee, and established thee? Remember the days of old, consider the years of many generations: ask thy father, and he will show thee; thy elders, and they will tell thee. When the most High divided to the nations their inheritance, when he separated the sons of Adam, he set the bounds of the people according to the number of the children of Israel."*

(The word Israel means "He strives with God and Prevails). With this definition, the word could also mean all of the people that strived with the Most High God at the beginning of man who would be the sons of Adam. The number of the children of Israel, those that strived with the Most High God was divided among his staff those that he intended to leave behind when he departed the earth. They were the crewmen who had taken human wives and had families. They were the supervisors of the labour force before the flood and became the minor or other gods after the flood.

When the Highest God, the creator of Man, divided his earthly property between the members of the staff he was going to leave behind, he specifically gave Jacob and his descendants to Jehovah because was his grandson. Jehovah took Jacob under his wing. They travelled and lived together for some period of time, during which time Jacob became fat and lazy and began to side with the sons and daughters of Jehovah in order to tease and provoke him. They did this by making a game of worshipping devils, and strange gods, and by creating new ones.

It is, I believe, possible that the reason Jacob was given to Jehovah as an inheritance in addition to his duties as the earthly administrator was a punishment placed upon him by the Lord God for his indiscretions, for co-habitation with earth women.

Genesis 21:1 *"And the Lord visited Sarah as he had said, and the Lord did unto Sarah as he had spoken."*

Sarah conceived and had a son. That son was Isaac who was not the son of Sarah and Abraham but Sarah and Jehovah. As such Jacob and Esau were his grandsons and the descendents of both his blood and kin. Jacob became the chosen one because when he was given to Jehovah he became property thereby giving Jehovah added power and authority as the new Lord God on earth. The Jewish Nation as the descendents of Jacob are rightly called the children of God. So too are the descendents of Esau but because he his status was never change by God he remained a servant.

Today both nations as the descendents of God worship the same God of Abraham only by different names and ideology.

It is an explanation which justifies the story that Abraham was willing to offer up Isaac as a sacrifice to his God and this is what God wanted who was he to object? It should also be remembered that Sarah was ninety years old and had been unable to conceive a child with Abraham. We know that this was not the fault of Abraham because he fathered Ishmael. So the fault had to be with Sarah. Since Abraham could not give her a child then it had to be Jehovah who was the father of Isaac. Jacob and Esau as the sons of Isaac made them the grandsons of Jehovah. As such they could not inherit the land of Canaan because they did not come from the loins of Abraham. This is the reason that that Jehovah changed his covenant with Abraham and gave the land to his son Isaac.

When Jacob was casted aside it was with a curse that allowed the children of Jacob to become slaves in Egypt, burned with hunger in the desert, devoured with burning heat, eaten by wild beast and poisoned by the serpents of the dust.

The Hebrews died by the sword, cut down not only by their enemies but from within their own camp. They suffered the heat of the desert thirst, hunger, plagues, the poison of serpents and during the last decades scattered throughout the world.

Even the threat of making the remembrance of them to cease from among men has been attempted by various nations at various times. The latest attempt was the gas chambers at Auschwitz.

Jehovah, like the Godfathers of today, maintained his control through fear. He gave Moses a command. Moses questioned that command and Jehovah tried to kill him for his insolence.

Exodus 4:24: *"And it came to pass by the way in the inn, that the Lord met him, and sought to kill him."*

The Jehovah could not defeat Moses and he could not defeat Jacob. How can any being that cannot defeat a mortal be an all-powerful immortal?

Once Jehovah obtained control of the Israelites, he organized the people according to the sons of Jacob. Each family was to have a certain obligation towards the whole, and were to reinforce each other. That concept is still being followed in Israel today. It is one of the main reasons that Israel has remained so strong throughout all of the years of their adversity.

The Israelites suffered under the hard cruel yoke of Jehovah. They only enjoyed a reward for their labour after they had conquered, destroyed, enslaved the people of Canaan and destroyed to some extent the gods and the people who worshipped the gods which had ridiculed Jehovah.

Jehovah began his organization by selecting the strongest family of the Hebrews, the tribe of Levi, as his immediate guardians. He made them into his priests. They were the only ones who could serve and be the closest to him. This tribe may have been selected because it was the tribe of Moses, but it is more likely that they were selected because they has no aversion to lying, cheating, stealing or murder.

Genesis 34:25-29: *"And it came to pass on the third day, when they were sore, that two of the sons of Jacob, Simeon and Levi, Dinah's brethren, took each man his sword, and came upon the city boldly, and slew all the males. And they slew Hamor and Shechem his son with the edge of the sword, and took Dinah out of Shechem's" house, and went out. The sons of Jacob came upon the slain, and spoiled the city, because they defied their sister They took their sheep, and their oxen, and their asses, and that which was in the city, and that which was in the field. And all their wealth, and all their little ones, and their wives took them captive, and spoiled even all that was in the house."*

Genesis 49:5: *"Simeon and Levi are brethren; instruments of cruelty are in their habitations."*

> Jehovah needed a strong family without scruples or morals to do his bidding. He knew that at times there would be trouble with the people. He needed a group of individuals who would not buckle under the threat of the people or to the commands which he knew he would be giving. Moses also needed such a family to assist him in bring the people out of Egypt.

Once in the desert and in the months that followed, God created an organization that would be duplicated by the modern-day brethren called the Mafia. To look at one is to look at the other.

For the disciples of both organizations, the church and the Mafia, blessings and the forgiveness of sins can be obtained by blood sacrifices, gifts of gold, silver, fine raiment, wine and special foods. Jehovah demanded one more thing not requested by the brotherhood, he demanded that all new life which opened the matrix of the womb be given to him as a sacrifice. These gifts appeased him. These gifts also gave the priests many servants, free labour, and increased their herds and flocks many fold.

While the laws of God and/or Moses were given only to the Israelites, they are nevertheless obeyed by the Gentiles of today who follow the teaching of Christianity, an offshoot of the Jewish faith.

As the religion of God, the Jewish faith, became modified and explained by, his son Jesus, the teaching of Jesus came to be called Christianity. This modified faith has spread into most of the countries of the world. The demands of God given to Moses for the rule and control of the Israelites, has been adapted by the Christians.

Christians, however, believing in the teachings of Jesus, have changed the meaning of biblical scripture to better suit their lifestyle and their purposes. They have come to believe what the preachers have told us the Bible means, rather than what it actually says.

For God and the Godfathers, the priesthood and Mafia families, it is complete control by the demonstration of discipline that guarantees a continued source of wealth and power to both families.

The church started with Moses offering hope and salvation to the slaves of Egypt. God offered protection, land wealth, power and many descendants to the people. Jesus offered salvation and a heavenly kingdom beyond the suffering of the earthly body.

The church today offers hope, peace, and a good life here on earth and a life everlasting in that heavenly kingdom of Jesus. The church survives by feeding hope to the deprived of spirit. The earthly brotherhood offers a chance to make a living, to feed the body and to enjoy many of the pleasures which exist on earth today. While the church stresses moral values determined to be in the best interest of mankind, the brotherhood believes that man is a free spirit and should control his own desires.

This is a concept also preached by the church. Man is given the choice of self determination of what is right and what is wrong. They are both saying the same thing.

As a member of a church congregation, one is expected to contribute a portion of one's income to support the priest and the church. One is to help maintain the building and property, help finance the larger organization, and follow the rules of conduct laid down by the leaders of the faith. From all reports and news stories, the Mafia brotherhood operates in much the same way. Both are very successful.

The brotherhood or Mafia is said to have started in the 1600's as a small organization combating corruption and tyranny. Its principles and ideas were brought to the United States by the immigrants from Sicily and Italy.

When the Italian immigrants entered this country they encountered many problems with the local citizens. When they tried to make a living, to support their families, many were taken unfair advantage of. To combat these injustices, the immigrants reverted to the protective principles of the old country. They began with neighbourhood protection. They selected a small group of individuals who banded together as a protective force to ensure that their families and neighbours were not abused. For this protection, usually provided only to the locality of the select group, a small fee was paid by each member of the business community. The protective group guaranteed that each member would be able to conduct business in peace. The fee was just enough to cover the expenses of the protective group. But just as with all benevolent enterprises, greed and corruption slowly became a standard rather than an exception. As the neighbourhoods grew, so too did both families, the families of God and the Godfather. Like giant spiders sitting in the middle of their webs waiting for its next victim, they spin their web throughout the land and the world. Everywhere the web touches it trapped the unlucky victims in its silky threads. Once trapped, a person could only struggle while their lives, both spiritually and physically, are drained away until only a shell remained.

The religion, like any good and thriving business depends upon expansion, new denominations, new congregations and new members to support and maintain the fundamental organization. This maintenance and support meant more wealth, power, property and prestige for the church. The brotherhood also grew. They added new territories, stores, customers, products and enterprises which catered to the physical needs of man. As the needs of man changed so too did both organizations. Each new change meant new, different and better stores, new customers and an increased in profits and power for the organization. At one time both of these organizations were run and controlled by cold, hard, ruthless uneducated individuals with a lot of street smarts and very little conscience. Today the organizations are ruled and controlled by well educated, sophisticated individuals, many times considered as the pillars of the community.

Jehovah and the Godfathers are shown by the bible and history to be greedy, egotistical and vindictive: perfect examples of all the vain traits of man. They both demand wealth, power and abject obedience. They obtain all of these things by preying on the weakness of man, a weakness that did not come from God the Creator or from the Lord God, the "Living Creature", the creator of man, but from Jehovah, and from his culture.

Somewhere back in the dawn of time, along with the creation of matter, the laws of physics, chemistry, biology, logic and all of the other sciences, life began. Inorganic matter or elements combined into particular patterns, given a spark of life, became organic, and capable of reproducing itself. This happened sometime during the evening and morning of the third day of creation. This beginning of organic life is said to have started with the advent of what are termed "grass, fruit and herb yielding seed.

Gen. 1:11. And God said, Let the earth bring forth grass, the herb yielding seed, and the fruit-tree yielding fruit after his kind, whose seed is in itself, upon the earth: and it was so."

This statement of the beginning of organic life had to have been made by an individual from a culture familiar with plants and the differences between reproductive plants and those which produce eatable fruits. Only a civilized individual would make such a distinction. It is certain that the Universal Creator would not.

Plants or organic life began at sometime during the fourth biblical age when the stars, solar systems, the sun and moon, were being formed. At the beginning of the fifth period of time, organic life, capable of motion, began to evolve into living matter, the moving creature that hath life, fowl that flew above the earth, the great whales and all manner of life in the seas.

Sometime after the evening and morning of the sixth day the Living Creature, beasts of the field, cattle and creeping things are said to have come into existence.

Whether the above creatures evolved from a lower life form is immaterial. They existed. How they came into being is open to debate. The fact that they are said to have existed long before the advent of man is a fact of biblical record. The question is, is that record accurate? If it is, then life, the Living Creature, beasts, cattle and creeping things exist not only on this planet, the one we call earth, but throughout the universe.

Genesis 1:24: "*And God said, Let the earth (meaning solid matter, the combination of elements), bring forth the living creature after his kind, cattle, and creeping thing, and beast of the earth after his kind, and it was so.*"

As a part of the creative process and the organization of all matter in all of its diverse forms, stages and dimensions the action, reaction and interaction of all of the above, resulted in what is described in scripture as a living creature. It was conceived, grew and flourished. How it was conceived is a mystery known only to the one true GOD.

These creatures in their struggle for survival grew in wisdom and in knowledge. After a time they, like us, began the exploration of space. During their evolutionary period we must assume that they, like man, accumulated a vast amount of knowledge. Obtained over countless generations, this gave to them, just as it has to man, a feeling of superiority over all that they surveyed. They came to believe themselves like unto the Universal Creator, omnipotent and gods. This feeling of power and superiority was strengthened as they ventured further and further into space. Never meeting their equal, who was there to question their claim to immortality and the deity of gods? In essence, the creatures were gods. But they were gods that had no power greater than their own intellect and technology.

It can be assumed that during their travels through space they stepped down onto many planets, one of which was this one. This assumption offers us an explanation for many of the unexplained artefacts found throughout the world. One such artefact is an imprint believed to be that of a boot or shoe of some kind found in a seam of coal in Nevada. Another such print was found in a slab of sandstone taken from the Gobi desert. These prints are estimated to have been made over 15,000,000 years ago.

The most plausible explanation for their occurrence is that they belonged to alien space travellers, who, for whatever reason, found it necessary to land on this planet in locations where the stone had yet to solidify.

The landings may have been accidental or they may have been a prelude to exploration and colonization. I believe that it was a combination of both.

This would be really immaterial if we were using the biblical story of Genesis just as a foundation upon which to base the biblical relationship which existed between the gods and man. However, it becomes crucial if we are attempting to ascertain the truth contained in the scriptures in a manner which unites many of the scriptural verses with odd bits and pieces of archaeology with the history of man as told by biblical scripture.

To analyze the scripture in light of history and archaeology we might begin almost anywhere, but I would like to start with the passage found in Genesis 1:26, the description of the beginning of man and biblical history.

It is unlikely that any mortal, writer or otherwise would have known the thoughts and commands of the Creative God during the process of the creation of the universe. It seems unlikely that even if they knew what God was thinking, he would not have used the words cattle, grass, and trees bearing fruit. These are the words used by a civilized, language speaking culture to express ideas, thoughts and objects. Therefore the passages, words and ideas are those expressed by civilization and not by the creative essence which created the universe.

But if the above passage is taken literally, it is highly possible that the Living Creatures mentioned it that verse is the gods who created us. We are formed in their image. As such they are also in our image. If we are not mirror images, we were at least created from the basic genetic material. Any differences in our appearances would be the result of the modification made to our genetic makeup in order for us to be able to adapt, survive and reproduce on this planet.

Biologically we are identical to the gods. As such we are also physically compatible. Because we are biologically and physically alike, we can also assume that we are alike mentally, and emotionally. From this compatibility, and from the biblical records, we can make a few reasonable assumptions and comparisons between the living creatures their society, culture and ourselves.

Just as trappers, fur traders, prospectors, miners and settlers of early America went west looking for fortunes, land, homes and adventure, so, too, must the spirit of adventure moved the race of living creatures.

Just as our pioneers braved the dangers of a new western frontier in order to achieve their dreams, so, too, did the alien creatures a few million years ago. Their frontiers were the regions of space.

When they arrived on our planet, they were met by its inhabitants, the dinosaurs. These creatures posed no threat to the visitors until they decided to colonize the planet.

When the first alien colonists arrived, their ships were equipped with protective weapons. These powerful, destructive weapons were turned against the dinosaurs and any other animals that threatened the newly arrived colonists.

Even with their knowledge and technology, it appears that the original colonization attempt failed. Whether the colonists were killed by a natural calamity, the animals that were left or died of disease, accidents, or old age, are unknown. But when an expedition from their home world returned to this planet there was little or no evidence of the original colonists.

We can safely assume that there was an attempt at colonization by the artefacts which have been discovered around the world, legends, ancient pictographs and the following statement made by the Lord God, leader and commander of the new expeditionary force. It was a command for man to be fruitful, to reproduce and replenish the earth.

The command to replenish the earth would not have been given to first man unless there had actually been inhabitants in existence on this planet before man. You do not replenish something which has never existed.

One possibility which could have contributed to the demise of the original colonists was a natural disaster, an impact between the earth and a giant asteroid which caused the mantel of the earth to rotate on its axis destroying almost all life. Geological evidence has been found which indicated that the mantel of the earth have over the last billion years rotated at least three times on its axis. Such a rotation would help to explain the last ice age and the archaeological finds which support such a claim.

A few of the original colonists may have survived the catastrophe. If they did in their effort to survived they digressed from their civilized culture into a primordial state where survival became of paramount importance. These may have been the manlike creatures that scientist call '1470 Man', a tool-making creature more advanced than Homo habilis, and a creature previously thought to be the connecting link between man and ape.

The original colonists without additional supplies, repair parts for their equipment or reinforcements from their home world, gradually began to regress culturally.

During their regression the colonists tried to maintain their equipment and obtain the required spare parts by using the technology of their own primitive past. This left behind relics like the ceramic spark plug found deep in a coal vein, the ceramic jugs containing acid and copper wires, believed to have been a primitive type of electrical generating device, celestial maps of the planet showing, what has just been recently verified, the correct configuration of the land mass which lies below the ice of Antarctica. The knowledge of this configuration could only have been obtained from space and before the time of man.

It is possible that the same destructive force, the impact between the earth and an asteroid, which caused the flood and the near annihilation of mankind, might well have caused the death of the original colonists. And if the Lord God and his crew had not been here at the time of our flood to intervene and assisted man, it is possible that man too might well have become, like the earlier alien colonists, a forgotten part of the long history of the planet.

Once the flood, experienced by the generation of Noah was over nothing remained in the destroyed area. It is reasonable to assume that Noah and the people who followed him used caves as natural shelters for their lives and homes. This would explain the underground caves which have been found which give us the impression of being underground cities. The original alien colonists, faced with a similar disaster, may have reverted to the same kind of existence.

Once the alien colonists were established on this planet, their ships returned to their home world. When they returned it was to find an unfamiliar environment. The earth had been changed by natural events. There were alterations in the planet surface, changes in the atmospheric makeup, drifting land masses, changes in the fauna and flora and possibly the entire rotation of the planet surface over the underlying magna bed.

According to a formula worked out by Professor Ackeret, in association with Einstein's theory of relativity, time passes almost ten times faster on earth than it does for those travelling through space at approximately the speed of light.

What was a thousand years to the people of earth was a mere hundred to those in space.

When God and his crew returned to this planet, there were no colonists to welcome them. There was no labour force to assist the new arrivals in the tasks that had to be accomplished. This required the Lord God and his crew, if they wanted to replenish the planet population with new colonists they had to start over from scratch. They had to create man.

At one time or another it has been stated that to look into the past is to look into the future, for nothing really changes except the time place and faces. When we go back into the history of the United States and review the steps in its development, it seems possible that the same steps taken by man to establish a new country may have been taken by our ancestors the gods themselves to establish a new planet.

During the exploration and expansion periods of our world, many explorers went in all directions into the unknown world in search of adventure and wealth.

Marco Polo, Magellan, and Christopher Columbus are just a few whose stories are well documented. But what of all the others which are not recorded? How many fur traders, mountain men, settlers and adventurers came, and died, never having left a mark to show that they were ever here?

After the discovery of the Americas, men of power and wealth began to send groups of men to this country in order to establish territorial rights to whatever lay within its borders. Some were successful, many perished, and many went home as failures.

To those who were successful, new possibilities opened up. Instead of the gold, silk and spices originally hoped for, there was land, agriculture and profits from new products.

The colonists of America came to the new world to map out a fresh existence. Once cities were established as a base, men began to spread out in all directions. One of these groups of adventurers was the miners. They went looking for gold, silver, and other valuable ores. When ore was found, claims staked, mining companies followed.

When the mines were established, there was a need for transportation to carry the ore from the mines to the smelter; Food was required for the workers. And most of all, workers themselves were needed. In our frontier, they came from everywhere; anyone who wanted to work was given a chance.

Many came and many grew tired of working the mines and left to pursue other opportunities. Some acquired land and cattle, some laboured on the land as farmers while others searched for their own bonanza.

When the aliens came to this planet, it was their new frontier. They came as miners. The similarity between their history and America's can be found in the first chapters of Genesis.

When the aliens first arrived on earth they must have been running low on many supplies, especially food. When they found that no civilization existed to replenish that supply, they planted a garden to supplement whatever food was available to them at the time.

They came as miners. They needed workers to mine the ore, methods of transporting it to the smelter, and people to refine it. Since there were no workers available, Adam, Eve and many others, all humans, earthlings, were created. They became the foundation upon which mankind was established. Since there was more than one camp of alien miners, there were more than one set of Adam and Eves.

The alien instructors, the crew of the Lord god and his counterparts in the other camps around the world, taught the created workers all the skills which they needed to know in order for them to do their jobs, mine the minerals of this planet and serve the gods.

The first biblical Adam and Eves created by the Lord God were taught how to plant and tend a garden. Their children, in the case of the biblical Adam, was Cain, Abel and Seth. Cain was taught to plant, harvest, mill grain, and make flour for bread. Later he was taught how to build cities. Abel was taught to tend sheep and cattle.

The children born later were taught how to shear the sheep, weave wool into fibre, and the fibre into cloth. They were taught to make and play musical instruments, extract metal from ore and refine that metal into brass and iron.

Sheep and cattle were raised for to supply meat for the table of God and the materials like wool and leather used for other purposes. These were the service obligations of man before the flood. After the flood they became the misunderstood sacrificial and religious rituals and traditions of the church.

The raising, killing and preparation of meat for the table of the Lord before the flood was perpetuated by the story of Noah's offering of thanks after the flood became the basis for the bloody sacrificial offerings of the religions which followed.

The wool of the sheep was made into clothes and tents. The animal hides were processed into leather goods. The grain grown by Cain was made into bread, and the vegetables, herbs, and fruits of the garden fed both the gods and man.

For grain, milling, flour and bread we have the following:

Genesis 3:19. *In the sweat of thy face shall thou eat bread, till thou return unto the ground?*

In order for man to eat bread, he must first have flour. To get flour one must have grain. To grow grain, mill that grain into flour and use that flour to make bread requires at least some small degree of civilization. Man of his own volition could not have arrived at the process of making bread unless he had been taught.

For entertainment the gods showed man how to make and play musical instruments;

Gen. 4:21: *"And his brother's name was Jubal: he was the father of all such as handle the harp and organ. Where did these terms originate over 5,000 years unless they were terms used by the gods as a part of their culture?"*

These are pretty sophisticated instruments for creatures living naked and eating nothings but fruit, nuts, grass and vegetables.

Early man, before the flood, walked, talked, worked, and was instructed by the gods, the Living Creatures. They taught man their laws, customs, and traditions. They taught him some of their skills and gave man the ability to work and survive. Man was given the expertise of the gods. These they brought with them when they came to this planet.

An example of their laws is the ones given as to Adam and Eve, as commandments, when they were first created.

They were told to unite and become one flesh, to procreate and have children. This was a union of a male and female which became the prerequisite of humans, which formed family traditions.

Gen. 2:24: *"Therefore shall a man leave his father and his mother, and shall cleave unto his wife: and they shall be one flesh (bare children).*

Along with the arts of agriculture, animal husbandry, weaving, and musical culture man was also taught the art of mining and construction. He learned how to build the cities which were required as housing by the aliens. And he was taught to work metal into usable objects.

Gen. 4:22: *"And Zillah, she also bare Tubal-Cain, an instructor of every artificer in brass and iron: and the sister of Tubal-Cain was Naamah.*

Why have an instructor in iron and brass unless it was to fashion the ore that the gods were mining into something useful?"

Gen. 4:17: *"And Cain knew his wife, and she conceived, and bare Enoch: and be built a city, and call the name of the city after the name of his son Enoch."*

While the cities were being built, the sons of Cain and their families were being taught other skills which both they and the aliens needed for survival. One of those skills, taught to Tubalcain, was the art of working in iron and brass. To obtain the necessary materials for the forging of these metals, one must obtain the raw ore. To get the ore one must mine for the minerals.

Man was taught how to mine the ore, transport it to the smelter and refine it in order to obtain the minerals it contained.

When it became apparent to the Lord God that the man needed help in his labours, the Lord God created special animals thought to be of assistance to man. After a while it was found that those specially created animals were not compatible with man and other companions were required. It was at this time that females were created.

The aliens had been on the planet for over a thousand years when it was announced that a giant asteroid had entered the solar system and was on a collision course with the earth. Such an impact should it occur would almost certainly destroy almost all life on the planet. When it became apparent to the Lord God's around the world that a global catastrophe was imminent they began to make preparations for saving as much of the planet life as possible.

Each expeditionary commander, using the materials available in their particular locations, taught a selected group of their charges on how to make survival floatation devices.

The gods knew that the following events were likely to occur when the earth was struck by the giant incoming asteroid.

As the two masses grew closer together weather patterns would change. There would be giant tidal waves caused by the gravitational pull of the new mass. Rains and winds would become hurricane of great force. The gravitational pull between the two masses would create earthquakes the likes of which man had never before experienced. As these earthquakes occurred, volcanos would erupt, poisonous gasses would be released, the atmosphere would become polluted and death and disease would be rampart.

The gods could not prevent this disaster from occurring but they could make preparations to save as much of life as possible.

For the Uros of Bolivia their floatation device, their ark was floating islands made of reeds. They still live on those islands today.

In China it might have been junks and sampans. In the biblical story of the Lord God, it was the ark, a box made of gopher wood and sealed within and without with tar or pitch.

In preparation for the expect disaster, the Lord God had Noah and his family build an ark. In that floating device, in addition to Noah, his family and as much livestock, birds, insects and reptiles as possible, there was stored food and water for the expected flood. All of these things were a part of the cargo, which the Lord God hoped would survive.

Noah the ark and all aboard survived, thanks to the stability and ark design.

Noah and those on board were cooped up in an enclosed container for a year if the biblical story is true. With the ark pitched inside and out with tar to make it waterproof and with one 19" x 18" sealed window, how did they survive without fresh air and water? How did eight people feed, water and dispose of the animal waste if the ark was sealed? How did they survive the toxic ammonia fumes generated by such a huge amount of waste?

There are, of course, two possible explanations for the above survival. One is that every living thing on board, like the bear in winter was placed into some kind of hibernation, or two, there was, like the space platform of the astronauts of today, a mechanical regeneration device which recycled waste into useable products. In either event it would have required very sophisticated medical and technical expertise, which was beyond the mechanical and technical abilities of early man. The ability to create a hibernation environment or to recycle waste products into useable products can only come from a highly advance civilization, one to which the alien gods belonged.

After the flood an assessment was made by the Lord God of the property, both men and material, under his control.

The earthquakes and floods had destroyed the mines and equipment. Personnel, except for Noah and his family were gone. It would take years to recoup the animal herds, raise and train a new crop of workers, find new deposits and begin mining operation again. Noah and his family, due to the high winds and flood conditions created by the asteroid impact found themselves miles away from the mines in a new territory called the Mountains of Ararat.

The Lord God and his crew celebrated the survival of the catastrophe with Noah and his family by having a big barbeque. The gods stayed around long enough to ensure that Noah, his family and the animals would survive. When the Lord god was satisfied that life would continue on earth he made plans to return to his home planet and reports what had happened. He delegated to certain of his subordinates, those which he intended to leave behind as stewards, certain areas of responsibilities along with the authority to carry out his instructions. When this was completed as outlined in Deuteronomy 32. The Lord departed the earth. He left behind as stewards several members of his crew, those who had made wives of the earth women and who had children by them. This we can only assume from the scriptures, which state that Jehovah himself had many sons and daughters. Again this is mentioned in Deuteronomy 32.

One of the subordinate left behind was Yahweh, an individual who became a friend and the God of Abraham. He was the one who later called himself I AM THAT I AM. In order to prevent taking his name in vane the Hebrews began to call him Jehovah. He was the administrator and steward of the Lord God, left in charge of the planet's affairs. He was an administrator before and as such had no group of humans under his command and control. After the flood as the administrator he was placed in charge of the earth's affairs and as such had the right to assume, by the right of his authority, the title of the Lord God.

Job 1:6. *"Now there was a day when the sons of God came to present themselves before the Lord, and Satan came also among them."*

The humans which descended from the survivors of the flood were placed under the command and control of the other gods. These are the gods who through mythology have become known by many names. In Jewish myths and legend they are known as Samael or Satan, Baal, Moloch and the other gods, who were responsible for certain areas and groups of people. They reported to the Lord God the status of the people and their territories. These gods were the supervisors of the people before the flood. It had been their task and obligation to trained, care for and protects their workers before the flood and now their responsibility to looked after them they began to scat around the world.

The people in remembrance of their gods, built houses for their gods called temples, ordained priest to serve them, established religious ritual to prepare their food, to feed them and to continue to sacrifice and to bring offerings and gifts to them.

In time, jealous of the attention paid to his subordinates, the ridicule and jokes made against him by his children, Jacob, and the other gods, Jehovah decide to become more than an administrator, he decided to become a god like the rest of his companions. But, the only people over whom he had any authority and control were Jacob and his descendants and they were slaves in Egypt.

He was no god and had no power over man therefore he needed some kind of a plan which would allow him to get the attention of the Hebrew slaves long enough for him to convince them to accept his as their gods. Once he was accepted, he could then delegate authority to individuals to act on his behalf. These individuals would be his priest. They would establish the sacrificial rituals he deemed appropriate to honour and glorify him. They would build him a temple, a place where he could live and administer to his people. He would then be able to establish a name for himself as a respected and feared god. He had the people, the children of Jacob, a responsibility delegated to him by the Lord God. Getting them to worship him was another thing altogether.

It has been said that it is an ill wind which does not blow someone some good. Such a wind blew for Jehovah. It gave him a plan and a way by which he could begin obtaining control of the Hebrew slaves in Egypt. It was the eruption of the volcano on the isle of Crete in the

Mediterranean Sea approximately three hundred miles from the land of Egypt. When the volcano erupted, the after effects of the eruption created the events which are described in the Bible as the plagues of Egypt. Jehovah used these events to scare Pharaoh and the people into believing that he was an all powerful god.

We are the descendants and distance relatives of the gods. We have inherited the laws and customs of their culture and their civilization which they have passed down to us through the various examples of government they have established on earth. These examples can be found in scripture and in the ancient relics, the stone and clay tablets which have been found which predate the Jewish faith by a couple of thousand years.

Many new laws have been added to the civil code of man and many have been changed to suit our purposes, but the moral and civil laws, the basis upon which civilize man exists and our attitude toward the laws instilled in us at the time of our creation still exists.

Today basic civil codes or laws go back to the time of Hammurabi, King of Babylon. These codes ancient and in existence almost a thousand years Jehovah modified and passed them onto the Hebrew as the laws of Moses. These codes were first found on clay tablets found in what was once called Shinar, the biblical name for Sumer, the early name of Mesopotamia. The estimated date of these tablets is from around 3100 B.C. The time of Jehovah and Moses was around 1500 B.C.

As a civilized culture we have inherited, whether we wanted to or not the laws, traditions, customs and traits of the gods themselves.

From their culture we learned how to grow crops, herd cattle and sheep, build cities, mine and process the minerals of the earth. We learned to make and play musical instruments. They taught us how to use the wool from the sheep to make the threads used to weave the cloth made into the clothes which are used warm, protect, adorn and cover our nakedness. They learned how to procreate and how to survive as a species. The gods taught us how to kill and destroy. Every distasteful trait of man, from greed and envy to murder and destruction, we learned from the acts of the gods either as examples or by their command.

The beginning of our instructions began with the command for man to be fruitful, to multiply and to replenish the earth. This could have been a simple process of a male and female uniting as the animals do. Children would have been born and the species would have survived but this was not the way by which the Lord God intended for men to bond. He instituted a ritual called which bonded a man and a woman to each other. This ritual has come to be called marriage. Through the union between a man and a woman, new life, children, are created and born through a natural biological process.

Family traditions and values began when the first man and woman, Adam and Eve, were commanded to unite become one flesh and reproduce the species.

Adam and Eve had no biological parents, yet they were commanded to leave a father and mother which did not exist except in the culture of the aliens, a culture which included gardening, tending and herding animals, music, construction, industry, mining and war.

And war was a part of the alien culture.

Gen. 3:24: "*So, he drove out the man: and he placed at the east of the garden Cherubim, and a flaming sword which turned every way, to keep the way of the tree of life.*"

The gods used the word sword. To us this is a weapon of war. It could not mean anything else because Jehovah himself used it in that context.

Isaiah 34:5-6. *For my sword shall be bathed in heaven: behold it shall come down upon Idumea, and upon the people of my curse, to judgement. The sword of the Lord is filled with blood, it is made fat with fatness, and with the blood of lambs and goats, with the fat of the kidneys of rams: for the lord hath a sacrifice in Bozrah, and a great slaughter in the land of Idumea.*"

The above is a reality only as long as one believes in the truth of the Bible and the messages within. Is what is written in the Bible the truth or a religious fictional tale told and believed by those who would have a God?

If one believes in the truth of the Bible one must also believe that Jehovah was one of the alien travellers and a part of the expedition of the Lord god to mine this planet. As such, the story of Genesis added to the bits and pieces of history, when combined with the biblical saga, the pieces of each, like a giant jig-saw puzzle, begins to take shape. They form a clear picture of the real relationship which exists between God, man, and religion.

What are some of those bits and pieces?

One, for example, was the recent discovery of a nest of baby dinosaur bones. They appear to have been destroyed by a blast of high intensity radiation. The radiation reading of the bones and the background was so high (that it is believed) that the only way this could have happened was if they were blasted by a radioactive weapon of some kind. Who existed at the time of the dinosaurs that would have had such weapon? The answer, of course, is "The Living Creature", our gods the aliens, our creators, kin and ancestors.

Another piece of the puzzle is a system of mine tunnels recently discovered in Central and South America. These tunnels are described in Erich Von Daniken's novel, "The Gold of the Gods". In his book he says:

> *"What I saw was not the product of dreams or imagination, it was real and tangible. A gigantic system of tunnels, thousands of miles in length and built by unknown constructors at some unknown date, lies hidden deep below the South American continent. Hundreds of miles of underground passages have already been explored and measured in Ecuador and Peru."*

Juan Moriez born in Hungary, an Argentine citizen by naturalization and finder of these tunnels states *"In my capacity as a scholar, I was carrying out research into the folklore and the ethnological and linguistic aspects of Ecuadorian tribes... The objects I found are of the following kinds: 1. Stone and metal objects of different sizes and colours. 2. Metal plaques (leaves) engraved with signs and writing.*

These form a veritable metal library which might contain a synopsis of the history of humanity, as well as an account of the origin of mankind on earth and information about a vanished civilization."

Baby dinosaur's eggs have been found believed destroyed by radiation and tunnels with passages formed with perfect right angles, smooth, almost polished walls, with evenly spaced air shafts 750 feet below the surface. All of these items speak of a civilization with tremendous engineering skills.

Found within these tunnels, along with many others artefacts of unknown origin was *the skeleton of a man, carved out of stone, I counted ten pairs of ribs, all anatomically accurate.*, says Von Daniken. The significance of that skeleton with its ten sets of ribs will be discussed later.

It is a possibility that these tunnels were part of one of the mines of the aliens, from which the ore was taken to a smelter, refined and transported to the landing sites which we call the Nazca Lines.

The Nazca Lines are images of animals and insects of gigantic proportions. They can only be seen and identified from the air.

These sites had a dual purposed. They served, not only as a storage and landing site for the incoming space craft, but more importantly, these symbols which can only be seen from the air or space and are the identity markings of the company which owned the mineral rights to that part of the world.

These symbols are laid out in patterns which we are able to recognize as life forms. There is one that looks like a jaguar, one a scorpion, a dragonfly and one that is very unique in that it is a vertical design placed upon the side of a mountain and can only be seen from the sea. That particular design is a trident. But it serves a very useful purpose. It is a directional symbol, a starting point from which to navigate the plant.

Just as we recognize the Exxon tiger, the Texaco star, the Shell, the Eagle and other symbols of our corporate entities, so, too, did the monkey, jaguar, scorpion, and other lines, identify various mining companies and their locations here on earth.

If a spaceship were approaching earth, what better way for them to know where they were to go and where to land than by sighting the symbol of the company to which it belonged? When approaching the planet from space, going from west to east the giant trident on the face of the west coast of South America would point the new arrival inland and provide a point of reference from which to navigate the planet.

If we are to believe any of the circumstantial evidence uncovered over the years we have: 1. what appears to be the skeleton of a humanoid with ten set of ribs carved out of stone, 2. Footprints embedded in 15,000,000 year old sandstone. 3. Animals killed by localized radiation blasts. 4. Unexplained symbols that can only be identified from space and last but not the least, very ancient tunnels and underground cities which appear to have been made with a technology that man has only recently achieved.

When these are correlated with biblical scripture, we must believe in alien life and the truth of the Bible. The Bible becomes a written record, without religious significance, of the beginning saga of man. The Bible is the cultured man version of history. What of those beliefs in man's beginning which belong to less cultured people? What of the legends of people who believe they either came from the stars or served the gods who did?

There are the Uros, an Indian tribe which still lives on reed islands in Lake Titicaca, Bolivia, who believe that their ancestors came from the stars long before the white man was created, and the Dogon, a very ancient tribe of aborigines found in Africa who believed they served those same gods.

Were the reed islands of the Uros actually the arks they were commanded to construct in order for them to survive the flood?

"The Uros, who live on reed islands in Lake Titicaca, Bolivia, claim that their people are older than that of the Incas, indeed, that they already existed before To Ti Tu, the father of heaven, who created the white man. The Uros swear black and blue that they were not men, for they had black blood and were alive when the earth still lay in darkness. We are not as other men, for we came from another planet. The few Uros who are still alive avoid any contact with the rest of the world. Proudly and stubbornly they defend their otherness as the heritage they brought with them from another planet." Von Daniken's "The Gold Of The Gods."

If the legend of the Uros is based upon a truth then the Uros were in existence before man was created by the Lord God. If this is also true then it would appear that the Uros are either the descendants of the original colonists, a part of the remnant of the mining exposition left behind or a closely knit group of people who sprang from the mixed marriages between the aliens and the first created men? Either of these possibilities would result in the belief that they existed before the first true human was created?

The Bible mentions sexual relationships between the sons of God and the daughters of men. This account, is of course, one which took place in Africa when the Lord God and his crew created Adam and Eve and planted their garden of Eden.

If my hypothesis is true, there was also a Lord Commander in South America. This would account for the mines tunnels the Nazca lines, the legend of the Uros and the Temple of the Sun at Lake Tiahuanaco in Bolivia. If the aliens had sexual relationships with the women of one camp, would they not have had such unions in all the camps? These various relationships would account for the different blood lines and types found around the world while still retaining the basic blood groups.

I cannot speak for true Gods, but sexual release and the desire for sexual union seems to be a common denominator for each and every known life form.

The biblical life forms we call the gods, were flesh and blood beings. They had sexual encounters. Children were born of these encounters. That biblical fact either makes the gods human or human's gods.

When the aliens, the biblical "Living Creatures", returned to this planet a few thousand years ago, they brought with them their technology, equipment, agriculture know-how, medical expertise and weapons.

The new expeditionary force, unsure of what they would find on earth after such a long absence would have prepared for the worse possible scenario.

Not knowing what edible foods might be available and compatible to their digestive system they brought with them their own seeds and special plants. These they planted in the "Biblical Garden of Eden." They also brought with them embryos of domesticated cattle, sheep and every animal they considered good for food. They also brought their medical expertise.

It is possible, that while yet in space, the creation and instruction of man was began. When the aliens arrived on the planet man would be ready to assume his duties as slave and gardener to the gods. A garden was planted and man was placed in that garden to care for it. That is a possibility, but I believe that the most likely scenario was slightly different.

The creation of man was not started until after the aliens had arrived on the planet. It was only after they had tested the atmosphere, examined the plants, water and environment did they make a decision as to what kind of an individual their new creation was to be. A major part of their decision on what to create, outside of the physical structure necessary to survive on the planet, was the most appropriate structure necessary for the work which the new creation was to do.

Regardless of what one's religious beliefs may be, and no matter what religious leaders expound from the pulpit, the truth of the matter is, the aliens came to this planet for the sole purpose of mining for minerals. This is clearly indicated by the Bible in the first few chapters of the Book of genesis.

The aliens evidently had no intentions of an extended stay on the planet. They were here to get their minerals and depart. From the length of the tunnels found in South America and the legends of the richness of King Solomon's mine, they were unable to bring themselves to abandon such richness. The belief that they only intended to stay a short while is supported by the fact that they originally had not made plans for a female and reproduction of the new species.

They created the men and special animals helpers for them to assist in working the mine and refining the ore for it mineral content. When the job was finished the aliens intended to depart the planet and the workers, their slaves, while a sub species, would no longer be required or wanted. Man as an indigenous species of this planet alone would be left to fend for themselves until they eventually died of old age.

It was fortunate for man that the planet proved to be so profitable that the aliens decided to prolonged their stay. When that decision was made to stay as long as the minerals made the stay profitable, it was easier for them to create women and let the workers reproduce themselves through natural birth rather than through machines and cloning.

Women were an afterthought and were not a part of the original plan of the Lord God.

Genesis 2:18-19,21-22: *"And the Lord God said, It is not good that the man should be alone: I will make him an help meet for him. 19. And out of the ground the Lord God formed every beast of the field, and every fowl of the air, and brought them unto Adam to see what he would call them; and whatsoever Adam called every living creature, that was the name thereof. 21. And the Lord God caused a deep sleep to fall upon Adam, and he slept; and he took one of his ribs, and closed up the flesh instead thereof: 22. And the rib, which the Lord God had taken from man, made he a woman, and brought her unto the man."*

Here I am confused. In Genesis 1:21-25 doesn't the scriptures say that GOD, not the Lord God, created the living creatures, cattle, creeping things, fowl, whales, beasts and every living thing that moved? This was before the creation of man. Now in Genesis 2:19 we have the Lord God, not GOD creating the same things all over again and bringing them to the man for him to name. Was man created before or after the other life that has movement?

Here the biblical record clearly and distinctly identified two Gods. One is the universal creator and the second is a mortal, flesh and blood being. One with endless and unlimited power and the other with technical and medical expertise.

Unless there are two distinct beings, GOD the creator of the universe, and the Lord God who created man, there is a biblical discrepancy here. That is unless the animals created by the Lord God, and called by the same names, are in reality, different from those animals and other life forms scattered throughout the universe, the ones created by GOD. However, while some of the animals may have been the same, the method of reproduction was different. One type of life evolved by a natural process over countless millennia and the other was the result of a creative process utilizing the eggs, sperm and or DNA cells taken from the creatures already in existence. Those created by GOD and reproduced by the Lord God.

How man was created has always been considered a mystery. Today with our knowledge of medical technology, and the biblical records, that creation is no longer a mystery. Mankind began as created clones of the alien gods. He was created in a laboratory by genetic engineering. He is a clone, a modified reproduction of the Living Creature.

According to Zecharia Sitchin in his book "the 12th Planet", cuneiform dating back almost 3000 B.C. say the same thing. Man was a clone created by the beings from the 12th planet as workers to mine the minerals of this planet.

As beings from a planet different from our own their physical structure would also be different. This difference would be in their physical structure.

The distance the 12th planet is from the sun would confirm the idea that the sun's rays are weak. This would account for the large eyes dark eyes of aliens depicted by those individuals who have claimed to have seem them. Large dark eyes would be appropriate on such a distant planet in order to capture more of the available sunlight. The inhabitants of the 12th planet would also have a physical structure different from man because their bodies would be based upon the gravity and atmosphere of their world.

The scriptures indicate that there are many diverse species and forms of life found throughout the universe. Not all of it intelligent. We must assume that this is true because this is what Moses was told by Jehovah. Moses could not have written Genesis without that information. And if Jehovah was one of the aliens, gods or not, as an a heavenly space traveller, would he not know of other life?

The commander of this alien group, in considering which type could be best adapted to the earth and the work which had to be accomplished, decided that his own species was the best and the most likely to survive the physical structural modification, the work and the earthly environment.

We know that it is possible to clone or create a living organism from the cell structure of another life form because our scientist and medical profession have done it. We also know that the genetic structure of a selected life form can be altered by genetic manipulation, in order to produce, if not a new species than a highly altered one. It is not only religion and the tremendous legal ramifications, but the ethical and moral dilemmas which would be incurred if the cloning of humans would ever take place. These have, until now, prevented such procedures from taking place.

Today's scientists have cloned sheep, monkeys, salamanders and a human embryo.(Time Magazine, Nov. 8, 1993.) If we can clone a human embryo today, how much easier must it have been for the aliens who had the technology to travel the stars? Their medical achievements must have been at least as advanced as we like to believe ours to be.

The gods made images of themselves. They called those images Man. But, because man was not born of natural parents but in a laboratory, as far as the aliens were concerned he had no status. He was disposal property create to serve at the whim of the gods.

Regardless of how are why we were created, the net result is that mankind is by DNA, the kin and descendants of God, Jehovah and the members of his crew who found their creation, the women of earth attractive and produced children by them.

Our research scientists have found that the richest source of cloning material most suitable for the creation of a species is found to be the blood cells found in the bone marrow of that species. These cells can be genetically manipulated in order to create a specific new organism, enhance an old one, or duplicate the original.

The Lord God and his crew used their own blood cells, altered and enhanced through genetic engineering, to create Adam and the men which came after him. Eve was created from the red blood cells taken from the marrow of the rib removed from Adam. Through genetic engineering and technology the blood cells of the Lord God and his crew were altered and modified so that the first created men would be adapted to this planet and it's environment. By using the DNA of the aliens man inherited all of the traits, abilities and characteristics of the living creatures except for those traits and physical characteristics of the aliens indigenous to their particular planet.

Their DNA was modified by genetic engineering so that man would have a greater chance of survival in a new and completed different environment.

Based on the life span of the Lord God, which appears to be approximately one thousand years, man had the ability to be very productive for a very long period of time. He was thus a very valuable and cost effective piece of property.

Adam was the prototype for the workers which followed his creation. The workers which were created later were created as individually programmed individuals with their own specific set of rules, traits, skills and abilities. These men created after Adam were created from the blood cells taken from the crew of the expedition. Their blood cells determined what traits, abilities and characteristics were to be inherited by the men especially created as their work force and under their command. These individuals groups, controlled by a particular supervisor or god formed a kind of guild, the first trade unions, but one without the right of arbitration.

There were farmers, construction crews, miners, herdsmen and domestics. Each group was a close knit organization which kept to themselves. Wary of outsiders, a new member was not accepted without some kind of conflict within the group. This was one of the reasons why Cain was afraid of the men which he would have to meet when he was forced from the sight and protection of God. He would have to belong to one of these groups in order to survive. He was accepted by the construction crew. This crew were the ones who were building the housing or city for the gods.

The genetic alteration of the blood cells of the aliens was a modification to the makeup of the DNA, RNA, and chromosome structures of the genes used in the cloning process. This modification included a change in the bone structure of man, his lungs and his blood chemistry. But, it did not affect the DNA, RNA and chromosome patterns to such a degree that man would be entirely different from the aliens. In fact, even after his modification man was still completely in tune with, and compatible with, the aliens; biological, physically, and mentally.

When we look at the skeleton of the stone carving of the man with ten sets of ribs and combine it with the legends of the Uros, we get, not only the following assumption, but a picture of our ancestors, the Gods.

The skeleton with ten sets of ribs indicates that the beings it represented came come from a planet with a rarefied atmosphere, where a tremendous set of lungs was required in order to survive. To protect these extra large lungs, an extra large rib cage was necessary. A rarefied atmosphere, would create a blood chemistry slightly different from Man's. The lack of oxygen in such blood would give that blood the appearance of being black. The blood of Man on the other hand, because of the high oxygen rich content of our atmosphere, gives our blood the appearance of being red.

When the aliens gods with their black blood mated with the daughters of men with red blood, children born as a result of those interracial affairs may well have had blood with a different hue. The black blood of the aliens, when mixed with the red blood of man, produced half-breed offspring with blood having a blue tint. These individuals, are called by scripture, the mighty men of old. Half god and half man, they became the blue-blooded aristocracy, the rulers of man by the right of God.

There was one other special purpose that could be served by the blood difference. No man could claim to be other than what he was. With one prick of the finger, a positive identification could be made of any individual: Red: man. Black: God. Blue: half breed. There is one other unusual characteristic about blood. There is a definite and distinct difference in its makeup which can be contributed to the idea that there were more that one beginning man.

There are "O" positive and negative, "A" positive and negative, "B" positive and negative and "AB" positive and negative.

If all of mankind had descended from one man and one woman,, Adam and Eve , logically all blood type would be the same. However, if we originated from different sources the above diversification of blood types makes sense.

Eve created from the blood of Adam taken from the blood of God would have been the same. The other groups and combinations would have come from different beings.

Man, when first created was naked. He lived, ate, worked and slept in the elements with the animals. Once produced, he, like the animals, was a very cost effective worker. He was intelligent and easily trained.

After the creation of a female, together they were able to reproduce the species.

When humans began to multiply, cloning, except under special or unusual circumstances was no longer necessary.

Adam, servant to the Lord God, became the prototype for mankind. Once he was found to be functional other workers followed. Instead of using the blood cells of God, the cells of crew were used. From each member of the crew a series of individual workers were cloned from their particular cells. The individual crew members of the Lord God became the supervisor of all who were cloned from their cells. Later these supervisors came to be called gods by the workers under their control. Each crew, group or guild, specialized in the area of the expertise of its supervisor.

As time passed, it became evident that the men could use some help in the tasks assigned to them. Replacements were needed for those who died by accident, disease or became disabled.

Women were yet to be created, so in order to assist man in his labours, specific animals were cloned or genetically created. When these animals were found to be incompatible with man, rather than clone more workers, the decision was made to clone mates which would allow the workers to reproduce their own replacements. A woman, a female was created. (Gen. 2:18-20).

The last time I was in a hospital for surgery, a doctor did the same thing to me as the Lord God did to Adam. He put me to sleep, removed a part, and closed up the flesh. To read the above passage of scripture in the light of today's knowledge, suggests the very same thing occurred to Adam. He was anaesthetized and operated on, a rib was surgically removed and the incision was closed.

The creation of woman, if it were a miracle, was a medical one. Once we realize that the biblical story is based on real life, the mysticism is removed. When we read the scriptures with this new reality in mind, it is easy to realized that the biblical passages are no longer mythical mysteries but stories we can relate to wherein the author has made a god the central character. We have only to change our perspective on how and why man was created in order to understand the Bible.

The rib which was removed from Adam was sent to a genetic laboratory. There scientists, using the altered red blood cells of Adam, cloned or created a female from those cells.

Eve, because she was created from the cells of Adam, was automatically adapted to his environment, and biologically compatible with him. She and the women who were cloned from her cells were also biologically compatible with man and the alien gods.

In time, the daughters of Eve, and the women cloned from her cells, were ready to marry and reproduce.

During the time of Adam, this was a medical miracle. Today medical science has advanced by leaps and bounds over what man was able to accomplish a mere fifty years ago.

During our lifetime there have been experiments and research done in the field of cybernetics and in the possibility of what are called cyborgs: These are individual which are half human and half machine. They have the bodies of a machine, operated and control by a human mind. Today we have individuals with mechanical hearts, dialysis machines, the iron lung and a host of other crude devices which are able to control the bodily functions of a person and help to keep them alive. We look at these devices and marvel at the progress and ingenuity of medical science.

There is a saying and a belief that in every myth there can be found an element of truth. If this is true, then the gargoyle, the centaur, the sphinx and a host of other mystical creatures could have existed not only as genetic experiments but as the creatures specifically designed to do the work that the space beings, our ancestors, wanted done.

Such a creatures is mentioned in Genesis as the "Cherubim", the guardians of God. Others are mentioned in Revelation 4:7: *"And the first beast was like a lion, and the second beast like a calf, and the third beast had a face as a man, and the fourth beast was like a flying eagle."*

This description sounds similar to the Gods of Egypt who protected the holy places. They also sound like a description of the Sphinx, the Minotaur, the Centaur and the Falcon god of Egypt.

Today medical science can genetically engineer a living creatures with specific traits and characteristics. Once they become functional, identical units called clones can be produced without the benefit of a father or mother.

Babies are now conceived in test tubes, and the fertilized eggs of one species carried in the womb of another. It is only a matter of time before man has developed an incubation machine for humans. This machine will be capable of acting just like a mother. It will nurture, protect and incubate the embryo of any living creature put into it until the time is appropriate for that being to be born.

The new living being, if it is human, will have been conceived, nurtured and born all without the benefit of parents. The new being will be born without the addiction of alcohol, drugs, diseases, malformation, and birth defects. Each and every child born in this manner will be whole and perfect.

Today we have medical facilities where males are able to donate their sperm for later use by women and couples who are unable to have children through the natural process of childbirth. The donated sperm of males, stored in these facilities, are used by medical personnel to fertilize the egg of a woman unable to conceive. If the mother to be is unable to carry the desired child the fertilized egg can be placed in and carried by surrogate mothers. Tomorrow the surrogate mothers may well be the incubation machines.

Adults who desire a child will be able to go to a baby factory and order a child to their own specifications.

These children will be created as special entities. Later, those individuals which required more than one child can receive, if desired, that additional being as a cloned of the original. It is possible that these cloned individuals could some day, like automobiles on an assembly line, become individual series of created beings, individuals which could be created, grown, worked and reproduced as the need arises.

What will become of the libido of man, we cannot begin to imagine. Will women feel deprived of motherhood because they will no longer have to go through the nine months of pain, labour and childbirth? Will the child ordered to specifications take the place and create the excitement of the unexpected? Will the elimination of birth defects and disease, giving every mother a perfect child be compensation for the forsaken maternal instinct of self mutation by natural childbirth? And at what point in time will people stop desiring children, leaving the perpetuation of the species to the government? What effect will this lack of responsible have on the emotional stability of the cloned individuals deprived of the love and devotion of a loving parent? Will a father and a mother become a new profession? Will these individuals be professionally trained persons with degrees who will be paid by society to perform the tasks that some parents love and others hate?

For the few individual throwbacks that would still insist upon having a child the old fashion way, by natural birth, and allowed to raise that child, what guarantee will they have that they will be allowed free will in the matter?

There may come a time when the world population becomes so staggering that children will only be available upon special request. Those children going only to those parents capable of caring for and funding their development. There may also come a time when governments will requires all children to be created and born with specified programming: programming which eliminates criminal, mental and/or physical disabilities.

China and India are a couple of the countries already experimenting with or considering the above scenario needed to reduce or control their already over populated lands.

We can clone animals, and we can clone humans. We have this technology today. It is only reasonable to assume that any race of beings capable of travelling the stars, would also possess the same or greater knowledge.

All of the animals created to help Adam were genetically created clones or modification of existing species that were owned or controlled by the aliens. Just as we have adapted and breed certain animals for our purposes, so, too, did the aliens.

The Minotaur with his huge eyes, worked the dark labyrinth of the mines. The Centaur, with the strength of a horse pulled the ore carts from the mines and the Sphinx, with it's powerful wings, carried the heavy loads from the mines to the smelter, and from the smelter to the landing sites.

The process of genetically manipulating the DNA of the cells through the cloning process did occur. In a man, the DNA, RNA, and Chromosomes, along with other protein materials, carry the genetic information of each individual in the form of genes. These individual genes are responsible for the determination, and transmission of, hereditary characteristics.

In Adam, as in most males, the chromosome pattern is "XY". In most females the pattern is "XX".

It was therefore relative easy for the medical science of the Lord God to double the "x" chromosomes pattern of a male in order to create a female.

There are times when the patterns have become mutated. In these cases the patterns become "X-Y-X" and "Y-X-Y." These individuals are known as "hermaphrodites", having the characteristics of both male and female. The chromosome sequences determines which will be the more dominate sex role of that individual.

For beings capable of travelling the stars it must have been a simple procedure to genetically isolate and double the "X" chromosome of a male, making it possible to create a female from a male.

Gen. 2:23. *"And Adam said, this is now bone of my bones, and flesh of my flesh: she shall be called woman, because she was taken out of man."*

The statement that Adam was put to sleep, operated on and the wound closed, certainly reinforces the idea that Adam and Eve were products of a medical procedure of some kind. The removal of the rib, and Adam's statement concerning his bones, make cloning the most likely possibility.

Once he was created, the Lord God passed to Man instructions which outlined his expected behaviour and provided him some insight into the culture of the alien beings themselves.

In order for the cloned slaves of the aliens to be able to function within the accepted social structure and society of the aliens, it became necessary for the aliens to instruct Man in their laws and customs. The following is one of the customs and traditions that Man was expected to obey:

Genesis 2:24-25: *"Therefore shall a man leave his father and his mother, and shall cleave unto his wife: and they shall be one flesh. 25. And they were both naked, the man and his wife, and were not ashamed."*

With the above statement, the institution of marriage began. Like many biblical laws and customs, these changed over the years to gratify man himself and not to conform to the laws of the Lord God.

Where did the idea of a father and a mother come from? It could not have come from the omnipotent GOD, creator of the universe. Such an entity is believed to be complete within itself, without the need for either a father or a mother. If this commandment did not come from the Universal Creator, it must have come from a being to whom the custom meant something special. Since it came from the Lord God than it is logical to assume that it was an established custom of his civilized society. A society to which the Lord God and his crew belonged.

Adam and Eve became parents only when there were children. Until then Adam and Eve were husband and wife, male and female companions.

When this command was given to Adam and Eve, the Lord God was passing down to them a number of things. First, within the culture of the aliens, men and women were bonded together. They became husband and wife. When this happened, it became the duty of the male to leave his parents, and begin the care of his wife. They were commanded to become one flesh, in other words, to unite and procreate new life.

We can assume that the creator of Adam and Eve was married. We can also assume that the race to which he belonged was given in marriage and that the gods had fathers and mothers. This is an assumption that we can make because the scripture clearly indicates that the gods took the daughters of men as wives. They had children, therefore they were parents.

It is said that we are the image of God and since he demands this of us, it seems logical to assume that the same requirements applied to him. Certainly Adam and Eve did not, of their own volition, choose to institute a custom which had never existed before for man. If the custom was not a part of the culture why would it be necessary for man to follow this concept?

Marriage as a social custom does not seem to apply to the rest of creation, so why is man, alone, singled out?

If such a custom is the tradition of the race of aliens, can we still consider them to be gods?

Because man was a modified duplicate of the aliens, biologically identical and compatible to them, he was, in essence, also an alien being. Therefore, as a member of this alien race, slave that he might be, he was still required to abide by the same rules and regulations that governed the conduct of the aliens. Even the aliens observed this custom.

Genesis 6:2: *"That the sons of God saw the daughters of men that they were fair; and they took them wives of all that they chose."*

Children were born of these unions; physical reproductions that could not have been possible unless both man and the aliens, were biologically compatible. Because of this compatibility, the gods were able to successfully have intercourse with the women, the daughters of men. From this intercourse children were conceived, were born and called the mighty men of old.

In order for this to happen both the gods and man, both species, must be flesh and blood kin. (Gen. 6:1-2). (Gen. 6:4). In creating Man, the gods, changed our genetic makeup so that our life span would not be equal to theirs.

Genesis 6:3: *"And the Lord said, My spirit shall not always strive with man, for that he also is flesh: yet his days shall be an hundred and twenty years."*

Somewhere in the genetic code of man is the gene that determines the length of his life. This gene was manipulated by the scientists when they decided on the makeup of man. The first men created lived for a very long time. It is possible that the length of their lives was first determined by the length of time the aliens expected to be on the planet. When they left those men who were still alive would be abandoned. This was before women and reproduction became a fact of life.

When God determined that it was about time for him to leave the planet he stated that the lifespan of man was to be cut to one hundred and twenty years. There must have been a reason for God to make this statement.

God and his crew owned, and supervised the humans under their control. They built a new society of alien beings. Only they were called man. Because man was created on this planet, he also came to be called an earthling.

All visitors from heavens will always be classified as alien whether we wish to call them gods or living creatures.

One day man will clone himself? When he does, will that clone be considered a slave, an individual little more than an animal? Will clones be recognized as true life forms? Will they have any legal rights or moral obligations because they were created by scientists outside the realm of natural childbirth? When they are created will these creations be considered as inferior beings and therefore slaves? To whom will they belong? Will the doctors and scientists who are able to being this new life into existence be worshipped as gods? And, if we should ever return to the dark ages, will our stories and legends of the above events make the ivory towers of today's medicine, the temples of tomorrow's worship?

When our gods, landed on earth, holy writ says that they planted a garden from which grew every tree which was pleasant to see and good for food. This statement indicates a planned and organized garden, one with specific plants. A garden by GOD would be randomly selected plants normally found in the wilds of nature not one under cultivation.

As living beings our gods required food and sustenance. After their long voyage through space, their food supplies would have been in short supply. Without the mother ship, those who were left behind on the planet had to establish a new and more readily available supply of food. They planted a garden in a temperate climate where crops could be raised year round. According to scripture, that location was on the east coast of central Africa in the land of Ethiopia.

Some have suggested, with good reason, that the original landing site of the aliens was somewhere in Central or South America. This reasoning is derived from the existence of the tunnels, the Nazca Lines and the Temple of the Sun in Tiahuanaco. The temple walls are lined with sculptured stone faces of men of almost every facial characteristic indicating that the temple might have been the cradle of mankind. This may be so, but, we are interested only in the company unit identified by the biblical records which indicate that mankind, as we know it today, had its' roots in east Africa. It was the unit of the Lord God, the creator of Man, as we know him today, and his subordinate, the Hebrew God Jehovah.

Both groups, the one in South America and the one in Africa, may have been a part of the same expedition, perhaps from the same culture, but representing different companies. The African unit is the one which we are concerned with. It was the camp of the Lord God, and man. It was set-up in Ethiopia, East Africa. This may well have been the camp of the original alien colonists, the first alien colonization attempt. The reason for this assumption are the enormous amount of skeletal remains found in Ethiopia dating back almost two million years.

Found here are the oldest skeletons known to exist. They are believed to be man's earliest ancestors. It is also the place the Bible indicates as the location of the Garden of Eden.

Saudi Arabia, Iraq, Iran and Syria, areas known as the fertile crescent are not known for such minerals. But Ethiopia and the mines of King Solomon are.

The above passage indicates that Eden might have been the name of the base camp only: it was situated at the head waters of the four rivers. From this location water went out of Eden to water the garden at some other location. It could not have been very far because the Lord God walked there in the cool of the evening.

A garden had been planted on the instructions of the Commander of the expedition, the Lord God. His crew knew how to accomplish such a task. Adam did not. Once the garden was growing Adam was taught how to tend it.

Adam was created as a naked dirt farmer, a slave to the Commander, the Lord God. Like the animals, he ate the herbs, seeds and fruit that he found around him. If Adam had a shelter it was one he made himself. Man did not wear clothes until Adam and Eve were given clothes by God when they were banned from the garden. Of course being near the equator, the climate was such that Adam and the other humans did not need protective clothing. Created as animals they were also not ashamed of their physical condition.

There were two other unusual things placed in the garden of God along with Adam and Eve. It was the "tree of life" and "the tree of the knowledge of good and evil."

Adam and Eve were forbidden to touch or go near the tree of knowledge so if it was not for the use of man who was it for, and why was it so important that it was planted in midst of the Garden? What purpose did it serve?

If the creator of Man was GOD, what would an omnipotent being, a spirit without form or substance, capable of living forever, need with a tree of life, or of a tree of the knowledge of good and evil, or of any of the things found in this garden?

It has been said by religious leader that evil cannot abide in the presence of God. This is not true. Evil is a civilized concept. It is any action that is considered by a civilized society to be beyond the best interest of that society.

Scripture say that Satan was evil because he convinced Eve to violated a commandment of the Lord God. Yet he stood face to face with the Jehovah when they discussed Job, a faithful servant of Jehovah.

The existence of tree of the knowledge of good and evil indicates that evil existed before the creation of man and that the tree or it's fruit had some connection with what was considered by the gods to be good and what they deemed evil. Evil is a concept. What is determined to be evil is in the mind of the receiver.

The Lord God and his alien race brought this tree with them and planted that particular tree in their garden. Man was not to touch this tree so how was he to tend it?

Evil, therefore, is a tenant of God himself. What kind of a tree might it have been, and why was it linked to the tree of life? The following is a suggested possibility.

The tree of the knowledge of good and evil was the coco plant. Why? Because it's leave have the power to alter the mind and consciousness of man? The effects of this plant are both good and bad.

Gods do not need the power or fruit of a particular tree in order for them to enjoy long life. For a god this would be a trait of his species. To obtain long life by eating of certain fruits and vegetables are the necessities of organic life, prolonged by the vitamins and minerals of those particular foods. The gods of early man enjoyed long life, and they knew the difference between good and evil, so there must be a logical explanation which explains the reasoning behind the planting and special care given to these two special plants.

One explanation which comes to mind is that the gods needed the tree of life for food. We know, or at least we are told indirectly that the tree of life was required by them as a part of their diet and their longevity.

Gen. 3:22: *"And the Lord God said, Behold the man is become as one of us, to know good and evil; and now lest he put forth his hand, and take also of the tree of life, and eat, and live forever."*

This is an unusual statement, since man had already been given permission to eat from this tree. Just to eat of the tree did not in itself guarantee immortality. If it had then the gods would not have needed to eat its fruit at regular intervals. Man was forbidden to eat or to touch only one plant, the tree of the knowledge of good and evil.

Whatever these two trees were, they were a part of the alien diet. One gave them life, and the other expanded their consciousness. It seems that the criteria for becoming a god was two fold. First, one must have access to the tree of life and second, one needed the knowledge of good and evil. Evil, therefore, existed long before man was created. It was the privileged domain of the gods.

If the gods never died once they had eaten of the tree of life, and they already knew the difference between good and evil, why did they plant these two special trees in the garden?

The tree of the knowledge of good and evil was evidently more prized to them than the tree of life because they forbid man even to touch it, much less eat its fruit. It must have been so important for their existence that they transported it across the galaxies in order to plant it here on earth.

When man was created he was innocent in all things. He only knew how to obey. When he did commit an act which was considered by the gods to be against their best interests he was punished. The act in it self was not evil but what we now call sin. Anything that is contrary to the will and commandments of the gods is classified by religion, as sin, Since there is a difference between sin that is not necessarily evil, evil must be something else.

Here the story of Adam, Eve, and original sin comes into play.

Eve committed a sin when she disobeyed the commandment not to eat or touch the fruit of the tree which was in the midst of the garden. But she knew only to obey the commands of the gods. If she was commanded or given permission to touch and eat of the tree of knowledge by Satan she did not commit a sin or do evil.

Man did not die, and the serpent did not lie. Gen. 3:22 confirms this. What did happen was that the minds of Adam and Eve were altered and expanded. They could understand the concept of good and evil. One ingredient which would create such a condition are the leaves of the coco shrub, which yield cocaine and other alkaloids.

The leaves of this shrub are sometimes chewed for their stimulant properties and used in the religious ceremonies of some South American Indians. The coco leaf, their legends say, was a gift to them from their gods. It controlled their hunger, warmed them on cold nights and eased their pain from the labours of the day.

Could this stimulant have been used by the gods to soothe the days and nights of their long journeys through space? If so they were addicted to it and brought their supply with them.

They would have planted such a tree in the middle of the garden where it would received the greatest protection. It would have guaranteed a steady supply of the drug required to meet their needs. It is the one tree that they would have forbidden the man to have access to.

Once Adam and Eve chewed the leaves of this tree, they experienced the effects of it's stimulants. Their minds expanded. They became aware of the sensations of the drug that has addicted so many thousands of individuals today. They may not have become addicted by just one use, but the experienced, the expansion of their mind, may have led to further use had they been allowed to remain in the garden.

The one thing which tends to support the idea that the tree of the knowledge of good and evil was the coco or a type of tree which had mine altering properties are the actions of Adam and Eve after they took the drug and began to feel it effects.

Gen. 3:6-7: "*And when the woman saw that the tree was good for food, and that it was pleasant to the eyes, and a tree to be desired to make one wise; she took of the fruit thereof, and did eat; and gave also unto her husband with her, and he did eat. 7. And the eyes of them both were opened, and they knew that they were naked: and they sewed fig-leaves together, and made themselves aprons.*"

Adam and Eve were like innocent children. They did not know nor does it appear that they had any idea as to what was and was not considered evil. When they ate from the tree they began to experience the kind of euphoria usually associated with mind expanding drugs. Even before they took the drug they knew they were naked. This was a natural condition to them and they were not embarrassed by that condition. Therefore, this was not the reason they tried to sew fig leaves together to make a covering for themselves. They also knew that the gods were different. They wore an outer coat of skin. They wore clothes.

Eve had been told by the serpent that once she ate from the tree that she would be as the gods to know not good from evil but good and evil.

Adam and Eve did know good and evil. They knew the good, the effects of the drug, a state of euphoria. When they came down from that euphoria and realized what they had done they knew that they had done something they had been forbidden to do and they were afraid. But, while under the influence of the drug they tried to imitate the gods. They tried to make themselves coats of skin. The most suitable material available were the leaves of the trees in the garden, the largest being the leaves of the fig tree. They chose that leaf to use as their material because the leaves of the fig tend to stick together when pressed against each other.

If they did in fact try to sew the leaves together, the idea of sewing pieces of material together had to have come from their observance of domestic servants doing the same thing to the clothes of the masters. They certainly did not learn to sew or to have obtain the idea out of thin air on the spur of the moment.

Adam and Eve, like our children today, were trying to play mama and daddy. Instead of mama's lipstick, and daddy's hat and tie, they tried to make and put on clothes. When the euphoria began to wear off and they began to come back to earth they realized what they had done and were ashamed. That is the reason they hid from the presence of the Lord God. Once Lord God realized what had happened, he knew that man had to be removed from the garden and no longer allowed access to the tree. If and when Adam and Eve became addicted they would no longer be trustworthy or dependable. Once the affects of the tree became know to the other humans, they to might try to obtain leaves for themselves. The gods would have trouble controlling the workers and the gods began to fear man.

Gen. 3:22-24. *And the Lord God said, Behold, the man is become as one of us, to know good and evil: and now, lest he put forth his hand, and take also of the tree of life, and eat, and live foe ever: 23. Therefore the Lord God sent him forth from the garden of Eden, to till the ground from whence he was taken. 24. So he drove out the man; and he placed at the east of the garden of Eden Cherubim, and a flaming sword which turned every way, to keep the way of the tree of life.*

This the Lord God could not allow Man to come to know the feeling and the euphoria of an expanded mind. He did not nor could he know from the one experience whether this was good or evil. This concept can only comes from the experiences, good or bad which result from taking the drug.

The continued experience with the drug would have made man completely unreliably. We know this from the problems society now experiences with addicts around the world.

It was the death of Man's innocence which was predicted by God, not his physical death. The death of man's innocence was also the end of the trustworthy relationship which existed between the Lord God and man. Man was no longer allowed to be in the presence of the Lord God himself.

When Eve yielded to temptation and tried the drug, it activated a part of her conscious mind beyond what was desired for Man at the time of his creation.

The disobedience to an order of God was and is considered a sin only by the church. Now that man was capable of independent thought, he became a danger to the creators.

The gods could no longer trust man to act or behave as they had been programmed to do. There was no way that Adam and Eve could explain to the other workers their expulsion from the garden without explaining why. Should the other workers attempt to gain access to the same drug, there would be havoc in the work place. The one compensation that Adam and Eve received were the coats of skin, clothes given to them to help protect them from the elements and identify them to the other workers as individual with special privileges. Their clothes set them apart from the other workers, perhaps even to the extent as to place them in a kind of isolated condition.

Gen. 3:17-19: *"And unto Adam he said, Because thou hast hearkened unto the voice of thy wife, and hast eaten of the tree of which I commanded thee, saying Thou shalt not eat of it: cursed is the ground for thy sake; in sorrow shalt thou eat of it all the days of thy life; 18. Thorns also and thistles shall it bring forth to thee; and thou shalt eat the herb of the field: 19. In te sweat of thy face shalt thou eat bread, till thou return unto the ground; for out of it wast thou taken: for dust thou art, and unto dust shalt thou return."*

In fear of man it became necessary for God and his men to forbid access to the garden. Not only was man forbidden to enter the garden, but to ensure that he obeyed, a protective shield was placed around the garden and guard dogs turned loose. The gods fully intend that the fruit of this particular tree remain secure for their private use only.

God's who can create universes, if they are gods, do not need to fear the actions of their creations. Men of science and technology do. The biblical gods were such beings. They were intelligent, but they were, nevertheless, afraid of Man. When our children try to imitates us by using our personal belongings they receive a scolding or a spanking, depending on the severity of what they have done. The punishment for Adam and Eve was to be placed outside of the protection of the garden, away from the Lord God.

They were no longer allowed access to the food, the special equipment of the gods, or the medical facilities. Adam had to work without implements. He had to work hard. Even then his reward was thorns and thistles.

The gods were like man, flesh and blood. They ate, drank, lusted, made laws and wore clothes. And according to their culture married and mated as husband and wife.

Adam and Eve were mated and Adam was told to leave a father and a mother which did not exist to care for the wife. They were commanded to unite and become one flesh, the reproduction of offspring, a condition that they knew nothing about because it had never happened before. They were given orders, and commands in terms which meant nothing to them. These commands did mean something to the gods. They constituted a stable way of life, a culture and tradition to the gods.

Where did all of these terms and 1conditions originate? They did not come from the air so they must have come from the social customs of the gods on the planet from which they came.

When the Lord God sent Adam and Eve from the garden he placed a barrier across the entrance. It was not to protect the tree of life but to ensure that Adam, Eve, and the other humans did not have access to the tree of knowledge.

In order to do this God placed "a flaming sword which turned every way, to keep the way of the tree of life." (Gen. 3:24.) This is so close to the description of a rotating searchlight, that it is hard to believe that it could have been anything else. Especially since it is described as a flaming sword. If man had been created by the Almighty, GOD, what and why would he need a flaming sword to protect the garden? The word sword is not a term which would mean anything to an omnipotent incorporeal being.

This flaming sword was placed at the garden entrance and lighted the entire area. It is possible that the garden was located in an area where it was also protected and surrounded by a compound barrier. It had to be in order to protect the garden from the predators of the night.

To a primitive, like Adam, the moving light of a searchlight would appear to be a flaming sword provided that he understood what a sword was.

How did the term sword, enter into the vocabulary of two innocent people like Adam and Eve? Probably the same way that words such as cattle, sheep and herbs became familiar to man. They were a part of the language, and the culture of the aliens.

In addition to the perimeter lights, the garden (or the base camp) of the aliens was protected by the Cherubim. They were animals similar to the guard dogs we use today, but far more sophisticated. They both protected the compound and gave the Lord God his transportation.

2 Sam.22:11: *"And he rode upon a cherub, and did fly: and he was seen upon the wings of the wind."*

Were the Cherubim genetic clones, who served the living creatures, the Lord God and his crew, or were they a race of beings which were under the control and servitude of the gods?

The Lord God and his crew, like Man, knew what fear was. For God and his crew, fear was not knowing the results of Man's actions when under the influence of the tree of knowledge.

God controlled, but he required both protection and transportation. This he obtained from his servants, the Cherubim. With them and their power, he was the ultimate authority. And in accordance with biblical scripture he used that authority with kindness and tolerance. He owned, controlled, was feared and protected by those who served him.

They called upon his name, paid homage, tribute and respect. It was his due because of his position of authority and it was not out of any fear of retribution.

The title of "The First Godfather" is reserved for Jehovah, the God of the Hebrews, Abraham, Isaac and Jacob. He was a lowly sub lieutenant of the Lord God.

Able and not Cain was the first true human, a hybrid from a cloned father and mother created out of the DNA material of the Lord God. They were created beings. Cain however was not. He was born to a human mother but sired by an alien father. Like Isaac, Sampson, and Jesus he was one of the mighty men of old, half human and half god.

The creation of Adam and Eve as a modified species of the aliens, makes mankind a sub species of their race and therefore through their DNA their descendants.

If Adam did not "know" Eve until after they were expelled from the garden, then sex was not the cause of the sin which the religious community believes caused their expulsion from the garden. They were commanded by God to be fruitful and multiply. They could not do this without sex, therefore sex was not their sin. But the statement made by Eve, "I have gotten a man from the Lord", clearly indicates that the Lord had something to do with the birth of Cain.

Even though Adam "knew" his wife, did the Serpent, her immediate supervisor also "know" her just as Jehovah is said to "know" Mary? Is it possible that Cain was the son of the Lord God and Eve, just as Jesus was suppose to be the son of Jehovah and Mary? Could Adam have been the earthly and surrogate father of Cain, just as Joseph was the father of Jesus?

In "Hebrew Myths, The Book of Genesis", by Graves and Patai, chapter 14, "THE BIRTHS OF CAIN AND ABEL" Samael or Satan is mentioned as the father of Cain. It also indicated that Eve was not the first woman, but Lilith, a woman of demonic passions. She is said to have been the mother of Cain.

The confusion concerning these two women and the beginning of the human race is justified by the statement made by Eve in certain translations of scripture, which say, "I have gotten a man-child from Yahweh!"

Cain is therefore the first human being born by natural birth on the planet, but for discussion purposes, the father of Cain becomes a critical issue. Was it Yahweh, Samael, or Adam? If it were Yahweh or Samael, then Cain is half god and half man and like Adam, not a true human. Abel, on the other hand, was by his birth to Adam and Eve, the first true human. After his death, Seth became the father of all true humans.

Gen. 4:25: *"And Adam knew his wife again, and she bare a son, and called his name Seth: For God, said she, hath appointed me another seed instead of Abel, whom Cain slew."*

Cain is not mentioned as having been her son or seed. The passage indicated that Abel was her only son until she bare Seth. Therefore, if this passage is true, then Cain could have been the son of either Lilith or Eve.

The children of Seth were nomads, farmers, and sheep herders. The descendants of Cain, the blue-blooded aristocracy became the builders, the innovators, the thinkers and rulers.

Cain was the progenitor of a new race of beings. As half a god, he was marked and protected by the Lord God for the accidental death of Abel. The Lord God could not destroy one of his own kind, even a half breed, for the death of a slave.

On the other hand if Adam was the true father of Cain. then the Lord may have assisted in the pregnancy and birth of Cain in order to insure that the reproduction of Man was certain. In any event, it was through Cain and his descendants that mankind can thank for its progress, culture and civilization.

For centuries Cain has been chastised because of the death of Abel. If one analysed the biblical passages relating to the incident that resulted in Abel's death one finds the following:

Adam, Eve, Cain and Abel were the caretakers and personal property of the leader of the expedition, the Lord God. Abel was responsible for raising, the sheep and cattle used for meat, wool and milk. Cain rise the grain that was made into flour and bread. Adam and Eve cared for the garden and raised the vegetables used by the gods in their daily meals. When required, they all served and presented food items to God for his table.

At some time during one of those presentations, the grain and or vegetables offered by Cain were either meagre or of such poor quality, that he was admonished by the Lord God.

It is evident that Abel's sheep were fat and healthy, because God was pleased with them. What did Abel feed his sheep that made them so fat and healthy? Upon what did they graze? There were no fences, so they grazed wherever they wanted or wherever they were lead by Abel.

It is highly possible that Abel allowed his sheep to graze in the fields of Cain. When they did, they ate or destroyed his crop. What he was able to present to the Lord was what he was able to salvage from his field.

I am only guessing but I would image that after being admonishment by God, Cain talked with Abel and asked him to keep his sheep out of his fields. Abel made a joke out of the incident, teased Cain, and deliberately allowed his sheep to get into Cain's field again, otherwise, Abel would not have been in the same field with Cain when he was killed. Cain would have been there tending to his crops, but Abel and his sheep should have been in other pastures where they belonged. If Abel had not been in Cain's field, there would not have been an argument, no fight, and Cain would not have accidentally killed Abel.

Cain was merely trying to protect his crop from being eaten and destroyed by the sheep of Abel. He was trying to get them out of his field. The killing of Abel was not deliberate, but accidental.

Gen. 4:8: *"And Cain talked with Abel his brother: and it came to pass when they were in the field, that Cain rose up against Abel his brother, and slew him."*

Today we are aware of the many problems which confront members of the same family. These problems often lead to violence, and sometimes to accidental death. Individuals can only accept so much punishment and abuse before they retaliate and begin defending themselves. Cain was no different. Abel pushed him to far and Cain retaliated. Since death was unknown to humans at the time, there was no way that Cain could have known that his actions would result in the death of Abel. Since the act of killing was not deliberate it becomes an accident.

Because of this, the Lord did not punish Cain, but transferred him to another groups of individuals located away from the garden and presence of the Lord God. When he did, he also placed on Cain a condition which would ensure his protection and safety from the people which he was to meet. The Lord God place a mark on Cain so that all who saw him, would know and fear him. They would also know that he was under the protection of the Lord God. And if the Lord God protected Cain and did not find fault with the death of Abel why does man feel justified in forever condemning him as a murderer, which he was not.

Gen. 4:15: *"And the Lord said unto him, Therefore whosoever slayeth Cain, vengeance shall be taken on him sevenfold. And the Lord set a mark upon Cain, lest any finding him should kill him."*

When Adam and Eve were dismissed from the presence of God they were given a suit of clothes, or coats of skins, which identify them as the property of God himself. Cain was identified as the property of God by a special mark place upon him to ensure that everyone knew that he was under the protection of God himself.

Since then, that mark has been one of the great mysteries of man. It still is, but we can make some assumptions as to what it might have been by a review of myths and legends Over the years many theories have been suggested as to what or how Cain was marked. Here is one more.

The garden of Eden, and the area where Cain lived at the time of his expulsion was in Ethiopia. The skin of Cain was dark, as are the skins of all those who are native to the tropics.

There is one condition of Man, one identifying mark, existing to this day, in every culture around the world which promotes fear and awe in people. That mark or stigma promotes fear, avoidance, awe and/or respect in everyone who comes into direct contact with the individual who bears that mark. Those who bear this mark or affliction are avoided by his fellows as if they carried the plague. That condition is a bleached skin, or the lack of skin pigment, causing a person to be labelled an Albino. There is no other mark like it i the world. It is unique unto itself.

Even the native American Indians on the warpath, having had very little contact with white men, were said to avoid a person with this affliction. Even their legends said that to have a bleached skin was a mark of God. This mark placed albinos under the protection of God and as such, they were never to be harmed without the fear of Gods' wrath.

When Cain left the camp of God it was as an albino, he went east to the land of Nod.

According to the "New Compact Bible Dictionary", he began to wander. Out of the presence of the Lord, he "knew" his wife, had a child, and built a city.

Cain's pigmentation was altered in order to make him an albino, that change may have been carried forward into the genetic makeup of his children. The combination of the white skin of Cain and the black skin of his wife might account for the beginning of the Caucasian race. The subtle changes of the skin pigmentation came about over many decades due to both the environment and change in diet.

As the children and descendants of Cain moved out into the world and away from Africa, the changes in their environment, food and sun intensity, over time, lighten and changed the colour of their skin. The heavy pigmentation of the African jungle was no longer needed for their survival. The further north the descendants went the lighter their skin became.

Cain and his descendants gave us many things besides the beginning of the Caucasian race and his claim to fame as the first killer of Man.

1. He was a farmer and a builder of cities: from him we obtained agriculture and construction.
2. His children gave us:
    a. Jabal: "the father of such as dwell in tents, and of such as have cattle.": herding livestock.
    b. Jubal: "the father of all such as handle the harp and organ.": music and instruments.

c. Tubalcain: "an instructor of every artificer in brass and iron.": business and industry.

In order for the above to have taken place someone had to teach early Man. There had to be instructors. Those instructors were the aliens, "The Living Creatures".

As the workers reproduced, their children were taught, not only the skills of their parents but those which made the lives of the aliens a little more tolerable.

The descendants of Cain learned how to make threads from the sheep's wool, weave it into the cloth that make the clothes and tents which protected the aliens and human from the weather, the rain, heat and cold. Humans were taught how to make and to play musical instruments, and they were taught how to process ore, smelt and refined the metals into brass and iron implements.

Who determined what was to be mined and the type of work to be done? It was the Lord God.

Gen. 2:11-12: *"The name of the first is Pison: that is it which compasseth the whole land of Havilah, where there is gold; 12. And the gold of that land is good: there is bdellium and the onyx-stone."*

What was valuable to God has become valuable to man.

During all of the time the created men were doing the work of the Lord God, they were under the supervision of the crewmen of God. These crewmen, are called by us today angels or messengers. During the time of Adam they were called the sons of God. After the time of the flood and the departure of the lord God to his home planet, the sons of God left behind as his stewards became the gods and entities worshipped by the descendants of those who had been under their command and control. They are the other gods which made Jehovah so angry and jealous that he pledged to remove their memory from the mind of man.

During the beginning time the Bible says that men began to call upon the name of God, their individual supervisors for their help, protection and guidance. Today this passage (Gen. 4:26) is taken to mean the beginning of worship and sacrifice to God.

At the beginning it was not so. As man began to multiply it became necessary for him, as a slaves to have a protector, as well as a supervisor and overseer. The name of the individual supervisor, owner, or God of each special group became their way of identification.

I am the property of this God or that god. I am under his protection. I belong to this tribe or that tribe.

When the slaves began to offer gifts, thought pleasing to their god, it was because they believed those gifts would help them to obtain favours, blessings, and relief from oppression. It was also their obligation, their duty and their daily chore.

Genesis 4:26: *"And to Seth, to him also there was born a son; and he called his name Enos; then began men to call upon the name of the Lord."*

Calling upon the name of the Lord" has been confused with the offer of sacrifices and gifts to God. Offerings and gifts were the food which the servants brought to the table of the Lord from the very beginning. The killing and cooking of meat was a part of the service that pleased the gods. Later Man forgot the original purpose of these gifts and wanton sacrificial killing was begun.

When Cain and Abel brought their foods to the table of the Lord it was not as a sacrifice but as a duty, a daily chore. When men began to call upon the name of the Lord it was with a different purpose in mind. The gifts were given to the individual gods, their supervisors, in much the same way that we use our gifts today. The gifts were given with the intension of obtaining a hearing, a petition to obtain redress for a wrong, grievance, or to receive a particular favour.

The supervisors accepted these gifts on behalf of the Lord God and supposedly relayed the gifts and the requests to the Lord God. The supervisors would then relay back to the petitioner, the ruling of the Lord God.

In time, the gifts never left the possession of the supervisor to which they and their grievances were first presented. This custom must have made some of the supervisors very rich and very powerful.

The presentation of gifts is a custom which has been handed down to us from generation to generation. Rulers, men of authority and even Jehovah demanded and received such gifts in return for favours rendered. Today religious disciples of all faiths offer gifts to their god in the hope of the forgiveness of sin, a reward or to give thanks for blessings received.

These offerings, given to the individual gods, are not used by that god, but by the heads of the particular faiths. The gifts are used by the clergy of the faith as they deem best. Usually what is deemed best by the clergy is what is in their best interest.

The giving of gifts, in the hope of a reward such as forgiveness or blessings, has been handed down to us from the laws and commandments given to the Hebrew nation as the will of Jehovah. It was certainly not required as such by the Lord God. At least such a practice is not mentioned before the time of the flood.

The practice of gift giving is so prevalent that it extends to the halls of industry, where gift-giving is done in the hope of a promotion, a sale, or some favourable consideration.

Early Man served the gods as a normal part of their everyday lives. It was at this period of time that the half-breed children, the offspring of the aliens and daughters of men, began to be born. And it was at this time that God is supposed to have said that evil was in the hearts of men and that he was going to destroy them all.

There was no evil in the hearts of men except what was put there by the gods themselves. Problems did arise between men but it was as a result of the half breed children born out of wedlock between the aliens and man. These half breed children, because of their father's power, began to exercise their authority over their human companions. This created conflict. A conflict which the oppressed humans tried to resolve by gifts and petitions to their immediate supervisors. Man had learned even then that certain things seem to please the gods more than others.

I am sure that sometimes justice was rendered by the god supervisors, but I believe that in time the idea became a nuances to God and he told the crew, his supervisors to take care of those matters themselves. The gifts intended for God, were kept by the supervisors. They rendered justice according to their own rules. And granted favours as they deem best.

It is no different today. Employers today, and as the kings, and rulers of the past have always done, continue to except the gifts of subordinates as a part of their role as the ruler, leader and master of the masses.

The Lord God, walked and talked with man. While he and his crew mingled with and used the slaves, under their control they also taught and looked after them.

The gifts of today, given to the church as gifts to God, have made many of the servants of God very rich. Today, instead of the crew of god getting rich within the religious communities, it is the pastors, and the intermediaries that enjoy the gifts and make the decisions for God.

When mankind was left alone by the Lord God after the flood and was no longer required to serve and offer up sacrifices, out of habit and tradition he began to initiate his own religious rituals. These rituals, revised, and amplified to suit changing conditions and circumstances have continued until today. Some of those manmade religious rituals included the sacrificial killing of animals, virgins and children.

The killing and preparation of meat and food for the table of the Lord God was one of the job tasks assigned to early man before the flood. This service ritual was renewed by Jehovah and Noah after the flood. It continued until the time of Abraham when even the killing of children was considered a required ritual. It was a ritual that Abraham must have been familiar with and might even have practiced at sometime in his travels. Otherwise he would not have been familiar enough with the ceremonial rites required when he took his son Isaac to the mountain altar to become one of those sacrifices to God. He was prepared with all of the essentials required for a blood sacrifice.

Religious sacrifices, during the time of Abraham, all seem to have had the same basic criteria. Only certain living things were allowed to be offered. They had to be killed, cooked and the remains disposed of in a specific way. What made these burnt offerings so desirable to the people were the thoughts of the biblical writers who, by tradition, stated the thoughts the Lord God is supposed to have uttered in his heart when he smelled a sweet savour, the roasting meat, the burning flesh of the animals being sacrificed. This was not for man but the gods.

Gen. 8:21-22: *"And the Lord smelled a sweet savour; and the Lord said in his heart, I will not again curse the ground any more for man's sake; for the imagination of man's heart is evil from his youth: neither will I again smite any more every thing living, as I have done. 22. While the earth remaineth, seed-time and harvest, and cold and heat, and summer and winter, and day and night, shall not cease."*

How can this be a true statement if Revelation is also true. This same God who claims he will never again destroy every living thing on earth turns right around and in Revelation plans to destroy man, and life as we know it to be. That is unless the reader realizes that the above statement was made by the Lord God, the creator of man and that the destruction of the world related in Revelation will be by the hand of Jehovah, the God of the Christian and Jew.

The God of Revelation is the Hebrew God Jehovah. It is he and not the Lord God and Satan who will be the destroyer of the world.

Sacrificial burnt offering to the gods have been carried over into almost every culture in the world. This practice of burning sacrifices to please the senses of the gods has evolved into the process of cremation which exists even today.

In some parts of the world, humans are still sacrificed to the gods and the spirits of ancestors. Today, however, the sacrifices, unlike those of the past, are already dead. It is the way of some individual cultures which required that the remains of the dead be cremated.

In some parts of the world the cremation occurs on open pyres which allow the departing spirit of those who have died to be carried on the ascending smoke, heat and winds to heaven, to the abode of the gods. In others, like the United States, the cremation takes place in a crematorium.

What nobler way can a devoted disciple offer themselves to their God than as a burnt offering. An offering that is sure to please the senses of the gods.

Since the gods can enjoy the sweet smell of roasting meat, it is far better to offer them a roasting cadaver than a decayed corpse, filled with disease and corruption rotting in a grave.

With fire, all of the disease and corruption of a man is cleansed away and his purified spirit is free to rise up and stand up in judgement before his god.

History records that Children were, in many religions, a vital part of some local religious sacrificial offerings. Why has been a question which has perplexed mankind for many decades. Added to this mystery was the strange command given by Jehovah that every firstborn, human or animal, that opened the matrix was to be given to him. What would a god want with all of these new born creatures?

Recently certain medical practices, occurring in private clinics around the world, have been made public. It may be a coincidence but it brings a very harsh reality to God, his demands, his longevity and the practice of child sacrifices.

In some countries of Europe there are clinics where those individuals of exception wealth and a desire to appear young can go for rejuvenation treatments. This treatment calls for the cells of certain organs from either newborn babies or unborn fetus to be injected into a receptive host. The effect of these new cells upon the host are said to do remarkable things.

There is no bodily rejection of these new cells. Evidently the new cells are able to enhance or replace the old dying and dead cells of the brain and body. This rejuvenation process gives to the host a new feeling of health and vibrancy. The whole physical structure of the host takes on the appearance of youth.

Could this medical procedure been one of the ways by which the gods stayed young or at least lived to become very old? Did the gods feed on the very young? Or where the children offered up to God, medically used to increase their longevity? Was this the basis or one of the reasons that people, in their misunderstanding of the medical procedure of god, offer up their children as religious sacrifices to the god of their particular culture? Was this the reason that God said the following:

Exodus 22:29-30: *"Thou shalt not delay to offer the first of thy ripe fruits, and of thy liquors: the firstborn of thy sons shalt thou give unto me. 30. Likewise shalt thou do with thine oxen, and with thy sheep: seven days it shall be with his dam; on the eighth day thou shalt give it to me."*

Was God using the cells of the new born of each of these individuals in some special way which prolonged his life and that of his crew? A case could certainly be made to that affect. It should ne noted that this was not a demand from the Lord God by his subordinate after he had left the planet and his power as Lord God to Jehovah.

From Cain and his descendants we have received agriculture, industry, civilized society, music and culture. From Seth and his descendants we have received the debased morals of Abraham, the atrocities of Joshua, the pacification of Jesus and the laws of Jehovah, the Godfather.

Much of what we are today, our morals, our altitudes, and our beliefs are those which were intertwined with what our fathers were taught, observed or learned from the Living Creature, and the half breeds that controlled and ruled our cultures over the eons of the past. We are the end result of the blue blooded rulers of man, the sons and daughters of the interbreeding between the man and the aliens sons of god.

Gen. 6:1-7 *"And it came to pass, when men began to multiply on the face of the earth, and daughters were born unto them. The sons of God saw the daughters of men that they were fair; and they took them wives of all which they chose. And the Lord God said my Spirit shall not always strive with man, for that he also is flesh; yet his days shall be an hundred and twenty years. There were giants in the earth in those days; and also after that, when the sons of God came in unto the daughters of men, and they bore children to them: the same became mighty men, which were of old, men of renown. And God saw that the wickedness of man was great in the earth, and that every imagination of the thoughts of his heart was only evil continually. And it repented the Lord that he had made man on the earth, and it grieved him at his heart. And the Lord said, I will destroy man whom I have created from the face of the earth; both man and beast, and the creeping thing, and the fowls of the air; for it repented me that I have made them."*

From the above scripture the following becomes quite evident:

That the sons of God were different from the daughters of men. They were in control because they, like the slave owners of the old south, could take whatever they wanted from man, their slaves. Either the sons of gods were his actual sons, which means that he was married, or the sons were the beings that we call angels, messengers, or crewmen of God. They were not the sons of Adam, as is so often implied by the church clergy.

Though there is a cultural distinction between the two races, verse three indicates that both were flesh and blood. The difference between the two was not biological but their life span and intellectual level. Even this is debatable when one reads Gen. 11:6. *"And the Lord said, Behold, the people is one, and they have all one language; and this they begin to do: and now nothing will be restrained from them, which they have imagined to do."*

Gen 6:3 also implies that God and his crew were working together, striving for a common goal. A situation which God says will not continue forever. There would come a time when the Lord God would either die or have to leave the earth, and man would no longer be under his protection. This occurrence may have been indicated by Gen. 5:22-24, when God left the earth and took Enoch with him.

The Lord God and his angels, or crewmen, used the women of early man, just as men of wealth and power have always used women. They were used as, slaves, mistresses or as prostitutes, to satisfy their sexual desires. The children born of these unions having the genetic characteristics and intelligence capability of their fathers, possessed a greater potential for power and intellectual achievement than their more human counterparts. They used that power to become the kings and rulers of men.

They were the mighty men of old, the half-breed children of gods and humans. They became the blue blooded aristocracy, the rulers by the divine authority of God.

This co-habitation between the god race and the human sub species is what generated the Lord God declared to be the wickedness of man. It was not man, but the acts of the gods with man which troubled the Lord God and caused him to regret creating man in the first place.

The Lord God was faced with a dilemma no different than that faced by every army general who has ever commanded a fighting force during a war of conquest and occupation.

During both world wars, the men and women of our nation co-habited with the men and women of the conquered countries. As long as the fraternization between our forces and the those of the enemy were by mutual consent and was strictly sexual in nature, there appear to have been no problems.

When fraternization went beyond those bounds problems arose for the generals and commanding officers of every force.

There were always a few individuals who desired to go beyond simple relationships. These individuals wanted to marry and bring home to this nation and to their families, brides and spouses from the nations which had been our enemy. The men of their armed forces had attacked and killed many of the neighbours, friends and family of this country. They were not welcomed here. They were considered inferior individuals.

The Lord God was faced the same problems as our generals. Members of his crew had married and had children from the women of slaves, a sub species, the ones he called human.

The sexual acts of his crew, and those acts which led to marriage and children, were blamed on the seductive power of the daughters of men.

He could not take these slaves home with him. They were inferior beings. It is possible that a few of his men refused to return to their home world and wished to remain here on earth with their families. Here they would be gods and their families rich and powerful. At home they would be considered little more than the slaves they brought home with them. After our world wars we found the same kind of reality among our own military. There were many individuals who wished to remain in the country of occupation rather than return to what they considered a lesser existence in this country.

With the choice between the life styles and the living conditions between here and their home world a few of the crew of God decided to stay on this planet.

The choice for the Lord God was made easier by the knowledge of the incoming asteroid and the impending collision. The destruction of this world, the flooding and environmental changes which were about to occur would help resolve many of his social problems. The slave women and their children would be destroyed and the problem eliminated.

However, the Lord God, as the representative of his company, and in good conscious, was obligated to at least try and salvage as much of his property and the colonizing attempt as possible. He had Noah construct the ark as a possible solution.

A couple of hundred years after the flood when it had been determined that the mines were no longer workable due to the lack of adequate equipment and skilled labour a decision was made to return to the home world. It was at that time that the Lord God decided to leave behind those individual crewmen who had earthly wives and children. They would act as his stewards and would look after his or rather the company property until such a time when a return to the planet was possible.

He transferred his authority to Jehovah and divided his earthly possessions and responsibilities amongst those crewmen who were to remain on the earth.

It would appear that according to Hebrew history these gods remained active in their use of earth women for their sexual gratification. It appears that every time a great man is mentioned in the Bible an angel has always been somehow involved:
1. Ishmael - Gen.16:11,
2. Isaac - Gen. 17:21,
3. Samson - Judges 13:3,
4. Samuel - 1 Samuel 2:21,
5. John the Baptist - St. Luke 1:13
6. Jesus - St. Luke 1:28.

There are many other individuals, in the religious literature of many nationalities who are believed to have been the sons and perhaps the daughters of the gods. These men and women were all considered to have been born to greatness.

There was the Buddha, whose birth brought light and healing to the whole world. There were also men like Pythagoras, Zoroaster,

Apollonius of Tyana, and Alexander the Great. These were all men credited with great powers and believed to have had mixed parents-one human and the other a god.

Like the early daughters of men, Mary, the mother of Jesus, was visited and impregnated by one of the beings the Christian religion calls the Lord God or the Holy Ghost? Even though Jesus is called the son of God, it appears in religious text that he may actually have been the son of one of the angels, a being called Gabriel.

According to St. Luke, one of the gospel writers of the Christian New Testament, the Angel Gabriel appeared before Mary and informed her that she was to bear a son, conceived by the Holy Ghost.

A couple of things need to be mention about these particular passages.

In Gen. 6:4 it reads, *There were giants in the earth in those days; and also after that, when the sons of God (came in unto) the daughters of men, and they bore children to them, the same became mighty men which were of old, men of renown.*

If the words "came in unto" in Gen. 6:4 refers to sexual intercourse, then the same words spoken to Mary must mean the same thing. Gabriel was speaking of a sexual relationship. Jesus became one of those mighty men of old.

He was promised the throne of his ancestor David which was the throne of Israel, an earthly throne. It never came to pass. Even though Jesus was the heir apparent to the throne of Israel, he never became its King. He was believed by many to be the Messiah that would free the Israelites for the yoke of their Roman oppressors. He was not.

As I understand from Hebrew myths and legends there have been many Messiahs which have come and gone down through the ages. Even though these Messiahs have had their followers, the Jewish people still believe that the true Messiah is still to come. While Christians believe that the promised Messiah was Jesus, the Jewish nation does not. They are still waiting.

There is ample reason why the Jewish people have followed different Leaders and believe them to be holy and inspired by their god. When one reads and studies the history and the writings of their prophets, it seems that most of the truly great men of Israel were in some way or another connected to the angels of God.

After the flood, men began to multiply and to put to use the skills taught to them by the gods, their fathers, and the sons of Noah. Their first attempt was the recorded edifice known as the Tower of Babel. It was started by the people who desiring to make a name for themselves and to build a stairway that would reach to the heavens and the abode of God.

Today we realize how foolish this idea was. The gods however, knowing the degree of intelligence and the training they had given man, fearful of what he might be capable of doing, separated the people and scattered them across the face of the earth. To further complicate the issue and to add to the confusion, the one basic language of man was changed and divided into many dialects.

In order to do this God and his staff had to come down from heaven because he had no divine heavenly power. Men, women and children were picked up and transported to the far reaches of the globe by the space ships of God. The memory of this event have been kept alive over the centuries in the legends of flying carpets.

Gen. 11:5: *"And the Lord came down to see the city and the tower, which the children of men built."*

If the Lord God was an omnipotent spirit why was it necessary for him to come to the earth in order to see for himself what he should have known as a god with divine and heavenly power? When he did, what he saw made them afraid.

Gen. 11:6-9: *"And the Lord said, behold, the people is one and they have all one language: and this they begin to do: and now nothing will be restricted from them, which they imagined to do. Go to, let us go down, and there confound their language, that they may not understand one another's speech So the Lord scattered them abroad from thence upon the face of all the earth: and they left off to build the city. Therefore is the name of it called Babel, because the Lord did there confound the language of all the earth: and from thence did the Lord scatter them abroad upon the face of all the earth."*

The Bible indicates that it was about this time that the Lord God departed the earth. When he did, he left Jehovah in charge, and willed to Jehovah and the other members of the occupational force their inheritance and areas of responsibility.

To Jehovah he gave only his authority and his grandson Jacob as property. To the other crewmembers he entrusted the care and responsibility of the humans under their control.

It should be noted that the children of Israel in the above passage does not refer to the descendants of Jacob but to the people who worked with the Lord God before his departure from earth, for the word Israel as defined in the Zondervan Compact Bible dictionary means, "He strives with God and prevails". This term strongly indicates that the term was in existence before Jacob, and referred to all of those humans who worked, walked and talked with the Lord God before the flood.

Jehovah became the overseer of the property of God. This property included the descendants of Adam and Eve through Seth, Methuselah, Lamech, Noah and Shem, the oldest son of Noah, to Abraham, Isaac and finally Jacob. Were Jehovah the Lord God of all the descendants of Adam and Eve then this would have included the descendants of Noah's other two sons as well. This might possibly have been true if only Noah and his sons had survived the flood. But according to scripture they were not.

Nowhere does the bible give any indication that Jehovah was more than an administrative assistant to the Lord God. He had no slaves of his own, or his inheritance would have included them along with Jacob and his descendants.

The other members of Gods' crew did own property. Their slaves were the workers who were under their command and control before the flood. They were the gods spoken of in Deu. 32.

Jehovah had more to worry about beside Jacob and his administrative responsibilities. He had his own rebellious sons and daughters to contend with. And according to Deu.32, they made his life a living hell.

Jehovah did not marry yet he managed to accumulate many sons and daughters. Who were the mothers? If he did not obtain them through marriage, he must have either own slaves of some kind or as a son of the Lord God, he took wives of all the women he desired, including Sarah and later Mary.

This idea of taking a female companion when ever the urge to procreate occurred appears to have been a custom that Jehovah and his men continued down through the years. It was a custom which produced men like Isaac, Samson, Samuel, John the Baptist and Jesus.

Before the flood, the gods and Man worked together. It was this close relationnship, and the intermarriages between the races which generated the problems with other humans that led to the evil the Lord God referred to in Genesis 6:5-6.

The evil which is referred to in biblical scripture is defined in the New Compact Bible Dictionary as "that which is not in harmony with the divine order."

For the gods of the universe, that meant the elevation of a lessor species to the status of the gods themselves. This happened when the gods began to take advantage of their power and position in order to possess the women of earth. This led to children, who became the mighty men of old. They like their fathers, also used their status to abused their fellow humans.

This abomination got out of hand, and created problems which the Lord God, as the alien Commander, found difficult to resolve. This accounts for his statement of regret in creating man and a desire to destroy what was.

The fact that animals were included in this plan of destruction could only have resulted from the degenerative habits of man which included animals in their mating rituals, ceremonies and orgies.

These rituals have been verified by archeological finds. While interbreeding between man and animals was an impossibility, the sexual rituals were not. This mating between man and animals began with the Lord God and his desire to create animals capable of assisting Adam and early man with their earthly chores.

Again man is being punished for the acts of the gods. The gods created the animals and brought them to Adam as help mates.

Out of all of these especially created animals none were found to be sexually compatible with Adam. They could not have been the same animals and fowl as those created before Man, those which are mentioned in Gen.1:21-25. Therefore the animals made for Adam were genetic hybrids designed to work side by side with him.

Mans' sexual escapades with animals, and the interbreeding between the gods and Man, were no different than similar situations which occur during every war or operation of conquest throughout the long history of Man.

Conquering armies, often raped, pillaged, and consider as spoils of war, the women, children and wealth of the conquered people. To the men of battle, if there were no normally acceptable outlets for sexual gratification available at the time, often found unorthodox ways of satisfying those desires. It may have been with one's self, with the same gender, with animals or by artificial means, but gratification was found. This tradition of rape and pillage was amply demonstrated not only by the Germans and the Japanese during World War II but by the Hebrew nation on their way to the promise land.

Even Jehovah recognized this weakness in man. In was so prevalent that specific laws were laid down to forbid such practices. These laws still exist. They are strictly enforced by our military courts today.

Exod. 22:19: *"Whoever lieth with a beast shall be put to death."*

Lev. 20:13: *"If a man also lie with mankind, as he lieth with a woman, both of them have committed an abomination: they shall surely be put to death; their blood shall be upon them."*

With a couple of exceptions found in the Bible and Jewish history, rape was an accepted practice by all invading armies. Since then it has been condemned by almost every civilized society. On the other hand prostitution and fraternization have not.

In the history of the Israelite nation, in at least one special circumstance, rape was decreed by the congregation as an accepted solution to a situation they created for themselves. Judges 20:6-25.

When the angels of God were said to have visited Lot in Sodom, the men of Sodom wanted to know them. Lot was so afraid of the what the men of the city might do to him and his male guests that he was willing to allow his two virgin daughters to be raped in order to satisfy the desires of the townsmen rather than turn the strangers over to them.

Gen. 19:5-8: *"And they called unto Lot, and said unto him, Where are the men which came in to thee this night? Bring them out unto us, that we may know them. And Lot went out at the door unto them, and shut the door after him and said, I pray you, brethren, do not so wickedly. Behold now, I have two daughters which have not known man; let me, I pray you, bring them out unto you, and do ye to them as is good in your eyes only unto these men do nothing; for therefore came they under the shadow of my roof."*

Another, but similar incident occurred involving a Levite. This time the consequences were different.

A Levite was travelling with his wife, a concubine, when he stopped for the night in a village of the tribe of Benjamin. He was given shelter by an old man of the town. The young men of the village, hearing of this, like the men of Sodom, wanted the Levite to come out and let the men of the town know him.

Again, like Lot, the Levite and the old man offered to the men of the town the daughter of the old man and the wife of the Levite. They were offered to the men of the city to do with them whatever they desire. The men took the concubine and abused her all night. In the morning she crawled back to the door of the old man's house and there she died. In the morning when the Levite was leaving he made no effort to care for her wounds. He told her to get up so that they could be on their way.

When the Levite realized that she was dead and unable to get up, he picked her up, put her on the back of an ass and took her to his house. There he cut her into twelve pieces and sent the pieces to the twelve tribes with his version of the death of the concubine. The congregations of the tribes were horrified by this act of atrocity committed against the concubine.

Were they horrified by the rape or that the Levite had cut her up into pieces and had the gall to sent these pieces of rotting flesh to the congregations of the tribes?

Judges 19: 20-30: *"And the old man said, Peace be with thee; howsoever, let all thy wants lie upon me; only lodge not in the street. So he brought him into his house, and gave provender unto the asses: and they washed their feet, and did eat and drink. Now as they were making their hearts merry, behold, the men of the city, certain sons of Belial, beset the house round about, and beat at the door, and spake to the master of the house, the old man, saying, Bring forth the man that came into thine house, that we may know him. And the man, the master of the house, went out unto them, and said unto them, Nay, my brethren, nay, I pray you, do not so wickedly; seeing that this man is come into mine house, do not this folly. Behold, here is my daughter, a maiden, and his concubine; them I will bring out now, and humble ye them, and do with them what seemeth good unto you: but unto this man do not so vile a thing. But the men would not hearken to him: so the man took his concubine, and brought her forth unto them; and they knew her, and abused her all the night until the morning: and when the day began to spring, they let her go. Then came the women in the dawning of the day and fell down at the door of the man's house where her lord was, till it was light. And her lord rose up in the morning, and opened the doors of the house, and went out to go his way: and behold, the woman his concubine was fallen down at the door of the house, and her ands were upon the threshold. And he said unto her, Up, and let us be going. But none answered. Then the man took her up upon an ass, and the man rose up, and gat him unto his place. And when he was come into his house, he took a knife, and laid hold on his concubine, and divided her, together with her bones, into twelve pieces, and sent her into all the coasts of Israel. And it was so, that all that saw it, said, There was no such deed done nor seen from the day that the children of Israel came up out of the land of Egypt unto this day: consider of it, take advice, and speak your minds."*

The Levite was not concerned about the welfare of his wife. Only about his own pride, self image, and ego or he would have at least tried to protect her.

Except for the tribe of Jabesh-gilead, the tribes of the Israelites congregation retaliated against the tribe of Benjamin. As a result, 30,000 of the Israelites led by God were destroyed before the Israelites destroyed 25,100 of the tribe of Benjamin.

During the destruction of the tribe of Benjamin, all but 600 of the men of the tribe were said to have been killed. Their cities were burned and their beasts destroyed. All because of a jealous Levite, whose wife leaves him and returns to her father's house.

Her husband, the Levite, follows her and persuades her to come back to him. On the way back to his home he is required to stop because night was about to fall. He is offered shelter by an old man of the town as Lot had offered shelter to the angels at Sodom. This town was one which belonged to the tribe of Benjamin. There the men of the town, as in Sodom, wanted to know the Levite. In fear of his safety, and to appease the carnal desires of the men of the town the Levite gave them his runaway concubine, the woman he considered an unfaithful wife, and the woman who had played a whore against him.

Judges 19:2: *"And the concubine played the whore against him, and went away from him unto her father's house to Beth-lehem-judah, and was there four whole months."*

The wife of the Levite could not stand to be with him. She leaves and returns to her father's house. For this transgression she is identified as a whore. For humiliating him he allows her to be used and abused all night long. When she was released she crawled back to the house of the old man before she died on his doorstep. Neither the Levite not the old man made any effort to help or protect the girl.

The Levite took his dead wife home and instead of burying and giving her a decent funeral in his anger at her he cuts her into 12 pieces and sends those pieces to the leaders of the Israelite nation.

The anger of the people was great. But was it because the men of an Israelite tribe gang raped a woman or because she was the wife of a Levite, or because he though so little of her that he chopped her into pieces and advertised his act.

What kind of a man was the Levite that his wife should leave him in the first place? Scripture indicates that he was a drunkard. He spent five days with his father-in law before heading home. He found bread and wine in Gibeah and when he found lodging with the old man, he also found drink. When he was challenged by the men of the town this drunk fearing for his own life and dignity gave up his wife. In his anger at her death, he cut her into pieces.

In order to justify his crime he sent the pieces to the tribes laying the blame of her death on the men of Gibeah. This brutal act of dismemberment arouse the leaders so much that they overlooked the act of the Levite and demanded that Gibeah surrender the men who committed the rape so that they could be tried and sentenced to death.

Gibeah refused. The other tribes, accept for the tribe of Jabesh-gilead, gathered together and made war against Gibeah and the tribe of Benjamin.

Because of the act of the Levite, forty thousand Israelites and forty three thousand of the tribe of Benjamin was slain, their cities burned. The Israelites destroyed all but six hundred men of the tribe of Benjamin.

Judges 20:48: *"And the men of Israel turned again upon the children of Benjamin, and smoke them with the edge of the sword, as well the men of every city, as the beast, and all that came to hand: also they set on fire all the cities that they came to."*

After the blood lust of the Israelites cooled and they began to realized that they had all but destroyed one of their tribes, they began to look around to make amends for their actions.

There were six hundred men of Benjamin left alive, but in order for them to multiply they needed wives, which means that the tribes which fought again the tribe of Benjamin destroyed not only the men of the cities but their wives and children as well.

The tribes which fought against the tribe of Benjamin would not let the men of Benjamin marry their daughters so other means of obtaining wives had to be considered if the tribe was to again grow and be a part of the Israelite community.

The tribe of Jabesh-gilead had refused to go against the tribe of Benjamin. For this failure the worthy leaders of Israel in order to obtain wives for the surviving men of the tribe which they had just slain gave orders that the tribe of Jabesh-gilead was to be destroyed except for the virgin girls. The Israelites lamenting the destruction of one tribe is now going to destroyed another to justify their guilt.

Judges 21:5-12: *"And the children of Israel said, Who is there among all the tribes of Israel that came not up with the congregation unto the Lord? For they had made a great oath concerning him that came not up to the Lord to Mizpeh, saying, He shall surely be put to death. And the children of Israel repented them for Benjamin their brother, and said, There is one tribe cut off from Israel this day. How shall we do for wives for them that remain, seeing we have sworn by the Lord, that we will not give them of our daughters to wives? And they said, What one is there of the tribes of Israel that came not up to Mizpeh to the Lord? And behold, there came none to the camp from Jabesh-gilead to the assembly. For the people were numbered, and behold there were none of the inhabitants of Jabesh-gilead there. And the congregation sent thither twelve thousand men of the valiantest, and commanded them saying, go and smite the inhabitants of Jabesh-gilead with the edge of the sword, with the women and the children. And this is the thing that ye shall do, Ye shall utterly destroy every male, and every woman that hath lain by man and they found among the inhabitants of Jabesh-gilead four hundred young virgins that had known no man by lying with any male: and they brought them unto the camp to Shiloh, which is in the land of Canaan."*

To revenge the rape of one woman and the atrocious act of one man over eighty thousand men, women and children were slaughtered. And all of this was considered the will and command of God.

Judges 20:18: *"And the children of Israel arose, and went up to the house of God, and asked counsel of God, and said, Which of us shall go up first to the battle against the children of Benjamin. And the Lord said, Judah shall go up first."*

In order to obtain virgin wives for the six hundred surviving men of Benjamin, the tribes sent twelve thousand of their best fighters to destroy the inhabitants of Jabesh-gilead, because they had not joined in the battle against the tribe of Benjamin.

The four hundred young virgins were given to the six hundred men of Benjamin. This left two hundred men without wives.

The remaining Benjamin members without wives were given permission to steal the wives that they needed from another tribe during the dances of a "feast of the Lord in Shiloh." (Judges 21:1-25.)

The Israelites were under a great oath not to allow the men of Benjamin to marry their daughters but they were allowed to steal what they wanted from one of the tribes during a certain feast.

For the rape and death of the concubine it is the priest that is to be condemned and not the tribe of Benjamin. It was the priest that offered up his concubine for the prostitution, rape and the sexual perversions of the men of the town. It was the priest that mutilated his wife. His crime is miniscule compared to the atrocities, the death and destruction committed by the whole Israelite congregation on his behalf.

We cannot say that this wholesale destruction of a people could not happen again. Hitler, in his purification plan for the German people, intended to destroy the Jewish people by enslavement and their death though his concentration camps.

This country was almost ready to go to war with Iran over the capture of it's embassy personnel and the civilians who chose to stay in Iran when the regime of the Shaw of Iran was overthrown by religious factions.

Before we condemn the men of the town of Gilbeah for their sexual customs, we need to remember that the priests of those days were no better than many of the servants of God today. Sex was rampant then and is still rampant today.

The carnal desires of man have not changed over the ages. If anything is different it is the laws which forbid such practices. These laws have been in affect since before the time of the Exodus. But sexual perversions, especially if it were associated with the religious festivals and the worship of a god was acceptable.

Only recently has International Law, forbidding the above behaviour been enforced. This is a direct result of the trials at Nuremberg. These laws have not eliminate the need by humans to experience sexual release in one form or another or to practice such behaviour. It has only reaffirmed the penalties for those who are caught committing such acts.

Military personnel, by the command of their government, often find themselves far from home. They have been placed in an unnatural environment that is not of their choosing and under conditions for which they have no control. They are lonely and often crave the companionship of the opposite sex. This is within the natural order of all things. If these craving for companionship and sexual releases cannot be satisfied within the confines placed upon an individual by circumstances, it will be and is found in the release by other means. Sometimes it is among themselves in the company of a conquered enemy or in fashions and manners not deem appropriate by polite society.

The conquered enemy has also suffered the lost of loved ones. They too hurt and have needs and desires. Many men of the conquered land have been killed or wounded. The women, in order to survive physically and emotionally, submit to the sexual desires and needs of the occupying armies. It becomes a mutual   benefit for both armies. In most instances, the relationships are temporary, there are no commitments, and for these individuals there are no problems. The problems begin when a few of the personnel involved desire a deeper relationship, including marriage.

This was especially true during World War I and II, when the young men with a highly religious background found themselves in such relationships. No matter how temporary their relationships were intended to be, they sometimes became permanent, especially when children became involved.

The Lord God might have had the same problem with his crew. Some of them may have wanted to marry the human women, who were beneath their status as gods. This created a conflict between his obligations as the authority required to maintain discipline and decorum among his crew and the situations involving a lower life form.

This dilemma was later resolved for him when the earth was hit by an incoming asteroid. The impact of this asteroid which is believed to have landed in the Carribean Ocean caused a gigantic flood to occur. This flood destroyed almost all life in the areas that it touched. It is recorded in the Bible as the flood which destroyed all life except that which was on board a box like boat called the ark.

We know that the gods were flesh and blood because they were biologically compatible with human women. Nowhere in the biological kingdom can any life form mate and reproduce the species unless both life forms are biologically compatible. So it was with human women and the gods that "came in unto" them. These unions between different ethnic groups, produced the mighty men of old, and the special people of the Hebrew nation.

In the genealogy of Jesus, as recorded by Luke, Adam was classified not as a human creation but as a son of God.

Luke 3:38: *"Which was the son of Enos, which was the son of Seth, which was the son of Adam, which was the son of God."*

Without a father or a mother the only way that Adam could be considered as a son of God outside of the process of natural birth would be through the creative process of cloning.

When the Bible speaks of the "sons of God" it refers to the crew of God. These individuals are those who later became the other gods worshipped by their followers and the ones to whom the Lord God divided his property. (Deu.32)

Adam and Eve were clones of the Lord God.

When Cain was born Eve is supposed to have said she that she has gotten a man from the Lord. If Adam was the son of one of the gods, and Cain was his son, then Eve was correct. Cain did come from the Lord and was the grandson of a God. Whether that god was the Lord God or Samael we do not know. Is it any wonder that when Cain killed Abel he was protected by the Lord God?

Religion claims that impregnation of Mary was by the power of the Holy Ghost. It does not seem like since he was said to have been present when he impregnate Sarah?

The Lord visited Sarah and she conceived.

Genesis 21:1-2: *"And the Lord visited Sarah as he had said, and the Lord did unto Sarah as he had spoken. For Sarah conceived, and bare Abraham a son in his old age, at the set time of which God had spoken to him."*

Sarah did bear a child. Was that child a son from the loins of Abraham or from the loins of Jehovah? Until the visit of Jehovah and the angels to the camp of Abraham, Sarah was not able to conceive.

Something special was introduced into the mating of Sarah which allowed her to conceive and bear Isaac. The fact that Jehovah might well have had intercourse with Sarah should not be considered outside of the realm of possibilities. Remember that it was the custom, during the time of Abraham, that honoured guests were allowed such privileges.

When one remembers that at various times during his life Abraham encouraged his wife to lay with men of high rank. It should not come as a surprise that he would allow her to lay with Jehovah who to him his God.

In any event that son, Isaac was a son whom Abraham did not hesitate to offer up as a blood sacrifice when it was demanded of him by God. Abraham knew that the son was not his, but God's. If God wanted his own son as a sacrifice, then who was Abraham to argue? If this seems unlikely that such an event could occurs ones has only to read the New Testament, where the Jesus another son of God is again offered up as a human sacrifice.

Whether the Lord God, the creator of man, was involved with any of the human women is unclear. What is positive is the involvement of his subordinate. Jehovah and the other members of his staff. They did use the earth women to satisfy their sexual appetites.

There is the recorded incidence in the field between the mother of Samson and an angel.

Judges 13:3: *"And the angel of the Lord appeared unto the woman, and said unto her, Behold, now, thou art barren, and bearest not: but thou shalt conceive, and bear a son."*

I Samuel 2:21: *"And the Lord visited Hannah, so that she conceived, and bare three sons and two daughters. And the child Samuel grew before the Lord."*

There may have been many other children born of these clandestine unions affecting not only the history of the Hebrew people, but of the world.

Of all of the men who have affected or changed the world around them, none have been more affective from a religious aspect than Moses, John the Baptist, Mohammed, Buddha, and for the Christian, the most noted of all, Jesus of Nazareth.

In Luke 1:25: *"The Lord appeared to Elizabeth and she conceived. Thus hath the Lord dealt with me in the days wherein he looked on me, to 'take away my reproach among men."*

Again with Mary. Luke 1:28. *And the angel (came in unto) her, and said, Hail thou that art highly favoured, the Lord is with thee: blessed art thou among women.*

Luke 1:31: *"And behold, thou shalt conceive in thy womb, and bring forth a son, and shalt call his name Jesus."*

Jesus a son of Jehovah, born to an earthly mother and raised by an earthly father, Joseph, became one of the mighty man of old. He was called a prophet, master and teacher, by his disciples and followers. The Christians believe him to be the Messiah, the saviour of the world.

What made him different from Isaac?

Both were sons of God, born to earthly women, raised by earthly fathers, and were demanded by God as offerings to him. Isaac was to demonstrate the faith and obedience of Abraham, and the other to redeem the transgressions of man. Both were demanded as sacrifices to please the ego of a god.

Isaac was lucky he did not have to die. The world was not ready to become slaves and servants again. The sacrifice of Isaac would have meant nothing because there was no one, except Abraham who would have known if the story were true or not.

The saving of Isaac and the biblical telling of the story has two significant points. First if Isaac had died there would have been no Jacob, no sons, no Egypt, no Exodus and no Jewish nation. Second without a the nation of Israel there would have been no King David and no story to justify the birth of Jesus as the Messiah.

The Christians believe that Jesus came as the saviour of mankind. He came as a willing sacrifice in order that the people of the world would have a way by which they could cleanse their hearts, minds, bodies and souls and return to his embraces pure, simple and worthy. This belief is based on fantasy and not on fact. When the world was destroyed by the flood, and Noah, his family and the animals were saved aboard the ark, the transgressions of sin were supposedly wiped out. Only the good and faithful were saved.

Only in man's attempt to remain faithful and obedient to the will and commands of the gods did perversion, sin and evil again become a part of man's daily life.

But was sin ever wiped out? Were blood sacrifices necessary or were they the result of the misunderstood rituals derived from the acts of waiting on and serving the gods before the flood?

Gen. 6:13-17: "*And God said unto Noah, The end of all flesh is come before me; for the earth is filled with violence through them: and behold, I will destroy them with the earth. Make thee an ark of gopher wood: rooms shalt thou make in the ark, and shall pitch it within and without with pitch. And this is the fashion which thou shalt make it of: The length of the ark shall be three hundred cubits, the breadth of it fifty cubits, and the height of it thirty cubits A window shalt thou make to the ark, and in a cubit shalt thou finish it above; and the door of the ark shalt thou set in the side thereof: with lower, second and third stories shalt thou make it. And behold, I, even I, do bring a flood of water upon the earth, to destroy all flesh, wherein is the breath of life, from under heaven: and every thing that is in the earth shall die.*"

Did God lie or does the scripture mislead us in order to justify the statement and biblical belief that all life except for what was in the ark was destroyed?

We know that there are living creatures on this planet, whose species seem to go back many thousands of years. Many of these species are located on remote and isolated locations, and are found no where else on earth. The komodo lizard, the platypus duck, polar bear, and kangaroo are only a few such animals that we know about. Were they a part of the species of life which was taken aboard the ark? If they were how did they get to the isolated location where they are found today?

What exactly did God mean when he said he was going to "destroy" every living substance that I have made will I destroy from off the face of the earth. He must have been referring, not to those animals, found in the wilderness and scattered around the world, but to those special species of animals created as the helpmeets for Adam. They were the genetically created creatures that assisted Adam, God and his crew in their mining operations.

According to biblical scripture, except for Noah, his family, and the animals which boarded the ark, all land life on the planet was destroyed by the flood. This did not happen. The location of the isolated animals and their particular species justifies such a statement.

Was there a flood? Yes, there was.

Excavations indicate mud and silt deposited by the flood in some specific locations to be as much as one hundred feet in depth.

Did God cause the flood or was there some other explanation for its occurrence?

In Gen 6:13 God makes the statement that "The end of all flesh is come before me." It is a curious statement and the following is a logical explanation which coincides precisely with the recorded biblical account.

The statement does not say that the Lord God is going to destroy all life himself. The statement merely indicates that information concerning the end of all life has been made available to him.

As travellers from the stars, the aliens had to be aware of all of the events which took place within this solar system. They would be especially concerned with any happening directly affecting this planet and their mining operations. Such an event did take place.

When a massive asteroid entered the solar system it was detected and reported to he Lord God. The trajectory of the asteroid mass indicated that it was on a possible collision course with earth. Evidently the mass of the asteroid was too great for the defensive technology of the Lord God to effectively prevent a collision and the possible destruction of all life. This information resulted in the above statement *that the end of all life has come before me.*

God, as the commander, was notified as verification was made that a disaster was imminent. Meetings were held, options discussed, and decisions made. The aliens did not want to lose their valuable property here on earth, but with the impending disaster they had no choice. They could not save all of the people but they could attempt to save as many as possible. This applied not only to the Lord God and his crew but also to the other alien company commanders around the world. Each had his own contingency to deal with.

The Lord God selected his most trusted servant Noah, his family, a total of four men and four women, along with whatever animals were available, built an ark, and placed them all on board.

They were to be the nucleus for a new generation of life after the flood. The gods believed, that with the new generation, they would be better able to control man and the evil he represented.

Noah, in Ethiopia, was instructed in the building of a boat, which scripture identifies as an ark. It was to be made of gopher wood.

The Uros of South America, also in danger from the earth's collision, with the asteroid built their own ark. It was an island built of reeds.

In the legends of almost every culture around the world, they tell of similar efforts made by their particular god and Noah.

There is evidence that a giant asteroid did strike the planet.

The particular one which create the flood landed in the Caribbean Ocean just off of the coast of Central America. The time of the hit by this giant asteroid is determined to be approximately the same time as that of the great flood.

If the hit was in the Caribbean, as many scientists believe, it would have destroyed many of the animals living in Central and South America. Records and stone drawings of that area, made before the flood, show pictures of animals which are now extinct, animals believed to have perished at the time of the flood.

However, an impact in the Caribbean would have had a minimal effect on animals in other parts of the world. But, the floods caused by the rains and changes in the atmosphere and weather patterns would have.

If, as the Bible says, it rained for forty days and forty nights around the world, there would have been massive flooding everywhere. But there would also have been men and animals in dry areas where no rain fell and those inland at higher levels where the waters did not reach.

This helps to explain why there are species of animals found only in certain parts of the world and nowhere else. It also provides a plausible explanation as to why certain animals, depicted on ancient artefacts found in Central and South America, no longer exist in that area.

Even if, as the Christians and Jews believe, all of the species of animals on earth were saved by Noah, and were on board the Ark, the present locations of the animals themselves contradict the ark theory.

God and his crew understood, as we do today what was to be expected as the impact between the earth and the asteroid became imminent. As the two great masses drew closer together the magnetic attraction between them would become stronger as the distance between them diminished. As a result of this attraction there would be massive tidal waves, earthquakes of gigantic proportions, cyclonic winds of tremendous intensity and incalculable changes in the earth's atmosphere and environment.

In an attempt to save some of the workers and the animals, the various commanders, or Lord Gods around the world had their people, and in the Lord Gods' case, Noah and his family, build themselves a boat, an ark, a floating device which would carry the occupants through the upcoming catastrophe. Those who were to be saved were to stock their arks with enough provisions to support the animals, themselves, and their families for a long period of time. The fact that man survived the impact indicates the venture was successful.

It is said that once Noah began his preparations, it took him and his family almost two years to complete their work. There were timbers to be cut and carried to the boat site. Pitch had to be obtained for waterproofing the ark, construction materials gathered, and scaffolds erected. Pens had to be built for the animals. Food planted, gathered and stored.

The bible does not say that Noah and his family had help in building the ark, but they must have. They could not have accomplished what had to be done on their own. Therefore it can be assumed that for he moment until the danger of the asteroid passed all work ceased in order to complete the ark.

The outside dimensions of the ark were approximately 450 feet long, 75 feet wide and 45 feet high. Inside, the space was divide into three floors. These floors were sub-divided into individual compartments and access from one level to another was built. Noah and his family could not have had the time nor expertise to gather the building materials, build the pens, gather the animals, grow the food, and build the ark, all at the same time.

They could not have fed and watered the stock, built the ark, and constructed the pens which held the animals until they boarded the ark. The only way all of this could have been accomplished was if God and his crew assisted. They could have hired the help, but who paid the workers during the interval of construction?

Right before the impact of the asteroid, Noah and his family were told to load the animals, and to go aboard the ark. Once they were all on board, the loading ramp was shut, the opening cracks sealed with pitch and the ark made waterproof.

Gen. 7:16. *And they that went in, went in male and female of all flesh, as God had commanded him: and the Lord shut him in.*

As the asteroid drew closer to the earth the magnetic attractions between the two gigantic masses began to cause drastic changes the weather pattern. There were changes in the wind and rain patterns. This caused cyclones, tornadoes, hurricanes and typhoons, and forty days of rain befotr the asteroid struck the earth.

As the gravitational pull of the masses increased, the tides began to rise. There were gigantic tidal waves that flooded the coastal areas. The increased rains caused the rivers and lakes to overflow and devastate the interior as well.

Before the collision there were massive earthquakes and tremors that began to literally tear the world apart. The cracks in the earths surface, created by these upheavals were so great that the fountains of the deep erupted and overflowed. Along with the lava from the volcanic fissures came poisonous and noxious gasses that began to spread around the world by the changing winds. Steam and all manner of elements were released into the atmosphere, blown into the air and the environment, by the released pressures from below the earths' surface. These elements contaminated not only the atmosphere but also the land itself. During this upheaval period, certain area must have become death traps. The contaminated atmosphere greatly decreased the chances of surface life anywhere surviving the event. But, because of the wind patterns and the stability of some remote regions, miraculously man and many species of life did survive. They are the animals and birds found in the isolated and remote regions of the earth. The komoda lizard, the polar bear, the panda, the platypus duck, the kangaroo, and koala are just a few of these surviving individual life species.

Gen. 7:11-12. *In the six hundredth year of Noah's life, in the second month, the seventeenth day of the month, the same day were all the fountains of the great deep broken up, and the windows of heaven were opened.*

During the turbulence that followed the collision between earth and the asteroid, the flood waters and the cyclonic winds generated by the impact carried the ark of Noah from Ethiopia, where it was built, into the mountains of Ararat where it is said to have finally come to rest.

When the collision occurred it may have had enough force to caused the earth to wobble upon its axis. As the earth gradually assumed its' equilibrium the winds began to die down, the rains stopped and the waters began to recede.

Gen. 7:12, *And the rains were upon the earth for forty days and forty nights.* Newsweek Magazine, November 23, 1992, there appeared an article entitled "The Science of Doom, by Sharon Begley. In this article she explains the affect of comets and asteroids on the planet and our chances of survival should we experience a hit of gigantic proportions.

Such hits have occurred in the past. Some have had a devastating effect on the life of the planet/ She says, quote "City size: Asteroids or comets larger than three miles across, like Swift-Tuttle, hit every 10 million to 30 million years. According to one calculation, if the dinosaur comet thought to have been about six miles across- hit in the Gulf of Mexico, it would have created a wave three miles high. Nine hundred miles away, the mammoth wall of water would still be 1,500 feet high. Such an asteroid landing in the Gulf of Mexico would cause floods in Kansas City. The impact would make entire continents burst into flame, block sunlight and make agriculture impossible. Humans might go the way of the trilobites."

Such an asteroid hit has been found in the Carribean Sea.

As the planet began to recover from the hit, the flood waters receded, the atmosphere stabilized and vegetation began to appear.

For twelve months, Noah and his family were cooped up inside a watertight boat with one window that was one cubit by one cubic, or 18 inches by 18 inches wide.

According to scripture, the ark came to rest on the top of a mountain on July 17th. On the 1st of October, Noah looked out of his cubit window and saw the tops of the mountains. On the 10th of November he opened the window of the ark and sent forth a raven and a dove. The dove returned. On January the 1st, Noah removed the covering from the ark. The waters were dried up and dry land could be seen. But Noah did not leave the ark for another 58 days.

Evidence has been found to clearly indicate that a flood did happen. Was there more than one global flood during the earth's long history? We cannot know for certain. Was the evidence of the flood that was found the flood of Noah? Again we may never know. What we do know is that there was an impact collision between the earth and an asteroid. It is also possible that a boat or boats of some kind were used to prevent the complete annihilation of man. Even the size, purpose and configuration of the ark is possible, but to house all of the animals, birds, amphibians, insects and man for a year is beyond comprehension. It could not have happened as it is recorded.

If the purpose of the aliens was to mine the earth, as I have proposed, why did the people fail to return to the mining trade and to the obedience of the aliens after the flood?

It is possible that in some areas they did. However, in most of the world the mines were flooded, collapsed, or destroyed by the earthquakes, tremors and gas. The equipment left at the mines was destroyed. There were no workers, and the brood stock, Noah and his family, who represented man and the workers, would take generations to recover their previous numbers. Also Noah and his family were now in the mountains of Ararat and the mines they had worked were in Ethiopia, a couple of thousand miles away.

God and his crew of miners did not have the equipment necessary to recover the mines, even if workers had been available. With everything gone, the Lord God had to make a decision, should he return to his home world for new equipment, return and continue the mining operations or was the project so far gone as to make it so unprofitable that it should be abandoned?

If he decided that the planet was worth the expense of a return journey to his home world, what was he to do about the planet while he was gone, and until he returned?

Deu. 32 gives us his answer. He decided to leave behind a governing crew, caretakers, to watch over the planet. This would not have been necessary if his race of beings were the only travellers of space.

When he divided the land, and his property he gave to each of his assigned crew different responsibilities. When he returns he intends to have those individuals account for their stewardship of the planet.

It was about this time that the gods ceased their physical interaction with man. There were not enough humans left to justify their time and efforts.

Mankind was left to himself, to become his own man.

Once the mines were gone, the original purpose of the aliens no longer existed. The gods had no need to walk, talk, supervise or control man. For approximately three hundred years after the flood, the gods elected to keep to themselves.

They did keep a watch on man. They were aware that he was trying to build a tower to heaven. That effort, in itself, was not as significant to the gods, as the fact that men, working together, would be able to accomplish great things. Man was on his way to competing with the gods themselves and this he was not allowed to do. So the gods separated the people.

Gen. 11-5-8. *And the Lord came down to see the city and the tower, which the children of men had built. And the Lord said, Behold, the people is one, and they have all one language; and this they begin to do: and now nothing will be restrained from them, which they have imagined to do. go to, let us go down, and there confound their language, that they may not understand one another's speech.. So the Lord scattered them abroad from thence upon the face of all the earth: and they left to build the city.*

This separation of man by the gods gives us a reasonable explanation for the various locations of man, found even in the remotest corners of the globe.

It was not until the time of Abraham, a time before the Lord God departed the earth, did one of the gods make himself known to man. That god was Elohim. Later he was to be called Jehovah, the God of the Israelite nation.

Why he chose to guide and become the mentor of Abraham is debatable. They may have become acquainted through the knowledge, stories and personal relationship which existed between Jehovah and Noah, the patriarch and ancestor of Abraham.

Noah was alive during the time of Abraham and through his tales of the flood, his personal belief in Jehovah, as the one and only god and protector, Abraham came to believe in him as the one and only true god.

True god or not, the stories of the flood told by Noah to his descendants, including Abraham were only half truths according to what was believed by Noah.

Let's assume for the moment that all of the species of life found on the earth today were on board the ark and saved from the flood by Noah. As these animals disembarked from the ark, where were they to go? They were in the mountains of Ararat. Did they spread out on their own accord, or were they transported to various locations around the world by God and his crew?

Did God say to his angels, "We will take the platypus duck, the koala bear, and the kangaroo to Australia. We locate the panda in inland China but the best place for the buffalo must be to the grass plains of America and northern Europe. The komodo lizard is a mean little rascal so we will place him on his own little island a couple of hundred miles in the middle of an ocean.

Does this sound logical? Of course not. These animals are located where they are because that is where they had migrated to long before the flood. They survived the flood because while devastating in some parts of the world it did not destroy all life in others.

If all the animals on earth were on the ark, as religion teaches, then as they disembarked and began to spread out from Ararat, they would have left some indication that their species had been there. Remains of some kind would have been found somewhere in the surrounding lands. This is not so. No animal leaves a location where there is food and water and travel several thousand miles before settling into only one remote area of the world without leaving some trace behind.

Birds and animals indigenous to a particular locality did not cross hundreds of miles of mountains, desert, or water, just to find a spot that they could call their own. Logic dictates otherwise.

If the Lord God was the all powerful creator of heaven and earth, why was it necessary for him to require man to build a boat to protect himself from the coming flood? Couldn't God destroy or save what he wanted without the help of man?

If man and the animals had become wicked enough to require annihilation, why select a flood as the method of destruction?

Think of all of the rotted bodies everywhere, the stink, the polluted water, the diseases and the contamination which was spread throughout the land. Why require Noah to take on board the ark, mating pairs of all of the species, that God said he intended to destroy?

Noah, his family, and mankind were vegetarians. Therefore Noah saved the animals because they were the foods of the gods. It was only after the flood that man was given permission to eat meat as well as the green herbs.

Gen. 9:3: *"Every moving thing that liveth shall be meat for you, even as the green herb have I given you all things."*

So during the time that Noah, his family, the beasts, the cattle, the birds and the creeping things were cooped up within the ark, what did Noah and his family eat? What and how did they feed all of the animals, the birds, snakes and amphibians. They did not eat each other or there would have been none to repopulate the land.

Approximately how many individuals birds, animals, insects and creepy things went aboard the ark?

Scientists have identified over 9,000 different species of birds found in the world today. This means that there were basically 18,000 plus birds aboard the ark. Then increase this amount by multiplying those that could fly by seven.(Gen. 7:3) If 8,000 species of fowl fit into this category you have approximately 56,000 flying birds and 2,000 birds that did not fly, a total of 58,000 flying, screeching creatures trying to find water and food over a period of a year. This took care of the upper level of the ark. But being birds we know that they would have been flying, feeding and messing all over the entire ark.

The other species taken on aboard the ark had to included the following groups and are composed of:
1. 800,000 different kinds of insects,
2. 6000 kinds of reptiles,
3. 3000 kinds of amphibians
4. 4000 kinds of mammals.

Now when we add to the 58,000 birds, 1,600,000 insects, 12,000 reptiles, 6000 amphibians and 8,000 plus mammals, you a grand total of 1,682,000 individuals life forms living in a boat 450 feet long by 75 feet wide by 45 feet high.

Suppose for the sake of discussion, we assume that the three stories that Noah was told to put into the ark were in fact there. The lower section housed the reptiles and the amphibians, a total of 18,000 individuals.

The second section was reserved for the 8,000 basic animal pairs, plus those eatable animals, which like the birds, were increased by seven. If 2000 animals were considered in this category than there were 22,000 animals on the second level. Where did Noah place his family? Where did he store the food and water that was going to be required to feed and water the life on board the ark for the time it took before they were able to disembark? It this instance a full year.

On the second level, 450' x 75' you have 33,750 sq. ft. When you divide this by 22,000 animals, you have 1,53 sq. ft. per unit. Unless they were sleeping on top of each other they could not have fit into the ark.

The ark was sealed inside and out. The rains stopped" *And the ark rested in the seventh month, on the seventeenth day of the month, upon the mountains of Ararat."* (Gen.8:4.)

Noah did not open the window of the ark until sometime in December. For 10 months there was no food or water taken in from the outside. There were eight people on board the ark. How did eight people feed and water 22,000 animals, 58,000 birds, reptiles and amphibians?

It was not only necessary to feed and water the various lives on board but to clean the stalls and dispose of the waste. We are led to believed that the ark was watertight and with only one window almost airtight. How could the waste matter be disposed of without breaking the seal? The urine from the large animals on the second deck would naturally flow downward to the first, and the waste from the birds would be everywhere. Everywhere there would be the insects, 1,600,000 of them breeding and multiplying and ready to spread disease.

There was only one window in the ark and it was one cubit square, 18 inches by 18 inches. It was not open for almost ten months, so there was no fresh air in the ark. The ammonia fumes from the urine and animals waste must have been at toxic levels. With no fresh air circulation, nothing on board the ark could have survived. They would have suffocated, died of starvation or dehydration due to a lack of water. Even if all the life on boad was place in hibernation as suggest by religious organization they still had to breath replacing oxygen with carbon dioxide.

There is, however, one reasonable possibility. The ark of Noah may have had some very special features provided by God and his crew. They could have had some kind of recycling and oxygen regenerating system similar to that used by today's modern atomic submarines and our astronauts in space. The waste and urine was captured, purified, separated, and recycled as supplements. The air was recycled through purifiers and sent throughout the ship via supply lines to all the compartments of the ark. The air, food and water were also treated with chemicals which reduced the metabolism of all on board. They were in essence placed in a state of suspended animation. In this way, they could have survived. In either case the survival of those on the ark was due entirely on the aid and assistance and technology of the aliens gods.

When Noah was allowed to leave the ark he built an altar and offered up sacrifices to God, his saviour.

Gen.8:20: *"And Noah built an altar unto the Lord, and took of every clean beast, and of every clean fowl, and offered burnt-offerings on the altar."*

Noah built a barbeque grill which called an alter. He, his family, the Lord God, and the crew of the Lord God had a giant barbecue to celebrate their survival of the catastrophe. It must have taken Noah and his family quite a while to kill and cook one of each clean beast and fowl as demanded by God.

If the Lord god had been a spirit instead of flesh and blood, and Noah just wanted to give thanks to the Lord for his deliverance, one sacrifice would have been enough, especially after all of the death and destruction which had just taken place.

But the Lord God and his crew were flesh and blood. They ate, drank and reproduced like all species of life. After a year they were hungry for the taste of meat. Noah was commanded to build an alter, a barbeque grill and a celebration took place.

How does the writer know what was in the heart or thoughts of God and man? But it is a of justifying the change in the diet of man from a vegetarian to a meat eater.

God and his crew were meat eaters, a fact supported by the lamb presented by Abel at the table of the Lord. The survivors of the flood had a barbecue. Noah and his family were the caterers and allowed to participate. After the flood Noah and his family became farmers. One of their crops were grapes that was used to make the wine served to the Lord with his meals.

Gen.9:20-21: *"And Noah began to be a husbandman, and he planted a vineyard, And he drank of the vine, and was drunken; and he was uncovered within his tent."*

Were did Noah get the vines for the grapes? The ark landed in the mountains of Ararat. Did he carry the grape vines with him or did he discover them in the valley after they had come down from the mountain?

I can understand a need for wanting a garden for food, but why did he also plant a vineyard? If there were grapes in the area he could have harvested them and made them into wine even as a farmer. If Noah grew grapes and made wine it is almost certain that he was at times drunk. One drunken stupor is considered to have been so important that it has become part of holy writ.

Of all of the events which happened to man before and after the flood, why was it necessary for the biblical writers to included in their most holy writings, this particular fact and to relate a particular incident of one of his drunken stupors?

This event must have occurred some years after the flood because it concerned Canaan, the son of Ham, and grandson of Noah.

Gen. 9:21-27: *"And he drank of the wine, and was drunken; and he was uncovered within his tent. And Ham, the father of Canaan, saw the nakedness of his father, and told his two brothers without. And Shem and Japheth took a garment, and laid it upon both their shoulders, and went backward, and covered the nakedness of their father: and their faces were backward, and they saw not their father's nakedness. And Noah awoke from his wine, and knew what his younger son had done unto him. And he said, Cursed be Canaan: a servant of servants shall he be unto his brethren. And he said, Blessed be the Lord God of Shem; and Canaan shall be his servant. God shall enlarge Japheth; and he shall dwell in the tents of Shem; and Canaan shall be his servant."*

The story of a drunk Noah is no more unusual than Noah building a large grill, calling it an altar, and barbecuing many of the animals which had been save from the flood only to be killed and roasted for food. One would think that after all the deaths which occurred because of the flood, Noah would be more concerned with saving life rather than roasting it upon a spit.

But if, as I contend, the gods ate, then they were hungry after the year aboard their ships. Noah barbecued the animals and the gods had a feast. Along with the meat was wine to drink.

Noah was a caterer to the Lord God. God demanded wine. Noah made the wine, and became a servant to its power. Noah made the wine because the Lord God and his crew required wine with their meals.

Exodus 29:40. *And with the one lamb a tenth-deal of flour mingled with the fourth part of an hin of beaten oil: and the fourth part of an hin of wine for a drink-offering.*

If Noah became a husbandman and raised the grapes, he did so on the orders of God. Getting drunk was not a part of those orders, but he might have done so for a number of reasons. He was sampling the quality of the wine which he had just made, was celebrating the first of his new crop or he was drinking because he had a problem.

We are not told exactly what it might have been, but it was something did occur because of that drunkenness that had dire consequences for his descendants and biblical history.

Could this be the reason the Jewish people believe that all of those who descended from Canaan are servants to the rest of the Jewish nation? Did this become their justification for trying to annihilate or enslave them all by command of their Lord God? Are the people of Palestine and Lebanon descendants of Canaan? Could this be the reason that there is so much bloodshed, hatred and conflict between these three nations?

What was it about the nakedness of Noah that was so reprehensible that thousands upon thousands of people yet unborn would be required to suffer? It could not be simply that he was drunk or that he was naked.

Noah, while drunk, was caught by his son in performing some unspeakable act. Somehow Canaan the youngest son of Ham was involved. Whatever Noah did that was so unspeakable he believed that Canaan was responsible for his embarrassment. Whether Canaan told his father, or his father came upon Noah by accident, it was Canaan and his descendants who were to suffer the humiliation of servitude in the ages yet to come.

What was the nakedness that his son Ham uncovered, and what did Ham relay to his brothers? Those are the big questions.

It had to be more than the sight of a old man drunk with wine. Was Canaan, the youngest son of Ham involved? If so did the nakedness of Noah mean an affair with his grandson? Or, more realistically, was Noah involved with someone else and Canaan saw the incident and related it to his father? When Ham related the information to his brothers, was he in fact asking for advice as to what they should do about the matter? Whatever it was, the brothers decided to cover Noah while he slept, to hide his shame.

After the flood, Noah lived three hundred and fifty years. He and his children had a positive relationship with God. They knew him personally. God helped them to build the ark, gather the animals, and load them onto the ark. He was with them after the flood, when he told them that it was all right to leave the boat. He was there for the banquet feast celebrating their survival. He also let them become a part of that celebration by allowing them, for the first time to eat meat, which, until this time, had been denied to them.

Gen. 9:3. *Every moving thing that liveth shall be meat for you; even as the green herb have I given you all things.*

This close association with God must have been known to the children, grandchildren, and great grandchildren of Noah, even to the time of Abraham. Why, then, were there so many other gods being worshipped by those who had been so close to the Lord God himself? Was it because the Lord God did not require man to worship and sacrifice to him? He had no temples, no priests and no religion.

All of these things came about later as man began to spread across the land. All of these came from the imagination of man himself in his belief that he was still serving the gods. Religion, sacrifices, temples and priests were not an edict of the Lord God, but of man.

As mankind began to spread across the land he retained the memory of his servitude to the gods. Since the gods were no longer readily available to him on a day by day basis, he continued that servitude in the only way possible to him. He established places where he set up statues and symbols which represented his god. There he was able to meet and honour them according to his beliefs.

The gods most humans remembered after the flood, were the gods who were their supervisors before the flood. These were the gods which taught and protected them. In time, according to circumstances, time, place, and ideas of the people, new gods were created or old gods changed to meet the needs of the people. Each god was considered individually with different desires and wants. So each entity was worship in its own particular way. The many gods of Egypt are an excellent example of a people who found it desirable to have many different gods to worship, rituals to follow, sacrifices to be made and a religion to believe in.

The Hebrews, residing in Egypt for four hundred years, were well aware of all of these gods. In their Exodus from Egypt they learned of one more, god, "I Am That I Am."

When the Hebrews were finally convinced that circumstance were such that it was in their best interests to leave Egypt, scripture says that they were led by Moses as he was instructed by God himself.

The people were witnesses to his supposed power and the devastation left behind in Egypt. Jehovah chose to call his destruction of life an example of his power and his glory. It flattered his ego to put fear into the hearts of the people.

Even after living through the death and destruction in Egypt, escaping the bondage of Pharaoh, and witnessing the supposed power of God at the parting of the Red Sea, the people, in the absence of Moses, elected to build and worship a golden calf in the place of their new god. Why?

The abandon calf temple was the temple Jehovah chose to be his first and the mountain he selected was to be use as his beginning rule over the people.

When Moses returned from the mountain and his talk with his new god, he found the people worshipping a golden calf and enjoying a feast. They were out of control and no longer believing in or worshipping Jehovah, who was to them a god in name only.

In anger Moses regained control by slaughtering his own people.

Exodus 32:27-28. *And he said unto them, Thus saith the Lord God of Israel, Put every man his sword by his side and go in and out from gate to gate throughout the camp, and slay every man his brother, and every man his companion, and every man his neighbour. And the children of Levi did according to the word of Moses: and there fell of the people that day about three thousand men. Thus the new god of the Hebrews began the rule of his new disciples with the death of around three thousand of his descendents.*

After Moses and his Levite brethren, by the command of God had killed three thousand of their own kin, friends and neighbours, the people came under the complete subjugation of the Lord Jehovah.

It was then that he began to establish his dynasty. He first established laws, ordained priests to administer those laws, outlined the sacrificial rituals he desired and established a government by which control was made and maintain by his organization. Thus the Jewish nation, and a government was founded, controlled and govern by a religion and a set of religious beliefs.

The god that saved Noah, his family and the animals was the Lord God, the creator of man. The god which saved the Hebrews from the yoke of Pharaoh was Jehovah, a subservient underling to the Lord God. But he was also the controlling authority on earth due to the departure of the Lord God.

Jehovah called and worshipped as a god was no more or less a ruler, a power and authority of a king. He commanded and the people obeyed. As long as they were under his jurisdiction and control, they did what was demanded of them or suffered the consequences.

As the people began to multiply they began to scattered abroad. As they went they met other people and came to know other gods and different ways of worship. Some created their own gods, religion, commandments, rituals and sacrifices.

Most of the other gods were based on the superstition and legends of the local people, superstitions and legends which had been passed down to them from their forefathers. That is why it is so unusual for Abraham to suddenly be the advocate of a one and only supreme god. This belief in one god was probably a carry over from the tales of Noah his great, great grandfather.

Noah lived three hundred and fifty years, after the flood. Abraham was born approximately fifty eight years before Noah died. Did Noah relay to Abraham his story of God and the flood? If Abraham believed in the stories told by Noah then when he met Jehovah, the representative of God, he believed him to be the one true god, the Lord God the creator of man.

The Bible says that Terah and Nahor, the father and grandfather of Abraham, lived on the other side of the flood and worshipped other gods. If so who were those gods? It does not seem to have been Jehovah.

Joshua 24:2-3. *And Joshua said unto all the people, Thus saith the Lord God of Israel, Your fathers dwelt on the other side of the flood in old times, even Terah, the father of Abraham, and the father of Nahor: and they served other gods And I took your father Abraham from the other side of the flood, and led him throughout all the land of Canaan, and multiplied his seed, and gave him Isaac.*

Who is lying, Jehovah, Joshua, or the biblical writers?

If Terah, Nahor and Abraham lived on the other side of the flood then all men did not die in the flood as the Bible indicates. If these men lived on the other side of the flood and worshipped other gods, did the flood really happen? Who were the other gods? Who was the god to which Noah offered his burnt offerings? Was it to all of the gods which were on the other side of the flood who also survived the cataclysmic event?

If the Bible is in error in any one part, then everything in it is suspect to interpretation and suspect and should be taken as an informative saga with historic significance rather than an absolute truth.

Was there a flood? The Bible and history says yes. Legends of many culture confirm that at some time in the history of a people the event did happen. The question become when and to what degree.

Were all of the people except Noah and his family destroyed by that flood?

No.

The passage of text indicating that Jehovah himself told Joshua, that Nahor and Terah and Abraham lived before the flood confirms the hypothesis that Noah and his family were not the only survivals of mankind.

If they survived the flood, were they saved by their gods or was it possible that they were in a location were the floods did not occur?

Terah worshipped other gods. Abraham, the son of Terah, raised in his house must, at some time or other worshipped those same gods. For

Abraham to break with family traditions and begin to worship Jehovah, who he believed to be the Lord God, must have known someone who knew him personally, someone who could instill in Abraham a sense of worship for a being no longer considered supreme by his people. That someone had to be Noah, the Patriarch of his family.

Jehovah, thought by Abraham to be the Lord God led him throughout the land of Canaan and made promises to him for his faithfulness? But it seems that Jehovah made no effort to care for Abrahams physical needs.

There was a famine in the land and in order to survive, Abraham had to journey into Egypt to find food. There he prostituted his wife in order to survive. Because of her willingness to be used as he dictated, they became rich.

During the time that Abraham was following and talking with his god, that god made him a promise.

Gen.12:6-7. *And Abram passed through the land unto the place of Sichem, unto the plain of Moreh. And the Canaanite was in the land. And the Lord appeared unto Abram, and said, Unto thy seed will I give this land: and there builded he an alter unto the Lord, who appeared unto him.*

Who were the seed of Abraham?

We understand the term to mean his descendants, all of those who came after Abraham whose roots began with him. There is definitely Ishmael and all of his descendants, Zimran, Jokshan, Medan, Midian, Ishbak and Shuah. (Gen. 25:2.)

Though the scriptures say that these children were born of concubines, it also say's that these concubines were the wives of Abraham and the mothers of his children. Therefore these children, along with Ishmael but not Isaac, are also the legitimate the seeds of Abraham. As such they too are his heirs and their children are his descendants. As such they are as equally entitled to the promised land of Canaan as are the children which came through Isaac, Esau and Jacob.

And if Isaac was the son of Jehovah and Sarah and not Abraham, then the land of Canaan belongs not to Isaac, Esau and Jacob and their descendants, who came from Jehovah, but to the true descendants of Abraham, the seeds of his lions and not those of Jehovah.

According to the promises made to Abraham unless the seeds are from the loins of Abraham they have no claim, by the right of God to the land of Canaan.

This must be so if the promise of the Lord God of Israel is the true and only God and if his promises are to be believed.

Genesis 13:14-18 repeats the promise made to Abraham that the land of Canaan would be for his children, and their descendants. This promise was made at least three times. The promise is further amplified in Genesis 15:4.

Gen.15:4. *And, behold, the word of the Lord came unto him saying, This shall not be thine heir; but he that shall come forth out of thine own bowels shall be thine heir.*

Who came out of the bowls of Abraham? Again it was Ishmael, Zimran, Joksan, Medan, Midian, Ishbak and Shuah. There is one son missing from the above and that is Isaac.

Why is he considered the only son and heir of Abraham?

Gen. 17:4-11 says that God will make Abraham the father of many nations.

How can this become a reality if only the sons of Jacob and the twelve tribes of Israel be considered the people of God? It becomes possible for this statement to become true if one believes that the twenty four elders of Zion, sitting around the throne of God shall become the kings which shall rule the kingdoms of God at the end time of Revelation.

The seed of Abraham did form many nations, but they were destroyed by the children of Israel, the descendants, not of Abraham but of Isaac, Esau and Jacob, the son and grandsons of God.

Isaac was the son of God and Sarah and not the son of Abraham.

Gen. 21:1-2. *And the Lord visited Sarah as he had said, and the Lord did unto Sarah as he had spoken. For Sarah conceived, and bare Abraham a son in his old age, at the set time of which God had spoken to him.*

Gen. 25:11. *And it came to pass after the death of Abraham, that God blessed his son Isaac; and Isaac dwelt by the well Lahai-roi.*

Religious leaders have always assumed the above passage to mean that God is blessing the son of Abraham, but the passage could well have been taken exactly as it is written. God blessed his own son Isaac.

Isaac was the son of God and Sarah not Abraham and Sarah. This makes Jacob and Esau the grandchildren of Jehovah. Which also helps to explain many of the myths which imply that the Jewish people are special people to God.

God and Abraham had made a covenant or a contract which was suppose to bind God to the promise that Abraham would have an heir, but he did not stipulate that the heir was to come from Sarah. Abraham had many heirs but not from Sarah.

There was acommand given to Abraham that all of the male children born to Abraham and his children's children were to undergo a certain bloody ritual. This ritual is called circumcision. This ritual marked and identified all of the men who carried the mark as the seed of Abraham. This mark gave to them the right to the land of Canaan and the promises of God.

The act of circumcision today is the continued renewing of the covenant between God and Abraham which gave to the seed of Abraham the land of Canaan.

In Genesis 17:15-16, God made another promise. *And God said unto Abraham, As for Sarai thy wife, thou shall not call her name Sarai, but Sarah shall her name be. And I will bless her, and give thee a son also of her; yea, I will bless her, and she shall be a mother of nations; kings of people shall be of her.*

God said that he would give Abraham a son from Sarah. He did not say that the son would be from the loins of Abraham.

We know that Ishmael was the first son born of Abraham, we also know that after the death of Sarah, Abraham married again or at least had several consorts. From his wife Keturah came Zimran, Jokshan, Medan, Midian, Ishbak and Shuah.

These were the true seeds of Abraham and the inheritors of the land of Canaan according to God, his contract and the Torah.

What about Isaac? Was he a true son of Abraham or was he the son of Sarah and God?

Remember that Sarah had been trying to have children all of her life and had never succeeded. Abraham was still fertile, a fact proven by the children born to him once he changed wives. It was Sarah who was not able to conceive. Not only could she not conceive, but she had long passed the age when nature would allow such an event. How, then, was she able to conceive and bear Isaac?

In Genesis 17:16, God says that he will give to Abraham a son of Sarah. He does not say that Isaac would come from the loins of Abraham but that he would have a son by Sarah. Isaac was not Abraham's' doing but God's doing. It is said that from him "nations: kings of people shall be of her."

Gen. 18:10,14. *And he said, I will certainly return unto thee according to the time of life; and lo Sarah thy wife shall have a son. And Sarah heard it in the tent-door, which was behind him. Is there anything too hard for the Lord? At the time appointed I will return unto thee, according to the time of life, and Sarah shall have a son.*

Gen. 21:1-2. *And the Lord visited Sarah as he had said, and the Lord did unto Sarah as he had spoken. For Sarah conceived, and bare Abraham a son in his old age, at the set time of which God had spoken to him.*

Was Sarah artificially inseminated or did she have a sexual encounter with Jehovah?

Such a relationship would not have been strange or out of the question considering the fact that Abraham had in the past allowed Sarah to be used as a concubine by at least two men of power. If he allowed Sarah to be the bed companion to men why not to his God?

If Isaac was the son of Sarah and God and I scripture verifies this assumption, then it becomes understandable why Abraham was willing to give up Isaac as a living sacrifice to Jehovah at his command. Isaac was the son of a god. If that god wanted to have his own son killed as an offering to his ego that was his affair.

The idea that a god would desire the death of his son is not beyond the realm of reality. Remember that history has recorded another such event determined to be the will and desire of God. It was the death of his son Jesus. He was believed by the Christians to have been the one and only son of the Jewish god, a fact not supported by scripture.

It would appear that Jehovah had an obsession with requiring his sons and those of his congregation to be offered up as sacrifices to him.

Deu. Chapter 32 indicates that Jehovah have many sons and daughters. What difference does the death of one son, a half-breed mean to someone who had so many. One more son, the result of a little affair with an earth woman would mean nothing to a god, especially a god who had many sons and daughters.

If one is to believe the scriptures, (Deu. 32:18-21), this statement applies to Jehovah.

The promises he made to Abraham was that the descendants of Abraham would inherit the land. No particular child of any particular woman was to be the primary recipient of this promise. Since it was Ishmael, who according to custom was the first born son from the loins of Abraham, then it is to him and his descendants that the promised of the land of Canaan, truly belongs.

This promise was made before the birth of Ishmael and Isaac. The misunderstanding of this promise has been the cause of the longest and bloodiest feud in the history of mankind.

The land of Canaan, a land belonging to the descendants of the youngest son of Ham, was taken away from them by a curse made by a drunken man. It was then given to the children, not of Seth nor of Abraham, but to Jacob, the grandson of God, a liar and a thief. But Jacob was one more thing. He was, at one time the apple of Gods eye before he became the object of his rage and frustrations.

When Jacob became fat and lazy and began to mock his grandfather, his god and protector, he and his descendants became the recipients of the fury and anger of a frustrated god.

The Jewish people are still under that curse placed upon Jacob by his grandfather before he took his family and journeyed into the land of Egypt.

The people may believe that they are the blessed and chosen people of a god, and perhaps they are, but, they are also his slaves and servants.

Once they allowed themselves to be led into the Sinai wilderness, they allowed themselves to become the subjects of a maniacal god.

They are suffering today, as they have suffered since they first followed Moses into the wilderness. It all because of their religious faith and belief in a being who was never a god.

Were Jacob and the Hebrew Nation ever loved, by Jehovah or were they the objects of his hatred, anger and frustration for being left behind on the earth with basically nothing but Jacob as a piece of property and a title. Compared to the other gods he was nobody. They have slaves, temples, riches and power.

It seems that for a little while Jehovah was satisfied with what he had been given before Jacob and his children began to mock him. He was kind, loving and benevolent.

When he became a mockery he became a god with a curse. He was filled with rage and anger at both Jacob and his children for their blasphemy against him. That rage, over four thousand years old, appears to still be prevalent today.

When the Lord Commander, left the earth some time after the collision between the earth and the giant asteroid, he left behind a part of his crew to act in a capacity similar to what we call today military or resident governors. To each of these individuals, his subordinates, he delegated certain responsibilities and areas of control.

It was their job to take care of the life that had survived the collision. They were to watch over the company property which included man, who not only their creation and slaves but their kin and descendents as sub-culture of their race.

These individuals gods are referred to in the Book of Job verse 1:6 as the sons of God.

Along with Jehovah there were Baal, Satan, and Moloch. There were other ancient gods included along with this group but their names have long been forgotten or have since then passed in oblivion.

Jehovah was one of those sons of God. His responsibility, in addition to his administrative duties, was the care of Jacob and his descendants.

Nothing has been said concerning the care of the other descendants of Adam, Cain or Seth. These too were the property.

From scripture, it can be assumed that Jehovah was high up in the inner circle of the Lord God because he was given the title, power and authority of the Lord God when there was a change in leadership.

For any new leader there is always some doubt to how they will be accepted by their subordinates. If Jehovah was afraid or had any doubts concerning his power and position or that he was in complete charge with absolute power, command and authority over the gods themselves it did not affect his command responsibility. In the beginning he was a god with property, Jacob and he had the authority of the Lord God. For his race and culture that was enough.

It would not have been the descendants of Abraham, because he later orders their death and destruction.

Jacob was Jehovah's inheritance. It was Jacob's descendants whom Jehovah guided , trained, and took into battle. It was Jacob that Jehovah loved, hated, and placed a curse upon him and his descendants. It was a curse which, began in Egypt and has been carried out in each successive generation to it's present day society.

As a people and as a nation, the Israelite people were burned in the heat of the desert, fought demons within and enemies without. They have felt the arrows of hate, tasted the blood of their sufferings and known the torment of the serpents sting about them. They felt the self-righteousness of Moses and the destructive power of Jehovah himself.

It is my understanding the it has always been the belief of the Jewish people that everything that has ever happened to them was by the will and command of God. Their misfortunes were the results of their failure in their commitments to God, or the transgression of his law which somehow displeased God.

They, therefore, believe that their sufferings are justified. They do not ask why. It is the will of God and that is sufficient justification for their suffering.

The instruments used by God to implement their purgatory has many times been obscure but, there were times when they were told and understood the reasons for their predicament. One of those times was the time that the Lord Jehovah himself sold his people into slavery. This is merely one illustration.

Judges 4:1-3. *And the children of Israel again did evil in the sight of the Lord when Ehud was dead. And the Lord sold them into the hand of Jabin king of Canaan that reigned in Hazor, the captain of whose host was Sisera, which dwelt in Harosheth of the Gentiles. And the children of Israel cried unto the Lord; for he had nine hundred chariots of iron; and twenty years he mightily oppressed the children of Israel.*

Another example is the complete annihilation of his people at Masada.

Looking through the biblical history of the Jewish people, and their suffering by the hand of Jehovah it is surprising that very few people have ever suggested that Hitler, like Jabin, the king of Canaan, might have been one of the instruments used by God to demonstrate his wrath. This was just another example in the long line of examples of his justice, love and benevolence for his chosen people.

Were the concentration camps of Germany another example of Jehovah love for his people? Was their suffering a continuation of his hate and his curse against them?

Deu. 32:26. *I said, I would scatter them into the corners. I would make the remembrance of them to cease from among men.*

It seems that Hitler, no matter what one may think, was attempting to carry out this will of God.

Long before the Hebrew people became the Jewish Nation there was conflict. Jacob; the father of all, the beloved of God was a liar and a thief, a legacy he passed on to his children. They too were liars, deceivers, thieves and murderers.

When Shechem, the son of Hamor (the Hivite, prince of the country in which Jacob and his family were living at the time), saw Dinah, the daughter of Jacob, he took her. He fell in love and wanted to marry her. Hamor and Shechem went to Jacob and asked for his permission to marry Dinah. Jacob agreed, but only under a certain condition: All of the men of Hamor had to be circumcised as were the men of Jacob. This was done. But when the men were sore and unable to defend themselves, two sons of Jacob came into their camp and murdered all of the men of the city. They then spoiled the city by stealing the sheep, oxen, and asses from both the fields and the city. After they had stolen the wealth of the town, they plundered all that was in the homes, they capture and made slaves of the wives and children.

For one rape, the sons of Jacob raped, murdered, and plundered an entire city. It was the descendants of one of these two brothers that the Holy God, Jehovah, chose to reward and made them into his priests and closest servants. It was the tribe of Levi, the tribe of Moses and Aaron. They were Levites. One became the prophet of God and the other his High Priest.

Except for the biblical references of Moses which refer to his physical being, and the references in the Kabbalah which refer to his spiritual enlightenment, we do not know how much of his story is true and how much is fiction. For some reason his linage and that of Aaron were not considered important enough to be included as a part of the Torah and the historical record of Jewish history.

What is recorded is used as a basis for believing that Moses did exist, and that he played a major part in the building of the Jewish nation. I believed that he did existed and that he was the leader who led the Hebrews out of Egypt. What I do not believe is the story of his beginning. His story according to scripture bears an uncanny resemblance to many of the religious fairy tales of ancient heros and saviours found in the myths and legends of many other cultures.

His story is like those of other religious saviours who were chosen by the gods as a champion of the people. They individuals were heros specially selected by the gods, born in unusual circumstances, and given great power by the gods so that they might free their enslaved people. Usually these great hero's are given some instrument which is used to demonstrate their power and to show that they have been chosen by the gods as a saviour. The staff or rod of Moses was just such an instrument.

Exodus 4:17. *And thou shalt take this rod in thine hand herewith thou shalt do signs.*

And Moses did signs.

His rod turned itself into a serpent which swallowed the serpents rods of the priests of Egypt. With his rod Moses struck the Nile River and turned it and the waters of Egypt into blood. With his rod Moses parted the Red Sea, brought water forth from a rock and standing upon a mountain raised his rod and defeated the army of the Amalek.

Exodus 17:9-13. And Moses said unto Joshua, choose us out men, and go out, fight with Amalek: tomorrow I will stand on the top of the hill with the rod of God in my hand So Joshua did as Moses had said to him. And fought with the Amalek: and Moses, Aaron, and Hur, went up to the top of the hill And it came to pass, when Moses held up his hand, that Israel prevailed: and when he let down his hand Amalek prevailed But Moses' hands were heavy; and they took a stone, and put it under him, and he sat thereon and Aaron and Hur stayed up his hands, the one on the one side, and the other on the other side; and his hands were steady until the going down of the sun. And Joshua discomfited Amalek and his people with the edge of the sword.

Moses, like the hero's of other mythical sagas, did mighty things with the rod of God, but how much of his beginning is true and how much is fiction?

The mother of Moses, fearful of the death of her son, because of a decree of Pharaoh that all Hebrew males be put to death, took and put him into a basket and placed him in the river.

Exodus 1:22. *And Pharaoh charged all his people, saying, Every son that is born ye shall cast into the river, and every daughter ye shall save alive.*

This edict applied only to the Hebrew families.

It is hard to believe that any mother who professing to loves her child, would kill that child or submit that child to the punishment that Moses would have suffered had he not been seen, taken in and adopted by Pharaoh's daughter.

His mother is supposed to have put him into a basket, covered the basket, and placed that basket in the reeds of the Nile River, a river known to be infested with crocodiles. If Moses had not been found, as the story goes, he would have died from the desert heat, thirst, or hunger if he was not eaten first by one of the Nile gods, the crocodile.

But as the story goes, Moses was found, not by just anyone, but a royal princess, the daughter of the Pharaoh himself. Many legends have heroes which that were found in similar circumstance. They were rescued by fair maidens, given extraordinary powers by the gods, and later use those powers to save a people in distress.

In addition to the unusual powers given to them by the gods, hero's were often presented magical swords, staffs, or other adornments which protect them from mortal men. Moses was one such person.

He was born to a people in bondage. He was saved by a princess, and under her protection he became well educated. He grew in strength and wisdom and as a surrogate son of Pharaoh and in the shadow of Egyptian religion. From the priests he learned many things about the gods and power.

When it was his time, according to the legend, he defended one of his Hebrew brothers from punishment by killing an Egyptian. To avoid execution for his crime, Moses escapes into the desert. There he underwent the trials and tribulations that conditioned him for his role as the saviour of his people. He was instructed by a god, whom he was told, was the god and savour of his forefathers Jacob, Isaac and Abraham.

Exodus 3:6. *Moreover he said, I am the God of thy father, the God of Abraham, the God of Isaac, and the God of Jacob. And Moses hid his face; for he was afraid to look upon God.*

I find it strange that the linage of Moses is not mentioned in a society where the family linage is considered a sacred trust, the absence of such linage cast a shadow upon the reality of the truth it there is any to be found in his story.

Like all true heroes, when Moses was told of the prophecies he was to fulfil, he replied, with humility, "Who am I, that I should go unto Pharaoh, and that I should bring forth the children of Israel out of Egypt?" (Exodus 3:11).

The Lord Jehovah replied that he had heard the cries of the people. He now intended to release them from their condition of bondage. Moses was to be his emissary to Pharaoh.(Exodus.2:23-25).

Today the terms 'bondage' and 'slavery' are considered by the religious communities as synonymous terms. This was not always so.

During the time of the Hebrews, slavery was a condition imposed upon a person without their consent, usually by a conquering enemy or by sale. The individuals who were captured as the result of a battle and found themselves in this condition were called slaves. They had no rights and no hope of redemption. The wives and children of Hamor and his people were such captives. They were brutalized, punished, used, or sold according to the whims of their owners, Simeon and Levi, the sons of Jacob.

Bondage was different. This was a condition where one placed themselves in a condition of servitude, usually for a specific period time and under detailed conditions. It was usually done to settle a debt of some kind. When the debt was settled, either by labour or fee, the bondage was lifted and the individual was freed of all obligations.

This country was make great by the indentured servants who submitted themselves to become servants in order to obtain passage to this country. Once their obligation was over they and their children made homes, built factories, established schools which helped to created our government. Those immigrants also included those of Jewish ancestry.

The church has long taught that slavery was an abomination and was against the will and commandment of God. This, like so many other fabrications of the church, was a condition which if God did not approve he at least practiced.

While he, as king and ruler, was able to sell his people into twenty years of labour and servitude under Jabin the congregation was only allowed to submit themselves into self styled servitude for a period of seven years. It was different for those outside of the congregation who were captured as plunder and spoils of war.

Scripture indicates that the Hebrews were originally in a condition of bondage, not slavery. Slavery was a condition they brought upon themselves.

In Egypt, especially the during the times of drought or famine, Pharaoh had a custom which allowed a person to pledge themselves, their families and their labour in exchange for food and sustenance.

The length of the pledge of service was determined by the amount received by a particular person or family. Sometimes it was the father who was pledged, but often it was the other family members. In time, if the severity of the conditions continued, and the family was unable to repay their debt, their bondage, in essence, became a form of slavery.

This is believed to have been the condition under which the Hebrews were living at the time of Moses.

Their servitude to Pharaoh was in repayment for goods and services received during the various droughts and famines which had hit Egypt in the years which followed the time of Joseph.

Since Pharaoh owned everything, it was to him that the people had to pay tribute in order to survive.

When Jehovah decided to become a God, not just in name but in reality, he had to have at least four things if he was to be respect and worshipped as a great god.

First he needed servants who would offer up gifts and sacrifices, to wait on and worship him. Second he needed priests, individuals who would accept the gifts of the congregation in his name and who would serve and offer up sacrifices to him. Third he needed a temple to which the people could come and worship. And fourth he needed a land which he could call his own.

At the time of the Exodus Jehovah had none of these things.

When Jehovah and Moses first met on the mountain natural conditions were such that Jehovah figured that the time was right for him to make his move and to fulfil his divine ambition. He decided to form his own dynasty. Until then he was merely a name to the Hebrew people. He was the mythical god of their forefathers, a name which had been passed down to them by word of mouth from the time of Jacob. He had no temples, no priest, no established rituals, sacrifices, territory, or worshippers. He was a nobody god.

All of the other gods, those of Egypt and the surrounding country had everything. They had priests, temples, sacrifices, rituals, worshippers and land.

Since Jehovah had nothing, he was a god with no power, no name, and a god which no one but the Hebrews of Egypt had ever heard of.

The Hebrews at least knew his name. They knew that he had promised them the land of Canaan. They were use to serving, obeying without question, and surviving under the harshest of conditions. They were therefore the perfect subjects, once under the control of Jehovah, by which he could begin building his dynasty and justify his claim to be a great god of might and power.

The Hebrews can be considered a chosen people for one reasons other than those which they claim as a result of their religion and their faith. According scripture they, as the descendants of Jacob, are genetically related to their God Jehovah through their ancestor Isaac, the son of Jehovah and Sarah and not Abraham. They are family.

If they choose not to accept the above as fact then they must accept that they are genetically related to the Lord God through Adam, Seth, Noah and Shem. As such, they were by genetics, the descendants and blood line, however diluted, of the Lord God himself and not to the blood line of Jehovah.

The Hebrews of Egypt were the descendent of Jehovah. It is easy to understand why they were chosen to become his subjects when decided to become a god of power and prestiage. He was also fulfilling his obligations as their earthly overseer.

As the owner of Jacob and is descendents the Hebrews were in fact his inheritance and his by right. As slaves, it was relatively easy for him to return them to the yoke under which they originally existed. They already knew his name and were aware of his existence from the tales passed down to them through their legends.

The Hebrews would make excellent slaves and worshippers. Who better to serve a new god than a people who were already slaves used to worshipping many gods? They would merely change the name of one master to that of another.

Jehovah believed that with his superior knowledge, mental expertise and alien technology, it should have been an easy task for him to get the Hebrews from under the yoke of Pharaoh, into the desert and under his direct control.

He found that Pharaoh was not so easily manipulated by Moses or out of the fear of a new and unknown god.

Every time a request was laid on Pharaoh and Pharaoh refused Jehovah claimed that it was his doing. He declared that he had harden the heart of Pharaoh only to be able to eventually demonstrate his full power and his glory before all of the people.

The people of Egypt suffered greatly during this time and thousands suffered and died. Their suffering was not due to the hardening of Pharaoh's heart, his power or his glory, but to a series of natural disasters which had just taken place.

Jehovah told Moses and Moses told the people that these natural events were the result of the power of their god and he was demonstrating that power to them for his glory.

Moses had a difficult time convincing Pharaoh to allow his Hebrews subjects to leave Egypt even for a few days. The people had no reason to leave. Jehovah had nothing to offer them as an inducement to follow and serve him except promises. He promised them freedom from their Egyptian bondage, debts, and obligations. He promised them a land of their own, wealth, prosperity, and freedom from the plagues and diseases which he claims he had afflicted on the Egyptians.

Whether the Hebrews believed or did not believe the promises of God and Moses, when Pharaoh gave Moses permission for the Hebrews to leave they were forced by circumstances to depart from Egypt. Their condition of bondage was great before the plagues and suffering of Pharaoh. How much greater would they be after the plagues were over and the grief of Pharaoh turned into anger.

As slaves, anything was better than the poverty and pain they had to endure day after day in the land of Egypt. This they did not fear as much as the wrath of Pharaoh which followed the last plague, all due to the actions of Jehovah their God and Moses their prophet.

To ease their fear and to give them a need to hurry their departure, Moses told the people that their new God Jehovah had given them permission to spoil the Egyptians. They were to take of their neighbours gold, silver, jewels and raiment, compensation for their years of bondage. This also allowed the Hebrew an opportunity to obtain what they would need to survive in the desert. Since they had no money to buy anything, they used the grief of the Egyptians and the empty households due to death from the plagues to steal what they wanted. They have down through the ages given God credit, blessings and thanks for his permission and his assistance during their times of trouble.

I am sure that there are many who would say that the Hebrews only took from those who were dead and only what was necessary but this is not what the scriptures say. It is true that the dead had no further use for their worldly possessions but they may have meant a great deal to the relatives of those who had died. There are some who will say that the Egyptians loaned these things to the Hebrews for their journey to their new land in order to get them out of Egypt and to stop the plagues. This also may be true. But according to scripture the Hebrews, regardless of the circumstances stole from a people suffering and dying. They have never nor is there any indications or evidence that the Hebrews ever made or attempted any kind of restitution for what they stole during the time of the Exodus. Such compensation is not considered necessary by any religious group as the result of any act committed in the name of God.

When one practices a religion, they are expected to make sacrifices and to obey the orders of the priests or clergy presiding over their faith or congregation. The laws, words or declarations of the clergy are supposed to be the words and will of God handed down to them. In return the clergy, by the authority of God make promises to the people in return for their service and dedication. One can only hope that the promises made to them by the priests will someday be kept by the gods.

In beginning of his quest for worshippers, Jehovah was not interested in freeing the Hebrews from the power and control of Pharaoh. He was interested only in obtaining their allegiance, services, gifts and sacrifices. Of course the Hebrews, as bonded servants, had nothing to give as gifts except the animals which the Lord demanded as sacrifices.

The first priority of the Lord Jehovah was to get the people to obey Moses. If they agreed, Moses was to lead them into the desert, to a certain mountain. There they were to offer up sacrifices and begin their worship of him as their new one and only god. They desired this, not out of love and reverence, but out of fear.

Moses asked Pharaoh to allow the Hebrews to quit work for seven days just so they could their cattle and their possessions into the desert to worship a god which Pharaoh did not know and the Hebrews had not worshipped in almost four hundred years. Once in the desert their was no reason for the Hebrews to return to Egypt and their bondage. Pharaoh knew this and refused to let them go unless they went without their cattle and possessions.

Moses offered no guarantees that once their worship was complete the Hebrews would return to their labours, especially when they were three days away from the control of Pharaoh and his armies.

Had Pharaoh allowed the Hebrews to journey into the desert to worship, Jehovah would have had the best of both worlds. Pharaoh would be responsible for their physical well being and control, while Jehovah received all of the godly benefits, the worship, sacrifices, gifts, honour and glory.

When Pharaoh refused to allow the Hebrews a possibility to escape into the desert it forced Jehovah to use other means by which he could achieved him goals. That was the beginning of the plagues.

If the Hebrews were ever allowed to journey into the desert Moses was to lead them to a particular mountain, he called, the Mountain of God. That mountain has been found to have the ruins of an abandon temple, believed to have belonged to the Calf Cult of Egypt.

Modern archaeology has uncovered what appears to have been a temple, high on a mountain, approximately three walking days distance from one of the ancient sites of a royal palace. At this site appear symbols of the cow or calf cult of ancient Egypt. This was a cult or religion the Hebrews, after four hundred years could identify with. It may have been the real reason the Hebrews had Aaron forge a golden calf and began to worship it so soon after their escape from Egypt? Since they are said to have had a feast and an orgy it must be assumed that they were familiar the custom and the ceremony.

While the people were in Egypt it appears that the power of Jehovah was not able enough to allow him to free the people by himself. He needed Moses, and he needed an excuse to use his technical and scientific knowledge, along with his weapons of destruction. He did not have the magical powers of a god, but he did have a superior knowledge of physics and the natural world. He also had the abilities and mentality of a military commander. It is possible that one of the reasons Jehovah was left in charge of the planet by the Lord God when he departed the earth was his background and his military expertise.

This expertise, along with certain other weapons, he evidently passed on to both Moses and Joshua.

Under his command, Moses and later Joshua led the people to the promised land. It took forty years to train and discipline the people to follow their leaders without question.

Once the Hebrews began their wandering in the desert and under the control of God, he fulfilled his first criteria to becoming a god. He had a congregation.

He had a congregation but the people were not convinced that he was a god, and if they were, they still had not decided to follow him as true believers. This is evident by their desire to worship the calf.

When Jehovah convinced Moses, and then Aaron that he was what he claimed to be then Moses believed and became his prophet.

With Moses and Aaron as his prophet and spokesperson he offered the Hebrews bribes, and made promises to them of freedom, land, power and riches.

They would not follow Moses and a nobody god for nothing. They must have asked Moses what was in it for them before they dared to face the wrath of Pharaoh.

Moses, as the prophet of Jehovah, promised the people that he, under the power and protection of Jehovah would lead them out of the land of Egypt and out of bondage. He promised to lead them to the promised land of Canaan. But in order for this to happen the people had to be willing to obey his commands, to worshipped and served Jehovah and accept him as their god. In return for their obedience, they would be led and would occupy the land of Canaan, a land flowing with milk and honey.

The people followed Moses. Whether it was out of fear or belief is not important to history or to the present day Jewish nation.

It seems ironic that the Hebrews seem to have forgotten that the reason they were in Egypt and bondage in the first place was because they had almost starved and died of thirst during the drought and famines in that promised land of milk and honey.

The Hebrews cursed the Egyptians once they were free from the control of Pharaoh and they seem to have forgotten that at least twice before, during a time of draught and starvation, that it was Egypt and not Jehovah who had been their salvation.

Pharaoh was not about to let his slaves go, or to allow anyone, especially some unknown god, to dictate to him what he could or could not do with his slaves. Jehovah knew this before he ever made his demands.

Exodus 3:19-20. *And I an sure that the king of Egypt will not let you go, no, not by a mighty hand. And I will stretch out my hand, and smite Egypt with all my wonders which I will do in the midst thereof: and after that he will let you go.*

Each and every time that Moses made a demand on Pharaoh to release the people, God is supposed to have somehow intervened and prevented Pharaoh from giving in to his own demands. In each instance it was an excuse for Jehovah to place a plague of some kind on the Egyptian people.

These plagues were the holocaust of Egyptians brought on by the supposed might and power of God. This almighty power destroyed the lives of the Egyptians out of spite, hatred and vengeance. These demonstrations of power and the events, as they occurred, were supposed to have give to Jehovah power, might, and prestige.

Today, we realize that the events which occurred in Egypt were not the result of some heavenly power but the result of events which occurred from a natural disaster.

The Egyptians, the Hebrews, and all of the nations down through the years, who have believed that the plagues of Egypt were the result of a god's power should now realize through modern science, technology and investigation that the plagues were the result of a natural phenomenon, the volcanic eruption of the isle of Crete. This created an earthquake and the natural events which followed a volcanic eruption. It also had a direct bearing on the events which happened in Egypt, events which Jehovah claimed were the result of his power.

Jehovah, with his scientific instruments, knew that an eruption was about to take place on the Isle of Crete. He had some idea of what was going to happen when the eruption took place. He used those events to his advantage.

When the eruption occurred Moses was told to go to the river and turn it into blood.

Exodus 7:15-18. *Get thee unto Pharaoh in the morning; lo, he goeth out unto the water; and thou shalt stand by the river's brink against he come; and the rod which was turned to a serpent shalt thou take in thine hand. And thou shalt say unto him, The Lord God of the Hebrews hath sent me unto thee, saying, Let my people go, that they may serve me in the wilderness: and, behold, hitherto thou wouldest not hear. Thus saith the Lord, In this thou shalt know that I am the Lord: behold, I will smite with the rod that is in my hand upon the waters which are in the river, and they shall be turned to blood. And the fish that is in the river shall die, and the river shall stink; and the Egyptians shall loathe to drink of the water of the river.*

Did the water actually turn into blood or was the water polluted by the river silt due to the volcanic eruption that the fish were unable to breathe and dies. This would result in the stink and cause the frogs to leave the river. This led to the rest of the plagues Jehovah claimed was due to his power.

This was the beginning of the plagues and the magic power of the Lord God. After all of the generations which have passed, it still causes the people of the Jewish and Christian faiths to stand in awe of these events. But were they the acts of a vindictive god or the natural results of an act of nature, the volcanic eruption.

As far as I know, no one has ever shown a correlation between the volcanic eruption of Crete and the sequence of events in Egypt. Suppose we try.

In any earthquake or eruption, shock waves and tremors travel far beyond the immediate local of the area and the event. When the volcano erupted on Crete, it caused cracks in the earth surface from which hot molten lava flowed. This upheaval beneath the sea stirred up the silt and robbed the fish and sea life of the ability to breath. The tremors extended to Egypt, and the Nile River underwent the same changes as the waters around Crete. It is possible that the earth cracked beneath the river and molten lava came forth, turning the river red. The escaping gases, especially if there was sulphur involved, would have given the area the smell of rotten eggs as it robbed the water of it's oxygen which, along with the heavy silt, killed the fish and river life. When Moses mentioned the word blood, the combination of the red river and the rotten smell would have convinced the people that it was just that.

The fish died because they could not breathe in the silt laden, oxygen deprived, water of the river; they floated to the surface and began to stink. The water was polluted. It took seven days for the silt to settle and the river to return to its natural state.

Exodus 7:25. *And seven days were fulfilled, after the Lord had smitten the river.*

When the river became contaminated, the fish died and the stink became unbearable. There was no clean water for the frogs that lived in and by the river. They had no choice but to leave the river. They covered the whole land. But without water they too perished.

Pharaoh approached Moses and asked him to remove the frogs and in return the people were free to go and worship their god.

Exodus 8:8. *Then Pharaoh called for Moses and Aaron, and said, Entreat the Lord that he may take away the frogs from me, and from my people: and I will let the people go, that they may do sacrifice unto the Lord.*

Moses agreed and promised to return the frogs to the river but he was unable to do so. Pharaoh realized that the God of Moses had no real power. The frogs continued to died from lack of water and had to be gathered up, leaving a stink on the land. When Moses was unable to fulfil his promise, Pharaoh had a change of heart and would not let the people go. Unable to return the frogs to the river both the word of Moses and the power of his god was without worth. Their words were no good.

Exodus 8:13-15. *And the Lord did according to the word of Moses and the frogs died out of the houses, out of the villages, and out of the fields. And they gathered them together upon heaps: and the land stank.. But when Pharaoh saw that there was respite, he hardened his heart, and hearkened not unto them as the Lord had said.*

The stink of the river, the lack of fresh water and the rotted frogs were merely a prelude to the next event, the infestation of lice, parasites, flies and locusts.

Exodus 8:16-21. *And the Lord said unto Moses, Say unto Aaron, Stretch out thy rod, and smite the dust of the land, that it may become lice throughout all the land of Egypt. And they did so; for Aaron stretched out his hand with his rod, and smote the dust of the earth, and it became lice in man and in beast: all the dust of the land became lice throughout all the land of Egypt. And the magicians did so with their enchantments to bring forth lice, but they could not: so there were lice upon man, and upon beast. The one thing that is not mentioned are discussed is the time span between the time Moses struck the earth and an event occurred.*

Today we know that lice, diseases and parasites cannot be erased by magic spells but by clean water and good hygiene.

The plagues were the natural result of the volcanic eruption and occurred in an expected sequence.

Another supposed miracle and power display of Jehovah is found in:

Exodus 8:22. *And I will sever in that day the land of Goshen in which my people dwell, that no swarm of flies shall be there; to the end thou mayest know that I am the Lord in the midst of the earth.*

There is a good reason why there were no swarm of flies in Goshen. The land of Goshen was located fairly close to the Mediterranean Sea, where breezes blew, the rains came, and the river delta cleared up faster than the surrounding area. There were no flies because there was no stink or rotting flesh.

As the winds blew they also blew the flies from the house of Pharaoh.

Exodus 8:31. *And the Lord did according to the word of Moses; and he removed the swarms of flies from Pharaoh, from his servants, and from his people; there remained not one.*

The contaminated water, lice, flies and parasites left behind another problem: animal diseases, one of which we now believe was anthrax.

Exodus 9:3. *Behold, the hand of the Lord is upon thy cattle which is in the field, upon the horses, upon the asses, upon the camels, upon the oxen, and upon the sheep and there shall be a very grievous murrain.*

Today' definition of the word "murrain", taken from the Reader's Digest Illustrated Encyclopedic Dictionary states:

"Murrain (mur'in)n. 1. Any highly infectious and malignant disease of cattle, such as anthrax. 2. Archaic. Any pestilence or dire disease..."

The Hebrew herds in the delta, away from the herds of the Egyptians, did not suffer or become infected because of their fresh water and freedom from the lice infestation.

Exodus 9:4. *And the Lord shall sever between the cattle of Israel, and the cattle of Egypt: and there shall nothing die of all that is the children's of Israel.*

The Egyptians, however, eating the meat of their diseased animals, and drinking the milk of their sick cattle and goats broke out in blisters and sores, and what the Bible describes as blains. Blains is described in modern terminology as an inflammatory swelling or some kind of sore.

When the eruption of Crete occurred, ash and debris were blown into the atmosphere. During the length of time it took for the eruption to diminish many things occurred. The atmosphere was contaminated. Depending upon the winds at that time of the year, the fallout of the ash and debris would extended over a very large area. The ash suspended in the upper atmosphere may have lasted for days before it began to settle.

Today we know a little more about volcanic eruptions and their effects than was known at the time of the Exodus. In this century alone we have seen and felt the effects of at least three major eruptions.

When the volcano Krakatoa erupted, the ash it threw into the atmosphere circled the globe for almost ten years. We know of the results of the eruption of Mt. Vesuvius in 79. A.D. Recently we have obtain a lot more information on volcanic eruptions from the eruptions which have occurred in the United states, Mexico and the Philippines.

When the eruption on Crete occurred, the ash and hot fires stones from that eruption were blown as far south as the land of Egypt. The escaping hot lava, rocks and gasses, created wind turbulent, cyclones, electrical storms, thunder, and hail. These events were the foundations upon which the plagues of Egypt were based. The results were air and water pollution, disease, death, ruined crops and destroyed property.

The stink of the dead fish, and rotten flesh of the dead frogs multiplied the plague of the lice and disease parasites. This resulted in the diseases which affected both man and animal.

The winds brought the locusts which fed on what was left of the destroyed crops. When the winds changed the locusts and flies, which were the result of the deaths, stink and rotting flesh, were blown away to other areas.

The fine ash blown into the atmosphere from the volcano was so thick that it blocked out the light from the sun for approximately three days.

After these plagues came the last of the plagues, "The Angel of Death".

Whether the "Angel of Death" was the result of malaria caused by mosquitoes, typhoid fever, ptomaine poisoning, cholera or some other disease as the result of the contaminated water, disease meat, milk or poisonous gases is not known. Death among both the Hebrews and the Egyptians did occur.

For those who survived the night was it the result of the power, might and glory of Jehovah or was it the fires which were used to roast the meat? Did the fires burn up the gases, the Angel of Death, and allow those who were waiting to survive?

The Hebrews who followed the commands of Moses survived. These he later led into the wilderness. Were the people saved because they obeyed Moses or was it because of the specific way and the type of food they prepared?

There is no way to verify that only the first born child of each family died. We only have the word of the writer that the event even took place.

I believe that many died, both Hebrews and Egyptians and it was not always the first born. If that were the case Pharaoh himself, as the first born, would also have died. He did not. But the last plague it was enough for Pharaoh. He did not want his people to suffer any more. Believing that the events were the work of the Hebrew god, he gave Moses permission to take the Hebrews, their cattle, all their livestock and possessions and leave the land of Egypt.

While the Egyptians were in mourning, the Hebrews did leave. They took advantage of the death, suffering and mourning of the Egyptians in order to rob them of much of their jewels, silver, gold, and raiment. They did this as a command of their new god. The Hebrews began their journey to freedom, their faith, religion and ans status as a nation as thieves.

Exod. 11:2. *Speak now in the ears of the people, and let every man borrow of his neighbour, and every woman of her neighbour, jewels of silver, and jewels of gold,*

Exod. 12:35. *And the children of Israel did according to the word of Moses; and they borrowed of the Egyptians jewels of silver, and jewels of gold, and raiment.*

The thinking of those who began the Exodus was that most of the Egyptians were too sick, dead or dying to stop them from the looting which took place. The Egyptians who were alive were too busy being sick, mourning, and burying their dead to care or stop the looting.

The Hebrews packed up what few possessions they had, and what they could steal, and began their journey to the magical land of Canaan. A journey led by Moses, a murderer and an angry, vindictive, remorseless, alien, who would be a god.

Once in the desert, the people were at the mercy and control of God and Moses. It was then that Jehovah began to show his true identify and his intentions.

He began by issuing the rules which the people were to live by, rules which would make him a god. He began by demanding gifts which were called sacrifices. These gifts or sacrifices, would not only make him a very rich and powerful individual, but they would feed, enrich and give power and control to Moses and his family, the Levites, the priests who he chose to served him. He also demanded other souls as his servants and slaves. Those he elected not to keep were to be redeem. He sold them back to their parents. He collected a tax.

Exod. 13:1-2. *And the Lord spake unto Moses, saying, Sanctify unto me all the firstborn, whatsoever openeth the womb among the children of Israel, both of man and of beast: it is mine.*

Exod. 13:12-13. *That thou shalt set apart unto the Lord all that openeth the matrix, and every firstling that cometh of a beast which thou hast; the males shall be the Lord's. And every firstling of an ass thou shall redeem with a lamb; and if thou wilt not redeem it, then thou shalt break his neck: and all the firstborn of man among the children shalt thou redeem."*

It is a curious demand to place upon an enslaved people. They have just been released from the yoke of one oppressor only to be oppressed by another. Now they are to be taxed for every firstborn already alive. Those yet to be born are to be given to God himself to do with as he or his priest pleases or they are to be redeemed with a lamb because that was what fed God and his priests.

If the lamb was not used for food, it increased the herds and wealth of the family of Levi.

Who was to accept the newborns? To whom was the redemption fee given, and to whom did the dead, unredeemed animals go? Were these really sacrifices or tribute? Since there were no ritual rules or procedures to follow, no altar on which to spread the blood, then the demand was tribute, rather than an official sacrifices to a deity. Such tribute is not too hard to understand if one remembers that the God Jehovah was a godfather taking over a new territory and needed funds by which he could buy the things which he desired.

His demand for newborns animals and infants has always been a mystery to theologians. What did he do with the souls presented to him? This practice has come to be understood as placing the newborn into the service of God. Until recently it was a reasonable assumption, except that only the priest of Levi could administer to God. Therefore the dedicated souls became slaves or servants, not to God but to the priests themselves.

There is another explanation for the demands of God for newborn life, especially male children.

Medical science have found that the cell and organ tissues of newborn infants, when implanted into the body of an older person is not rejected but accepted and helps to regenerate the body of the receiving host. These cells injected into a host can and is utilized by the host body to rebuild, repair, and regenerate the old cells of the various organs and different parts of the human body. When these new cells are injected into a host, the host experiences a feeling of revitalized health, vigour and youth.

Did Jehovah demand these newborn infants been out of necessity? As he and his people aged were they required, at periodic intervals, to undergo cell regenerated, in order to enjoy a very long and vigorous life? Was this the way that they, as flesh and blood beings, live for long periods of time? If so, it becomes apparent that Jehovah's sacrificial demands for newborn children was for him a very necessary and practical need. As a demand of a God, who would refuse his command?

When one considers his age and like man, flesh and blood, with physical and medical needs, he had a need to be forever young. To maintain that youth, he demanded special foods prepared in a special way, wine to drink, and special sacrifices which catered to his physical, mental, and egotistical needs.

Jehovah's race with their advanced technology, were able to clone men and animals. How much easier would it have been for them to extend their lives and meet many of their physical and medical needs by using the fresh cells of the newborn infants provided as sacrifices from his people, his slaves, servants and property.

As flesh and blood individuals, with the same, DNA, RNA and Chromosomes as man, their cells structure would be completely compatible with almost all human life. There would be no rejection by any of their organs or parts of their bodies when human cells were injected into them.

Jehovah did not have to replace anything. All he had to do in order to maintain the look, feel, and strength of a young, healthy and vibrant individual was to have his body, from time to time, injected with the living cells of a newborn infant. Once injected into his body the new cells became active, regenerating his old tissue so that his organs or fading parts were made whole and functional again.

This process, called cell regeneration, is a procedure found only in certain specialized clinics around the world. This process is said to have a very high success rate of youth regeneration.

From these special laboratories or clinics found only in certain countries around the globe, there have been reports of highly successful experiments where cell implantation has caused unhealthy organs to regenerate and become both functional and healthy again. This treatment is said to be not only successful but highly sought-after by the rich and famous. If we are able to accomplish these medical miracles today, how could a god, who could create a man do less?

Whether one calls the demand for animals or firstborns infants, a tribute or a sacrifice is immaterial. The people had to be made to sacrifice something in order for Jehovah to become a god. Without sacrifices he was just another nobody entity: a god in name only.

Under the leadership of Moses, the Israelites began their long journey from Egypt to the promised land of Canaan.

While Moses appeared to be the leader it was actually Jehovah who was in charge. When he said "move", they moved. When he said "stop", they stopped. The people obeyed without question remembering what happened to the Egyptians before the Exodus, and the incident at the Red Sea.

Soon after the Hebrews had left Egypt, they found themselves being pursued by the Egyptian Army. Jehovah claimed that it was because he had harden the heart of Pharaoh in order to bring further power and glory to his name. Jehovah destroy that army. How could the destruction of hundreds of additional Egyptians bring any more power and glory to the ego of this god? He had already caused the Egyptians untold suffering, famine, disease, death and destruction; how much death does it take to bring him his honour and glory?

The army of Pharaoh was not chasing the Hebrews became God had harden his heart but because they had robbed the Egyptians. The army was chasing a bunch of thieves in order to recapture what had been stolen from them, to punish the Hebrews for their crime and to return them to the power of Pharaoh.

Whether the Egyptian army was destroyed by the technical power of Jehovah or by natural forces of nature is not as important as the reason the army had to perish.

While Jehovah claimed it was for his honour and glory it was also to ensure that the Egyptians developed a hatred against the Hebrews. It was to be a hatred so intense that the Hebrews would never again be allowed sanctuary in Egypt. It also guaranteed that no mattered what would happen in the future, the Hebrews would never again be allowed to return to Egypt. They were doomed to wander in the wilderness at the mercy of God and Moses until they became strong enough to conquer a people and claim a land for themselves. Regardless of what torment they had to endure under the yoke and leadership of Moses and Jehovah, they could not change their minds and return to a land where they were not welcomed. Wherever they were led they had to go because they had nowhere else available to them except the wilderness of Sinai. They were banned from Egypt, and the countries in their path were too strong for them to pass through without a fight.

The deceitful reputation of Jacob and his sons, passed down to the people of the area, from one generation to the next, was so bad that no tribe or nation would trust the Hebrews to coexist with them as neighbours. And once the people of the surrounding nations learned of the Exodus, the destruction of the Egyptians and the robberies committed by the Hebrews, no one would ever trust them to abide in their midst.

Jehovah was not a god of love and peace. He was a god of war and vengeance. He was not the Lord, God and creator of the universe, he was a mortal being. He did not exist in heavens but here on earth.

Exodus 15:1-3. *Then sang Moses and the children of Israel this song unto the Lord, and spake, saying, I will sing unto the Lord, for he hath triumphed gloriously: the horse and the rider hath he thrown into the sea. The Lord is my strength and song, and he is become my salvation: he is my God, and I will prepare him an habitation: my father's God, and I will exalt him. The Lord is a man of war: the Lord is his name.*

God's purpose for the Hebrews other than to make himself a god, was to obtain an army, train and lead that army into battle against the people who worshipped of the other gods, his enemies. He intended to destroy the people, which would destroy the gods. He intended to bask in the honour and glory and to enjoy the blood, the plunder of war and the defeat of his enemies. In this quest he and his army, by his command, showed no mercy.

Exodus 15:14-18. *The people shall hear and be afraid: sorrow shall take hold on the inhabitants of Palestine. Then the dukes of Edom shall be amazed; the mighty men of Moab, trembling shall take hold upon them; all the inhabitants of Canaan shall melt away. Fear and dread shall fall upon them; by the greatness of thine arm they shall be still as a stone; till thy people pass over, O Lord, till the people pass over, which thou hast purchased. Thou shall bring them in, and plant them in the mountain of thine inheritance, in the place, O Lord, which thou hast made for thee to dwell in, in the Sanctuary, O Lord, which thy hands have established. The Lord shall reign fo ever and ever.*

The reign of God began when the Israelites entered the wilderness. They agreed to follow him out of fear. Now they followed because they were tired, hungry, and thirsty.

There had been no firm commitment binding them to Moses and Jehovah until they let themselves be led into the wilderness of Shur. For three days they went without water. (Exo. 15:22). They began to thirst, to worry and to complain.

Soon they found water, the waters of Marah, but it was too bitter to drink. It was here that Moses and God, using the thirst of the people as a weapon demanded that a commitment from the people follow the Lord or die of thirst in the desert.

They could not go back to Egypt. There was no country which would allow them into their camp. They had no army which could fight or obtain a place for them to live, sp where else could they go and what could they do?

Through the use of bribery, fear, intimation, and corruption God and Moses began the Nation of Israel.

Exodus 15:22-27. *So Moses brought Israel from the Red sea, and they went out into the wilderness of Shur; and they went three days in the wilderness, and found no water. And when they came to Marah, they could not drink of the waters of Marah; for they were bitter: therefore the name of it was called Marah And the people murmured against Moses, saying, What shall we drink? And he cried unto the Lord; and the Lord shewed him a tree, which when he had cast into the waters, the waters were made sweet: there he made for them a statute and an ordinance, and there he proved them. .And he said, If thou wilt diligently hearken to the voice of the Lord thy God, and wilt do what is right in his sight, and wilt give ear to his commandments, and keep all his statutes, I will put none of these diseases upon thee, which I have brought upon the Egyptians: for I am the Lord that healeth thee. And they came to Elim, where were twelve wells of water, and threescore and ten palm-trees: and they encamped there by the waters.*

Nothing has changed since those days in the desert when the Lord God Jehovah became the First Godfather.

It did not take the Israelites long to realize that the situation in which they now found themselves was not to different from the one which they had just left in Egypt. True they no longer had to make bricks from mud and straw but now they had to struggle day by day merely to survive. In Egypt, they at least did not grow hungry or thirsty. Under Pharaoh, they had meat and bread to eat. Under the rule of God, until the time be began to feed them manna, they went hungry. They had the meat, they had their sheep and cattle so why did they lust for meat?

The people in a desire for freedom exchanged one form of slavery for another. Now, like their bondage to Pharaoh they had committed themselves to servitude of a new god with no hope of a reprieve.

Exodus. 16:2-3. *And the whole congregation of the children of Israel murmured against Moses and Aaron in the wilderness. And the children of Israel said unto them, Would to God we had died by the hand of the Lord in the land of Egypt, where we sat by the flesh-pots, and we did eat bread to the full: for ye have brought us forth into this wilderness, to kill this whole assembly with hunger.*

Like Pharaoh, the Lord promise to feed and take care of the people. He promised meat in the evening and bread in the morning.

Exod. 16:4,8, 13-15. *Then said the Lord unto Moses, Behold, I will rain bread from heaven for you; and the people shall go out and gather a certain rate every day, that I may prove them, whether they will walk in my law, or no. And Moses said, This shall be when the Lord shall give you in the evening flesh to eat, and in the morning bread to the full; for that the Lord heareth your murmurings which ye murmur against him: and what are we? Your murmurings are not against us, but against the Lord. And it came to pass, that at even the quails came up, and covered the camp: and in the morning the dew lay round about the camp .And when the dew that lay was gone up, behold, upon the face of the wilderness there lay a small round thing, as small as the hoar frost on the grounds: And when the children of Israel saw it, they said one to another, It is manna: for they wist not what it was. And Moses said unto them, This is the bread which the Lord hath given you to eat.*

When the people were the most vulnerable and were completely at the mercy of God and Moses, then and then only did God and Moses begin to show their true intentions.

They began their control through hunger, thirst and fear. These were the beginning tenets of the rule by "Jehovah The First Godfather."

If the people, his subjects and servants, did not obey his commands they were threaten with the diseases and plagues he claimed that he had inflicted upon the Egyptians. He would and did on occasions kill them en masse when it became necessary to have his way or to demonstrate his anger. Even the Godfathers of today are more merciful.

Suppose we review a couple of the acts and biblical miracles of God, the ones experienced by the Hebrews while they were wandering through the wilderness under the love, benevolence and protection of God.

These miracles were recorded as the remembered experiences of the people. They were told and they believed that the acts and events they experienced were demonstrations of the effective power, might and glory of their god.

When the people were thirsty they were led to a well of bitter water. Their thirst was quenched not by the power of God but by throwing herbs or organic matter into water which neutralized the bitter taste.

The bitterness in the water was removed by the chemicals in a plant. If this was a miracle it was not one of divine power but of natural science. Anyone with an advanced knowledge of botany and chemistry would have been able to do the same thing. If it was a miracle it was not divine but a scientific or chemical one.

Then there was the supposed miracle of the quails, when the Lord fed his people poisoned or contaminated meat because they loath the manna and lusted after fresh meat. The people had lots of meat but it was for sacrifices which went to the tables of the Lord and the priests while the people had to survive on manna and what they could find in the desert that was fir to eat.

Numbers 11:1, 4-6, 10, 18-20, 31-33. *And when the people complained, it displeased the Lord; and the Lord heard it: and his anger was kindled; and the fire of the Lord burnt among them, and consumed them that were in the uttermost parts of the camp. And the mixed multitude that was among them fell a lusting: and the children of Israel also wept again, and said, Who shall give us flesh to eat? We remember the fish which we did eat in Egypt freely; the cucumbers, and the melons, and the leeks, and the onions, and the garlic. But now our soul is dried away; there is nothing at all, besides this manna, before our eyes. Then Moses heard the people weep throughout their families, every man in the door of his tent: and the anger of the Lord was kindled greatly; Moses also was displeased. And say thou unto the people, Sanctify yourselves against to-morrow, and ye shall eat flesh: for ye have wept in the ears of the Lord, saying, who shall give us flesh to eat? For it was well with us in Egypt: therefore the Lord will give you flesh and ye shall eat. Ye shall not eat one day, nor two days, nor five days, neither ten days, nor twenty days but even a whole month, until it come out at your nostrils, and it be loathsome unto you: because that ye have displeased the Lord which is among you, and have wept before him, saying, Why came we forth out of Egypt. And there went forth a wind from the Lord, and brought quails from the sea, and let them fall by the camp, as it were a day's journey on this side, and as it were a day's journey on the*

This appears to be the way the Lord God of the Hebrews handled the complains of his people.

The people did not eat meat for a month because they died before they could chew and swallow their first bite.

This was the way that Moses and the Lord God handled the grumbling and dissatisfaction of the people with their command/ It was his way of power and controlled. He either kill them singularly or en masse according to his mood at the time of the offense. Those he did not personally kill or lay claim to he had Moses or the tribe of Levi do it for him.

It took the people approximately forty five days to learn that Jehovah as a god was a hoax, and that Moses, while a leader was also a con man. By that time the whole congregation began to murmur against Moses, Aaron, and indirectly their new god out of fear and intimidation they did nothing about it.

During their journey through the wilderness the Hebrews suffered hunger and thirst. They had committed themselves to Moses and to Jehovah. And like a king, Jehovah promised to be the supreme deity, the divine god and leader of his people. Moses was his intermediary, his prophet, the speaker of his divine wisdom and commandments.

Once God had destroyed the Egyptian army at the Red Sea, the Israelites were doomed to whatever fate he, Moses, time, and circumstances dictated for them.

In time the control of the people would passed from Moses to Joshua, a military ruler. After him came the elders, called judges and finally a king. But throughout the whole history of the Jewish Nation it has been the high priests and the priest of Levi who have held the real the power behind the throne.

For forty years the Israelites wandered through the wilderness. Led and instructed by God and Moses, they soon became proficient in the art of survival. They learned the secrets of the desert and more important they learned the art of warfare.

Through all of their wandering they carried the banner of Jehovah before them. He was their God and they became his army. Like the army ants of the Amazon, once they began their march to Canaan, they were such a destructive force that they destroyed almost everything and everyone who opposed their march to Canaan.

During this journey the Israelites either killed or enslaved all of those who opposed them. This included not only the men of the tribes or nations they conquered but their wives, their children and even their animals.

The fear of the Israelite God and the army of the Israelites spread throughout the land. The blood bath imposed by Jehovah began with the Amaleks and ended with the destruction of most of the people of Canaan, the promised land. This land for which Jehovah had no claim, he had promised to Abraham and his descendants. If the land had belonged to him he would not have had to fight for it. The land of Canaan belonged to the other gods. They were the gods which Jehovah envied and wished to destroy.

The Israelites did finally possess a portion of the land but what they obtained was not given to them by the power, might and glory of God, but by the spears, swords, arrows, death, suffering and might of the army of Moses and Joshua.

The tribes and small nations which occupied the the land of Canaan really had no choice but to surrender and become subjects of the Israelite. How many nations today can stand up and fight against a trained army of over half a million warriors. For the Israelites, they suffered too. They either killed the people of Canaan as they were commanded to do by God or he intended to inflict upon them what he demanded they do to those they conquered.

Lev. 26:7. *And ye shall chase your enemies, and they shall fall before you by the sword.*

Lev. 26:14-20. *But if ye will not hearken unto me, and will not do all these commandments. And if ye shall despise my statues, so that ye will not do all my commandments, but that ye break my covenant; I also will do this unto you; I will even appoint over you terror, consumption, and burning ague, that shall consume the eyes, and cause sorrow of heart: and ye shall sow your seed in vain, for your enemies shall eat it. And I will set my face against you, and ye shall be slain before your enemies; they that hate you shall reign over you; and ye shall flee when none pursueth you. And if you will not yet for all this hearken unto me, then I will punish you seven times more for your sins. And I will break the pride of your power; and I will make your heaven as iron, and your earth as brass. And your strength shall be spent in vain: for your land shall not yield her increase, neither shall the trees of the land yield their fruits.*

The Lord and Moses began to assemble their army on the first day of the second month in the second year after they had left Egypt. Num. 1:2-3.

On the eastern side of the tabernacle was the tribe of Judah. Next to them were to be the tribes of Issachar and then the tribe of Zebulun. To the south were the tribes of Reuben, Simeon and Gad. To the west were the tribes of Ephraim, Manasseh, and Benjamin. On the northern side were located the tribes of Dan, Asher, and Naphtali. In the middle surrounded and protected on all sides was the tabernacle and the thirteenth tribe of Israel. It was that of Moses, Aaron and the Levi.

The Israelite god ensured his personal protection by surrounding himself with his army. He ensured himself that when he walked about the camp on an inspection he could do so unafraid. A part of his inspection was to ensure that the Israelites maintained a clean camp and orderly camp. This is not normally the type of thing that would concern a god but it is something which every military commander demands and expects. Jehovah was no different. He lived in the camp and expected it to clean because he intended to walk through it.

Deu. 23:12-14. *Thou shalt have a place also without the camp, whither thou shalt go forth abroad:(a camp latrine) remember there were an estimated six millions individusls along with their pets and animals. And thou shalt have a paddle upon thy weapon: and it shall be when thou wilt ease thyself abroad, thou shalt dig therein, and shall turn back, and cover that which cometh from thee 14. For the Lord thy God walketh in the midst of thy camp, to deliver thee, and to give up thine enemies before thee; therefore shall thy camp be holy: that he see no unclean thing in thee, and turn away from thee.*

While the Hebrews wandered through the wilderness, eating manna instead of meat and vegetables, and trying to find suitable water to drink, they were still required to offer up their animals as a sacrifice to their god. He and his priest ate meat while the people either ate manna or went without.

Exodus 29:42-45. *This shall be a continual burnt offering throughout your generations at the door of the tabernacle of the congregation before the Lord: where I will meet you, to speak there unto you. And there I will meet with the children of Israel, and the tabernacle shall be sanctified by my glory. And I will sanctify the tabernacle of the congregation, and the alter: I will sanctify also both Aaron and his sons, to minister to me in the priest's office And I will dwell among the children of Israel and will be their God.*

And he would do this in kingly luxury. He ate from golden plates, sat in a golden chair, smelled the fragrance of special incense and consumed special foods prepared in a special way and cooked on an altar which resembled a large barbeque grill. Exodus 27:1-5.

The altar (i.e. barbeque grill) was used for cooking the food of God. Many call the food an offering and believe that the preparation was all symbolic, but the following passages indicate otherwise. The offerings were prepared according to the strict directions of Jehovah.

Exodus 29:38-46. *Now this is that which thou shalt offer upon the altar; two lambs of the first year day by day continually. The one lamb thou shalt offer in the morning; and the other lamb thou shalt offer at even: And with the one lamb a tenth eal of flour mingled with the fourth part of an hin of beaten oil; and the fourth part of a hin of wine for a drink offering. And the other lamb thou shalt offer at even, and shalt do thereto according to the meat offering of the morning, and according to the drink offering thereof, for a sweet savour, an offering made by fire unto the Lord.*

42. This shall be a continual burnt offering throughout your generations at the door of the tabernacle of the congregation before the Lord where I will meet you, to speak there unto you. And there I will meet with the children of Israel, and the tabernacle shall be sanctified by my glory. And I will sanctify the tabernacle of the congregation, and the altar: I will sanctify also both Aaron and his sons to dminister to me in the priest's office. And I will dwell among the children of Israel, and will be their God and they shall know that I am the Lord their God that brought them forth out of the land of Egypt that I may dwell among them: I am the Lord their God.

The above is a curious statement for a spiritual God to make; "that I brought them forth out of the land of Egypt, that I may dwell among them." If he were a god, why was he not able to dwell among them when they were in Egypt?

Would this statement ever have been made by the creator of the universe, who abides everywhere and in everything. I do not think so. But for a living being who wanted to live in luxury, ete, drink and demonstrated his fits of anger and paranoia, the idea that he lived, walked, talked and dwelt among the Hebrew is not unreasonable.

In order to mask the scent of the slaughtered animals offered daily, within the tabernacle, for the sacrificial feeding of God and the priests, a special incense was burnt.

Exodus 30:7-8. *And Aaron shall burn thereon sweet incense every morning when he dresseth the lamps, he shall burn incense upon it. And when Aaron lighteth the lamps at even, he shall burn incense upon it; a perpetual incense before the Lord, throughout your generations,*

He even created his own incense according to Exodus 30:22-27. *Moreover the Lord spake unto Moses, saying, Take thou also unto thee principle spices, of pure myrrh five hundred shekels, and sweet cinnamon half so much, even two hundred and fifty shekels ,and of sweet calamus two hundred and fifty shekels, And of cassia five hundred shekels, after the shekel of the sanctuary, and of oil olive an hin: And thou shalt make it an oil of holy ointment, an ointment compound after the art of the apothecary: it shall be an holy anointing oil. And thou shalt anoint the tabernacle of the congregation therewith, and the ark of the testimony, And the table and all his vessels, and the candlestick and all his vessels, and the altar of incense.*

Exodus 30:32. *Upon man's flesh shall it not be poured, neither shall ye make any other like it, after the composition of it: it is holy, and it shall be holy unto you.*

These are the instructions, given by God, on how to make a particular perfume or incense.to be used in his service and only in the tht he dictated. He even went so far as to specifically designate the specific individuals he wanted to do the work that he demanded. (Exodus 31:1-12.)

While Jehovah was dictating his desires to Moses, the people who decided that they were no longer under the direct control of God and Moses, decided to worship a different god one they could see and relate to. They went to Aaron, who, in the absence of Moses was considered their leader. They made a request for a new god in order to have a feast and to celebrate their freedom from Pharaoh. Aaron, who had been with Moses and was supposed to have seen and talked with God could not have been to impressed with him because he reverted back to the religions of Egypt and built a golden calf for the people to worship. The golden calf was a throwback to the calf cult of Egypt, with which the Israelites were familiar. If the Israelites had been in the presence of a God of divine might and power, (experiencing the Exodus, and the death of Egypt), would they have dared to have Aaron build them an artificial god?

The people, while in Egypt, were use to spiritual gods, represented by images. These they could relate to and worship. Jehovah was not such a god. He was a living, breathing life form that the people did not associated with as the gods which they had grown up with. He was a being to fear, not to worship. While Moses called him a god he was looked upon by the people as just another ruler, a king or leader. He was a flesh and blood, not a god. He was a being who could be seen, talked to and negotiated with. The Israelites did not give to Jehovah the service and respect that they had rendered to Pharaoh. Some of the congregation decided that they would like to have a different god to worship.

Hen Jehovah learned what the Israelites were trying to do his enormous ego demanded a retaliation. He began contemplating the destruction of the Israelites. His ego, paranoia, dementia and anger, he was at the point when he considered disregarding the promises he had made to Abraham , Isaac and Jacob When Moses reminded him of these things his anger dissipated and he relented his thoughts of destroying the Hebrews.

A true God is never wrong, and therefore has no reason to repent any thought or action. But Jehovah was not a true god. He was an enormously egotical spoiled mananical individual who acted like any normal, spoiled, fallible human when the individuals behaved contrary to what they are expected to do.

He congregation had gone to Aaron and again requested him to again construct another golden calf. When Moses returned to the camp and saw the calf his actions were those of an angry man. He commanded, in the name of God, the death of all those who were not on the side of the Lord. His family, the family of the Levi came to Moses. This family of priests, on or by the command of Moses, slaughtered approximately three thousand men that day. (Exodus 32:28.)

Even with the death of so many men, the anger of Jehovah was not appeased. He continued to punish the Israelites.

Exodus 32:33-35. *And the Lord said unto Moses, Whoever hath sinned against me, him will I blot out of my book. Therefore now go, lead the people unto the place of which I have spoken unto thee: behold, mine Angel shall go before thee: nevertheless in the day when I visit I will visit their sin upon them. And the Lord plagued the people, because they made the calf, which Aaron made.*

Even though Aaron had made the golden calf, he was not killed or punished because he was a Levi. Jehovah had a curious way of determining who and in what way he would deal with the transgressors to his commandments. For a god who was supposed to love his subjects, he dealt with them in a cruel, and vicious way. There was no love in his actions; only revenge and retribution.

The retribution of this 'holy god' was not a one time occurrence. He killed the Egyptians. He killed his own priests. He tried to kill Moses. He destroyed Sodom and Gomorrah and he had Moses hang everyone who had bowed down to a different god. On other dissenting tribes he placed a curse or plague, and caused the deaths of untold thousands of men, women, children and animals. He even claimed the credit for the death of his own people when they died of the plague.

Numbers 25:4-5. *And the Lord said unto Moses, Take all the heads of the people, and hang them up before the Lord against the sun, that the fierce anger of the Lord may be turned away from Israel And Moses said unto the judges of Israel, Slay ye every one his men that were joined unto Baalpeor.*

It was not only Moses who was able to kill with impunity and without penalty, but members of his family of priests, as well.

Numbers 25:7-9. *And when Phinehas, the son of Eleazar, the son of Aaron the priest, saw it, he rose up from among the congregation, and took a javelin in his hand; And he went after the man of Israel into the tent and thrust both of them through, the man of Israel and the woman through her belly. So the plague was stayed from the children of Israel And those that died in the plague were twenty and four thousand.*

What action did the Lord Jehovah take for this atrocity, the murder of two people, within his temple?

Numbers 25:12-13. *Wherefore say, Behold I give unto him my covenant of peace: And he shall have it, and his seed after him, even the covenant of an everlasting priesthood; because he was zealous for his God, and made an atonement for the children of Israel.*

How does killing two people stop a plague? How does killing two people become an atonement for the sins of the people? Is it any wonder, that according to the blessings given to this particular priest by God, that many pious have come to believe that the killing of infidels, unbelievers and human sacrifices of heathens is pleasing to God?

Based upon the same above passages is it any wonder that the idea of 'death to an infidel' came to be a part of the Moslem religious tradition. Such an idea seems to be the heritage of both the Jewish and Islamic religions. The death of anyone who is not a true believer of their God is deemed to be pleasing to him. Gender and age does not seem to have any bearing on who is to be killed. According to the faith of Islam and Judaism it is only a man's faith which either justifies life or death.

The woman killed by the priest was not an infidel, nor was her husband. He was a member of the congregation and she and her people were followers of Jehovah. She belonged to the tribe of Midian, a son of Abraham and was herself a believer in God. Her tribe were from one of the sons of Abraham and as such were his seed and heirs to the promises of God himself. They were promised the land of Canaan, not annihilation by kinsmen.

Jethro, the father-in law of Moses, was himself, a priest of Midian. He was a servant of the same God who demand the death of his whole tribe. Jethro was the man who helped Moses to set up the governing authority of the twelve tribes.

When God commanded Moses to destroy the Midianites, that destruction had to included his own father-in-law, wife and child.

What reward did Jethro receive for his years of good and faithful service. For Jethro it was the death of his tribe and his family. What did Moses receive for his years of good and faithful service? He was killed by the same god which he had served.

Why was Jethro and his tribe killed? They were destroyed by the command of God because a few of the Israelite men found the women of Midian fair to look upon and choose them as brides and lovers. This infatuation of a few men, who chose to worship God in the manner of the Midianites, instead of the particular manner prescribed by Jehovah for the Israelite congregation was through no fault of the women, yet thousands were executed as an example to the remaining Israelite men to stay within the bounds set by Jehovah, Moses and his priests.

The above death of an entire faithful people is a prime example of the egotism, brutality and blood thirst of Jehovah.

Numbers 25:16-18. *And the Lord spake unto Moses, saying, Vex the Midianites, and smite them: For they vex you with their wiles, wherewith they have beguiled you in the matter of Peor and in the matter of Cozbi, the daughter of a prince of Midian, their sister, which was slain in the day of the plague for Peor's sake.*

Numbers 31:3. *And Moses spake unto the people, saying, Arm some of yourselves unto war, and let them go against the Midianites, and avenge the Lord of Midian.*

Numbers 31:7-12. *And they warred against the Midianites as the Lord commanded Moses; and they slew all the males. And they slew the kings of Midian, beside the rest of them that were slain; namely, Evi, and Rekem, and Zur, and Hur, and Reba, five kings of Midian: Balaam also the son of Beor they slew with the sword. And the children of Israel took all the women of Midian captives, and their little ones, and took the spoil of all of their cattle, and all their flocks, and all their goods. And they burnt all their cities wherein they dwelt, and all their goodly castles, with fire and they took all the spoil, and all the prey, both of men and of beasts. And they brought the captives, and the prey, and the spoil, unto Moses, and Eleazar the pries, and unto the congregation of the children of Israel, unto the camp at the plains of Moab, which are by Jordan near Jericho.*

Numbers 31:15-18. *And Moses said unto them, Have ye saved all the women alive? Behold, these caused the children of Israel through the counsel of Balaam, to commit trespass against the Lord in the matter of Peor, and there was a plague among the congregation of the Lord. Now therefore kill every male among the little ones, and kill every woman that hath known man by lying with him. But all the women children, that have not known a man by lying with him, keep alive for yourself.*

How can anyone in their study of history not see or understand that acts of Hitler were in essence a mirror image of the acts committed by the Lord God Jehovah and his prophet Moses.

The reason, given by Jehovah, for killing the people of Midian was the beauty of the women which turned the heads of the men of the congregation to the young women and against the worship of their Lord, Jehovah. Yet these same young girls would also grow into beauties and yet they were spared. What would happen to them and the men who took and kept them as the young girls grew older? Would the hearts of the men harden against these young girls out of the fear of death at the hand of God or would they become acceptable mates, wives and lovers to the Israelites men because they were slaves? What is not said in this story is the disposition of the wealth of Median obtained by the Israelites.

What kind of a god, was Jehovah?

He was a god of war, brutal, arrogant, egotistical, filled with anger and revenge. This was a vital part of his psyche.

Exodus 15:3. *The Lord is a man of war: the Lord is his name.*

Exodus 15:7. *Thy right hand, O Lord, is become glorious in power: thy right hand, O Lord, hath dashed in pieces the enemy.*

Exodus 15:15-16. *Then the dukes of Edom shall be amazed; the mighty men of Moab, trembling shall take hold upon them; all the inhabitants of Canaan shall melt away. Fear and dread shall fall upon them; by the greatness of thine arm they shall be as still as a stone; till the people pass over, which thou hast purchased.*

This fear can also be seen in the lives of the European community as the Army of Germany advanced under the order of their lord and god Adolf Hitler.

The Israelites were completely under the control of Moses and God, could not go back to Egypt. They were not welcomed in any territory or nation because of the known acts of Jacob and his sons and they were not yet powerful enough to conquer land for themselves. So they followed Jehovah and Moses. When they became thirsty, God made them agree to a covenant of servitude before he showed Moses where and how to find drinkable water for the them. In one instance, when the people complained about their hunger, and desired meat for their table, God gave them a feast of meat. It is called by the religious community, "the miracle of the quails".

The people ate, but it was not a feast of meat but of diseased and death. The people died while the quails meat was still in their mouths.

What kind of ruler feeds his people contaminated food? One who is either demented or has no compassion. Concerned only with his image, the egotistical Jehovah chose to kill and torture the people, rather than allow them to complain.

It is unthinkable that the Hebrews, long acquainted with the rigors of the desert, would believe that the fallen birds were safe to eat. Something must have caused the birds to fall out of the sky. There must have been thousands that died, for they covered the ground for miles around the camp and were piled a yard deep.

There is one explanation for the situation. Scriptures say that the birds came from the sea. There is a rare occurrence when the plankton of the sea absorb a chemical which turns into strychnine. In large doses it is a deadly poison. In small doses it acts as a mild stimulant. It is possible that the birds, immune to small doses of this poison, might have been feeding on the plankton before flying in the direction of the Israelite camp. The poison, activated by the flying, killed the birds or caused them to flutter on the ground, making it easy for the Israelites to capture them. Once the Israelites began to chew on the meat the poison killed or made them deathly ill. The fact that the birds were piled a yard deep indicates that those on the bottom were dead and rotting. Add to the heat of the desert, the two days that it took to gather up the birds, and the rotting flesh, added ptomaine poison to the strychnine. The meat of the birds was so toxic that those who ate the quails were almost guaranteed to die.

Thus did an angry, egotistical, and wrathful god obtain his revenge for the questions and complaints of the people.

After this experience, those who survived became as docile and obedient as sheep, They followed, without complaint all of the the dictates of God and Moses.

For a while the people became good, faithful and dutiful servants. They began to learn the ways of war. Untrained in its' art they were unprepared for the attack by the Amalek people, (the descendants of the son of Eliphaz, eldest son of Esau by his concubine Timna). Moses sent Joshua to do battle with the Amalek, while he stood on the top of a hill with the rod of God in his hand.

Exodus 17:11. *And it came to pass, when Moses held up his hand that Israel prevailed: and when he let down his hand, Amalek prevailed.*

The following scriptures however indicate that Jehovah was embarrassed by the above incident and the fact that Moses and the Israelites could not defeat the Amalek on their own. To cover this failure he made the following declaration.

Exodus 14-16. And the Lord said unto Moses, Write this for a memorial in a book, and rehearse it in the ears of Joshua for I will utterly put out the remembrance of Amalek from under heaven. And

Moses built an altar, and called the name of it Jehovahnissi: For he said, Because the Lord hath sworn that the Lord will have war with Amalek from generation to generation.

There are a couple of things that should be noted: God does not seem to have the power of a divine being. He cannot erase the name and the remembrance of the Amalek in a moment in time. He says that he will do battle with them from one generation to generation or in other words for all time. The very fact that this promise is in the Christian Bible almost guarantees that this will never happen. For all of the descendants of the Amalek race, be they Moslem, Christian or any other religion which worships this god, by whatever name they chose to call him, according to the above scriptural promise they will never be able to enter his presence because they are his mortal enemies.

There will never be a garden of paradise, nor a heavenly temple for the descendants of the Amalek because there is no salvation for them. That of course is assuming that there is salvation for all other believers.

During the beginning days of the Exodus, while the Hebrews' were wandering through the wilderness, there was no formal governing body. Moses settled all disputes. His was the final word on all things.

Exodus 18:16. *When they have a matter, they come unto me; and I judge between one and another, and I do make them know the statutes of God, and his laws.*

These were the words of Moses as he spoke to his father-in-law, while the Israelites were camped before the mountain of God. Jethro, priest of Midian and father-in-law to Moses, had some experience in governing people. He suggested to Moses that Moses should divide his authority between the elders of the tribes. In this way not only would justice be better served, but it would relieve Moses of some of his duties to the people. This Moses consented to do. This was the beginning of the governing authority over the congregation of the future Jewish Nation.

It would seem that there was never a definite decision made as to what constituted a great matter or a small matter. Eventually it must have been decided and agreed to by the people that anything having to do with God, the priests and religion was to be treated as a great matter and all other disputes as small ones.

It was about this time that God told Moses that he was going to come down from his mountain and speak to the people. When he spoke, it was with a voice of thunder, lightning, and fire. It was a voice that scripture says that only Moses could understand. It was also at this time that Moses and the people were given the Ten Commandants for the first time.

From the above description of the event one might almost believe that the voice of God was nothing more than the rumble of a smoking volcano. It was Moses who determined what it was that God had said and what he wanted the people to do.

This was not the original or the first recorded issue of the ten commandants or the real beginning of the law and a true understanding of the culture from which God and the original creators of man came. That information was first recorded ib h Code of Hammurabi almost 2500 years before the time of Moses.

This alien culture which created Adam and Eve, gave us the custom of marriage, the idea of a father and mother, servitude, husbandry, music and musical instruments, weaving, mining, swords and metallurgy. They taught Cain how to build cities and Noah how to build an ark and man to grow grain, make bread and how to survive.

Now Jehovah as the resident overseer of man passed down to him through the Jewish Nation further evidence of his ancient culture. With Moses as his spokesperson he relayed to the people, his standard of living, a code of conduct, and a check and balance kind of society. For this, Jehovah demanded strict obedience to all that he ordained. To disobey any of his commandants was to face his wrath and on many occasions death.

What is not stated or understood by most religious disciples regardless of their   faith is that these laws and civilized codes of conduct where given to the Israelites as the laws of God but are remarkably simular to the "Laws of Hammurabi". It was these laws that were in existence approximately 2500 years before the Exodus. While he Laws of Moses was given only to the Israelite people the laws of Hammurabi were universal. They are basically the standard by which the ancient race of beings, our earthly gods lived and obeyed. The reality of these laws transcends any particular people, nationality or culture.

For an Israelite, the disobedience of any laws of Moses or God, depending upon how they chose to interpret the law usually resulted in a very severe type of punishment. Not only did the transgressor stand trial for his disobedience but many times his whole family, including his animals and possessions. They so suffered as well.

If the offence was severe enough the whole congregation suffered.

Apparently this was another custom of the society from which Jehovah came. Another unique custom was that of circumcision. It was a positive way of identifying the men who belonged to a certain tribe in this case the tribe of Jehovah.

The custom of circumsion was first given to Abraham and apparently observed by the Hebrews during their long stay in Egypt. Apparently it was not observed during the time the Israelites were wandering through the desert. It only became important when the Israelites had crossed the Jordan and were about to invade the land of Canaan. This was to be a war which was to annihilate everyone in the land in order for the Israelites to inherit the land promised by their god to Abraham.

This was a promised that could only be fulfilled by violence and bloodshed.

The circumcision of every Israelite male guaranteed that, in the event of a dispute as to who was Israelite and who was not, identification could be made by circumcision.

Before the fighting began the Lord spoke to Joshua and said:

Joshua 5:2-7. *At that time the Lord said unto Joshua, Make thee sharp knives, and circumcise again the children of Israel the second time. And Joshua made him sharp knives, and circumcised the children of Israel at the hill of the foreskins. And this is the cause why Joshua did circumcise: All the people that came out of Egypt, that were males, even all the men of war, died in the wilderness by the way, after they came out of Egypt.*

Now all the people that came out were circumcised: but all the people that were born in the wilderness by the way as they came forth out of Egypt, them they had not circumcised. For the children of Israel walked forty years in the wilderness, till all the people that were men of war, which came out of Egypt, were consumed, because they obeyed not the voice of the Lord: unto whom the Lord swore that he would not shew them the land, which the Lord sware unto their fathers that he would give us, a land that flowed with milk and honey. And their children, whom he raised up in their stead, them Joshua circumcised: for they were uncircumcised, because they had not circumcised them by the way.

The act of circumcision was a positive way for the Israelite males to identify themselves to each other if the need every occurred.

Later circumcision seem to have lost its' meaning. In a letter to the Galatians 6:15 the Apostle Paul wrote, *For in Christ Jesus neither circumcision availeth anything, nor uncircumcision but a new creature.*

If circumcision does not serve any specific purpose it becomes just another bloody ritual serving the whims of a god, or possibly the renewal of a custom, derived from the culture from which the God of Man belonged.

If is was it was not required of Adam, and early man and the Lord God. This would have been on purpose because it served to maintain the separated between the gods and early.

Circumcision, the mutilation of one's body, is the one mark which denoting a Jewish male as a servant of God. For the Christians it is the symbolic marks of baptism upon the forehead of a child.

Ezekiel 9:3-6. *And the glory of the God of Israel was gone up from the cherub, whereupon he was, to the threshold of the house. And he called to the man clothed with linen, which had the writer's inkhorn by his side; And the Lord said unto him, Go through the midst of the city, through the midst of Jerusalem, and set a mark upon the foreheads of the men that sigh and that cry for all the abominations that be done in the midst thereof. And to the others he said in mine hearing, Go ye after him through the city, and smite: let not your eye spare, neither have ye pity: Slay utterly old and young, both maids, and little children, and women: but come not near any man upon whom is the mark; and begin at my sanctuary. Then they began at the ancient men which were before the house.*

Today male children of almost all civilized societies are circumcised at birth in the belief that it will prevent health and medical problems as the male grows older.

Almost every child born is believed to go before a member of the clergy of some faith in order to be given a name. This ceremony is called Christening. During this naming ceremony the child is blessed by a mark, the sign of the cross or some other religious symble symbolically placed upon the forehead of the child. The child is given a name by which the God of the believer might know the child. It is also a mark which makes that child a servant of God and a member of a particular religious faith.

But is that mark the mark of God or of Satan?

Revelation 14:9-10. *And the third angel followed them, saying with a loud voice, If any man worship the beast and his image, and receive his mark in his forehead, or in his hand, The same shall drink of the wine of the wrath of God, which is poured out without mixture into the cup of his indignation; and he shall be tormented with fire and brimstone in the presence of holy angels, and in the presence of the Lamb:*

But who worships the beast and his image and carries his mark?

Revelation 13:17. *And that no man might buy or sell, save he that had the mark, or the name of the beast, or the number of his name.*

If Jehovah has set a mark upon the foreheads of his followers as a sign of his protection and the same mark is required by the beast, the destructive god of Revelation who intends to destroy the world, are they not one and the same?

When one considers the bloody destruction of so many nations destroyed by the Israelites, by the command of God then reads the destruction prophesied in Revelation, it becomes plausible that Jehovah and the beast are one and the same.

If we are to believe that Jehovah was the creator of man, which he was not and if he chooses to take credit for the flood and the massive destruction of life on this planet so be It. If the power to destroy life through violence and bloodshed is his only claim to glory, outside of his claim to have brought the Israelites out of Egypt, then we must give credit where credit is due.

If Jehovah as the destroyer of life on a grand scale wishes to be worship as a god because it was believed that he had a hand in saving mankind it serves no purpose to deny him that pleasure. In reality he did not save man but he may have assisted Noah in the construction of the ark, gathering of the animals and helped the Lord God save Noah and his family. As a subordinate to the Lord God that was one of his responsibilities. He claims to have saved Abraham and his family while the Lord God was saving Noah which gives us a plausible explanation that explaines how and why be became the God of Abraham. Joshua 24:1-4.

It was the Lord God who created man, assisted Noah in the construction of the ark and not Jehovah, the God of Abraham and the Israelites.

If the original destruction of Man by the flood was the result of the evil of man nothing changed for the next few hundred years before Jehovah again made himself known to Abraham, sired Isaac and received Jacob as an inheritance.

He began his destructive reign as a fanatical crusader by claiming credit for the destruction of Sodom, Gomorrah and everything and everyone in these two cities. He also claimed responsibility for a number of other natural disasters among them the destruction of Jericho. Today we know that Jericho sits on top of a fault line and is subject to earthquakes and tremors. Jericho was destroyed by an earthquake not by the marching of men and the sounding of trumpets. Even though we also know that sound vibrations is a very powerful weapon.

Thousand of Egyptians died, or became deathly ill because of the disasters he claims to have generated. It would seem that death, plagues and diseases, which are a natural occurrence in nature are the favorite weapons of the Jewish God.

It was so during the time of the Exodus, the complete history of the Israelite people, and in the Revelation to come.

During the forty years the Israelites wandered through the Sinai wilderness under the control of God and Moses, it is recorded that thousands of Israelites died horrible deaths at the hand of Moses and or by the power of God himself.

Genesis 38:7-10. *And Er, Judah's firstborn, was wicked in the sigh of the Lord; and the Lord slew him .and Judah said unto Onan, Go in unto thy brother's wife, and marry her, and raise up seed to thy brother. And Onan knew that the seed should not be his; and it came to pass, when he went in unto his brother's wife, that he spilled in on the ground, lest that he should give seed to his brother. And the thing which he did displeased the Lord: wherefore he slew him also.*

Exodus 17:8-16. The Israelites were first attacked by the Amalek people the number of deaths that occurred that day is not recorded, but what is recorded is that the Lord swore that he would be at war with the Amalek from generation to generation. These were the descendants of Esau, the bother of Jacob and therefore his grandson ("Amalek, son of Eliphaz (eldest son of Esau) by his concubine Timna (Gen. 36:12; I Chron. 1:36). Duke of Edom (Gen. 36:16)(1).

God intended to war against the Amalek people and their descendants forever.

He wanted to remove their existence from the memory of man. But, according to other passages in scripture the Israelites are not allowed to make war against the Edomites which were their cousins and also the descendants of Easu.

Deu. 23:7. *Thou shalt not abhor an Edomite; for he is thy brother: thou shalt not abhor an Egyptian; because thou wast a stranger in his land.*

Yet the Israelites warred against them both for they were his enemies . (1 Sam. 24:47, II Sam. 8:14, II Kings 8:20, II Kings 14:7.). but to be fair he also did the same to his own people.

Lev. 10:1-2. *And Nadab and Abihu, the sons of Aaron, took either of them his censer, and put fire therein, and put incense thereon, and offered strange fire before the Lord, which he commanded them not. And there went out fire from the lord, and devoured them, and they died before the Lord.*

These men, priests of Jehovah, died because in presenting the fire and incense before God when they appeared to be drunk. This, God would not allow. We must assume that their death was due to alcohol because of the following passages and instructions which Jehovah gave to Moses so soon after the affair.

Lev. 10:8-9. *And the Lord spoke to Aaron, saying. Do not drink wine nor strong drink, thou, nor thy sons with thee, when they go into the tabernacle of the congregation, lest ye die: it shall be a statute for ever throughout your generations:*

It is ironic that this commandment, not to drink wine when one goes into the tabernacle or sanctuary to present oneself before God, has become in reverse, a holy ritual in the Christian Church. The drinking of wine as a part of what has come to be called the last supper, which was made holy by Jesus and his apostles and is in direct contradiction to a commandment of God himself.

Matt. 26:26-29. *And as they were eating, Jesus took bread, and blessed it, and brake it, and gave it to the disciples, and said, Take, eat; this is my body and he took the cup, and gave thanks, and gave it to them, saying, Drink ye all of it for this is my blood of the new testament, which is shed for many for the remission of sins. But I say unto you, I will not drink henceforth of this fruit of the vine, until that day when I drink it new with you in my Father's kingdom."*

This ritual has become known as the "Lord's Supper," where it is believed by the faithful, that the bread and wine, once taken by the believer, changes in form and substance to become a part of the actual body and blood of Jesus. As such, the partakers of this ritual are, in essence, participating in an act of cannibalism. This ritual, the act of drinking the wine which transforms itself into the blood of Jesus, although symbolic in nature, was condemned by God.

The Israelites were forbidden to ever eat or drink blood. But the Christian in partaking of the ritual of the last supper are drinking the blood of Christ in the wine served at this ritual.

Although the Israelites were forbidden to certain things as a part of their diet, the following was a prediction of what was to happen to them should they disobey his commands. They would be turned into cannibals.

Lev. 26:27-29. *And if ye will not for all this hearken unto me, but walk contrary unto me; Then I will walk contrary unto you also in fury;*

and I, even I, will chastise you seven times for your sins. And ye shall eat the flesh of your sons, and the flesh of your daughters shall ye eat.

The God of the Israelites showed no mercy or understanding what so ever whenever one of his ordinances was broken. Take for example the man who gathered sticks on the Sabbath. We are not told if the man had gathered sticks the day before or not. We are not told if the sticks were for a cooking fire or a fire needed to keep him warm on a cold day. Perhaps what he had gathered was not enough for his immediate needs and he required addition wood for his fire. Regardless of his circumstances, for disobeying the law which forbid any work on the Sabbath the man was put to death. Yet the man who had killed a fellow member of the congregation along with his wife in the temple was rewarded.

Numbers 15:35-36. *And the Lord said unto Moses, The man shall be surely put to death: all the congregation shall stone him with stones without the camp. And all of the congregation brought him without the camp, and stone him with stones, and he died; as the Lord commanded Moses.*

For failing in a small thing, this man was condemned to die. The congregation had to take the word of Moses that the man's death was the wish of God.

So too was the death of Korah, along with two hundred and fifty princes of the assembly, men of renown, famous in the congregation, men who had enough of the justice of Moses. They questioned him and his brother Aaron about their 'right' to have so much power over the people.

Numbers 16:3. *And they gathered themselves together against Moses and against Aaron, and said unto them, Ye take too much upon you, seeing all the congregation are holy, every one of them, and the Lord is among them: wherefore then lift ye up yourselves above the congregation of the Lord?*

Moses appealed to the Lord not to accept the offerings of these men. Korah and the princes were told to gather themselves before the tabernacle the next day and to bring their censers, vessels used to hold incense while it burned. The Lord is said to have appeared to all of the congregation. He spoke to Moses and to Aaron and told them to separate themselves from the congregation.

Numbers 16:21-22. *Separate yourselves from among the congregation, that I may consume them in a moment.. And they fell upon their faces, and said, O God, the God of the spirits of all flesh, shall one man sin, and wilt thou be wroth with all the congregation?*

This is reminiscent of the Abraham/Sodom story. Why punish the many for the sins of the few? Why punish the congregation because a few men question the authority of Moses? Rather than kill just those who were questioning the authority of Moses and Aaron, God did the following:

Numbers 16:28-35. *And Moses said, Hereby ye shall know that the Lord hath sent me to do all these works; for I have not done them of my own mind. If these men die the common death of all men or if they be visited after the visitation of all men; then the Lord hath not sent me. But if the Lord make a new thing, and the earth open her mouth, and swallow them up, with all that appertain unto them, and they go down quick into the pit; then ye shall understand that these men have provoked the lord. And it came to pass, as he had made an end of speaking all these words, that the ground clave asunder that was under them: And the earth opened her mouth, and swallowed them up, and their houses, and all the men that appertained unto Korah, and all their goods. They and all that appertained to them, went down alive into the pit, and the earth closed upon them: and they perished from among the congregation. And all Israel that were round about them fled at the cry of them: for they said, Lest the earth swallow us up also. And there came out a fire from the Lord, and consumed the two hundred and fifty men that offered incense.*

This fire and quake may have been the work of God but it was more likely the result of an earthquake. This possibility is suggested by verses 44 through 50. If there was an earthquake it is possible that poisonous gases were released into the surrounding area. Fire from the censer of Aaron may have ignited the gases that burst into flame and caused what the Israelites believed to be another plague of God.

Numbers 16:44-50. *And the Lord Spoke to Moses saying, Get you up from among this congregation, that I may consume them as in a moment.*

The plague was stayed because the poisonous gasses were soon dissipated by fire from the sensors and the affect of the winds. Soon they were no longer dangerous, but not before fourteen thousand, seven hundred people died because of it. Was this a natural disaster or the work of a god?

If these deaths were the result of a natural disaster we can understand them. But it is also possible that the seismic event was triggered by some technical device of Jehovah. It which case we would be correct in stating that he caused the death of fourteen thousand men women and children. If, as the Bible contends, that these deaths were the direct result of God's wrath, then we must ask ourselves the following questions.

What kind of a god kills thousands of innocent people because of the actions of a few individuals? If that god is in the habit of doing this type of thing to a whole nation, simply because his commands or his servants' action have been questioned, what can the religious believer of today expect as their reward for their faithful service and dedication if those around them failed in theirs?

This god of the Israelites did not punish individuals for their crimes; he punished almost everyone in order that his wrath be felt, realized and feared.

Aaron and Moses, both faithful servants, having spoken with and been in the presence of God himself, died like all other men. After all of their faithful service, they were led upon a mountain and killed. They died by the hand of God, himself.

For all of their faithful and devoted service there was no indication of any reward, no recognition, and no 'thank you my good and faithful servant. There was, however, a condemnation of Aaron because he and Moses did not do as they had been commanded by God at the waters of Meribah.

The people were thirsty. Moses and Aaron were told to speak to the rock for water. Instead Moses struck the rock which took the glory away from God. Because Aaron was a part of the incident he too was condemned, even though it was Moses and not Aaron that complained to God about the thirst of the people at Meribah.

Moses died, killed by God as was Aaron, only on a different mountain. Moses was not allowed to enter Canaan for basically the same reason Aaron died. He did not sanctify God before the people at the waters of Meribah.

During the journey through the wilderness the Israelites camped at a place infested with snakes. It was hot and dry, with no water or food. It is reasonable to assume that in any area were snakes are prevalent people will be bitten and if the snakes are poisonous people will die. It was no different with the Israelites.

They were tired, hungry, and thirty. When they had set up camp they began to complain of their condition. Moses complained to God and God knowing the nature of snakes and what was bound to happen in the natural order of things told Moses that he was going to punish the people for their complains. He was going to allow his people to be bitten and poisoned by the snakes, as if there was a choice.

The bites of serpents fulfilled another part of the curse he had placed on Jacob when he was banished from the presence of Jehovah and his family.

God did not take away the serpents. They still bit the people, but he did direct them to another location, and gave them a brass serpent, an idol, mounted upon a pole which was suppose to cure, by faith, anyone who was bitten by a serpent and who looked upon this idol. (Num. 21:8). Those who were healed were said to have had faith in the power of God. Those who died did so because they lacked the faith. They did not believe in the power of God. They died because they either did not look upon the idol or they did not believe that they would be cured.

There are in the mountains of Virginia cults who have taken the above incident to heart and use snakes in their religious worship as a way to test their faith. The individuals who handle these poisonous snakes do so in the belief that should they be bitten their faith will make them whole. If anyone dies it was because their faith in the healing power of god was not strong enough to save them.

Every time the Israelite congregation suffered a disaster, plague, or defeat, they were told by their priest that it was they had in some way displeased their god. Their failures were due to his anger. They had either complained too often about their condition, failed in some way to abide by the laws of Jehovah or they were beginning to follow false gods.

The Israelites were experiencing a conditioning phase in the life of their nation. They were being taught that no matter what happened to them in the future, good or bad they were to accept it and deem it the will of their Lord. They were never, under any circumstances to question that will. If they did, they would be made to suffer the consequences.

In time, the destructive nature of Jehovah began to change. At first he was an impulsive god, anxious to take the people into Canaan but unable to do so because of their timid nature. As a result he vented his frustration upon them. Judging by scripture, he looked for any excuse that could be found in order to vent that anger and frustration on the people. If he wasn't killing them as individuals, he was killing them en masse. As the Israelites became stronger they began to test themselves against the people with whom they came into contact. When they were victorious, they believed God had been with them and gave them the victory. If they were defeated, it was because God was angry for some reason and had chosen not to help. Usually the failure of God to assist them was blamed on some individual's failure to obey the commands of Moses, the High Priest, or God.

Whenever the Israelites went into battle, they were instructed to destroy everything. They were to leave no one alive and all precious metals and spoils of war were to be given to the priests for purification and were either added to the coffers of the house of Levi, (the treasures of god), or distributed among the congregation.

When the children of Israel went into battle to conquer the land of Canaan, they were led by Joshua but it has been said the Joshua was led by his god, Jehovah. For the most part the Israelites were successful. Whether this success was due to the battle skills of Joshua, the power of God or the strength and number of their army is debatable.

The church chooses to believe that it was the power of God. I choose to believe that it was the size and strength of their army and the fear of that army placed in the minds of the people before they ever went into battle against the Israelites. Their fear and the knowledge of the atrocities committed by the army of God cause the people to be psychologically defeated before they ever went into battle. This was due largely to the battle tactics used by Joshua.

Joshua, by the command and authority of God, showed no mercy. He and his troops slaughtered all life, burned the cities, and took as spoils of war, all of the material goods not destroyed in the fire and battle.

The children of Israel, under the leadership of Moses and Joshua, destroyed thousands of people, men, women and children in their march to Canaan. Joshua himself destroyed thirty one kings, all of their men, and many of their women and children. There were in some cases young women left alive to be sold as slaves, and some animals taken as the spoils of war. But there was no mercy for anyone who was not of the tribes of Israel.

God's battle plan was simple: Destroy everything except for what had material worth. A prime example of this strategy was the destruction of the Midianites. Numbers 31:3,7-12,15-19, 21-23,27-29.

The booty from this battle alone made the Israelites a wealthy nation. It is recorded that there were six hundred and seventy five thousand sheep, twelve thousand and sixty head of cattle, one thousand sixty asses and thirty two thousand persons, young women and girls who had not had sexual relations with a man. Just the gold booty alone, turned in to the priest amounted to sixteen thousand seven hundred and fifty shekels.

Today we are unable to place a comparative value on the above amount of gold shekels. We have no idea what that amount of gold would be worth on today's market. We can calculate how much the silver would be worth if we use the Biblical verse Exodus 21:32 as our standard. In this verse 30 shekels of silver was the price for a slave. In today's market, with gold selling at approximately three hundred and seventy five dollars an ounce and silver, at five dollars then one has a seventy five to one ratio. If sixteen thousand seven hundred and fifty shekels of silver would buy five hundred and fifty eight slaves, then multiply that amount by seventy five and you have enough gold to buy forty one thousand eight hundred and seventy five slaves at that time, a small nation.

A percentage of this wealth went to the priests, the tribe of Levi, to guard, to act as its' custodian and to hold in trust for Jehovah should he decide to claim his wealth.

Moses was granted one out of every fifty men or beasts and gave all to the Levites, according to the commandment of God.

Led by God, Moses and Joshua the children of Israel raped, plundered, and murdered most of the people who attempted to protect their own land or who came before the Israelites in the pursuit of their objective, the complete domination of the land of Canaan.

The Israelites, whether they believed that Jehovah was truly a God is immaterial. They, right or wrong, like the men of every country, fought out of fear and in obedience to what their leaders called their enemies.

Is it any wonder that the Jewish people have always been under attack and at war with their neighbours? Everything they had, they achieved by conquest. It was their blood and guts which conquered their enemies, not the words contributed by their God.

In their war of aggression the Congregation soon failed to expel all of the inhabitants of the land of Canaan a place where their god wanted to call home. It was the place where he wanted his temple and their worship to be.

Deu. 12:10-12. *But when ye go over Jordan, and dwell in the land which the Lord your God gives to you to inherit, and when he gives you rest from all your nemies round about, so that ye dwell in safety; Then there shall be a place which the Lord your God shall choose to cause his name to dwell there; and there shall you bring all that I command you; your burnt offering, and your choice vows which you have vowed unto the Lord:*

At what time in the history have the Jewish people known such peace. When have they ever been free of disease and plagues? They have been led down the primrose path by dedicated fanatics, who passed their belief in a god down to a people who were doomed to servitude and poverty all of their lives.

Desperate times breed desperate men, leaders and visionaries. Moses was such a person, Under his guidance so too was Joshua.

The Israelites followed mortal beings. They were not gods of creation, but flesh and blood beings who ate, drank, and desired all of the good things in life.

Was Jehovah a god or a mortal being? Many would call this question blasphemous but consider the following. The people of the Exodus lived within the supposed presence of a god. Scripture state that they witnessed and lived through the supposed power and glory of that god. Why was it then necessary for Joshua in reminding the people of the words of God when he made the following statement?

Joshua 24:13-15. And I have given you a land for which ye did not labour, and cities which ye built not, and ye dwell in them; of the vineyards and olive-yards which ye planted not do ye eat. Now therefore fear the Lord, and serve him in sincerity and in truth: and put away the gods which your fathers served on the other side of the flood, and in Egypt; and serve ye the Lord. And if it seem evil unto you to serve the Lord, chooses you this day whom ye will serve; whether the gods which your fathers served that were on the other side of the flood, or the gods of the Amorites, in whose land ye dwell: but as for me and my house, we will serve the Lord.

Today those gods, the original supervisors of man, are considered to be the false gods of heathen societies. We, the people of western culture, consider ourselves to be a more civilized and sophisticated people. We now have, basically, two gods: Jehovah, the good guy, and Satan, the bad guy. For some reason that I cannot understand is that whenever I study the scriptures I am never able to really separate the two.

Since the prescribed blood and ritual killing of animals in the worship of one is almost identical to the rituals of the other. The rituals and demand for blood sacrifices of both gods become strangely similar.

However to be fair there does appear to be a few small difference between the worship of Jehovah and that of Satan.

In the worship of Jehovah the worshipper is commanded not to drink of the blood, for in the blood was the life. In the worship of Satan the drinking the sacrificial blood is said to be a vital part of the religious ceremony. If you are a Christian and you partake of the bread and wine ritual called the last supper, you are following a commandment given by Jesus, the son of Jehovah, to his disciples which actually commands the symbolic drinking of his blood as a sign of faith.

While the Christian in drinking the wine is symbolically drinking the blood of Jesus, the Satan worshipper in drinking the actual blood of their victim have taken the commandment of Jesus at its face value. They believe that in drinking the actual blood they become one with their god.

From the above command it is easy to understand how a devoted worshipper, following the sacrificial commands of God and Jesus, could be following a practice that might easily be identified as that of "Devil Worship."

It is appalling to me that when I think of the millions of individuals who still believe in the deity of Jehovah when one considers the death and destruction which took place under his control and by his direct commands.

Think of the thousands of men, women and children who have suffered and died in the religious events, wars, inquisition and crusades initiated in his name. One only has to pick up the evening news to hear of the killing and mutilation taking place in Ireland, Israel and Palestine and to review the cataclysmic events of Revelation to equate Jehovah with an egotistical homicidal individual filled with rage, self pity and insecurity.

A critique of the Bible, devoid of any religious aspects, clearly indicates that it is a history of the Israelite nation who followed a maniacal bloodthirsty individual devoid of all human compassion in the mistaken belief that he was the God and creator of Man.

The Israelites believe that they are the chosen people of God, therefore of the human race. This belief, handed down to them from the time of Adam, is the reason for their belief in the concept of their own superiority.

Deu. 28:1-13. *And it shall come to pass, if thou shalt hearken diligently unto the voice of the Lord thy God, to observe and to do all his commandments which I command thee this day, that the Lord thy God will set thee on high above all nations of the earth: And all these blessings shall come on thee, and overtake thee, if thou shalt hearken unto the voice of the Lord thy God. Blessed shalt thou be in the city, and blessed shalt thou be in the field. Blessed shall be the fruit of thy body, and the fruit of thy ground, and the fruit of thy cattle, the increase of thy kine and the flocks of thy sheep. Blessed shall be thy basket and thy store. Blessed shalt thou be when thou comest in, and blessed shalt thou be when thou goest out. The Lord shall cause thine enemies that rise up against thee to be smitten before thy face: they shall come out against thee one way, and flee before thee seven ways. The Lord shall command the blessing upon thee in thy storehouses, and in all that thou settest thine hand unto; and he shall bless thee in the land which the Lord thy God giveth thee. The Lord shall establish thee an holy people unto himself, as he hath sworn unto thee, if thou shalt keep the commandments of the Lord thy God, and walk in his ways. And all people of the earth shall see that thou art called by the name of the Lord; and they shall be afraid of thee. And the Lord shall make thee plenteous in goods, in the fruit of thy body, and in the fruit of thy cattle, and in the fruit of the ground, in the land which the Lord sware unto thy fathers to give thee. The Lord shall open unto thee his good treasure, the heaven to give the rain unto the land in his season, and to bless all the works of thine hand: and thou shall lend unto many nations, and thou shalt not borrow. And the Lord shall make thee the head, and not the tail; and thou shalt be above only, and thou shalt not be beneath; if that thou hearken unto the commandments of the Lord thy God, which I command thee this day, to observe and to do them.*

With the above scripture as a guideline and philosophy, it is understandable how an author could write an article several years ago which accused the Jewish leaders, of plotting the overthrow of the world's nations. This plot was supposed to have been outlined in a published document entitled "Protocols of the Learned Elders of Zion".

According to an article published in the June 1995 issue of Reader's Digest by Lawrence Elliott, "The message was explosive: as a global conspiracy by which Jews meant to conquer the world. The plot was detailed in the supposedly verbatim record of 24 meetings of the secret Jewish government—the Learned Elders—said to have taken place during an 1897 Zionist congress in Basel, Switzerland…"

The Elders' goal, according to the Protocols, was a Messianic Age when the world would be united under Judaism and ruled by a member of the House of David.

The blueprint for this action was:
1. Corrupt the young by subversive education.
2. Dominate people through their vices-foster drunkenness and prostitution.
3. Religion would be discredited, war fomented, and pestilence let loose around the world. Starving, the masses would rise up to "shed the blood of those whom they envy" and loot their property.
4. And finally, the Jews would step in-taking charge as the saviours of civilization.

This document was thought to be the epitome of anti-Semitism. That may be true, but the above plan is similar to one outlined in scriture where the destruction of Man is to come from the hand of God. No one said that the Jews would not be instrumental in it's beginning.

It was their hand and not the hand of God which eliminated most of the native people of Canaan. The documents cited as the "Protocols of the Learned Elders of Zion", may have been an aspect of the events predicted by the Book of Revelation.

How does the plan of the Protocols coincide with Biblical prophecy?

Rev. 4:4. *And round about the throne were four and twenty seats: and upon the seats I saw four and twenty elders sitting, clothed in white raiment; and they had on their heads crowns of gold.*

The twenty four meetings of the Elders is symbolic of the twenty four elders around the throne of God.

Rev. 4:10-11. *The four and twenty elders fall down before him that sat on the throne, and worship him that lives forever and ever, and cast their crowns before the throne, saying, Thou art worthy, O Lord, to receive glory and honour and power: for thou hast created all things, and for thy pleasure they are and were created.*

For the pleasure of God were all things created. Man was one of those creations. He was created as a slave to serve God, a position he still maintains as a worshipper and temple servant. But who is to receive the power, honour and glory from man?

It is to be one of his son, a man called Jesus, a half breed of the house of David. It is he, who is to sit upon the throne of the world and rule with a hand of iron.

Rev. 22:12-13, 16. *And behold, I come quickly; and my reward is with me, to give every man according as his work shall be. I am Alpha and Omega, the beginning and the end, the first and the last. I Jesus have sent mine angel to testify unto you these things in the churches. I am the root and the offspring of David, and the bright and morning star.*

If the world is to be united under Judaism and ruled by a descendant of the House of David it appears that his rule will be the beginning of the holocaust, the destruction of independent man. Only those who bear his mark on their forehead can expect to survive. It is the the mark of the beast foretold in Revelation, so often contributed to Satan will be the mark of Jehovah. Those who carry his mark ill be his servants and the absolute slaves of the new ruler.

Rev. 5:5-6. *And one of the elders saith unto me, Weep not: behold, the Lion of the tribe of Juda, the Root of David, hath prevailed to open the book, and to loose the seven seals thereof. And I beheld, and, lo, in the midst of the throne and of the four beasts, and in the midst of the elders, stood a Lamb as it had been slain, having seven horns and seven eyes, which are the seven Spirits of God sent forth into the earth.*

Rev. 5:8-10. *And when he had taken the book, the four beasts and the four and twenty elders fell down before the Lamb, having every one of them harps, and golden vials full of odours, which are the prayers of saints. And they sung a new song, saying, Thou art worthy to take the book, and to open the seals thereof: for thou wast slain, and hast redeemed us to God by thy blood out of every kindred, and tongue, and people, and nation; And hast made us unto our God kings and priests: and we shall reign on the earth.*

And who shall the elders reign over?

Rev. 7:13-15. *And one of the elders answered saying unto me, What are these which are arrayed in white robes? And whence came they? And I said unto him, Sir, thou knowest. And he said to me, These are they which came out of great tribulation, and have washed their robes, and made them white in the blood of the Lamb. Therefore are they before the throne of God, and serve him day and night in his temple: and he that sitteth on the throne shall dwell among them.*

And where is the throne of God to be?

Rev. 21:10. *And he carried me away in the spirit to a great and high mountain, and shewed me that great city, the holy Jerusalem, descending out of the heaven from God,*

The new kingdom of God is to be upon this earth. The earth is to be ravaged by war, pestilence, famine, corruption, and degradation, things which are taking place within our society today.

The education of our young is slowly being eroded by the decrease of social and moral values. Our children are being taught that homosexual practices are an acceptable way of life. From this rent in the moral fabric of family life it is but a short step into other bizarre sexual practices, including the abuse of young children and animals.

Sex, drugs and alcohol are all advertised as necessary for one to enjoy and obtain the most that life has to offer. Religions are changing their old values in order to accommodate the new ideas around them. In order to be a good Christian one must learn to be more permissive, understanding and tolerant of the other person's views, ideas and life styles.

It is ironic that the Gentiles, the Christians, are the ones who are the most active in pursuing the goals outline in the Protocols agenda. I believe that this pursue is due to the misunderstandings of the faith and practices of the various religious denominations It is Catholics against Protestants, Jews against Moslems and the rest of the religions of the world each believing in the right and sanctity of their individual faith and misunderstanding.

All of this misunderstanding can be cleared away with an understanding that the religions of man are the creations of man and not of gods but individuals who wanted to be gods.

With an understanding of scripture from the new and unique perspective presented in this book the religions of the world can cease to exist replaced by an acceptance and respect for the race of ancient aliens who created man in their image and made him a sub-species of their culture society. They were our gods of yesterday we are the gods of our tomorrow.

The God of the Jewish people was no spiritual being but an individual who wanted to be a god. He declared that he brought the people out of Egypt, not out of love or caring but to obtain servants to wait on and serve him. He desired sacrifices, he wanted gifts, priests, temples, a place to stay and all of the other things normally expected to be bestowed upon a god. Pharaoh received all of these things and was he not more than Pharaoh?

He demanded to be treated as a god. His status as the overseer of the Most High God demanded that he claim what was his by right of ownership.

You are mine, says the Lord, therefore you belong to me and you will serve me as I see fit. I will dwell among you. I will be a god to you. I will hold court and speak to you at the door of the tabernacle.

This will be my dwelling. Your priests and my immediate servants are those I have chosen to wait on me, to do my bidding and serve me as I dictate. You will follow their commands and their instructions as if they were my own.

I have sanctified them with and by the death and blood of sacrifices. I have made my altar, my administrators, and even the clothes of my special servants, holy to me, by the blood and death of your sacrifices. Your sacrifices of meat bread and wine, shall feed me and my servants. I accept your offerings as a fitting tribute, paid to me in order that I remain your god, leader and ruler.

My meals will be served to me on golden plates in surroundings that I will make opulent. I have told you what I desire for my morning and evening meals. You have been instructed in how I desire those meals to be prepared. Do not forget less you suffer the consequences. I require a gallon of wine that is to come with every meal. What I do not eat, I will give to my servants, your priests.

Daily you will slaughter and barbeque two lambs on the grill that I call my altar. You will sprinkle the blood as I have commanded. Each day you will clean the grill and dispose of the remains of the slaughter as I have commanded.

To paraphrase Exodus 30: 7-10. 'In order to remove the stink of the slaughter you are to burn incense both morning and night so that I will not be offended by the smell of slaughtered flesh and the stink of rotting blood.

Not only are you to feed, clothe and care for me as your God, but every male over the age of twenty is to pay to me a tax for his soul, a tax of half a shekel. The money is to go into my treasury to be used by my priests in their duties as my servants. It is to be their reward for their faithful service to me.

The Godfather of the Israelites ordained his authority by the slaughter, blood and sacrifice of animals. He levied taxes in order to establish a standard of giving that would provide a steady income to his coffers and those of the Levi.

As the people spread throughout the land they took with them these ideas, customs and commandments.

Wherever there was a Jewish community there was a religious synagogue. This synagogue presided over by a member of the priestly tribe received the sacrifices and tribute offered up to God. Since God could only be in all of these isolated places in spirit, each individual religious synagogues more or less operated on its own. How faithfully did the priest serve the will of God is unknown. But, the more synagogues that were established the more the revenue of the tribe of Levi increased.

The same can be said about the churches of Christianity. Every time a new church is formed and become successful, so too is the increase in money tithes and gifts which makes that particular church organization richer and more powerful. Nothing can be a more vivid example than the wealth and power of the Pope, and the Roman Catholic Church.

The priesthood, the family of Levi, became one of the riches, strongest, and most powerful organizations in the land of Canaan. The treasurers of God became so powerful and wealthy that they have become the bankers of nations.

The God dictated to Moses and the Jewish people how he wanted his altar,(his barbeque grill), built. He gave the people an exacting formula that they were to use in making the special incense he desired to be used in the temple and he gave them specific instructions for making the holy oil that was to be used in the anointing ceremonies. Exodus 30:19-38.

The God of the Israelites was a physical being capable of being seen, felt and spoken to. He walked and talked with man. He wrestled with Jacob, had intercourse with Mary, ate with Abraham and instructed Moses. Physically, he was evidently so ugly and horrifying that to look upon his face was to die. When he spoke to Moses he said to him:

Exodus 33:20-23. *And he said, Thou canst not see my face: for there shall no man see me, and live. And the Lord said, Behold, there is a place by me, and thou shalt stand upon a rock: And it shall come to pass, while my glory passeth by, that I will put thee in a cleft of the rock, and will cover thee with my hand while I pass by: 23. And I will take away mine hand, and thou shalt see my back parts but my face shall not be seen.*

Could it be that the face of God is in actuality the face of Satan and of evil? Where is the glory, the light and the love that is portrayed as the face of God? What is the face of a Godfather? Is it the face of good or of evil?

To paraphrase Exodus 35:2, If any member of the Jewish congregation worked on the day dedicated for worship they are to be condemned to death. I often wonder what the people did when someone got sick? Was the healing and services of a doctor considered as something other than work?

When the members did work they were required to share the rewards of their labour with God and the Levi.

If anyone committed or thought that they had committed a sin or a trespass against any commandments of God, they were to offer up a blood sacrifice as atonement for that offence. All offerings were to be without blemish. If the offering was cattle then it was to be slaughtered at the door of the tabernacle and the blood sprinkled around the altar. The animal was to be cut into pieces and cooked upon the altar of grill. If the meat was that of a sheep or goat, it was to be butchered on the north side of the altar facing the abode of the Lord. The blood was again to be sprinkled around the altar. If birds were offered, they were to be young pigeons or turtle doves. They were to be killed by wringing their heads off. Then they were to be placed over the fire to remove their feathers. Their blood was wrung out at the side of the altar. These were meat offerings whose roasting aromas were savoured by God.

These meat offering were cooked in a certain way. Those instructions are specified in Lev. 2:1-16.

In addition to the sacrificial offerings received by God, the priests also benefited from these efforts. For example, the scripture verses found in Lev. 5:11-13, is a small illustration of just how much the priests were able to make as a result of their priestly duties.

Lev.5:11-13. *But if he be not able to bring two turtle-doves, or two young pigeons, then he that sinneth shall bring for his offering the tenth part of an ephah of fine flour for a sin offering; he shall put no oil upon it, neither shall he put any frankincense thereon: for it is a sin offering. Then shall he bring it to the priest, and the priest shall take his handful of it, even a memorial thereof, and burn it on the altar, according to the offerings made by fire unto the Lord: it is a sin offering. And the priest shall make an atonement for him as touching his sin that he hath sinned in one of these, and it shall be forgiven him: and the remnant shall be the priest's as a meat offering.*

It is an enviable job, telling people when they have sinned and making a comfortable living from the offerings meant to nullify those sins.

The priests served an alien god, if he did in fact exist. If he did not exist, then the priests served an imaginary god, absorbing from the people, ten percent of the wealth of the nation. Like the modern day Godfather, the High Priest and his family fed on the blood, sweat, and tears of the people. In return the people were forgiven for sins that were merely the disobedience of a religious edict or figment of their imagination. If there was no god, then there would be no edict and therefore no sin. Some of the supposed sins requiring sacrifices are so ridiculous as to defy the imagination.

The following is an example of a religious sin committed by a woman who must atone for that sin. It is by the commandment of the God Jehovah. Lev. 12:1-8.

If a woman becomes pregnant and has a boy she shall be considered as unclean for seven days. On the eight day the baby boy is to be mutilated by circumcised. For the next thirty three days the mother is forbidden to touch anything that is considered holy. She is even barred from coming into the sanctuary of the congregation. But, if the woman is unfortunate enough to have a baby girl, then she is to be considered unclean for twice as long. She must go fourteen days as her separation time and continue in the blood of her purification for a total of sixty six days. For the God Jehovah there was clearly gender discrimination. He preferred males to females. Even his sacrifices were predominately males without blemish.

The sex of a child determined the length of time it's mother was required to undergo purification rites. For the sin of giving birth to a child, sacrifices were required to be made to the priests in order for the woman to atone for her sins. What were her sins? She was merely obeying the commands of her creator to go forth be fruitful and multiply.

How can a Johnny Come Lately tell her that she has committed a sin when she is obeying the command of her god? Something is definitely wrong with at least one of these commandments. I believe that it is the one from the Lord Jehovah. It is his commandments that brings food, drink and riches into the coffers of the high priest and the houses of Levi.

According to Jehovah a woman sins when she became pregnant, again when she gives to her child, and again according to the sex of her offspring. In all three the priests receive a reward. The more prolific the congregation, the richer the families of the priesthood became.

Whether the child was male or female, a lamb and either a young pigeon or a turtle-dove was required to be offered as the atonement for the woman's sin and to make her clean again.

In other words, the God of the Jews considered pregnancy and childbirth to be unclean, sinful acts. But the creator of Man, The Most High God, to him this was no sin, but the normal procreation of a species.

Aside from accepting the tithes and offerings of the people, preforming the sacrificial duties required by God, the priests were also considered ordained doctors and healers. They possessed the power of healing from God himself.

Whenever someone was sick they went go to the priest. The priest would then determine if the sick individual was to be considered clean or unclean. If declared unclean by the priest, that individual was locked up for seven days. If their condition had not changed in that time, they were locked away for another seven days. If after fourteen days the priest declared the sick individual clean they were allowed to mingle again with the congregation. If, on the other hand, at the end of fourteen days the sick individual was still considered unclean by the priest, they were declared to have the plague. That sick person was to rent their clothes, bare their head, put a covering upon their upper lip, and cry to all that they were unclean. They were banished from their families and required to dwell alone outside of the camp. All based upon nothing more than the word of a priest with no formal medical training. Lev. 13:1-59.

The Jewish priest, like an African witchdoctor, performed his cures, if there were any through the belief of the people in the imaginary power of God and the hypnotic rituals practiced in the offering of sacrifices.

If an individual was declared by the priest to have a plague, or to be a leper, and found themselves healed, then the cure was credited to the power of God. The priest then performed the following ritual in order to declare the individual cleansed of their affliction.

Lev. chap. 14 contains this witchdoctor remedy given by Jehovah to the Jewish congregation for curing leprosy in an individual and from what the priest declared to be a contaminated house.

It is an excellent example of the religious mumbo jumbo practiced by the ancient Jewish religious hierarchy. It is a clear indication of the true power and insight of God and the priest of Gods.

An individual, believed to have the plague was to take the following ingredients and at the command of the priest perform the following ceremony.

They were to take two live birds, along with cedar wood, scarlet and hyssop, and kill one of the birds in an earthen vessel over running water. When this was accomplished they were to then take the remaining living bird, the cedar wood, the scarlet and the hyssop and dip all of these ingredients into the blood of the bird that was killed. The priest was then to sprinkle the blood of the dead bird upon the person who was to be cured. The priest was to perform this ceremony seven times. When the ceremony was completed the priest was then to declare the person clean and cured of leprosy. The live bird was then to be set free in an open field. The cured person was to wash their clothes, shave off their hair, wash themselves, and return to their tent where they were to remain outside of it for seven days. On the eight day they were to take two he lambs and one ewe without blemish, fine flour mingled with oil, and one log of oil to the door of the tabernacle.

The priest who was to make the man clean, presented him and his offerings to the Lord. The priest was to slay one of the lambs, burned the offering, and take some of the blood of the offering and put it upon the tip of the right ear of the diseased person who was to be cleansed. Blood was also placed upon the thumb of their right hand and upon the big toe of their right foot. The priest was to then take some of the oil, brought by the diseased individual, pour some of it into his left hand. The priest then dipped the finger of his right hand into the oil in his left hand. The priest then sprinkled the oil from his right finger seven times before the Lord. The oil that is left in the hand of the priest was put with the blood of the lamb onto the tip of the right ear, the thumb of the right hand, and the big toe of the right foot of the ill person. What remained was poured upon the head of the person being cleansed. What was left of the offering belonged to the priest as his fee for acting as an intermediary between the diseased man and God.

Lev. 14:13. And he shall slay the lamb in the place where he shall kill the sin offering and the burnt offering, in the holy place: for as the sin offering is the priest's, so is the trepass offering: it is most holy:

The above procedure was based upon the instructions of the God Jehovah. This was his idea of a cure, his medical remedy for cleansing an individual of leprosy. Just as it was his idea that looking at a brass snake hung on a pole in the wilderness would cure a person of snake bite. Equally baffing is the following remedy for removing the curse of leprosy from a house.

Lev. 14:33-34. *And the Lord spake unto Moses and unto Aaron saying,. When ye be come into the land of Canaan, which I give to you for a possession, and I put the plague of leprosy in a house of the land of your possession.*

The Lord not only give the people a receipt for removing the curse of leprosy from a house, he also put the curse in. If he curses a house, I suppose that it is only right that he be able to cure his own curse. Just what was his cure?

The congregation went into a land where leprosy existed. In spite of all the power of God, the prayers and the sacrifices of the people over the millennium, leprosy still exists. The promises that God made to the people that he would heal, protect and care for them, as long as they were his people never materialized. Any existing conditions which

God was unable to eliminate, he claims to have created in order to test the faithfulness of the congregation.

When a man was convinced that his house was contaminated with a disease, he told a priest. The priest would command the man and his family to vacate the house. When the house was empty, the priest would go in and determine the cleanliness of the house. If there was a discolouration on the walls of the house, the priest would quarantine the house for a period of seven days. In seven days he inspected the house again. The section of the house that was believed to be contaminated was removed and the section repaired. The house was to be scraped clean and the dust taken to an unclean place. The house was to be replastered. If the disease reappears the house was to be torn down and taken to the dump. If the disease or discolouration did not reappear, the plague was considered to be removed and the house healed. Again the cleansing ceremony involving the two birds, cedar wood, scarlet, and hyssop and is preformed by the priest.

For the sins of the congregation, the high priest took two goats and cast lots to determine which goat was to die and which one was to be released. The goat set free was considered the scapegoat. He carries the sins of the congregation into the wilderness. The high priest then killed the second goat. The death of this goat was considered to be an offering for the sins of the people. The blood of this goat was sprinkled seven times, upon and before the mercy seat of God with the finger of the priest. Lev. 16:7-10,15.

It was not the death of the offerings themselves that seem important to God, but the spilled blood. It was the blood and not the death that atoned for the sins of the people.

Lev. 17:11. *For the life of the flesh is in the blood: and I have given it to you upon the altar to make an atonement for your souls: for it is the blood that maketh an atonement for the soul.*

Jehovah required not only the death of animals but also of his own congregation. He refused to accept subordination of any kind.

Everyone who cursed his father and or their mother was to be put to death. Lev. 20:9.

Anyone who committed adultery was to be put to death. Lev. 20:10.

Any man who slept with his father's wife, was to be put to death. Lev. 20:11.

Any man who slept with his daughter-in-law, was to be death, along with her.

Lev. 20:12.

If a man lay with another man they were both to be put to death. Lev. 20:13.

If a man lay with his wife and also her mother they were all to be burned with fire. Lev. 20:14.

If a man or woman laid with a beast they were to be put to death. Lev. 20:15. Even though the beast had done no wrong, it was also to be killed. Lev. 20:15-16.

These were only a few of the harsh, barbaric laws of conduct given to a civilized society by a tyrannical god.

Lev. 20:23. *And ye shall not walk in the manners of the nation which I cast out before you: for they committed all these things, and therefore I abhorred them.*

The god of the Jews did not love mankind. He did not love or care for the Jews themselves. He cares about their absolute obedience, his control and his power over them.

He did not accept anything that was imperfect, including his own servants the priests themselves.

Lev. 22:19-25. *Ye shall offer at your own will a male without blemish of the beeves, of the sheep, or of the goats. But whatsoever hath a blemish, that shall ye not offer: for it shall not be acceptable for you. And whosoever offers a sacrifice of peace-offering unto the Lord to accomplish his vow, or a free-will-offering in beeves, or sheep, it shall be perfect to be accepted: there shall be no blemish therein. Blind, or broken, or maimed, or having a wen, or scurvy, or scabbed, ye shall not offer these unto the Lord, nor make an offering by fire of them upon the alter unto the Lord. Either a bullock, or a lamb that hath anything superfluous or lacking in his parts, that mayest thou offer for a free-will-offering; but for a vow it shall not be accepted. Ye shall not offer unto the Lord that which is bruised, or crushed, or broken, or cut; neither shall ye make any offering thereof in your land. Neither from a stranger's hand shall ye offer the bread of your God of any of these; because their corruption is in them, and blemishes be in them: they shall not be accepted for you.*

Lev. 21:16-23. *And the Lord spoke to Moses saying, Speak unto Aaron, saying, Whosoever he be of thy seed in their generations that hath any blemish, let him not approach to offer the bread of his God. For whatsoever man he be that hath a blemish, he shall not approach: a blind man, or a lame, or he that hath a flat nose, or anything superfluous, or a man that is brokenfooted or brokenhanded. Or crookbackt, or a dwarf, or that hath a blemish in his eye, or be scurvy, or scabbed, or hath his stones broken; No man that hath a blemish of the seed of Aaron the priest shall come nigh to offer the offering of the Lord made by fire: he hath a blemish; he shall not come nigh to offer the bread of his God. He shall eat the bread of his God, both of the most holy, and of the holy. Only he shall not go in unto the vail, nor come nigh unto the altar, because he hath a blemish; that he profane not my sanctuaries: for I the Lord do sanctify them.*

After reading the above scriptural passages, is it wrong to assume that anyone with a blemish, injury, or disfigurement is while they may be acceptable to God, can never enter into the vail of service to him. If he does not want them to serve him within his sanctuaries in this life will they also be unacceptable to him in the life to come?

If everyone born is a creation of God, and he chooses which ones are to born with or without blemishes, will he also determine, regardless of earthly service, the ones he will accept as his servants in the hereafter?

It seems clear that anyone who chooses to be a devoted servant to God, yet fails to meet his physical criteria, is doomed to wander outside of the immediate presence of the holy one himself.

While the scriptures seem to indicate that while God is fairly exacting in what he desires in the physical appearances of his servants, he does not seem to care or place any special significance on their mental stability or moral values. It appears that the more fanatical a person is in their desire to please him the more pleasing that individual is to him It also means that one can break the laws of God himself and be blessed by him only according to the fanatical intentions of the perpetrator.

The following is a recorded example of the above statement.

Phinehas, the son of Eleazar, who was the son of Aaron the High Priest, broke the commandment, "Thou shall not kill" when he murdered a fellow Israelite and a Midianitish woman 'in the sight of Moses, and in the sight of all of the congregation of the children of Israel..." (Numbers 25:6). He did this at the height of a killing spree which had been ordered by God. Numbers 25:3-15

During this time the Israelites were intermingling with the inhabitants of a place called Shittim. Some of the Israelites began to worship Baal-Peor, a Moabite deity. Jehovah became so angry that he ordered Moses and the judges to killed every person who had participated in any religious ceremony to Baal-peor.

This defection to another god was considered to be a plague among the Israelite congregation. To put an immediate stop to any further deflection to another god and to make it definitely clear to anyone who should decided in the future to wander from the faith, death was to be their reward.

It was during the height of this slaughter that Phinehas got carried away and killed the man and the woman in the tabernacle. This act was enough to set the example desire by Moses and God. Phinehas was not punished for a couple of reasons. First he was the nephew of Moses. Moses was not about to kill a member of his own family. And second the congregation was made to believed that his act was pleasing to God.

How many times in the ages that have followed this incident has the killing en mass of individuals outside of the Israelite faith been considered justified because of the above event?

This contemptible act of Phinehas was made more despicable by the Lord God Jehovah himself when he ordered Moses to destroy the Midianite nation, the descendants of Esau, a grandson of Abraham and followers of Jehovah.

Why did he want them destroyed?

According to scripture it was because of the beauty of the Midian women which enticed the men of israel away from their service to Jehovah. He was jealous.

Reuel, the father-in-law of Moses, later called Jethro was himself a priest of Jehovah. He is said to have rejoiced at the good fortune and blessings which Jehovah had bestowed upon the Israelites and he even offered up sacrifices and burnt offering to honour him.

The Midianites were cousins and followers of Jehovah. As such they were some of the seeds of Abraham and were one of the recipients of God's promise to Abraham that his seed would inherit the promised land of Canaan.

Moses and Joshua, under the direction of God, eliminated all of the seed of Abraham so that only the descendants of Isaac through Jacob would be heirs. The descendants of Ishmael, although they too are the seed of Abraham, they have been denied forever of any chance of claiming any part of the land of Canaan except by the conquest of the Jewish nation.

According to the Zonderan Compact Bible Dictionary, the Midianite race, cousins to the Jewish nation, "have long since disappeared from among mankind."

In reviewing the Biblical conquest of Jehovah, Moses, and Joshua it is apparent that their crusade to capture, control, and own the land of Canaan was a war of ethnic cleansing. This was to ensure that the land of Canaan go not to the seed of Abraham but to the seed of Isaac who was his son.

As the god of the Jews, he was unable to do this by his own power. If he had the power chose not to use it. Even if he had been able to conquer Canaan on his own he had no one to take care of it for him so he needed people. These he obtained by bribery, intimidation, greed and promises. He chose the descendants of Jacob, to do his bloody work for him.

The tribes of the sons of Jacob were use to corrupt behaviour. They first came to biblical notice, when it is said that they sold their own brother into slavery, for nothing more than spite and jealousy.

Next they butchered the men of a city, stole their wealth and either butchered or enslaved their women and children.

Jehovah used their traits of greed, cruelty and their condition of bondage in order to get them to follow him and Moses. Because of the instructions, laws and desires that Moses said came from Jehovah the Israelites, through the training and leadership of Moses and Joshua became a mighty army and a great nation.

Whenever they were led into battle and prospered the congregation were told that it was the power and blessing of their god. When they failed in battle it was because their god was displeased and their failure was his punishment.

The Israelites during their wandering and even after they had conquered most of the land of Canaan knew death from diseases, hunger and plagues. Because of their suffering under the leadership and guidance of Jehovah he made them into a people without remorse, for whom the shedding of blood, be it animal or enemy, became a vital part of their lives and their religion.

When the people became tired of wandering through the wilderness, greedy for land, wealth and the fulfilment of the promises that had been made to them, Joshua, by the commands of God, led them down the road into the promised land of Canaan.

This road, which led the Jewish people into immortality, was a road covered in blood, brutality and mutilation. It was a road without mercy, or human compassion. It was the will of the God Jehovah that no life should be spared that might in any way threaten the future of the Jewish nation. Deu.1:1-8.

Jehovah did not do this out of the kindness of his heart. He did this because he did not want to give the congregation an opportunity to stray from the yoke he had placed around their necks.

After the Israelites had gained a foothold in the land of Canaan they had their land of promise. Israelite history states that this achievement was through the efforts power and glory of Jehovah. He had finally fulfilled the promise that he had made to Abraham. Yet he demanded payment for keeping his promises.

The congregation was required by his laws to offer to him payment. These payments were in the form of food, wealth, cattle, sheep and slaves. These were used to support his servants the priests, the tribe of Levi, the tribe and descendants of Moses.

A portion of every sacrifice made by the people belonged to the priest:

Deu. 18:3-4. *And this shall be the priest's due from the people, from them that offer a sacrifice, whether it be ox or sheep; and they shall give unto the priest the shoulder, and the two cheeks, and the maw. The first fruits also of thy corn, of thy wine, and of thine oil, and the first of the fleece of thy sheep, shalt thou give him.*

The priests, clergy and ministers of all religions, like the priests of the Jewish faith, seem to be cut from the same cloth. They all preach and try to enforce the laws of God and Moses and in their preaching and leadership they feed on the wealth of the congregation. The wealth that they obtain, offered to the church by the congregations out of their fear of death and hell. Their gifts, offerings and sacrifices are fed into the coffers of the church through the fear instilled by the false teachings of the servants of a God who are themselves nothing more than con men selling a pig in a poke that can never be proven or denied.

The laws of God can be reduced to two thoughts which were expressed by Moses to the congregation in Deu. 19:19,21. *Then shall ye do unto him, as he had thought to have done unto his brother: so shalt thou put the evil away from among you. And thine eye shall not pity; but life shall go for life, eye for eye, tooth for tooth, hand for hand, foot for foot.*

This is the law and the mentality of the God of the Jews. The Christians, following the teachings of Jesus, which in many instances are in direct opposition to the commands of God. Christians preach the opposite. Instead of slaughtering their enemies, they turn the other cheek. They try to do unto their brother not what he would do unto them but what they would like for him to do unto them. They are to treat everyone with love and kindness. They are not to shed the blood of another human. They are to love, care for, and protect the animals. They are not to take what they have not earned or that which does not belong to them. These are laws and concepts that are in direct opposition to each other. While Jehovah was a harsh disciplinarian, his son Jesus was a pacifist. While there is no mention of a Jewish heaven the Christians believe in a heavenly paradise they fail to mention where it will be because tht paradise is biblical hell.

Revelation 14: 9-11. *And the third angel followed them saying in a loud voice , if any man worship the beast and his image and receive his mark in his forehead or in his hand the same shall drink of the wine of the wrath of God, which is poured out without mixture into the cup of his indignation: and he shall be tormented with fire and brimstone in the presence of the Lamb. And the smoke of their ascendeth up forever and ever and they have no rest day or night who worship the beast and his image and whosoever receiveth the mark of his name.*

Who worships the idols and who has received the mark of the beast and who shall be spending eternity in the lake of fire and brimstone with Jesus and his angels. If not his servants?

The laws established by Moses under the direction of God were evidently many of those established by the alien society of the race to which Jehovah belonged. Many of those laws were in existence before Joseph, Jacob and the Hebrews went down into Egypt. They were issued by Hammurabi, King of Babylon approximated four hundred and fifty years before the time of Moses and the Exodus and were old even before then.

Either Jehovah stole those laws and claimed them for his own or else they were the standards by which all civilized people governed themselves. He might have been reinforcing them upon the Hebrews in order that they might begin their new existence as a nation with a firm and solid established system of laws by which they could govern themselves. Also these laws, passed down to the Hebrews, may well have been those laws which govern the alien society of the Lord God.

It has been man which has chosen to change those laws to suit himself and to establish what he considers a more humane way of handling social problems.

Many faiths preach that at the time of reckoning, every man will be called upon to account for his deeds and his life on earth. The premise is that a man is to be rewarded or punished accordingly.

But according to scripture, a transgression of the law, no matter how small or apparently insignificant can be costly not only for the person committing the offense but also for his beloved family.

In scripture, the god of the Jews destroyed, not only the material possessions of an offender, but also his entire family. If God is forever and he never changes, how can anyone believe that he will be more reasonable in his future judgement of mankind or if there will in fact e a judgement in the end time.

If Jehovah is so harsh with his own beloved people, the Jews, how much harsher will he be with the gentiles, that he has directed the Jews to destroy or enslave? The destruction of life and property was and still appears to be the way of the Jewish and God.

When Joshua and the congregation were told to destroyed the city of Jericho, they were also told to destroy all living things within the city: men, women and children, young and old, along with all of their livestock. The only material thing that appeared to be important and pleasing to God was the gold, silver, brass and iron that was to be captured. These were to be collected and given to the priest so that it could go into the treasury of the house of the Lord; in other words, the treasury of the house of Levi and eventually used to make the plates of gold for the table of the Lord.

Scripture says that one man violated that order. He took and withheld a garment, some silver and a wedge of gold. He was found out. For committing this trespass, a crime, again an order given by God, Joshua took the man, the garment, the silver, the gold, his sons, daughters, oxen, asses, sheep, his tent, and all that he had, and the congregation stoned them to death. When it was believed that they were all dead, the remains were burned. Those who were not dead were burned alive in the fire that followed. This was the justice, love, and benevolence of God and his servants, the twelve tribes of Israel. Joshua 8 and 9.

Jesus, the son and heir of Jehovah was conceived and born out of wedlock. He was half alien and half human, by definition a bastard. As such, by the law of God himself, he will not or should not be able to enter into the congregation much less be considered a High Priest by Christians. Deu. 23:2.

Jesus was a man. He was no different then the mighty men of old or the children born out of wedlock between the aliens sons of God, and the daughters of men during the time of Adam.

There was one minor difference between the degradation of Mary and her impregnated and that of the half-breed children born during the time of Adam. During the time of Adam there was no law which forbid the aliens gods from having intercourse with the daughters of men. There was during the time of Mary.

Mary was considered a virgin, a maiden who was espoused to Joseph. Depending upon how one interprets the scriptures, the act of impregnating Mary was a direct violation of one of the laws of God by God himself. This law did not exist during the time of Adam because it was n edict of Jehovah and not the Lord God.

Deu. 22:23-24. *If a damsel that is a virgin is betrothed to a husband, and a man find her in the city, and he lie with her; Then you shall bring them both out unto the gate of that city, and you shall stone them with stones that they die; the damsel, because she cried not, being in the city; and the man, because he hath humbled his neighbour's wife: so thou shalt put away evil from among you.*

God violated his own law. Mary was betrothed to Joseph, therefore to violate her virginity was a crime. According to the law Mary was supposed to have been stoned to death.

Mary, betrothed to Joseph and found to be pregnant, was bound by law to be stoned to death because she was pregnant by someone other than her espoused husband. Deu. 22:23-27.

To escape death Mary had to claim that her pregnancy was the work of the Lord God. Among a religious people who accepted the power of God as a natural part of everything who was there to argue? The priest could not refute the statement without negating the power of the God whom they professed to serve.

Upon conception Mary became not only a servant of Jehovah but she also became his concubine. She was therefore to be protected as his personal property. Since Joseph, her husband to be, made no accusations against her, who was there to punish her for her sin?

But did Mary, like Eve, obey the will of her god and let him have his way with her? Has it even been considered a sin to bow to the wishes and desires of a god? Has it ever been considered a sin for a maiden to bow to the wishes and desires of her king, lord or master? It has always been accepted as their right.

It has been said that in some culture it was the right of a master to participate in the marriage and be present if not participate in the consummation of the marriage.

Mary became the mother of Jesus, who has been declared the Messiah, the saviour of the human race. He was an individual who gave the impression of someone who had divine authority and heredity to God himself. This was the result of the transgression of the very law given to the people to prevent such occurrences.

So is the new testament story of Jesus, is it fact or fiction?

It has been said that the books of the New Testament were not written until years after the death and supposed resurrection of Jesus.

It was these writings along with the ideas and teachings of a prophet which made Jesus of Nazareth appear to be the Messiah and the hoped for saviour of the Jewish people. He was to come to them through the line of David. St. Matthew claims that right for Jesus because of the genealogy of his foster father Joseph. Since Joseph was not the genetic father of Jesus, this assumption cannot be true. In St. Matthew the genealogy of Joseph is traced back to Abraham through David. In St. Luke the genealogy of Jesus goes from Mary to David through his son Nathan, all the way back to Adam who, according to St. Luke, was also the son of God. Since there were no women before the time of Adam, the only way that Adam could have been the genetic son of God was by cloning. As a genetic alteration he was a direct descendant of God alone.

Mark 3:38. *Which was the son of Enos, which was the son of Seth, which was the son of Adam, which was the son of God.*

Even though Jesus did not come through the line of David through Joseph, he was of the Messianic line through Mary. It was through her lineage and not that of Joseph which gave Jesus the right to claim that he was the rightful king and high priest of the Jewish Nation.

There is a passage in St. Mark that can be read in either of two ways, depending upon where one places the emphasis. Read one way, it is Joseph that is of the house of David. Read another way it is Mary who is one of his descendants.

Since Jesus was of the House of David and the rightful High Priest of the congregation the prophecies concerning a messiah and the claim of Jesus to that right would have been accepted as true.

There is one significant fact about Jesus that is never mentioned or considered by theologians, ministers, or religious study groups. That fact was the hereditary right of Jesus to the throne of Israel and that of the high priest through Mary's heritage as one of the last descendents of Mattathias who was king, high priests and leaders of the Maccabaeans rebellion. This was the real reason that Herod became so upset when he learned of the birth of Jesus. Jesus threaten his right to the throne.

Herod was an Idumaean, a direct descendent of Esau on both his father and his mother's side, rather than a descendant of Jacob. His right to rule was the result of a political power play which made him king. It is understandable that he would attempt to destroy his rival Jesus by whatever means that was available. His soldiers were ordered to kill all of the male children under the age of two years. This was the time frame considered as the most likely to include the possible birth date of Jesus, based on the information he received from the wise men, the scholars from the east his scribes and the priests.

Even as a child, Jesus, as the heir to the throne, was a threat to Herod.

St. Matthew 2:13. *And when they were departed, behold, the angel of the Lord appeareth to Joseph in a dream, saying, Arise, and take the young child and his mother, and flee into Egypt; and be thou there until I bring thee word: for Herod will seek the young child to destroy him.*

If a god cannot protect his own son from a mortal, can he still be a god?

Herod certainly was not worried about a mortal god, but he was concerned about a new "King of the Jews."

The lineage of Jesus, through Mary, can be traced back to Mattathias, the father of the Maccabaeans, who were a family of Jewish faithful which led the Jewish people in a revolt for their freedom. As a result of this rebellion, the sons of Mattathias, a priest, became the rulers and high priests of the Jewish nation by acclamation of the people themselves. It was to Simon, the last remaining son of Old Mattathias, the leader, that the honour and glory for a successful revolution was given.

An insert found in the C.S.S. edition of the King James version of the Holy Bible, contains a brief information section regarding the history of the Jewish Nation from Malachi to Matthew. The above information is a part of Jewish history.

Mattathias began the revolution. His sons led the people. Except for Simon, all of the other sons of Mattathias were killed during the revolt. Simon, as the sole surviving son, became the undisputed leader of the rebellion. After the revolt, "Simon received Jewish independence at the hands of the monarch Demetrius, King of Syria. This little nation, free for the first time in nearly four and a half centuries, struck coins bearing Simon's likeness, and began to date documents and happenings from the 'first year of Simon, high priest and governor'. The following year he was appointed hereditary prince of the Jewish theocracy.

When Simon and two of his sons were killed, another son of Simon, then serving as high priest, succeeded Simon and ruled for thirty years. He had two sons, One of them, Aristobulus, who also served as high priest. He turned the theocracy into a kingdom, set himself upon the throne, yet retained his priestly prerogatives. A civil war erupted between him and his brother Alexander Jannaeus. Alexander took over the throne and ruled for the next twenty seven years. When he died, his widow took his place. For the next nine years the Jews were ruled by a queen. She had two sons, Hyrcanus II and Aristobulus II. They too fought for the throne. Hyrcanus wanted the priesthood and Aristobulus the secular authority. Another civil war ensued. At this time Roman authority began to be felt in the kingdom. They set Hyrcanus on the throne. This was known as the rule of the Hasmonaeans.

Hyrcanus ruled in name only. The real power behind the throne belonged to Antipas, or Antipater, an Idumaean and descendant of Esau. The Idumaean dynasty, that of Herod, had begun.

When Herod learned of another heir to the Hasmonaean dynasty, an heir to both the kingship and priesthood of Israel he had a right to be concerned.

Mary was a descendent of one John Hyrcanus I, a son of Simon.

When Jesus was touring the countryside preaching and teaching, he was supported by wealthy and influential people. This should be significant to the layman familiar with the customs and the traditions of Israel during the time of Christ. How could someone in the lowly position of a carpenter demand such respect?

Why would Joseph of Arimathaea, a very rich and influencial personage not only support the travels of Jesus, intercede with Pilot on his behalf, donate his private tomb, and provide expensive herbs for his burial had he not believed and had great respect for the heritage of Jesus?

There is very little recorded on the background of Mary except that she was said to have been raised in the temple was betrothed to Joseph, a carpenter and her cousin was Elizabeth, of the daughters of Aaron, and wife of Zacharis, a priest. So Mary was a descendent of a very rich and influential family.

It is important at this time to point out an obvious difference in the story of Jesus as told by two of the gospel writers, St. Matthew and St. Luke.

St. Matthew says that Jesus, Mary and Joseph, by order of God, went down into Egypt to escape the wrath of Herod and the death of Jesus. (Chapter 2 vs. 14-23)

St. Luke says Jesus, Mary, and Joseph never left Canaan. They did not go into Egypt. They were never told by an angel to go or to return. Instead, according to custom, eight days after Jesus was born he was circumcised. When Mary had fulfilled her period of purification, she took Jesus to the temple in order to make the sacrifices required for the sin, of giving birth.

Lev. 12:1-4. *And the Lord spoke to Moses, saying, Speak to the children of Israel, saying, If a woman has conceived seed, and born a man child: then she shall be unclean seven days; according to the days of the separation for infirmity shall she be unclean. And in the eight day the flesh of his foreskin shall be circumcised. And she shall then continue in the blood of her purification three and thirty days; she shall touch no hallowed thing, nor come into the sanctuary, until the days of her purifying be fulfilled.*

When the sacrifices had been offered, the family returned to Galilee, to the city of Nazareth, the home of Joseph.

St. Luke 2:39-41. *And when they had performed all things according to the law of the Lord, they returned into Galilee, to their own city Nazareth And the child grew, and waxed strong inspirit, filled with wisdom; and the grace of God was upon him. Now his parents went to Jerusalem every year at the feast of the Passover.*

Mary and Joseph lived in a small town in Galilee called Nazareth. This was the home to which they returned after the birth of Jesus. It is located approximately eighty miles north of Jerusalem. It was there that Jesus grew up.

Every year the family made their pilgrimage from Nazareth, through the land of Samaria to the city of Jerusalem in order to observe and celebrate the Feast of the Passover.

This would not have been possible if Jesus and his family had fled and lived in the land of Egypt.

One of the gospel writers erred in his writing. Since Luke is alleged to have been more factual in his account, then it must be assumed that it was Matthew who was wrong.

There is a book, now out of print, entitled "The Jesus Scroll". This book is an analyses of some of the events surrounding and leading up to the crucifixion and supposed death of Jesus. It helps to explain the New Testament writings in the light of an ancient scroll found hidden in an earthen pot during an excavation of the ruins of Masada.

The author of that scroll, according to Donovan Joyce, the author of "The Jesus Scroll" was Jesus himself. The scroll states, according to the archaeologist who found it, said that Jesus of Nazareth, supposedly wrote this document the night the people of Masada committed mass suicide in order to escape capture by the Romans the next day.

The scroll indicated that Jesus was attempting to recover the throne of Israel as the rightful heir of the Maccabaeans and not that of a heavenly saviour.

His capture, trial, and execution were all prearranged by his supporters in order to give the Romans and the Jewish people the impression that he died on the cross. The myth of his death and his subsequent resurrection, led to the belief that he was in fact a divine entity and the Messiah promised to the Jewish people by the old testament prophets.

With a crucified and resurrected martyr, the myth of Jesus became a new religious. It came to be called Christianity.

The divinity of Jesus is merely a continuation of the religious hoax perpetuated by man upon man, by the apostles, and followers of Jesus. Their fanatic belief in his deity as the son of God, and their dedication to his cause led them to continue his teachings. Teachings which they believed were inspired by God. To the apostles and the followers of Jesus, he was in line by right, to the position of High Priest and to the throne of Israel. In their belief in his status as heir apparent and his philosophy, they spread his gospel to all they met.

It was through the efforts, beliefs, fanaticism and writings of Paul, that evangelism and the Christian religion became a reality.

The life and death of Jesus was hardly noticed by the majority of the Jewish people. To them he was no more than an itinerant preacher, just another country prophet.

Except for the letters which are recorded in the bible, there appears to be very little officially documented evidence that he even existed. From writings and what documented evidence that we have today, the spread of Christianity and the remembrance of Jesus is due primarily to the efforts of the Apostle Paul.

If it had not been for his letters and evangelic work, there might not be a Christian religion today. The life, death and crucifixion of Jesus would be merely an extension of the other religious stories which add interest to the history and long list of sayings quoted by the Hebrew itinerant prophets.

The biblical belief in the holy participation by divine persons in the pregnancies of both Elizabeth and Mary, lend mystery and intrigue to the birth of two of Christianity's most prominent figures, John the Baptist and Jesus of Nazareth. They were relatives and of the divine house of Levi. Either they were a part of a hoax or, like the mothers of Sampson, Samuel, and Isaac they were impregnated by aliens, the ones who called themselves the gods. With the exception of Mary, all of the mothers of the great men of Israel, were women who claim to have been barren. Through prayers, they were visited by divine individuals which gave them the ability to bare children. After a visit by these angels of God, the women became pregnant.

Throughout the old testament the term "came in unto" was used to indicate a sexual union between a male and a female. During the time of Adam it referred to the union between the alien sons of Gods and the daughters of men. From these unions mighty men were born. There is every indication that Cain, Isaac, Sampson and Samuel, along with Jesus, were just a few of the men who were born as a result of a sexual encounter between an alien life force (the gods) and the daughters of man. There may even have been some women born of these unions, but in the Hebrew society they would have little or no status. Therefore it is the men who are noted by the biblical writers.

In the reference section of the King James Version of the Bible under "Women of the Bible" are the names 'Bithiah-daughter of Jehovah, Ali-Jehovah is father, and Noadiah-convened of Jehovah.'

Were these women the daughters of Jehovah and did Jehovah have more than one son Isaac? Was Jesus his son or the son of Gabriel?

In Deu. 32:19 it says that the Lord was provoked by his sons and daughters. He had children. In order to have children one must have sex.

The Christians try to justify this statement by claiming that all humans are the children of God. If so what makes Jesus any different from the rest of humanity?

It is evident that the Lord God of the Israelites and his entourage took advantage of their power and authority over man in order to have intercourse with the women under their control. From these unions children were born.

Was Jesus the son of Mary and Jehovah, or of Mary and the angel Gabriel?

St. Luke 1:28 states that the angel Gabriel "came in unto" her. If the term "came in unto her" means one thing in Genesis should it not mean the same during the time of Jesus? If so, then the father of Jesus was not Jehovah but one of the members of his staff. It really does not matter because Jesus, like the half-breed children, the mighty men of old, he would have inherited from his alien father not only some of his intellect but a lot of his mental powers and abilities. This gave Jesus the ability to perform feats that ordinary men thought miracles deemed to be by divine authority. The fact the Jesus at some time in his youth spent time in India under the instruction of the mystics.

The Christian faith is based on the belief that Jesus died an unjust death upon the cross as a death will by his father as a blood sacrifice to take away the sins of man. Many men, of all nationalities, and all faiths, have died unjust deaths in the belief that their death was the will of God. They all believed equally in their causes, yet none are revered and worshipped as a son of a god. It then becomes apparent that it was not the death of Jesus that is of the utmost importance, but his supposed resurrection from the dead. It is the belief in his apparent defeat of death which places him in the enviable position of portraying himself to his believers as the delivered son of God himself.

It was not the death of Jesus that gave special meaning to his teachings but the supposed belief that he somehow arose from death to live again. Had he remained dead there would be no religion. But, did he actually die and come back to life?

If he did, to the uninitiated, this could only be a miracle of God and proof of his divine heritage. Today we know different. Today this apparent miracle, the ability to bring one back from the dead is a medical fact. Doctors perform this seemingly miraculous feat daily. People in all walks of life, in many circumstances have been declared or believed dead and have been brought back to life by doctors with the medical skills and technical equipment to perform this apparent miracle.

The heart stops and is restarted. An individual has stopped breathing, resuscitated and returned to the living.

Today we know that there are drugs, which can be taken by an individual, which will slow their heart rate so low as to give that individual the appearance of death. It is undetectable by anyone unfamiliar with the drug. An antidote to that drug is all that is required to revive an individual from such a catatonic state.

At the time of Jesus there was a religious sect of Jewish individuals believed skilled in the use and administration of drugs. They were always dressed in white and called themselves the Essenes. Jesus, himself, is rumoured to have been a member of this group. If so, the Essenes, would have been familiar with the birth and background of Jesus. The Essenes believing in the birth right of Jesus as the true king of Israel, may well have collaborating with him in a scheme to fake his anticipated death on the cross, thereby convincing the High Priest, Herod and the Romans that he was dead and no longer a threat to the throne of Israel.

The plot was to give the High priest and the Romans the idea that they had succeeded in destroying Jesus. They wanted him dead, not because he claimed to be the Messiah, but because he was preaching insurrection and was a threat to the throne of Israel, Roman order and discipline.

The information that there was a plot to preserve the life of Jesus and convince Herod and Rome of his death was derived from the information found on that above mention buried scroll found in Masada a few years ago.

The plot was very elaborate. Its implementation began at what has been called the Lord's "Last Supper". The full plot, as it was revealed in the document found at Masada, can be found in a book entitled The Jesus Scroll" by Donovan Joyce. This information clearly indicated that Jesus succeeded in convincing both the Romans and the High Priest that he died on the cross.

The scriptural record of the events of the death, burial and resurrection of Jesus gives some credence to the scroll information.

One example, is the biblical description of the individual dressed in white, found in the tomb of Jesus. Christians believe and have been taught that the young man was an angel, sent by God to assist Jesus in his preparation to enter the kingdom of heaven.

The words recorded in Matt. 16:5-7, have all been taken out of context, and because of the ignorance of the people at the time completely misunderstood what they wer reading.

Matt.16:5-7. *And entering into the sepulchre, they saw a young man sitting on the right side, clothed in a long white garment; and they were affrighted. And he saith unto them, Be not affrighted: ye seek Jesus of Nazareth, which was crucified: he is risen; he is not here: behold the place where they laid him. But go your way, tell his disciples and Peter, that he goeth before you into Galilee: there shall ye see him, as he said unto you.*

This along with the statement made by Jesus to Mary not to touch him, clearly indicates that Jesus was still near the tomb had not completely recovered from the drug. It is also evidence that the Essenes were a part of the conspiracy to save Jesus and trick the High Priest and Romans into believing that he was dead.

It is rumored that during his youth, before he began his ministry, Jesus had travelled to both Egypt and the far east. In both places he would have had an opportunity to study under the mystics. There he would have learned the use of herbs, drugs, special healing techniques and mind control. These skills alone would have set him apart from the other prophets and holy men of the time.

When he left the tomb Jesus did not go into heaven but into Galilee. This was the place where he had instructed his disciples to meet him after his crucifixion indicating that he was confident that he would survive the ordeal.

Matt. 28:6-10. *He is not here: for he is risen, as he said. Come see the place where the Lord lay. And go quickly, and tell his disciples, that he is risen from the dead, and behold, he goeth before you into Galilee; there shall ye see him: lo, I have told you. And they departed quickly from the sepulchre, with fear and great joy: and did run to bring his disciples word.*

And as they went to tell his disciples, behold, Jesus met them saying, All hail. And they came, and held him by the feet, and worshipped him. Then said Jesus unto them, Be not afraid: go tell my brethren, that they go into Galilee, and there shall they see me.

Matt. 28:16. *Then the eleven disciples went away into Galilee into a mountain where Jesus had appointed them.*

The death of Jesus was a hoax, well executed and understood by very few individuals.

The key to the above passages has always been our understanding of the word "dead". If one had the appearance of death it was assumed that they had died. Today we know that this is not true. It has always been assumed that Jesus actually did die on the cross, was buried and was resurrected because of the words used to describe the event. But did the events actually happen as they are recorded in scripture?

If there was a hoax, then the big mystery, in the biblical death, burial and resurrection of Jesus, would be how was it accomplished.

Giving Jesus the drug which gave him the appearance of death was easy. Convincing the authorities, the Romans, that Jesus had died and getting permission to retrieving his body in time to administer the antidote was the difficult part.

The antidote had to be accomplished within a given length of time or Jesus would have died not of thev crucifix, but of the drug given to him on the cross.

In this part of the plot, Joseph of Arimathea relying on Jewish custom and his position in the community, play a very important part in this scheme. He had the body released to him in order to obey Jewish customs of burial, and to get Jesus off of the cross before sunset. This had to be accomplished because the next day was the Sabbath, a day in which no work was supposed to be done. Therefore the antidote had to be administered to Jesus when he was placed in the tomb.

The Essene's knowledge of medicine and their skills in its use, along with the skills and knowledge of Jesus, enabled him to escape death and carry on his mission as a revolutionary teacher and fighter against the Romans.

The Essenes administered a narcotic to Jesus while he was on the cross, and an antidote to that narcotic while he lay in the tomb. They brought Jesus back from a state of being which gave him the appearance of death.

The beauty of the plot was the way in which the drug was administered to him and the unwitting part played by the Centurion at the cross which gave the plot a real sense of reality.

The drug was administered to Jesus in a sponge filled with what is described as a mixture of wine and vinegar.

Mark 15:36-37. *And one ran and filled a sponge full of vinegar, and put it on a reed, and gave him to drink, saying, Let alone; let us see whether Elias will come to take him down. And Jesus cried with a loud voice, and gave up the ghost.*

Once Jesus sucked on the sponge and indigested the drug, he passed out. To the viewers it appeared that he died, he gave up the ghost.

His side was never pierced according to Matthew, Mark and Luke. John is the only writer of the four gospels to mention that the side of Jesus was pierced and this was only to connect Jesus as the Messiah mentioned in Old Testament scripture.

The legs bones of Jesus were not broken as required by Roman law because Jesus appeared to be already dead.

St. John 19:32-33. *Then came the soldiers and brake the legs of the first, and of the other which was crucified with him. But when they came to Jesus, and saw that he was dead already, they brake not his legs.*

John mentioned both of these things so that the Old Testament scripture might be fulfilled.

John 19:34-37. *But one of the soldiers with a spear pierced his side, and forthwith came thereout blood and water. And he that saw it, bare record, and his record is true: and he knoweth that he saith was true, that ye might believe. For these things were done, that the scripture should be fulfilled, A bone of him shall not be broken. And again another scripture saith, They shall look on him whom they pierce.*

It is only John who states that Jesus was pierced in the side?

That could have been the impression he received when the reed soaked with wine and vinegar was given to Jesus to drink. In the attempt to get the sponge to the mouth of Jesus, the sponge may well have touched his side on the way up or down. When it did it left a mark and the seeping wine may well have given one the impression of blood leaking from a wounded side.

Did Jesus ever really die or was his apparent death a charade performed for the benefit of the Sadducees, the High Priest, the Pharisees and the people?

The author of the "Jesus Scroll", based on his knowledge of Hebrew history and customs, along with his study of New Testament scripture, offers the following explanation concerning the death of Jesus.

No one questions the fact that Jesus under Roman law was crucified. Crucifixion was one of the standard forms of execution of the day. It was a custom practiced by the Phoenicians, Carthaginians, Egyptians and Romans. A person dying from this form of execution usually took two to three days to die. Death was normally brought about either by heart failure or suffocation. Sometimes, in order to hasten death, the legs of the victim were broken. Once the legs collapsed, there was no support for the body and suffocation occurred. None of these incidents are recorded in scripture as having been a part of the death of Jesus.

From the time that he ate the passover meal with his disciples, went to the garden on the Mount of Olives, prayed and was taken prisoner, brought before the High Priest, questioned by Pilot, scourged, sentenced, taken to the mount, crucified and taken down for burial, was less than one day.

The biblical description of the death of Jesus was written by individuals standing some distance away from the actual crucifixion site. It would have been impossible for them to see clearly everything that went on at the cross. What they did see and what they were told by the centurions cause them to believed that Jesus had actually been crucified and that he had died.

According to scripture and the author of the "Jesus Scroll", the following is what history and the scriptures do not say. The spear that is supposed to have pierced the side of Jesus never broke his flesh. This staff, having a sponge on the end, used to give Jesus a taste of vinegar, (wine) fell against his side. The red color of the vinegar gave to those who were watching, the idea that the soldier had pierced the side of Jesus with the staff. The red wine flowing from the side of Jesus where the sponge had touched him, appeared to be his blood flowing from a wound. This also accounts for the impression the spectators had that water was mixed with the flowing blood. Jesus did take a drink of the wine vinegar the second time that it was offered. Soon after taking a sip of the wine he is said to have died. Since his body gave the appearance of death, those who were observing at the time believed that he had died.

Matt.27:48-50. the wine vinegar was laced with a powerful narcotic. This not only relieved his suffering but also gave him the appearance of death. Because of the appearance of death, the legs of Jesus was not broken according to custom. This gave Joseph of Arimathaea, a follower of Jesus, as the rightful heir to the throne of Israel, an opportunity to beg Pilot for the right to bury Jesus. Once Jesus was taken down, the Essenes were able to administer an antidote to the narcotic which allowed Jesus to be able to walk away from the tomb.

Jesus was no poor itinerant preacher. It is believed that according to Jewish custom he did take a wife. She was the daughter to a very rich provider who raised doves for the temple sacrifices. She supported his travels and was with him on his journeys.

When Jesus was crucified the soldiers cast lots for his garments. One does not cast lots for the rags of beggars. The robe of Jesus was expensive.

John 19:23-24. *Then the soldiers, when they had crucified Jesus, took his garments, and made four parts, to every soldier a part; and also his coat: now the coat was without seam, woven from the top throughout. They said therefore among themselves, Let us not rend it, but cast lots for it whose it shall be that the scripture might be fulfilled, which saith, they parted my raiment among them, and for my vesture they did cast lots. These tings therefore the soldiers did.*

As the future king of Israel Jesus had many followers, besides Joseph of Arimathea, who probably donated to his cause, in the belief that he would one day gain his rightful place as the king of Israel.

Jesus is believed to have risen from the dead. To his followers this power over death made him the son of God. But if he did not die how did he rise from the dead?

We might ask ourselves this same question about those who have appeared to have died and have been restored to life by modern medicine. These individuals are not called messiahs and the sons of God.

In I Kings 17: 17-23 it is quoted that the prophet Elijah, through prayer, brought back to life the son of a widow.

Rev.11:7-11, speaks of two witnesses for God, in the days of tribulation, who will be killed by the beast. After laying dead in the streets for three and a half days, are to be revived, and brought back to life by some special power.

Jesus is also said to have arisen from death on the third day. It seems that in Jewish history and religious mythology three and forty are magic numbers. Three days appear to be the magic number for dead. Perhaps under the right circumstances a body can survive for that long a period of time before deterioration becomes so complete that the body and the mind are beyond recovery. But I might mention that here that Jesus was not dead for three days. If Jesus had died on Friday afternoon and placed in the tomb that day he would have had to lay there for at least one day, Saturday the Jewish Sabbath. The next day he was found to be missing from the tomb, a period of some thirty six hours, not seventy two hours or three days as preached by the various religious denominations.

Rev. 1:18. *I am he that liveth, and was dead; and behold, I am alive for evermore, Amen; and have the keys of hell and of death.*

The Jews and Christians believe their God Jehovah is immortal. If so how can he die? If he were dead how was he able to return to life without some kind of assistant, be it mechanical or medical? Who were the assistants which brought him back to life?

The god of Revelation says that he has the keys of hell and of death. Where are the keys to life, salvation and the paradise offered by organized religions? Are they to be found in the hands of the beast?

According to the Scroll, Jesus did not die on the cross. He continued his quest for the throne and the freedom of the Jewish people against the Romans. He died at Masada in approximately 70 A.D., as a revolutionary fighting the Romans.

During his time, the Jewish people were in a kind of bondage to Rome. It was not entirely unlike their condition in Egypt. Except now instead of being ruled, governed and controlled by Pharaoh they were under the yoke of Caesar.

For approximately 400 years from the time of Malachi, the last prophet, until the time of Jesus, the Jewish nation had suffered many forms of bondage. They were looking for the saviour, the Messiah promised by Malachi, who would be their deliverer. When Jesus appeared on the scene he was accepted by many to be the promised Elijah, the Messiah.

Malachi wrote in 3:5 Behold, I will send you Elijah the prophet before the great and terrible day the Lord comes. And he will turn the hearts of the fathers to their children and the hearts of the children to their fathers, lest I come and smite the land with a curse.

> When John the Baptist began preaching throughout the land many believed that he was the fulfilment of this prophecy. When Jesus appeared as a teacher, he was taken to be the promised Messiah. This belief, and the fact that he was of the line of David and a direct descendant of the Maccabees for the position of High Priest aided him in his quest for whatever his true intentions might have been.

Jesus might have been the new Messiah hoped for by the Jewish people, but he was also a revolutionary.

Unlike Moses, who promised the people, on behalf of God land, wealth, health and prosperity on earth, the promises of Jesus were to be fulfilled in an afterlife, in a place called paradise or heaven.

Moses and Jehovah catered to the physical greed of man. Jesus catered to the physical and spiritually deprived. He sought to ease the burden of the people here on earth by offering them equality in heaven after death. Jehovah was for the here and now, the land of Canaan, wealth, land and power. Jesus offered a better world in the future and the hereafter. The rewards for following him would not be material wealth but spiritual peace and contentment. It was a way by which the people would be able to find peace and contentment with whatever their conditions might be here on this earth.

The Jews in order to enter their promised land, the land of Canaan, which for them was paradise, under the leadership of Jehovah, they had to kill, destroy, enslave and rob all that they conquered. Their paradise was built on a bloodbath.

On the other hand, the requirements for entering the heavenly kingdom of Jesus are the very opposite to those demanded by Jehovah. Jesus required one to turn the other cheek, feed the poor, help the destitute and above all be honest and forthright in all affairs. A disciple of Jesus had to become a humble servant to all. In this way one humbles himself and make his servitude and himself more presentable to God.

Jehovah demanded that the Jews bow to no man.

Moses told the people to follow him and obey all of his laws and commandments and he would lead them to Canaan, the Promised Land. Jesus also said to follow him, obey his laws and his commandments and he too will lead the people to a promised land, a heavenly home after death, a place called by the Christians, paradise.

During the time of Jesus the old ways, obeying the laws of Moses, were not working. The promises of Jehovah were not being fulfilled. The people were suffering. There was sickness, disease and poverty throughout the land. The wealth of the people was slowly being taken away by the taxes of Caesar and the rule of King Herod. Both ruled the people with a hand of iron.

When Herod commanded the soldiers to go forth and slaughter every male child under the age of two, believing that this would eliminate Jesus as a threat to his throne, the soldiers did as they were commanded to do. Where was the god of the Jews during this time of horror and anguish?

If Jehovah was aware of the condition of the Jewish people at this time, he gave no indication of it.

When Jesus went before the rabble to gather support for his cause, he appealed to their oppressive condition. Due primarily to his teachings and their misunderstandings of what he was preaching, his followers began to believe that everything they did not have on earth they would be able to obtain in heaven. These rewards included, but were not limited to honour, riches, health, joy and prosperity.

At the time of Jesus there was really very little difference between the Jewish people and their forefathers who had suffered in Egypt. For those who had nothing, the promises of anything were better than what they had.

The people began to follow Jesus as their new Messiah in the hope that they might benefit from his cause should he be successful.

The promises of Jehovah and Moses appealed to the greed, lust and physical bondage of the Hebrews in Egypt. They were bribed with promises of land, freedom, riches and glory in order to get them to leave Egypt. Once the Hebrews were under complete control they were given demonstrations of the technical power and might of Jehovah. He became the First Godfather, not because he claimed to be a god, but by the abuse of his technical power and might.

Jehovah satisfied his desire to become a god, and in doing so eventually satisfied the promises made to the Israelites which satisfied their greed and lust for power.

Jesus, like Jehovah, also appealed to the greed and lust of the people. He provided them with a way by which they could justify their physical condition. He offered them a new way of looking at God and religion. He satisfied their need for a spiritual guide and ruler. He became the Godfather of the spirit.

In Lev. 25:44-46, Jehovah said: Both thy bondmen, and thy bondmaids, which thou shalt have, shall be of the heathen that are round about you; of them shall ye buy bondmen and bondmaids. Moreover of the children of the strangers that do sojourn among you, of them shall ye buy, and of their families that are with you, which they beget in your land: and they shall be your possession. And ye shall take them as an inheritance for your children after you, to inherit them fora possession; they shall be your bondmen fo ever; but over your brethren the children of Israel ye shall not rule one over the other with rigour.

How can anyone read the above passage and say with a certainty that the Jewish god did not believe in slavery. It was, until a few years ago, a fact of life.

Jesus says in Matt. 5:39-45. But I say unto you, that ye resist not evil: but whosoever shall smite thee on thy right cheek, turn to him the other also. And if any man shall sue thee at the law, and take away thy coat, let him have thy cloak also And whosoever shall compel thee to go a mile. Go with him twain.

Give him that asketh thee, and from him that would borrow of thee turn not thou away. Ye have heard that it hath been said, Thou shalt love thy neighbour, and hate thine enemy. But I say unto you, Love your enemies, bless them that curse you, do good to them that hate you, and pray for them which despitefully use you, and persecute you.

Matt. 6:19-21. *Lay not up for yourselves treasures upon earth, where moth and rust doth corrupt, and where thieves break through and steal: But lay up for yourselves treasures in heaven, where neither moth nor rust corrupt, and where thieves do not break through nor steal: For where your treasure is, there will your heart be also.*

Jehovah preached strength. Jesus advocated pacifism. Jehovah preached earthly wealth, power and glory. Jesus preached humility, poverty and servitude. If one follows the teachings and goals of Jesus it is a road leading man back to his original condition as the slave he was created to be.

If one followed the guidance of Jehovah, and was successful in accumulating treasures on earth they are on the road of becoming the gods man was create to be.

What is to become of those treasures accumulated on earth when one passes on to the great beyond? What happens to the results of the fruit of a person's time, labour, and years of privation? It goes to one's heirs. On the other hand what happens to the treasures one has accumulated in heaven if they are denied access to that realm in the end time? And of what use are treasures in heaven when none are need.

Jehovah commanded that the people give to his priests at least ten (10) percent of everything which they accumulated in this life. It was the right of the Levi, their due inheritance as the servants of Jehovah.

This practice of giving ten percent (10%) of one's income to the church to support the clergy, continues today.

The synagogues and churches founded in the names of Jehovah and Jesus are nothing more than organized business ventures which call themselves a religious order. In addition to the tithes, offerings and sacrifices given, in the name of god, to support these religious organizational structure, these organizations also expect a dedicated disciple to do support the poor, the destitute, and the under privileged.

The church proper, in the name of God, will first feed and support themselves and their organization. If and when there are any donations left, these religious organization claim that it is distributed, in the name of God, to those in need. They claim to help feed the hungry, clothe and shelter the homeless, and give to those who are to lazy or stupid to work.

By doing all of these things, the Christians are taught that they are laying up for themselves treasures in heaven.

Why?

Isn't heaven a place where treasures are not supposed to be needed? Do the preachers not tell us that heaven is a place of everlasting joy, a place where there are no tears, no sorrow, no pain and a place where every need will be taken care of? If so why would a saved soul need treasures in heavens? What are they suppose to do with it? Will one be able to go to a store, shopping mall or bazaar and buy what one does not have? This was certainly not a concept, promise or expectation of the Israelites as they journeyed to Canaan.

The Lord God of the Jews made no such promises. This was an idea that came from the teachings of Jesus, and from the words he is supposed to have spoken to one of the thieves hanging beside him on calvary. Those words are found only in Luke 23:43, when Jesus is quoted as saying to one of the thieves, "Truly I say to you, today you will be with me in Paradise."

The laws of Jehovah, and the practice of Judaism, placed the Israelites into a condition of physical slavery through their religious beliefs and practices. The followers of Jesus, the Christians, have also placed themselves into a similar condition of slavery. Instead of physical servitude they are under a mental, spiritual and emotional bondage.

When Jesus taught his disciples to pray, he gave them a prayer to pray. It is not a prayer of praise and homage to a god, but a prayer of a slave to render to their master, god or ruler. This prayer, called the Lord's Prayer is continually repeated by Christians in their religious rituals and home prayers. This prayer reinforces the subject's state of servitude. Jesus taught his disciples to pray thus:

Matt. 6:9-15. *After this manner therefore pray ye: Our father which are in heaven, Hallowed be thy name. Thy kingdom come. Thy will be done in earth, as it is in heaven. Give us this day our daily bread. And forgive us our debts, as we forgive our debtors And lead us not into temptation, but deliver us from evil: for thine is the kingdom, and the power, and the glory, forever. Amen*

What appears to be the point of the prayer? Where does it indicate that the petitioner is speaking to a Holy God? What is its purpose?

First of all the prayer is a petition addressed to a ruler identified not as God but as a Father, an overseer, one who resides in a place called heaven. Second, the petitioner is humbly and respectively praising the Father by flattering, not him but his name. (In the olden days it was believed, that if one knew the name of someone they possessed a power over that individual. To know and call upon the name of God, gives power to the requests of the petitioner.

Lord just as your will is obey by your servants in heaven so we your servants on earth will also obey your will. Only like the slaves and servants that we are, we humbly ask that you feed us today. Please give us our daily bread. If we have erred or failed in any of our tasks, or broken any of your laws, we ask that you do not punish but forgive us for our transgressions. In return for your forgiveness, we will, in turn, forgive those that have failed or wronged us.

This is a prayer of slaves. It is a plea to a master, a ruler or a king, to be merciful in his judgement. It is not a prayer in praise or honour to a God. It is a reinforcement and an acknowledgement of a condition of slavery.

How does God or Jesus acknowledge such requests?

Matt. 7:21-23. *Not everyone that saith unto me, Lord, Lord, shall enter into the kingdom of heaven; but he that doeth the will of my Father which is in heaven. It is not the will and desires of Jesus that will get a disciple into heaven but of will of Jehovah. But if it as the Jewish people believe that there is no heaven then what is he point? Many will say to me in that day, Lord, Lord have we not prophesied in thy name? And in thy name have cast out devils? And in thy name done many wonderful works And then will I profess unto them, I never knew you: depart from me, ye that work iniquity.*

In the New Testament there are four books written by the selected disciples of an iterant preacher, a Jewish prophet, a man called Jesus. These books are identified as the gospel books. They were written by the disciples of Jesus in order to create an illusion of who Jesus was. They were designed or written in order to create a belief in the holiness of Jesus, and that his teachings and his philosophy were divinely inspired. Their writing suggested that Jesus was the Messiah, the son of God, and the saviour of the people foretold in their scripture by the ancient prophets.

Over time Christian theologians, based on their interpretations of those scriptural writings and the teachings of Jesus, have come to believe that the Jewish God Jehovah was in reality, three beings in one which has created the religious confusion that exists today.

First he is God the creator, who is identified in scripture as the Father. There is Jesus, his Son and his human form, and finally there is his spirit known as God the Holy Spirit or Holy Ghost.

Each of the Trinity served a definite purpose in the forming of the Christian doctrine. God was the father to whom all things belonged. He was the authority to whom all creatures answered for the transgression of his law and command.

Man was corrupt, he had sinned and was therefore unworthy to stand before a Holy God or to be able to communicate with him in any way. Therefore god devised a plan whereby man would have a way of making restitution for his sins and be made holy again. The Christians believe that plan was the birth, death and resurrection of a man called Jesus. Jesus is said to have been God himself who came to the earth as a man, endured the hardships and offered himself up as a living sacrifice so man might have an atonement for his sins. Jehovah indicated as much when he establish the office of the High Priest. The High Priest became the intermediary between God and the people of the congregation until such a time when they themselves became worthy enough to stand before him. The Christians believe that Jesus replaced the High Priest and is therefore their intermediary.

What happened to the religious authority of that position during the time of Jesus is uncertain.

Christians believe that it is Jesus and not the High Priest who is now their intermediary to God the Father. Jesus, by his death on the cross and his resurrection, became the High Priest and it is he who now has access to God for the benefit of man. . Why Christians believe this is uncertain because this belief is certainly not the scriptures teachings or words of Jesus. For Jesus told his disciples they are their own intermediary and through prayer find and talk to God themself.

When Jesus was supposed to have died on the cross, his sacrifice was to be the ultimate sacrifice. No more bloody sacrifices were ever needed to talk to God or be necessary for the forgiveness of sins. Now the members of the congregation could speak directly to God. They no longer had to make sacrifices, rely on the apparent righteousness of their religious leader or a particular faith in order to pray or petition God for whatever they wanted or needed.

Mat. 6:5-6. *And when thou prayest, thou shalt not be as the hypocrites are: for they love to pray standing in the synagogues, and in the corners of the streets, that they may be seen of men. Verily I say unto you, They have their reward. But thou, when thou prayest, enter into thy closet, and when thou hast shut thy door, pray to thy Father, which is in secret; and thy Father, which seeth in secret, shall reward thee openly.*

The Christians have come to believe that because of their sins they are unworthy to pray directly to God the Father. Therefore, because of the righteousness of Jesus, and his position as the son of the Father, he is better able to carry their petitions to Jehovah.

The Holy Spirit is considered the power of God by which all things everywhere are united in celestial harmony. The Holy Spirit is considered as the way by which the union between God, Jesus and man is to be spread and the force which binds them all together. This precept by the theologians came about through their interpretations of the gospel texts and the writings of the Apostle Paul.

In an analysis of these scriptural texts it was not the original four gospels or the idea of the trinity which gave Christianity it's power and force, but the work of Paul, the fifth and most prolific of the biblical writer. Almost forty percent of the accepted New Testament was written by him. His writings bring all of the religion teachings and philosophy of Jesus together.

Without his evangelism to the gentiles it is doubtful that Christianity would have been anything more than a passing fad.

Like many of the religions which have come and gone down through the ages, Christianity might have lasted for a few years, but at the death of the original apostles, it would most likely have faded into oblivion.

It was the letters of Paul and his testimonies that not only kept the teachings of Jesus alive but also helped to spread those teachings abroad.

His conversion from a devout prosecutor of Christians to one of the most ardent followers of the path of Jesus gave force and credibility to the teachings and philosophy of Jesus. It is through the writings of Paul that the meanings and ideas of Jesus are expressed and explained. It is the quotes from his writings, along with those of Jesus, which have become the foundation upon which the sermons taught in the Christian church today are based.

There are times when the Christian religion should be called the religion of Paul. That is because the teachings of Paul through his letters seem to be the substance which not only binds but holds Christianity together.

In the Christian beliefs there are two gods, the Father and the Son. In the Jewish and Christian religions there are two saviours, Moses and Jesus.

In the Jewish religion Moses is supposed to have saved the Hebrews from physical bondage. Though the teachings of Jesus, he strives to teach the people how to live within their physical bondage through spiritual supplication. But the true aim of both saviours is to return the congregation to the yoke of religious oppression.

There are basically nine individuals writers in the New Testament united for the sole purposed of one thing, to advance the enslavement of man by preaching the salvation of his soul.

The foundation of Christianity is based upon the teachings of Jesus, reinforced by the explanations of Paul, which supports the belief that the man called Jesus was the Christ, the Anointed One. He is believed to have been the Holy Messiah promised by the old testament prophets.

Who was the man called Jesus?

First of all he was a bastard child born to a unwed woman who claimed to have been a virgin at the time of his conception. It is recorded that she was impregnated by the power of God, the Holy Spirit. Because of this propaganda, Christians believe that Jesus is, as the gospels writers have stated, to have been the son of God. It is believed that he was born out of the love and compassion of a god who desired to save his people from eternal damnation.

This love for mankind was so great, that the Lord God Jehovah, an entity who was supposed to have created and still controlled a universe beyond comprehension, allowed himself to be born a human, in order to suffered the trials and tribulations of the flesh of man.

God himself, came to the earth, in the form of a man, so that he might be humiliated, whipped, sacrificed and hung upon a cross to die like a common criminal in order to save the souls of the descendants of the cloned sub-species, the slaves, he had created. I do not think so.

Jesus was crucified not because he was the son of God, suffering and dying for the sins of man, but because he was a revolutionary and a threat to the order of Rome, the High Priest of Jerusalem and to Herod and the throne of Israel.

The New Testament version of the impregnation of Mary does not state that Jehovah and Jesus are one and the same entity. Theologians have made this determined by doctrine.

Religious leaders would have us believe that even if God and Jesus are not the same, Jesus was still put on this earth to do the will and command of his father, Jehovah. Jesus, if he is God or is the son of God and is doing the will of God, then he is God, and unlike the leopard, he has changed his spots.

He is no longer a fearful God, a god of wrath and vengeance, but a kind, loving and benevolent father doing everything in his power to prepare a home and a welcome to all of his repentant children.

This is unlikely if Jehovah was, is and always will be God.

Since there is such a vast difference between the laws of Jehovah and the teachings of Jesus we might ask ourselves if Jehovah was the actually father of Jesus. Like father, like son they are not.

If Jehovah was not the father of Jesus, who was?

Based on old testament scripture, Mary might have been impregnated by any one of the angels or members of God's crew. As such her claim to have been impregnated by a god would still be valid. Jesus could still justify the claim that his father was a heavenly being.

But the birth, and death of Jesus had nothing to do with his death as a sacrificial offering for the sins of man. Nor did it have anything to do with his claim to be the son of a god. According to scripture it was most likely that his father was the angel Gabriel and not Jehovah. Luke 1:26-28.

Gabriel went in unto Mary. He claimed that he was sent from God. Mary became pregnant. She said she was told that it was the will and desire of God.

With the threat of death by stoning, for having a child out of wedlock, what did Mary have to lose by blaming God for her condition. As a young woman, closely associated with the temple and having been a vestal virgin she was filled with religious zeal. She may well have believed that her impregnation was a part of a religious experience.

How many stories have we heard in our lifetime of both women and men who have had sexual relationships with members of the clergy convinced that such an experience was the will of the Lord and one of the ways to heaven. Such stupidity is not always limited to those of great faith.

Take for example the many Christians of today who believe that when they participate in the religious ritual identified as the Lord's Supper, that the bread and the wine which they consume before the altar is actually changed and becomes the body and blood of Christ. If not in physical substance then in spirit. Why not sex through his messenger, the priest and ministers. Should the impregnation of Mary be considered any different?

From her earliest childhood Mary was under the guidance and control of the High Priest. She knew, as a part of Israelite history, that the gods has come into the daughters of men and had bore great men to the gods.

She had sex and she became pregnant. She could not have conceived a child unless she had either been artificial impregnated or had a relationship with a biologically being, be it man or alien god. It has been found possible that a woman can conceive even if penetration had not been achieved. No matter how the sperm and the egg come into contact with other, if they are biological compatible, they will unite and a child will be conceived. There is one possible explanation that would allow Mary to become pregnant and conceive a child as a virgin with the assistance of a male sperm donor. She may have been born a hermaphrodite.

Hermaphrodites are individual life forms, born with both male and female sex organs. It may be that her female organ were somehow impregnated by male sperm from her own body. I have been unable to find out if such a thing is possible or if such an occurrence has ever been recorded. It does occur in nature but in humans, I am not sure.

I believe that it is safe to assume that the New Testament angel identified as Gabriel was no different than the "sons of God" referred to in the Book of Genesis. And, that the term "came in unto," as it is used in Genesis, refers to the act of intercourse.

Unless the meanings of these words have changed over time, Mary had an alien visitor. That visitor became the father of her child. That child was Jesus, an individual which became a man of renown. If Mary was in fact still a virgin, then contact was made, sperm ejaculate and impregnation occurred without penetration.

This occurrence is believed to have happened even in modern times, when young girls have become pregnant by males who ejaculate while rubbing their male organs against the vagina of the female.

After the birth of Jesus, the gospels state that Mary and Joseph, warned by an angel, took Jesus and went to live in the land of Egypt. They did this to prevent the death of Jesus by the militia of Herod. It is said and believed that they did not return to Israel until after the death of Herod when they were told that Herod was dead and it was safe to return.

This idea that Joseph, Mary and Jesus journeyed to Egypt is sometimes used explain certain passages of scripture prophesy found in the Old Testament. It would also offer us an explanation which would explain the means by which Jesus receive some of the training, the skills and wisdom he is said to have possessed.

According to the gospel of St. Luke Jesus and his family never ventured into the land of Egypt when he was a child. He spent his youth in Galilee with his parents. St. Luke 2:39-42.

After the age of twelve or at sometime during his youth and young manhood then he may well have gone to both Egypt and the fareast to study and obtain an education.

Except for the fact that Jesus was born an Israelite his birth and early life appears to be little different from the birth and lives other great men born under like circumstances. Men like Pythagoras, Apollonius of Tyanis, Zoroaster, and Alexander the Great, are all men who it has been said were born of immaculate conception, studied in Egypt and with the mystics of the far east.

It is said that all were to have on different occasions demonstrated strange and mystical powers. It is also rumoured that they were all ritually crucified and lay for three days in a tomb or a place where they underwent some kind of initiation rites into a mystical organization.

Upon their release, they were said to have been raised from the dead and had conquered death.

Jesus, the Christ, was not the first saviour of man or of the world. He was only one of many which spread a philosophy which was designed to help man overcome his earthly conditions and to give him an impetus to strive for a higher and better life.

They too were called the sons of God and called out. How many times have the readings of the scriptures been changed and interpreted to mean something other than what they were intended to say.

But, it was necessary for Matthew to connect Jesus with Egypt in order to show him as the fulfilment of the Jewish prophecy related to the coming of their Messiah.

Luke does not try to connect Jesus to the past prophesies. He relates the facts in the life of Jesus as he was able to determine them to be. If the parents of Jesus attended the Feast of the Passover every year how and when were they ever in Egypt?

One of the apostles is stretching the truth. Matthew is striving to bring together odd and miscellaneous elements of Old Testament prophecy in order to show the deity of Jesus and his right to the title as the foretold Messiah. Luke appears to be interested in a more realistic and factual approach.

In the belief of Matthew, God finds it necessary to send his son into Egypt in order to fulfil a prophecy. But the prophecy is not the main reason that Jesus is said to have made this journey. The real reason was that God was not able to protect his son from the sword and fear of Herod.

It became necessary for Jesus and his parents to play hide and seek with Herod in order for Jesus to survive. Evidently God, the father, is not able to do any more about protecting his son and family from the wrath of earthly powers than any other father.

Jesus was just another man. From his teachings one can assume that he was well educated and seemed to have had special powers and abilities. This can also be said about other religious leaders, from whom many other religious cults have developed. Zoroaster, Mohammed, Krishna and Buddha are just a few.

Jesus, as a teacher, can be compared with many other intellectuals individuals which have changed the relationships between people. Men like Hammurabi, Disraeli, Aristotle, Pythagoras, Plato, Voltaire and a thousand others which down through history have left their mark on the evolution of man.

The life and legend of Jesus is a duplication, a repeat of the lives of many other saviours of different cultures and civilizations which have gone before him. All the reader has to do is to obtain a book on ancient religions, myths, customs and legends to see the similarities.

An interest note on history is that according to some references Herod the Great, the one responsible for the slaughter of young children, in an attempt to kill Jesus, was the king and ruler of Israel from approximately 37 B.C. to 4 B.C.

Matthew 2:22 says that the son of Herod was king when Jesus returned from Egypt. That son was Archelaus, who ruled Israel from 4 B.C.E. to 6 A.C.E. Therefore, if the calendars are correct, Herod died before Jesus was even born. Of course calendars have been adjusted in order to bring about conformity in the time line of Jesus and events that occurred before his cruification

Matthew 2:23 *And he came and dwelt in a city called Nazareth: that it might be fulfilled which was spoken by the prophets, he shall be called a Nazarene.* It is difficult to understand how the life of Jesus and this passage can be a fulfilment of the Old Testament prophecy found in Judges which states:

Judges 13:5,7. *For lo, thou shalt conceive, and bear a son; and no razor shall come on his head; for the child shall be a Nazarite unto God from the womb: and he shall begin to deliver Israel out of the hands of the Philistines. This is the story of Samson not Jesus. And while Jesus lived in Nazareth he was not a Nazarene. He was not born in Nazareth and drank wine and strong drink.*

The references made to the terms and conditions of a Nazarite are found in Numbers 6:1-4. *And the Lord spoke to Moses, saying, Speak unto the children of Israel, and say unto them, when either man or woman shall separate themselves to vow a vow of a Nazarite, to separate themselves unto the Lord He shall separate himself from wine and strong drink, and shall drink no vinegar of wine, or vinegar of strong drink, neither shall he drink any liquor of grapes, nor eat moist grapes, or dried. All the days of his separation shall he eat nothing that is made of the vine tree, from the kernal even to the husk.*

If the above were the requirements for an Israelite to take a vow to God and to become and to stay a Nazarite, than Jesus was not one and the prophecy was not fulfilled. By his own words Jesus was not a Nazarite.

Matthew 11:18-19. Jesus says, speaking of John the Baptist, *For John came neither eating nor drinking, and they say, he hath a devil. The son of man cameating and drinking, and they say, behold a man gluttonous, and a winebibber, a friend of publicans and sinners.*

Matthew 26:29. *But I say unto you, I will not drink henceforth of this fruit of the vine, until that day when I drink it new with you in my father's kingdom."*

Another question that can be raised concerns the birth of Jesus.

Luke 2:1-2. *And it came to pass in those days, that there went out a decree from Caesar Augustus, that all the world should be taxed. And this taxing was first made when Cyrenius was governor of Syria.*

The revised edition of the Bible identifies Cyrenius as Quirinus. This is an anglicized form of the Greek rendering of his name. Quirinius was governor of Syria A.D. 6-9. It was during this time that the taxing and census was to have taken place. (Zondervan Compact Bible Dictionary.)

If this is true, then Joseph and Mary were going to Bethlehem to be taxed when Jesus was born. That places his birth sometime between 6 and 9 A.D., and 10 years after the death of Herod the Great.

If Jesus was not the son of God, nor the Messiah of the Jews, exactly who was he?

If we discount the time line and the references to the birth date of Jesus, we have the following.

Jesus, or some other individual was born at sometime during the rule of Herod. For some unknown reason the wise men of the court believed that this individual was of the line of David and therefore a rightful pretender for the throne of Israel. When Herod was told, he inquired as to the date of the birth of this individual. The wise men, unable to be certain of the date, caused Herod to issue an order that every male child born between certain dates were to be killed. In this way he believed that he was protecting his throne.

Certainly the rumour that the birth of Jesus was god-like would not have been enough to cause Herod to order the execution of all the males under two years of age. Another prophet more or less in Israel meant nothing to him. But, an heir, through the line of David was something else.

Herod ruled by the right and power of Rome. A rightful heir through the line of David would rule by the right and power of the people. This was the reason Herod feared the lost of his throne?

It has been stated that Jesus came to save the people. That he was the king of the Jews and High priest of God. By what right could these claims be made on behalf of Jesus? Was he the true King of Israel? Was he also the High Priest? Or was he just another religious prophet, the believed offspring of an earth woman and an alien god?

Religious writers say one thing, but historical scholars are hard pressed to find any records which support the claim of Jesus in one way or another.

If the teachings of Jesus and what he had to say were of such great importance to the welfare of the people, why weren't records made at the time of his preaching? Why wasn't there some historical references made at the time three thousand souls were said to have been saved by the reception of the Holy Ghost and the time of their remembrance? Why did the disciples wait almost forty years before finally writing down what they remembered of their experience, what they came to believed, and what they were taught?

One answer which could explain all of the above would be the fact that Jesus had not died. He was still alive and the disciples continued not only to follow him but to study under him.

Christians believe Jesus died on the cross at ge thirty-three. The scroll at Masada says he died in seventy A.D., forty years after his believed death on the cross This could be a possible explanation that explains why it took the gospels writers so long before writing what they remembered of the life of Jesus.

The first recorded scripture concerning the life of Jesus appeared at about the same time as that of an individual who, bearing the same name, died as a revolutionary at Masada, in 70 A.D.

When the gospel writers began to record their experiences they included conversations between individuals, angels, God, Jesus and Satan. They wrote as if they were privy to even the thoughts of their characters. Their dialogue and the stories which are told are written in order to make them interesting and believable if not necessarily factual.

The Christian faith is based on two things, the belief that Jesus lived, died and arose from the grave and thst his teachings or from the Lord himself.. Those teaching are those of a pacifist and they are in direct conflict with the laws laid down by Jehovah through Moses.

Today if a contract is made by a father and that contract is changed or voided by the son, who is the more powerful, the father or the son?

Jehovah indicated that his words and any contracts made by him are to be forever. Those words and contracts are either changed or voided by Jesus said toi be his son. If the words and contracts of the God Jehovah or null and void based on time and circumstances, can the word or contract of either the father or the son be accepted as worthy of any trust?

God promised the Jews one thing. Jesus promised his followers another. The big question then becomes which of the two, God or Jesus is the more powerful? Which one is worthy of trust? What alternative does a believer have if neither can be trusted to live up to their promises? Perhaps neither can be trusted because neither is a god but mere flesh and blood individuals who's ego made them into what man come to believe are gods.

Rev. 1:8. *I am, Alpha and Omega, the beginning and the ending, saith the Lord, which is, and which was, and which is to come, the almighty.*

Rev. 1:17-18. *And when I saw him, I fell at his feet as dead. And he laid his right hand upon me, saying unto me, fear not: I am the first and the last: I am he that liveth, and was dead; and behold, I am alive for evermore, Amen: and have the keys of hell and death.*

Can any being which claims to be immortal ever die? If that being can die is it immortal? If it can die, can it also bring itself back to life or must it have help of some kind?

The scriptures state that God claimed that he was once dead. Did his minions, the angels, bring him back to life, as our doctors are able to do today, and as the Christians believe they did for Jesus? Will the angels, the doctors and scientist of God, also be involved in the resurrection of the two servants of God who are to be killed by the beast in Rev. 11:1-12.

For three and a half days these two prophets of God shall lay dead in the streets of Sodom before the power of life (the Spirit of God), is returned to their bodies and they become alive again. When this happens the prophets will then ascend into heaven. The power of resurrection, is it by mythical power or by medical and technical skills?

God says that he has been brought back to life. If he can die just like the rest of us, and if he can be brought back to life then so can we. How long are we allowed to be dead and what would circumstances are we allowed to return to life?

During the last several years there have been several instances where people have fallen through the ice of frozen bodies of water and became trapped under the ice for long periods of time. In one instance the individual was under water for approximately thirty minutes before being rescued. Deprived of oxygen and frozen, these individuals have been returned to life without any apparent major medical difficulties all due to the quick and efficient actions of the rescue term and the medical personnel of the immediate area.

It is a fact that people around the world die every day from heart attacks. Many are returned to life by electric shock treatments which restart their hearts.

If man can perform these apparent miracles today, surely, a race of beings, capable of travelling the stars, and who had the medical and technical skills to created and clone new from that which already exist would certainly have the same capabilities as man does today.

When is one consider legally or medically dead? Is it when the heart stops, breathing ceases, or the brain no longer functions? Where does life really begin or end?

If by some miracle we do die and after death we are resurrected to a new life in the hereafter by some mythical power, what can we expect to happen to us at that time?

Rev. 2:7 says, *To him that over cometh will I give to eat of the tree of life, which is in the midst of the paradise of God.*

Where is this paradise of God and this "Tree of Life?"

Genesis 2:9 says that it is here on earth in the garden of God. If the tree of life is here on earth in the paradise of God is that paradise here also? It must be, because in Revelation 21:3 there is the following statement.

Rev. 21:3. *And I heard a great voice out of heaven, saying, Behold, the tabernacle of God is with men, and he will dwell with them, and they shall be his people, and God himself shall be with them, and be their God.*

Can anything be any clearer? There is no such place as a heavenly paradise. Heaven exists, but it is the universe, the stars, and the cosmos. It is not the religious paradise of believers in God. True it is the abode of the living beings, our creators, but it will not be the New Jerusalem and the kingdom of the earthly God of Man. That god and Christian paradise will be here on earth after the God of the Jews and Christians has destroyed almost everything in it.

After the plagues and destruction promised by the God of Revelation, any kind of a life at all could well be considered paradise. Just to be alive will be justification for one to be thankful. But at what price will one have to pay for this paradise a return to the dark ages of slavery without any hope of ever again knowing freedom without a god.

Rev. 2:17. To the angel of the church of Smyrna To him that over cometh shall not be hurt of the second death.

What is the second death? For Adam the first death came when he ate the fruit of the tree of the knowledge of good and evil. His eyes were opened his mind expanded and he lost his innocence. It was not a physical death but a mental, moral and spiritual death. But he was resurrected to a new life one which separated him from the gods and his master the Lord God.

Will the second death also be a separation from the presence of God or will it be eternity spent in the black emptiness of the grave?

Either way if I am involved in any way with the second death what happens to the treasures that I stored up in heaven during my earthly service to a god?

If I have stored up treasures in heaven what are they to be use for? If we are not allowed to get there what happens to our investments? Will the investments which we have made be taken over by the more affluent in God's court? Will the affluent help decide who will be the rulers and who will have the power over the nations which still abide on earth? In this new kingdom of God, who will be the ones who will rule over the nations?

The paradise of God, the heavenly kingdom is going to be a secret society of drug addicted slaves, ruled by the more dedicated worshippers of God. These rulers will be the fanatics who believe that any act in the name of God justifies the means to attain whatever their desires and goals might be.

Rev. 3:5. *To the angel of the church of Saris, He that over cometh, the same shall be clothed in white raiment; and I will not blot out his name out of the book of life, but I will confess his name before my father, and before his angel.*

What is to be overcome? If you do not know how can you be sure that your name will not be blotted out of the book of life. What happened to the promise of God that he will remember your sins and iniquities no more? If yours sins are forgiven, and God remembers those sins no more, what sins and crimes are you to be called upon to answer for in the last days?

It seems that the promises of God are only good as long as they are able to bring more slaves or disciples under his control.

Rev. 3:12. *To the angel of the church of Philadelphia To him that overcometh will I make a pillar in the temple of my God, and he shall go no more out: and I will write upon him the name of my God, and the name of the city of my God, which is new Jerusalem, which cometh down out of heaven from my God: and I will write upon him my new name.*

This passage of scripture sounds very much like a method or procedures used in marking slaves, their owners and the cities to which they belong. It also sounds very much like the numbering social sercurity system in use today. The slave owners of the old south use it and so did the Germans in World War Two.

To the Jewish people who have studied history, the above statements should bring to mind, not by the tinkling of a bell but a clasp of thunder, the stories of the Nazi concentration camps of World War II. Is there really any difference between the above statements of Revelation and the acts of the Nazi Gestapo?

Each disciple, each slave will be tattooed with a mark that shall identify each individual as to their name, their place of birth, residence and the owner to which they belong.

Rev. 22:3-4. *And there shall be no curse; but the throne of God and of the Lamb shall be in it; and his servants shall serve him: And they shall see his face; and his name shall be in their foreheads,*

How can Jesus be the Alpha and the Omega, the first and the last, he that liveth, and was dead, overcame death and also sits down with his father in his throne? How can Jesus, the Holy Spirit and God be one and the same yet be separate?

My son is the same but is as different from me as I am from my father. The son certainly is not the Holy Spirit. That is the name given to the breath of all life which has existed from the beginning of organic matter. It is the power of life created or given to all living beings by the creator of the universes, it is the power which moves life and controls all living things.

God, Jesus, you and I use that power every day in every way. It is the power which converts what we eat into the energy and building materials needed to repair and keep us functioning. It is the binding power which allows our broken bones to mend, our wounds to heal and our organs to continually rebuild and repair themselves. It is the power which converts physical matter into chemical, mechanical and electrical energies. It is the force which allows the body to reproduce itself and pass that life force down through our DNA, from one generation to the next.

Since this reproductive process appears to extend beyond man into every realm of living matter in can only be assumed that it is universal and is not limited to the whims of man made gods.

Who are the angels which are to go to these churches, and why is there a different promise made to each of them?

Many religions claim, that the seven churches represent the seven vices, or deadly sins of man. Vices and sins which man must overcome in order to receive his reward in heaven.

The Christians believed that Jesus is the one and only human to have been pure and upright enough to have overcome the trials and temptations of man. If this is so, then it can be argued, that it is not the overcoming of death, but the overcoming of the above seven vices which gets one into heaven.

I tend to disagree. According to scripture, Job was a perfect and an upright man, did he ever get to heaven, or will he ever sit with Jesus upon the throne? He was persecuted and suffered many tragic events in his life just because he was considered a perfect and upright man.

The Protestants believe that one cannot enter into the kingdom of heaven unless they have professed before men that they believed that Jesus Christ is their Lord and Saviour. The Lutherans believed that it is by faith alone that one is granted entrance into paradise, but according to Revelation Jesus is supposed to have said the following:

Rev. 22:12 says, *And behold, I come quickly; and my reward is with me, to give every man according as his work shall be.*

It there is a heaven and a paradise and a man's reward is to be, according to the words of Jesus, his work then the Christians are wrong. Paradise is not obtained by faith or by professing the name of Jesus.

The new kingdom of God will be like the castles of old. It will be an abode where the immediate servants, followers and accepted members of God community will reside. Those within the castle or city and be privy to the blessings and curses of God, their Lord and Master. Outside the temple and the city will reside all of those who are of no consequences, they are the serfs.

In many ways they will be more blessed than those of the castle because they are out of sight and therefore out of the mind of God.

Rev. 22:14-15. *Blessed are they that do his commandments, that they may have right to the tree of life, and may enter in through the gates into the city. For without are dogs, and sorcerers, and whoremongers, and murders, and idolaters, and whosoever loveth and maketh a lie.*

This clearly indicates that there is no such thing as a biblical hell unless that hell is in the presence of Jesus, his angels and the souls that will burn forever in everlasting fire. If there is going to be a hell it will be little different than the sordid squalor reminiscent of our ghettos of today.

If one is unable to overcome the seven deadly vices which are:
1. Labour and patience (church of Ephesus)
2. Tribulation and poverty (church of Smyrna)
3. Fornication and idol worship (church of Perganios)
4. Charity service and faith (church of Thyatira)
5. Lack of faith (church of Sardis)
6. Temptation (church of Philadelphia)
7. Apathy (church of Laodiceans)

The will receive the following reward:
1. The tree of life (church of Ephesus)
2. Will not be hurt by the second death (church of Smyrna)
3. Hidden manna and a new name (church of Perganios)
4. Power over nations (church of Thyatira)
5. White raiment's and his name (church of Sardis)
6. Made a pillar in the temple (church of Philadelphia)
7. Will sit on a throne (church of Laodiceans)

What will happen to the twenty four elders that are to be around the throne of God? How many thrones will there be in the heavenly paradise of god?

If everyone who has stored up treasures in heaven has a throne who then will be the subjects which will bow down, worship and serve before those thrones?

The twenty four elders are to be our rulers.

Rev. 5:9-10. *And they sung a new song, saying, Thou art worthy to take the book, and to open the seals thereof: for thou wast slain, and hast redeemed us to God by thy blood out of every kindred, and tongue, and people, and nation; And hast made us unto God kings and priests: and we shall reign on the earth.*

The elders which shall reign on earth will be the entourage of God, his cabinet and his advisors. Also around God will be his protectors, the Seraphim. These Creatures are of a particular species, cloned minions created with special abilities in order to serve and protect the ruling classes, in this case God. If they are not living beings than they are mechanical robots, built by an alien race and are forever.

Rev. 4:6-8. *And before the throne there was a sea of glass like unto crystal: And in the midst of the throne and round about the throne, were four beasts full, of eyes before and behind. And the first beast was like a lion, and the second beast like a calf, and the third beast had a face of a man, and the fourth beast was like a flying eagle. And the four beasts had each of them six wings about him; and they were full of eyes within: and they rest not day and night, saying, Holy, Holy, Holy Lord God Almighty, which was, and is, and is to come.*

What is to come is the new world order, an order which is strongly reminiscent of the type Hitler tried to establish in 1933. It will be similar to the Mafia, Italian, Russian, and Chinese Triads. There will be those in authority dictating to the people what they can and cannot do. There will be the wealthy class of heavenly hosts served by those who have nothing. Their wealth, according to scripture, will be determined by their earthly behaviour. This wealth will, by necessity, create a class society, a society which will demand a separation between the classes of those that have and those who do not. The poor will once again be subjected to the will of those who rule.

This accumulation of wealth to be stored in heaven is one of the strangest of all of the ideas proposed by the Christian Church.

Heaven is portrayed as a place without need or want? It is suppose to be a place where no sorrow exists? It is suppose to be a place of everlasting joy, a place where every wish will be granted and every desire fulfilled? If this is so why then is it so necessary for a believer to lay up treasures there if that treasure has no meaning?

If one is able to amass a fortune, what are they to do with it when they finally reach paradise? What will these treasures bring to someone who has everything?

Wealth is an earthly concept. Wealth only has value if it is desired by someone else, serves some useful purpose, affords one the opportunity to obtain something they do not have, or to obtain power and prestige over ones constituents.

What wealth, honour and prestige a man is not able to obtain on earth he hopes and expects to be able to achieve in heaven.

Rev. 5:13. *And every creature which is in heaven, and on earth, and under the earth, and such as are in the sea, and all that are in them, heard I saying, blessing, and honour and glory, and power, be unto him that sitteth upon the throne, and unto the, lamb forever and ever.*

Will all of the creatures who have ever lived, either in heaven or on earth, alive, dead, buried or in the sea, Will they be in heaven? If so it contradicts the beliefs of some religious communities, which believe, that heaven will be a paradise filled with the saved and righteous people serving with the angels before God. If all of the creatures ever created are to be among those in heaven, by who are they to be ruled?

What type of creatures are the scriptures talking about when it speaks of heaven? It cannot be the angels because they already serve and obey God. Are there other creatures besides the minions of God himself? We already know of the Living Creature, the Cherubim and the Seraphim. How many others forms of life are there spread across the galaxies which serve and obey the will and command the Universal Creator but not but the Gods of Man who is considered the ultimate authority within the culture of living creature?

Who is the ultimate ruler of heaven, the Universal Creator, the Lord God the creator of Man or his minion, the Jewish God Jehovah?

In order to answer this question we must open the book with the seven seals and ask ourselves a number of questions. One, when was this book with the names of the saved in God sealed? If it was sealed in the beginning of creation, then we are either in it or not as it was determined from that beginning moment. In other words, we are preordained to whatever destiny has already been declared and written there. On the other hand there may not be a book at all.

The "Book of Life" to which the preachers refer, is not of life but of death. It is the instructions and the authority for the destruction of man and the earth. And it is Jesus, the Lamb, the Lion of the tribe of Juda, the Root of David, who will open the book and break the seven seals. It is the Lamb, worshipped as the saviour of the world who will be its destroyer.

The scriptures say that no man was found worthy enough to break the seals and to open the book. No man, no matter how inhumane, could ever bring it upon himself to destroy man as it is described in the Book of Revelation. Only an alien being, without love or compassion, could be so violent in his quest for power.

Rev. 5:5-6. *And one of the elders saith unto me, weep not: behold, the lion of the tribe of Juda, the root of David, hath prevailed to open the book, and to loose the seven seals thereon. And I beheld, and lo, in the midst of the throne, and of the four beasts, and in the midst of the elders, stood a lamb as it had been slain, having seven horns and seven eyes, which are the seven spirits of God sent forth into the earth.*

Rev. 6:1-17. *And I saw when the Lamb opened one of the seals, and I heard as it were the noise of thunder, one of the four beasts, saying, Come and see. And I saw, and behold, a white horse: and he that sat on him had a bow; and a crown was given unto him: and he went forth conquering, and to conquer.*

And when he opened the second seal, I heard the second beast say, Come and see. And there went out another horse that was red: and power was given to him that sat thereon to take peace from the earth, and that they should kill one another: and there was given to him a great sword.

And when he had opened the third seal, I heard the third beast say, Come and see. And I beheld and lo, a black horse; and he that sat on him had a pair of balances in his hand. And I heard a voice in the midst of the four beasts, A measure of wheat for a penny, and three measures of barley for a penny; and see thou hurt not the oil and the wine.

And when he had opened the fourth seal, I heard the voice of the fourth beast say, Come and see. And I looked, and behold, a pale horse and his name that sat on him was death, and hell followed him. And power was given unto them over the fourth part of the earth, to kill with sword, and with hunger, and with death, and with the beasts of the earth.

And when he had opened the fifth seal, I saw under the alter the souls of them that were slain for the word of God, and for the testimony which they held: And they cried with a loud voice, saying, How long, O Lord, holy and true, dost thou not judge and avenge our blood on them that dwell on the earth. And white robes were given unto every one of them; and it was said unto them, that they should rest yet for a little season, until heir fellow-servants also and their brethren that should be killed as they were, should be fulfilled.

And I beheld when he opened the sixth seal, and lo, there was a great earthquake; and the sun became black as sackcloth of hair, and the moon became as blood: And the stars of heaven fell unto the earth, even as a fig-tree casteth her untimely figs, when she is shaken of a mighty wind. And the heaven departed as a scroll when it is rolled together; and every mountain and island were moved out of their places. And the kings of the earth, and the great men, and the rich men, and the chief captains, and the mighty men, and every bond-man, and every free-man, hid themselves in the dens and in the rocks of the mountains. And said to the mountains and the rocks, Fall on us, and hide us from the face of him that sitteth on the throne, and from the wrath of the Lamb. For the great day of his wrath is come; and who shall be able to stand.

What is hidden in the seventh seal that was not opened. Was it the instructions that sealed and protected the hundred and forty four thousand of the tribes of Israel before the destruction of earth began?

I could be mistaken but I have always thought that a lamb was a young sheep, one which had no horns. Goats have horns, and Satan is many times pictured as having horns and many eyes.

While the indication of these passage is to present Christ in his new form, it does an excellent job of indicating that he looks an awful lot like the images of Satan which are found throughout literature, pictures, myths, legends and descriptions.

From the destruction, horror and bloodshed which will be created when the seals are broken I would tend to believe that it is God and Jesus which are the Satanic forces of the world and not Satan, himself.

It is God and his minions, who then are the Satanic, or evil forces of the earth who have blinded man into believing just the opposite of what is true?

John, in writing Revelation, says that he is in the spirit. It is highly possible that what he is seeing is his vision of hell.

John, when he was supposed to have received this vision was a prisoner on the Isle of Patmos. Wheat, rye and barley grain was a common staple food during those days. It is possible that at some time or other before his vision John ate some contaminated grain and unknowing suffered from a mild dose of "lysergic acid diethylamide", LSD for short.

LSD is obtained from ergot, a fungus which has been found to grow on rye and wheat. This may also have been one of the contributing factors for many of the heavenly visions received by the devout religion prophets of the Old Testament.

The World Book Encyclopaedia 1, vol. 12, states, "LSD is an extremely powerful drug which causes distortions in thinking and feeling. These distortions include hallucinations, during which a person sees, hears, smells, or feels things which do not really exist. A dose of only 100 to 200 millionth of a gram of LSD can produce a mental and emotional experience called a trip which lasts from 8 to 12 hours. Most scientists believe that people who use LSD do not become physically dependent on the drug.

Two Swiss chemists, Arthur Stroll and Albert Hofmann, first made LSD in 1938. In 1943 Hofmann accidentally swallowed a small amount of LSD and discovered the drugs hallucinatory effects.

The effects of LSD can seem either pleasant or frightening. The drug may give users the feeling that they are gaining insights into their personality and past experiences.

LSD also makes individuals anxious, confused, or terrified. The user may panic and require medication to overcome the effects of LSD.

Some scientists believe the drug can cause birth defects in the babies of women who take LSD during pregnancy.

A person who takes LSD may see shifting patterns of light and hear colours. The sensory reactions become exaggerated and moods may alter rapidly from intense happiness to deep depression.

A user of LSD may experience a flashback when not under the influence of the drug. During a flashback, a person relives a frightening trip which occurred weeks or months before. The person may also become anxious or depressed and fear losing his or her mind.

It is not only possible that John was experiencing an hallucination, but it is also possible that many if not all of the prophets of God received their visions or messages from God under the same or similar circumstances.

Today we have been made aware of religious cult leaders and their followers who claim to have experienced similar effects during their religious ceremonies by the use of special mushrooms or special herbs.

The prophets would not have recorded any of their bad trips but only their good ones. Any bad or terrifying trips experienced by the prophets would naturally be considered by them as God's punishment for some sin or transgression which they had committed. Their bad experiences, dreams or hallucinations, was Gods way of rendering punishment.

John had a vision, and in that vision he saw a horned god who was about to administer his brand of justice. From scripture how can one tell the differences between the god John saw in his dreams and the god worshipped by the people?

Perhaps we can determined if the God of the Bible is God or Satan by reviewing the orders which he shall give to his angels in the last days. We should be able to decide which is which by the results of their action.

The Book of Revelation are the sealed orders, given to John by God himself in his vision. They are the seven sealed documents. Why are they sealed if everyone knows that they exist and what is to happen when the seals are broken?

Is it to create a feeling of love, respect and admiration for God the Father and his son Jesus or is it to create fear and intimidation?

Rev 6:2. From the first seal, a conqueror is to go forth, conquer and enslave the world.

Rev. 6:3 From the second seal, a messenger, or prophet is to go forth, remove peace from the world, turn brother again brother, and initiate the wholesale killing of one man against another.

Rev. 6:5. From the third seal, it is an order, a command, to buy up all of the available food, except for wine and oil. In addition to the enslavement, killing of brother against brother, God now adds hunger and starvation to his list of attributes.

Rev. 6:7. From the fourth seal is to come death for over a quarter of the planet. The people are to die of starvation, thirst, starving beasts, and murder.

Rev. 6:8. From the fifth seal, a cry for vengeance from the souls of heaven against the those still alive. A retribution against those alive for the torment suffered by those who had chosen to follow and worship the God Jehovah.

Rev. 6:12. From the sixth seal, destruction from earthquakes, tremors and cyclonic winds. The air will be filled with the dust of the earth, volcanic ash and poisonous gasses.

Before the final destruction begins, the people of God who will survive the holocaust are to be marked on their forehead with the mark of God or is it the mark of the beast?

Rev. 7:3-4. *Saying, Hurt not the earth, neither the sea, nor the trees, till we have sealed the servants of God in their forehead. And I heard the number of them which were sealed: and there sealed an hundred and forty and four thousand of all the tribes of the children of Israel.*

These are the only ones who will be saved, those who have been branded not by circumcision, but by the mark, a branded number across the forehead, a hundred and forty four thousand Israelites.

Rev. 8:1, from the seventh seal, silence in heaven before the beginning of the destruction of the earth by God.

The seven angels shall sound their trumpets and this will follow:

Rev. 8:7-10. *The first angel sounded and there followed hail and fire mingled with blood, and they were cast upon the earth: and the third part of trees was burnt up, and all green grass was burnt up.*

And the second angel sounded, and as it were a great mountain burning with fire was cast into the sea: and the third part of the sea became blood;

And the third part of the creatures which were in the sea, and had life, died; and the third part of the ships were destroyed.

And the third angel sounded, and there fell a great star from heaven, burning as it were a lamp, and it fell upon the third part of the rivers, and upon the fountain of waters.

This sounds like the earth will be hit by asteroids of gigantic sizes which will destroy various parts of the earth. From this destruction the Lord God will have returned to establish his kingdom on earth. It will be a ruined and devastated kingdom peopled tired, thirsty, starving and maniacal people.

Rev. 8:12. *And the fourth angel sounded, and the third part of the sun was smitten, and the third part of the moon, and the third part of the stars; so as the third part of them was darkened, and the day shone not for a third part of it, and the night likewise.*

The vision of John indicates that a gigantic solar mass will enter this solar system. When it does it will bring with it satellites the size of mountains. These satellites will crash into the earth creating massive death and destruction. The main body itself will be so large that it will cause an eclipse of both the sun and the moon for the third of a day.

Rev. 9:1. *And the fifth angel sounded, and I saw a star fall from heaven unto the earth: and to him was given the key of the bottomless pit.*

The star struck the earth with such impact that it created a great crater. From the crater came smoke as from a great furnace. From the smoke came locusts upon the earth. Unto them was given the power, as the scorpions of the earth.

Will that star be a spaceship loaded with warriors of an alien race sent not to assist Jehovah in his takeover bid for the earth but announce the return of the Lord God, the biblical Satan to claim his right to his descendents and his property?

Rev. 9:4. *And it was commanded them that they should not hurt the grass of the earth, neither any green thing, neither any tree; but only those men which have not the seal of God in their foreheads.*

Their purpose was to torment the men who had received the mark of god or the beast in their foreheads. These tormentors, whatever they are, will be controlled by a king. A king, which scriptures say was a fallen star.

If it looks like the devil, sounds like the devil, and acts like the devil then there is a very good chance that it is the devil.

The scriptures say that there are angels of God which were held in bondage. In the final days of judgement they will be set free to kill as dictated by God. After the angels of bondage have finished killing, maiming, burning, destroying and tormenting all of those who do not have the seal of God on their forehead, then there will be send out into the world four messengers. They are represented by the symbols of two-olives trees and the two candlesticks. Rev.11:3-8.

Jesus was crucified in Jerusalem. Is the New Jerusalem to become the corrupt Sodom and Egypt of tomorrow? Is it possible that the scriptures are not talking about Jesus but another being called Lord?

These witnesses which are to come, what will they testify to? The power, love, mercy and salvation of the beloved god of the Jews and Christians, or to the destruction, the blood craze, desolation, waste, droughts and contamination taking place throughout the world during all of this testimony?

Will they be testifying to the contamination plagues, infection and diseases' which will spread through man like a wildfire causing more death, a repeat of the plagues of Egypt?

Without water fit to drink, or water for crops to grow, all life will be in peril of extinction.

The beast from the bottomless pit, taught and believed by Christians to be Satan, will be in truth the Lord God, the creator of Man. He is the landowner, who will one day return to earth and call Jehovah, Satan, and his other stewards to account to him for their stewardship of his property, the earth and man. It is at this time that Jehovah will rebel and the war of Armageddon will begin. It will be between Gog, the Lord God and Magog, the Jewish God Jehovah. It will be this war which will come close to destroying the earth and all of mankind.

The forces of the Lord God, small in number will be unable to defeat the forces of Jehovah because of the vast number of disciples he has gathered together in the various religions which call upon his name.

The Lord God will be defeated and will be imprisoned for a thousand years uring which time Jehovah will rule the earth.

Jehovah is not the all powerful that his minions believe him to be. He allows and even predicts that the beast will for once be able to defeat him? If he can be defeated once, why not many times?

Jesus was crucified in Jerusalem which is the city of God. The new city of God and heaven wll be called the New Jerusalem and yet Jesus, speaking to John in his vision calls the city Sodom and Egypt. Why? Was it because of the perverse sexuality of Sodom and Egypt or because of the slavery and bondage that is to come? Is this to be mans' great reward for his faithful service to Jehovah?

Man will be used and abused as befits the needs, the desires, and the whims of the tyrant, that man, in his ignorance, has make into a God.

God, the Holy Father, the protector of man, the one who allowed his servants and his son to die and who will be responsible for the destruction of the earth, seeks disciples to follow, adore and worship him. He would have us believe that like his messengers, who died in the streets, that we to, after three and a half days will be restore to life, arise and be transported to heaven, the abode of Jehovah. It appears that his abode is nothing more than a space ship in orbit around the earth.

This ship with its medical facilities will evidently be capable of repairing the physical damage done to the messengers of God even after the three days they will lay dead in the streets.

This three day time schedule coincides with the three days which Jesus was supposed to have been in the grave. This same three day time period of death and resurrection is one indicated in many myths, legends and religious rituals and suffered by some of the more renown religious saviours of the world. Rev. 11:15.

The kingdoms of this world will be under the domination of the coming Lord. He will establish his kingdom here on earth. Here is where heaven and the heavenly salvation, preached by the religious ministers on Sunday mornings will be found.

This is the prophesy promised by the Jewish messiah. I is to bring joy, peace and happiness into the world during his predicted thousand years of peace, or is it?

The twelfth chapter of Revelation speaks of the wonders of heaven. The coming of the "Great Red Dragon." A beast with seven heads with seven crowns and ten horns. It will be the return of the Lord Commander, the creator of man, to demand an accounting by Jehovah of his stewardship of the planet. The Great Dragon will not like what he finds. Jehovah will not give up his kingdom. His forces will be far superior in numbers to those of the dragon.

Should the Lord God request reinforcements from his home world, it would take another thousand years for them to arrive. By that time it will be too late. Jehovah will have brought war against the Lord God and committed him to the pit for a thousand years.

Rev. 12:7-9. *And there was war in heaven: Michael and his angels fought against the dragon; and the dragon fought and his angels, And prevailed not; neither was their place found any more in heaven. And the great dragon was cast out, that old serpent, called the Devil and Satan, which deceiveth the whole world: he was cast out into the earth, and his angels were cast out with him.*

The real beast and dragon referred to in the above scripture is not the Lord God but Jehovah. During all of his reign on earth he has convinced man or rather man has convinced himself, that Jehovah is the true Lord God and that the Lord God was in reality the beast.

This has largely been due to man's misinterpretation of the scriptures and his understanding of his beginning.

It was the Great Red Dragon (God) and not Jehovah (the beast) which first came to earth and created man. It was the Red Dragon, the first commander, which cast man from the garden for disobedience. It was this same dragon which tried to save mankind from extinction at the time of the flood, when it became evident that the world was on a collision course with a giant asteroid which could obliterate all life on earth.

It did not happen because the intentions of the dragon was good. It was also this dragon which gave clothes to Adam and Eve and protected Cain from the anger of others when he accidentally killed his brother Abel.

Jehovah is another story.

From the time of his initial contact Abraham, Isaac and Jacob, as their god, he has demanded, persecuted and destroyed, in one way or another, almost all that came in contact with him. Biblical scriptures are a saga of his lust for power, slaves, land and riches. Through and because of his influence as a holy deity, there have been wars and rumours of wars throughout the whole history of his contact with man through the Jewish nation and their religious beliefs.

The words, laws and commandments of Jehovah were given to the Israelites, the Jewish nation, his chosen people, for order, and for his total control. He used those laws, which were a part of his culture and his traditions, to gain and control a group of men, the descendants of Jacob.

They, by virtue of their deprived condition, believed in and followed a being which they believed to be a god. From that belief and their continued condition of voluntary slavery they created for themselves the belief in a coming Messiah who would return them, not to paradise, but like Moses and Joshua, to freedom, and prosperity.

A believed saviour did come to the Jewish people. He was a man called Jesus, the Christ. He established a following among his people. Many believed in his teaching, but they misunderstood his motives. Because of this misunderstanding, it has been the gentiles, and not the Jews who have become the inheritors of the Jewish Messiah called Jesus.

Jesus, believed to be the son of God, has become a deity himself. Under his guidance or teachings, and those of Jehovah, man has known nothing but war, bloodshed, death and destruction throughout recent history. From the time of the Exodus, war, pestilence, poverty and death have been the legacy of both Jehovah and Jesus.

Jehovah is truth the biblical beast. He used his knowledge, technology and his position of power and authority to become the residence governor of earth in order to establish himself as a God.

Due to the limited number of people who had survived the flood it was not a heavy burden or one which would lead to any great reward. As time passed and man increased in number, the need to worship a god remained a dominate part of the consciousness of man. As such, when man had no gods to worship, pray to or serve he created them.

As other gods began to appear in man's worship to the divine powers which he did not understand, Jehovah began to renew his interest as the governing authority of man. As the interest, gifts, offerings, sacrifices, and number of worshippers increased for the minor gods under his control Jehovah became jealous, from envy and the reticule he received from them.

In time he decided that it was time for him to begin reaping some reward for his position on earth. He did not select the descendents of Adam and Eve to be his disciples, but the descendants of his grandson Jacob who were already trained as slaves and servants. They were his slaves and servants by his right of inheritance.

To enforce his authority he needed a priesthood to serve him in his task of governing his people that would become a new nation, He selected the tribe of Levi, the descendants of the cruellest son of Jacob for that purpose.

To them he gave the right to kill, rob and cheat and destroy all who opposed his right to become the god he desired to be. They were to do this by enforcing his laws and his commandments, laws and commandments which became the foundation of a new religion and form of government.

His followers then, today, and those of tomorrow will be like the bonded angels of Revelation. Once they have accomplished the bidding of God, they will become disposal commodities. They will be bonded, shackled and cast into prison until such a time as their Lord God Jehovah sees fit to let them be free for a little while.

If he keeps his angels in bondage, those who have lived and worked with him since his beginning, can man, who seems to be nothing but trouble and conflict, expect anything less?

Rev. 13:1-9. *And I stood upon the sand of the sea, and saw a beast rise up out of the sea, having seven heads and ten horns, and upon his horns ten crowns, and upon his head the name of blasphemy. And the beast which I saw was like unto a leopard, and his feet were as the feet of a bear, and his And I saw one of his heads as it were wounded to death; and his deadly wound was healed: and all the world wondered after the beast. And they worshipped the dragon which gave power unto the beast: and they worshipped the beast, saying, Who is like unto the beast? Who is able to and it was given unto him to make war with the saints, and to overcome them: and power was given him over all kingdoms, and tongues, and nations. And all that dwell upon the earth shall worship him, whose names are not written in the book of life of the Lamb slain from the foundations of the world.. If any man have an ear, let him hear.*

The beast will be given the power to overcome the saints and the tabernacle of God. He will have power over all of the kingdoms, nations and people of the world. And all of the people will worshipped him, those whose names are not written in the "Book of Life"

Who is great enough to give enough power to the beast to overcome the saints and the tabernacle of God? It cannot be Jehovah. He certainly would not give power to his enemies to defeat his own troops.

Who are the people of earth, who after living though the thousand years of peace under the rule of Jehovah, will be willing to leave is service to follow and serve the beast, who is in reality the Dragon, the Lord God who will eased from the bottomless pit at the end of that thousand years.

They will be the people who will have live through the thousand years of Jehovah brand righteousness. They will have been able to see his brand of justice in all that he will do. They will have lived through the killing, the destruction and the torment of man. There will be no wars because for a thousand years because the power and control of Jehovah will be so great that no one will dare challenge his authority.

Mankind will be slaves without any hope of every again enjoying any kind of freedom.

What mankind will not be able to see or understand is how all of the destruction of the earth by the hand of their God Jehovah, will be, according to him, for the future good of mankind?

John speaks of the lamb slain from the foundations of the world. Who is he talking about?

Is John talking about Jesus? If so, then how can he have been slain from the foundations of the world before man was created, sins committed and a need for redemption realized? If this is so, then the death of Jesus was a part of the plan of God from the beginning. If the lamb was slain in the beginning, or at least preordained, then the whole Christian belief in his death is a sham and a mockery. If the lamb was preordained as a part of Gods plan to redeem men, then he intended for man to commit all of his transgressions just so he, God, could use those transgressions as an excuse to come in and punish man.

If this was not his plan then he was and is not a God of all things. He becomes just what he was or is, an alien being abandon here on earth and is trying to make the best of his predicament by playing on the fears and superstitions of primitive men.

As sophisticated as modern man likes to believe himself to be, he is still lives day by day, filled with fear, superstition and bewilderment. He fears the unknown, a fear rooted deep within a sub-conscious which has no boundaries.

Rev. 13:11-14. *And I beheld another beast coming up out of the earth; and he had two horns like a lamb, and he spoke as a dragon. And he exercised all the power of the first beast before him, and causeth the earth and them that dwell therein to worship the first beast, whose deadly wound was healed. And he doeth great wonders, so that he maketh fire come down from heaven in the sight of men. And decieveth them that dwell on the earth, by the means of those miracles which he had power to do in the sight of the beast; saying to them that dwell on the earth, that they should make an image to the beast, which had the wound by a sword and did live.*

1 Kings 18:37-40. *Hear me, O Lord, hear me, that this people may know that thou art the Lord God, and that thou hast turned their*

heart back again. Then the fire of the Lord fell, and consumed the burnth sacrifice, and the wood, and the stones and the dust, and licked up the water that was in the trench. And when the people saw it, they fell on their faces: and they said, the Lord, he is the God; the Lord, he is the God. And Elijah said unto them, take the prophets of Baal; let not one of them escape. And they took them: and Elijah brought them down to the brook Kishon, and he slew them there.

One of the laws of the God Jehovah was that "thou shall not kill" but he failed to mention the times when man could kill and who that might be. It was a law intended to prevent one Hebrew from killing another. This may have been the intent until he abolished the law in flavour of the wholesale slaughter of all who opposed him in any way. Thus he changed the law to mean that the death and killing of any Jew or Gentile in and by his name was justified. To kill anyone who is outside of the Jewish family is considered by the prophets and by God as a fulfilment of his command, a fulfilment which was justified by a blessing and a reward.

Elijah, under and by the authority of Jehovah called for the destruction of the Alters of Baal. When they had been destroyed he was then to proceed to kill all of the servants of Baal. The destruction of the alters and priests of Baal is an occasion for the people who witness this event, to fall down and worship Jehovah. In Revelation one of the beast is said to have called down fire from heaven in the sight of men, which caused them to worship the beast. Those that did not worship the image of the beast were killed.

Was Elijah the beast of revelation? Was he the one who called down fire from heaven? Was he, the servant of Jehovah, the slayer of those which did not worship the image?

Rev. 13:16-18. *And he caused all, both small and great, rich and poor, free and bond, to receive a mark in their right hand, or in their foreheads; And that no man might buy or sell, save he that had the mark, or the name of the beast, or the number of his name. Here is wisdom. Let him that hath understanding count the number of the beast: for it is the number of a man; and his number is Six hundred threescore and six.*

Rev. 14:1-3. *And I looked, and lo, a lamb stood on the Mount Zion, and with him an hundred forty and four thousand, having his father's name written in their forehead. And I heard a voice from heaven, as the voice of many waters, and as the voice of a great thunder I heard the voice of harpers harping with their harps: And they sung as it were a new song before the throne, and before the four beasts, and the elders: and no man could learn that song but the hundred and forty and four thousand, which were redeemed from the earth.*

The beast and "the God", of Elijah appear to be one and the same. And who are the hundred and forty and four thousand who are standing before the four beasts and learning a new song? Who can identify which beast is the true god and which is the dragon? They have both, according to scripture, been guilty of the same acts of destruction.

The scripture say that both beasts are going to identify their slaves by marking their hands and or their foreheads. The fight between the two beasts will be for the domination of the world. The beast that is able to obtain the most disciples to fight and die for him will be declared the winner.

Rev. 14:9-11. *And the third angel followed them, saying with a loud, if any man worship the beast and his image, and receive his mark in his forehead, or in his hand, The same shall drink of the wine of the wrath of God, which is poured out without mixture into the cup of his indignation; and he shall be tormented with fire and brimstone in the presence of the holy angels, and in the presence of the lamb. And the smoke of their torment ascendeth up forever and ever: and they have no rest day or night who worship the beast and his image, and whosoever receiveth the mark of his name.*

Unless the scriptures are wrong, it will be the disciples of Jehovah, those who have or who will receive his name and his mark upon their forehead and who will be tormented by the fires of hell and brimstone. It is not those who have refused to bow down to the beast.

In today's society it has long been the custom of Christians to baptise a child when it is born. This is done in order to give the child a surname, identification, a blessing from God for a good life in the service of the church.

His is usually done in a church of some kind, it establishes the child as a child of God, and thereby protected by his holy powers. This custom seems to have been handed down from generation to generation in the Judian tradition of symbolically following the command of God that the first child to open the matrix is to be dedicated to him. There is also the fear in a family that should a child die or be killed in some kind of an accident without the forgiveness of God, that child is doomed to suffer the eternal fires of hell and damnation.

The baptism or christening ceremony of Christianity is accomplished by sprinkling or marking the forehead of the child with holy water. The sign of a cross is made on the forehead of the new born made by the priest or clergy in the name of God the Father, the Son and the Holy Ghost. With the mark of the beast on their forehead another servant is added to the membership of the church and army of God Jehovah.

This will be an army led by Jehovah the First Godfather the evil beast of mankind as it is recorded in Revelation. It will be a war of destruction which will demand the death of thousands upon thousands if not millions of men, women, children and animals. And it will be Jehovah the First Godfather, the Jewish and Christian God who will send the seven angels, with the seven last plaques that will be poured out into the world. And it will be Jehovah the First Godfather who will pour out upon mankind in the last days the following:

1. the first - sores
2. the second - to kill all of the souls in the sea
3. the third - to turn the water into blood
4. the fourth - to scorch man with fire
5. the fifth - to create pain
6. the sixth - to dry up the river Euphrates
7. the seventh - to create thunder, lightning, a great earthquake, and the plague of great hail.

Why so much destruction? Can it be that there will still be men who will continue to refuse to repent and worship this being. With all of the pain, sufferings, trials and tribulations, there will be those individuals who will not yield their bodies, minds and souls to this creature.

They will be the revolutionaries who will be after the thousand year reign of Jehovah join with and fight this dictator in the army of the Lord God, the biblical Dagon. The Lord God, the creator of man and his ancient ancestor will be the leader of humanity's last great fight against the tyranny and the right to survive as a culture regardless of whether it will be as free men of slaves.

The death, plagues and the destruction of the earth and mankind mentioned in Revelation will not be like the plagues of Egypt, the results of natural causes created by nature but a nuclear war created by man.

Each camp, that of Jehovah and the Lord God, will need as many bodies as they are able to get. Victory in this war to come, will go to the camp who has the greatest numbers of survivors. This war between the gods will be a rebellion of cosmic conflict for the control of the planet. While man will be in the middle he will be the loser no matter what the outcome of the battle will be.

Rev. 16:14. *For they are the spirits of devils, working miracles, which go forth unto the kings of the earth and of the whole world, to gather them to the battle of that great day of God Almighty.*

Who are the spirits of devils, working miracles? Who are those calling all to repentance and to the acceptance of Jesus as their Lord and Saviour? Who are the prophets who will work the miracles of God in the name of God?

It will not be the disciples of the dragon for they do not call upon miracles, but it will be the disciples of God and Jesus. And what is to be the great day of the Lord God Almighty?

It does not seem to be the day of the second coming, the day of resurrection or of judgement, but the battle between the resident governor Jehovah and the Lord God.

Hosea 2:16. *And it shall be at that day, saith the Lord, that thou s halt call me Ishi; and shall call me no more Baali.*

All through the old testament, it says that the Israelites kept going back to the worship of Baal. The priests of Baal are slaughtered by Elijah, a priest and prophet of Jehovah. Now according to Hosea

Jehovah now declares that he is the one who will no longer be called Baal.

According to "the compact bible dictionary, special crusade edition", the meaning of the word Baal is, "Lord, possessor, husband." Baali means, "my Lord, my master."

If Jehovah is to no longer be call Lord and Master, and is to now be call Ishi, what does Ishi mean? It means, "my man,"" my husband." Is he no longer to be called God?

Rev. 17:12-17. *And the ten horns which thou sawest are ten kings, which have received no kingdom as yet; but receive power as kings one hour with the beast. These have one mind, and shall give their power and strength to the beast. These shall make war with the Lamb, and the Lamb shall overcome them: for he is Lord of Lords, and King of Kings: and they that are with him are called, and chosen, and faithful. And he said unto me, the waters which thou sawest, where the whore sitteth, are people, and multitudes, and nations, and tongues And the ten horns which thou sawest upon the beast, these shall hate the whore, and shall make her desolate and naked, and shall eat her flesh, and burn her with fire. For God hath put in their hearts to fulfil his will, and to agree, and give their kingdom unto the beast until the words of God shall be fulfilled.*

After reading the above verse 17 I ask myself the following question. Why would God deliberately filled the hearts and minds of his servants and allow them to give their kingdom to the beast until the words of God shall be fulfilled unless God is the beast. And what are the words and what is to be fulfilled?

If the ten horns are the ten kings which are the servants of the beast and they are to make war against the Lamb why do they hate the whore, which is also an enemy of the Lamb? The whore then must be a servant or a representative of Jehovah the Holy God, the evil from which, man has been taught to avoid.

The Lamb, which is the Lord of Lords, according to Revelation 5:6, only has seven horns. He is the one that will make war against the ten kings. He will overcome them and then turn right around and input into their hearts the desire to fulfil his will, and to agree, and to give their kingdom unto the beast, until the words of God shall be fulfilled.

Exactly who is the biblical beast?

Rev. 17:8. *The beast (the dragon) that thou sawest, was, and is not; and shall ascend out of the bottomless pit, and go into perdition: and they that dwell on the earth shall wonder,(whose names were not written in the book of life from the foundation of the world, when they behold the beast that was, and is not and yet is.*

Didn't God tell John in Rev. 1:18, *I am he that liveth, and was dead; and, behold, I am alive forevermore, Amen; and have the keys of hell and of death.*

Behold the Lamb, was alive, was dead, and was raised to life.

Behold the God, " Alpha and Omega, the beginning and the ending, who lived, was dead and now is alive.

Behold the beast which was, and is not; and shall ascend out of the bottomless pit. He was alive, died and shall be raised to life.

Who is telling the truth? Who is the God, and who is the Dagon that John sees in his vision?

Rev. 5:12. *Saying with a loud voice, worthy is the Lamb that was slain to receive power, and riches, and wisdom, and strength, and honour, and glory, and blessings.*

Who is going to present all of these gifts to the Lamb if he is already the God, a part of the Holy Trinity?

Why is he deemed worthy by angels, beasts, elders and thousands of thousands to receive all of these rewards and honour if all is to come to naught?

Rev. 18:14. *And the fruits that thy soul lusted after are departed from thee, and all things which were dainty and goodly are departed from thee, and thou shalt find them no more at all.*

Exodus 25: 1-8. *And the Lord spoke to Moses, saying, Speak to the children of Israel, that they bring me an offering: of every man that giveth it willingly with his heart ye shall take my offering. And this is the offering which ye shall take of them; gold, silver, and brass, And blue, and purple, and scarlet, and fine linen, and goats hair, And rams' skins dyed red, and badgers' skin, and shittem wood, Oil for the light, spices for anointing oil, and for sweet incense, Onyx stones, and stones to be set in the ephod, and in the breastplate. And let them make me a sanctuary; that I may dwell among them.*

What does an immortal, spiritual and all-powerful God who has everything along with the power to command into existence all that he desires need of such things from man?

Unless the Lord God Jehovah is not the all powerful being that religious disciples have been led to believe him to be but a con artist then he does have a need for these things in his dealings with the other nations on the earth.

The followers of God and Jesus have been so blinded by the fear of purgatory and the greed of untold riches in heaven that they cannot see the trees for the forest.

For those that are alive after the great battle, they will find that there is nothing left to fight about. Food and water will be more precious that all of the gold, the silver and the treasures of today.

If everyone in paradise is to be rewarded beyond measure, then everyone will be equal and no one will ever need anything. If on the other hand one is rewarded greater than another then we have a heavenly paradise duplicating the conditions that exist on earth today. Nothing will have changed. It will be the rich over the poor and one race subservient to another.

Heaven will be the new paradise, the promised land, filled with jealousy, hate, distrust and envy. The New Jerusalem will be a remake of the dark ages. It will be the world of today.

In the New Jerusalem there will be murder, theft and all of the other sins and vices committed by man on earth today and for the very same reasons? It will have nothing to do with good and evil but power nd control.

Jehovah, the destroyer of mankind, will issue a decree of moral indignation against man. This is a being who lusted after the daughters of men. This is a being that drank the wine of man, ate their food, and sold them into slavery. This is a being which has committed every sin known to man, and yet he has the audacity to accused and punishes man for obeying his commands and for following his examples.

Rev. 20:1-3. *And I saw an angel come down from heaven, having the key of the bottomless pit and a great chain in his hand. And he laid hold on the dragon, the old serpent, which is the devil, and Satan, and bound him a thousand years. And cast him into the bottomless pit, and shut him in and set a seal upon him, that he should deceive the nations no more, till the thousand years should be fulfilled: and after that he must be loosed a little season.*

For some reason Jehovah cannot kill or rather did not choose not kill the Highest God, his superior, who he has called Satan and devil. This cannot be the same Satan which gathered with the sons of god as recorded in Job. So the word Satan may also be a title with power that was respected by a cultured tradition stilled honoured by the other minor gods.

In any case why must he be released after a thousand years? Why imprison the Lord God and his crew at all unless of course Jehovah is not quite sure of his position and his authority among the minor gods. This ploy may have just been a political maneuver to be used later if the necessity arises.

While Jehovah may be the Lord Commander of his earthly contingency, his fellow countrymen may not have allowed him the right to kill off a superior of their race. This could have lead to a revolt. This confrontation was best avoided by a term of imprisonment a specified period of time.

Before the earth was to be destroyed, the angels are told that they are not to destroy the earth, neither the sea, nor the trees, till they have sealed the servants of God in their foreheads, These were not the servants of the Lord God, but of Jehovah. The descriptions of the angels of Jehovah sound like and act like the elemental servants of evil rather than of a God of good and righteousness.

Rev. 20:4-7. *And I saw the thrones, and they sat upon them, and Judgement was given unto them: and I saw the souls of them that were beheaded for the witness of Jesus, and for the word of God, and which had not worshipped the beast, neither his image, neither had received his mark upon their foreheads, or in their hands; and they lived and reigned with*

Christ a thousand years. But the rest of the dead lived not again until the thousand years were finished. This is the first resurrection. Blessed and holy is he that hath part in the first resurrection: on such the second death hath no power, but they shall be priests of God and of Christ, and shall reign with him a thousand years. And when the thousand years are expired, Satan shall be loosed out of his prison.

In verse 4, those who had not received the mark of God upon their forehead or on their hand, were to be the priests which will reign with God. Isn't is strange that God is not going to destroy the world until he has placed his mark on all of his servants, yet those who have no mark are to be his closest attendants.

If one were to read Lev. 21:17. Tey will under why. Slaves are marked, servants are not.

Lev. 21:17. *Speak Aaron, saying, Whosoever he be of thy seed in their generations that hath any blemish, let him not approach to offer the bread of his God.*

God cannot tolerate a blemish within his presence. Any mark that is upon the body becomes a blemish. Those who have this visible mark will never be within the presence of God or Christ but will be his slaves and servants.

In the future concentration camps of the Jehovah every man will be branded upon his hand or forehead so that his lord and master will always know him.

Say what you will, to be a priest of God, is to be his slave and to do his bidding. To reign with him for a thousand years is merely another way of saying that you will live for that period of time only not within his presence. So where will the descendents of man, slaves of in servitude to an egotistical manicial god serve and exist?

They will be doing the same thing that Adam and Eve, Cain, Abel and the rest of mankind have been doing from the time of our creation as a sub-species of an advanced culture organic beings. Except that they will be doing it in a changed environment due radiation poisoning, polluted air and water surrounded by sickness, diseases, hunger and thirst.

Jehovah is said to be the God of Glory, the father of peace, the keeper of paradise and the righteous ruler of the thousand years of peace, happiness, and glory to the edification of man.

For those who will be alive and who will live with and serve God and Christ for this thousand years of peace and happiness, a time of no want, no pain, nor suffering, where is Satan is suppose to obtain those souls who are to be as the sands of the sea who will fight, suffer and die for him when he is released?

Perhaps this reign of God, Christ and the priests of paradise will not to be as peaceful and glorious as the reader is led to believe.

Where is the power and the glory of the God Jehovah?

It seems that all of his power and glory comes from, a fear put there by his acts of death and destruction. It is a fear created by Jesus, the priests, and religious leaders who claim that the names of those who do not believe in God and profess Jesus as their personal saviour, will not be in the book of life, they will not be allowed into heaven, and they shall cease to exist.

But what is this book of life everyone claims that Jesus will open in the end time? According to Revelation the book that Jesus will open will not be that of life but of death. When he sits upon his throne surrounded by death, destruction, disease and horror is the time he will be in his glory.

The beast which calls himself God, the Lord of earth, will be called upon to account for his actions and his stewardship of the earth when the Lord God, the rightful landowner returns.

At that Jehovah, the beast, fearful of what he has done and unwilling to relinquish his position as the Lord of earth will rebel against the Lord God his superior. He will capture the Lord God and throw him into prison for a thousand years. At that time the beast will begin his rule of the earth for that thousand years. After that time The Lord God will be release firmly believing that he is not the all powerful Almighty who is powerless to fight and defeat him.

It was predicted that the Almighty will be able to gather an army as of the sands of the sea, of those on the earth who will be fed up with the tyrannical rule of the glorious God of death and destruction. This army will attack and try to defeat the beast, the Lord God Jehovah and his son Jesus.

But the beast, Jehovah, will have a thousand years in which to prepare for this battle. He will gather his army, brainwash and train his subjects.

Jehovah knows that he will have a battle to fight but he does not believed it will be with the Almighty who he has thrown unto the bottomless pit but with the reinforcements of the Almighty from the home world. Reinforcements called for by the Almighty when he first called Jehovah to account for his rule of earth and found himself faced with prison.

These reinforcements will take a thousand years to reach this planet.

The second battle will be fought and won again by Jehovah the First Godfather. He will again cast the Lord God into prison. This time there will be for the Almighty no release. Jehovah will become the absolute ruler of the earth and his evil empire.

He can never return to his planet and his people, so he will establish his rule and his kingdom here on earth. Here he will live with man and be their God.

In order to ensure that there will never again be an uprising against him, he will purge their minds clean. All men will be reprogrammed to obey and to serve. There will be no more death, tears, sorrow, crying or pain. There will also be no more joy, gladness, nor happiness. For one cannot exist without the other.

Man will become a genetically clones race of servants, owned , controlled and disposed of as seen fit by Jehovah, the new Lord God and his servants, the priests.

Rev. 22:10-11. *And he said to me, Seal not the sayings of the prophecy of this book: for the time is at hand. He that is unjust, let him be unjust still: and he which is filthy , let him be filthy still: and he that is righteous, let him be righteous still: and he that is holy, let him be holy still.*

These words of the Bible and the promises of paradise, are for those who would be believers. For those who chose not to believe the following is for them. There is no hell, fire and damnation. That is a false premise if the words of the Bible are to be believed. The following passage explains why.

Rev. 21:8. *But the fearful, and unbelieving, and the abominable, and murderers, and whoremongers, and sorcerers, and idolators, and all liars, shall have their part in the lake which burneth with fire and brimstone: which is the second death.*

This passage is completely contradicted in: Rev. 22:14-15. *Blessed are they that do his commandments, that they may have the right to the tree of life, and may enter in through the gates into the city. For without are dogs, and sorcerers, and whoremongers, and murderers, and idolators, and hosoever loveth and maketh a lie.*

How can sinners be burned in the lake of fire and still reside outside of the city of God. It would seem that according to the above passages, everyone except the chosen few will live outside of the city. It will only be a few who will be able to go inside and be given the fruit of the tree of life in order that their lives be extended.

The others who will be forbidden entrance to the city and out of the sight of God will be the ones truly blessed.

This book is an agnostic's critique of God, the Bible and religion. It is an evaluation of the written words, sayings and actions of the biblical events and of the God Jehovah, as they have been revealed to me.

The religious disciple may not choose to believe the interpretations and explanations given here, but the words of the bible should speak for themselves. I did not change anything. I merely explained the words in a way by which the reader could better understand what has being said.

This review of the Bible is from a new perspective. The reader has only look at his faith, his religion and his God from this new perspective in order to begin to see and understand the realm of Gods and religion.

At death there is no tomorrow, no heavenly kingdom nor salvation. There is death and the emptiness of the tomb.

Ecclesiastes 9:1-13. *For all this I considered in my heart even to declare all this, that the righteous, and the wise, and their works, are in the hands of God: no man knoweth either love or hatred by all that is before them. All things come alike to all: there is one event to the righteous, and to the wicked; to the good and the clean, and to the unclean; to him that sacrificeth, and to him that sacrificeth not: as is the good, so is the sinner; and he that sweareth, as he that feareth an oath. This is an evil among all things that are done under the sun, that there is one event unto all: yea, also the heart of the sons of men is full of evil, and madness is in their heart while they live, and after that they go to the dead. For him that is joined to all the living there is hope: for a living dog is better than a dead lion. For the living know that they shall die: but the dead know not anything, neither have they any more a reward; for the memory of them is forgotten. Also their love, and their hatred, and their envy, is now perished; neither have they any more a portion for ever in any thing that is done under the sun. Go thy way, eat thy bread with joy, and drink thy wine with a merry heart; for God now accepteth thy works. Let thy garments be always white; and let thy head lack no ointment. Live joyfully with thy wife whom thou lovest all the days of the life of thy vanity, which he hath given thee under the sun, all the days of thy vanity: for that is thy portion in this life, and in thy labour which thou takest under the sun. Whatsoever thy hand findeth to do, do it with thy might; for there is no work, nor device, nor knowledge, nor wisdom, in the grave, whither thou goest. I returned, and saw under the sun, that the race is not to the swift, nor the battle to the strong, neither yet bread to the wise, nor yet riches to men of understanding, nor yet favour to men of skill; but time and chance happeneth to them all. For man also knoweth not his time: as the fishes that are taken in an evil net, and as the birds that are caught in the snare; so are the sons of men snared in an evil time, when it falleth suddenly upon them. This wisdom have I seen also under the sun, and it seemed great to me.*

SUMMARY

The Torah, the Koran and the Holy Bible of Christendom are religious texts, written by men in order to extol the glory and magnificence of an entity they call and believe to be GOD.

Their god they believe to be the creator of all things, including mankind itself. That is not a truth that can be substantiated by fact, or by their holy writings.

In reality their writings are nothing more than a collection of short stories, written by dedicated or fanatical individuals, who concerned themselves with specific people, places and events in the name of their god and their religion. These stories are the transcribed results of an oral tradition based upon legends, myths and religious beliefs which were handed down to the writers from one generation to another. They are nothing more than segments of a saga which concerns itself, not with mankind, GOD and the universal creation, but with a relationship between a man, his family, his descendants and their religious beliefs in an entity who they identify as God.

Their stories, those of the history of the Jewish nation, told time and time again, have over time taken on a holy and religious significance. This religious significance began with the Exodus from Egypt, the hardships and wilderness wanderings, and the yoke of oppression place upon the people by the religious and civil laws imposed upon them by their leader Moses and their God Jehovah. This religion and the laws imposed upon the people have evolved into an organized form of a religion, and the worship of a god which exists only in the imagination of man himself.

These biblical books are not the story of mankind nor are they a relationship between mankind and the universal creator. Rather they are a loose collection of individual episodes associated with one family which started, not with Adam and Eve and the beginning of mankind, but with Noah the first flood. From Noah the saga passes to one of his great, great, great grand children, a man named Abram who is known by the religion he formed as Abraham.

The religions of the Jews, Moslems, and Christians, while they are all originated or had their foundation in the faith and beliefs of Abraham, they have each separated into a different faith each with different beliefs, rites and organized religious organizations.

The alien god of Abraham, became Jehovah to the Jewish people, Allah to the Moslems and Baal to many of the other descendants of Abraham.

Jesus, one of the sons of Jehovah, the god of the Jews, has become the saviour and the messiah of the Christian faith.

The differences between the two major faiths of today, Judaism and Islam, lay in the beliefs and roots of their two great leaders. For the Jewish nation that leader was Moses. For the faithful of Allah their Messiah was Mohammed, their prophet of God. For the Christians it is Jesus.

These leaders brought to their believers their interpretations of the laws, rituals, customs, punishments, will and desires of their particular god. These they have each incorporated into their individual worship and believes according to what they believes best pleases their god.

The Jews follow the laws of Moses. The Moslem faithful bow to the teachings of Mohammed and the Christians follow the teachings of Jesus according to the writings of Paul and the apostles. Each faith believe themselves to be the true believers, the blessed and the most righteously faithful of God.

The Jewish faith of today, while it is based upon the beliefs of Abraham, was established and modified by God and Moses during their forty years of control over the Israelite in the Sinai wilderness.

It is difficult to determine if the faith of the Moslem people, while it too is based on the worship and beliefs of Abraham, began with Ishmael, the first son of Abraham or with Esau, the first son of Jacob.

Whatever the source of the faith of Islam, Mohammed, their prophet of God, brought stability to their beliefs, their faith, discipline, customs, and laws.

The Christians while proclaiming the Old Testament as fundamental their faith, use the teachings of Jesus, who they claim to be their prophet and their Messiah.

Religion, no matter what the faith, is based upon moral codes, human ideals, laws, rituals, customs and teachings of men. These men, the teachers of men, claim that what they are teaching are the words, thoughts and desires of GOD.

It has been so with every religion, cult and schism since the time of Noah.

The Hebrew, Israelite or Jewish nation, what ever the name, in an effort to justify their relationship with their God and to rationalize their commitments to him, trace their relationship and their beginning to the creation of what they believe to be the beginning of the human race, the first man and woman made or created by a being they call God.

The beginning of mankind, the first man and woman, is found in the myths and legends of almost every cultures around the world. The differences between the legends lay in the manner in which the biblical couple were conceived or created.

They were all created or came into being, in some way through the power of a God or gods.

My hypothesis, simply stated, does not disagree with that assumption. Man was created by other beings but they were flesh and blood beings basically little different from man.

Their creation of man was not by magic or supernatural power but through the process of medical and scientific knowledge. Man was created through the process of cloning. We are therefore relatives to our gods by blood and DNA.

I believe in GOD the universal creator. I differ with organized religion in my interpretation of their religious writings. Those writings lead me to believe that there are actually three mythical biblical gods. One is GOD the universal creator. He or it is responsible for all of nature, the universe and creation. The second biblical being is the Lord God. He was the authority by which man was allowed to be created, not as the love of God to his power and glory but as naked slaves to serve at his whim. Then there was Jehovah. He was probably not the god worshipped by Abram but it was the god he chose out of all those available to him. He passed on to his two sons, Ishmael and Isaac his beliefs. They to worshipped Jehovah as the one true god.

Jehovah the God of the Jews and Christians was not the creator of man nor was he the Almighty power of the universe. He was nothing more than another flesh and blood life form who convinced a weak and uneducated nomad to follow and worship him. He has no divine power and could do more than what his science and medical technology allowed his to do.

Even our creator, the biblical Lord God, was not a god in the present day term of reference unless the word god is used and assumed to be the title of someone with the highest authority. If so we have no disagreement.

There can be no disagreement between religion on how man was created or how he came into being, because no religion offers us an absolute explanation other than it was by the power of God. That power was not necessarily divine or heavenly.

The hypothesis stated in this book suggests, and is supported by scripture, that mankind began not by some magical or divine power, but by the medical skills and the advanced technology of another race of beings similar to ourselves.

Mankind began in a laboratory as genetically engineered individuals, created, designed and especially made and adapted to function and survive on this particular planet. We were created out of commercial and industrial necessity, not out of the love and benevolent of any particular god.

Our creators were not gods, but aliens from another world. They came to mine the earth for its minerals but we were not their first attempt at the colonization of this planet. Our existence is a fluke. When we were created the aliens had no intention of letting us survive on this planet. It was only after the creation of Eve that mankind ordered to populate and replenish the earth.

Long before man was created and told to replenish the earth, other life forms attempted to colonize this world.

We do not know how successful those attempts might have been because geological and archaeology evidence indicates that they, like early man suffered a cataclysmic event which destroyed almost all life on the earth more than once in the geological life of this planet.

Those other life forms, which I believe were the original colonists were from the world of the aliens race of beings which create us. Evidence of history strongly indicates that they may well have suffered and gone the way of the dinosaurs, destroyed as the result of a collision between the earth and a giant asteroid. At the time of that collision there was either a shift in the earth's axis or a rotation of the earth's mantel around its core. In either case almost all life perished.

Tropical vegetation and animals found frozen in the artic tundra, along with the aligned magnetic elements in the earth's mineral support this possibility.

When the aliens returned to this planet as a mining expedition to mine for minerals they found the world devoid of intelligent life forms. They needed workers so used their medical and scientific skills to created man. We were created as naked little different from the animals to work their claims and to serve their every whim and desire.

We were created form their DNA. Therefore we are biologically, emotionally and mentally created in their image. We are a modified extension of our aliens creators, the ones we now worship as gods.

The aliens using their knowledge of genetics, created a new sub-species of themselves which was more adaptable and productive to this planets environment than their own species.

They cloned Man from their own DNA. They modified that DNA in order to give man the ability to survive in a rich oxygenated atmosphere, higher gravity and a brighter sun than the environment of their home world.

Man was created to survived on the local vegetation of this planet and on the plants and animals brought to this planet by our gods from their home world. Man was also created to be able to reproduce his own species. He was a new creature, a sub-species of the gods themselves.

In order for him to become his most productive he was taught the laws, customs, and traditions of the alien culture he was created to serve.

Mankind, for all practical purposes were slaves, pieces of property that belonged to the individual members of the alien community, which at the time of our creation, were inhabiting the earth. In order for us to be our most productive the alien gods taught us how to serve them. We were taught how to grow, prepare and serve their food. They taught man how to tend their animals herds, make thread from fibers, weave cloth and make clothes. Early man was taught to build cities for their shelter and to make and play musical instruments for their pleasure. He was also taught how tho mine for gold and other the minerals. Man was taught how to smelt the ore, refine the metal and work the metal into the things desire by the gods.

The original creation and purpose for the creation of man, was to work the mines and to serve the gods. When the gods decided to departed the earth and return to their own planet, man would no longer needed. He was to be either destroyed or left behind to survive on his own. Originally man would have creased to exists because there were no females for the perpetuation of the species. It was only as a second thought that mates were created and man allowed to procreate.

After the flood, caused by a collision with an asteroid, the mines of the gods were destroyed. Man was no longer needed to work the mines which had either been destroyed by earthquakes, collapsed, flooded or unsafe for humans.

At sometime after the flood the Lord God departed the earth. When he did he left behind a few of the members of his crew to act as the guardians of what he considered his earth property. The members he left as his representatives were those whose sexual desires and lustful appetites had persuaded them to cohabited with the daughters of men. As a result of this racial intermingling half-breed children were born. While the these children became the mighty men of old, their fathers, the gods were ostracized by the Lord God and the other crewmen of his expedition. These abandoned lustful alien fathers of the mighty men of old became the gods worshipped by the descendants of the survivors of the flood.

Jehovah was one of those gods.

After the flood, as man began to spread throughout the land, the memory of his original condition of physical servitude to the gods began to fade in his mind. As time passed, out of fear and ignorance, new ideas of service came into being. New gods began to surface. With each new creation, new rituals of worship and offers of sacrifices began to appear.

The practice of serving the masters as slaves eventually changed to become a practice of religious sacrifice and godly worship. The alien masters, who no longer walked among us became figments of our imagination. In our confused memories they changed from our lords and masters into our gods.

Prior to the flood, they ruled man for at least a thousand years. That much we believe from the biblical age of Methuselah. For a least a thousand years man served the gods. He worked the mines, smelted the ores into the metals, worked the fields, tended the herds, entertained, grew, prepared the food and served the gods. When they were not doing this they built the cities in which the gods lived.

Our ancestors were not Adam and Eve but an alien life form which came from the stars. They created us as a sub species, of themselves, out of their own genetic material. We are therefore kin to the alien and the stars from which they came.

If it had not been for the accidental disobedience of a command by the first woman, man might still be a slave. But because of that disobedience we began the long journey towards our liberation. We are the gods of tomorrow. We have yet to learn all that they knew, but in time, we shall. In time we too will travel the stars. And when we step down on distant planets we will be the gods.

Sometime after the thousand years of alien domination, the earth experienced a great catastrophe. It collided with a giant asteroid. Our alien masters knew of this impending disaster. They also knew what was going to happen as the two giant masses drew closer together.

When the asteroid entered the gravitational field of the earth, the following effects took place. Weather patterns changed and rain became continuous. There were hurricanes, typhoons, and cyclonic winds which raged across the surface of the world. As the magnetic attraction between these two masses increased, there were gigantic earthquakes, cracks appeared in the earth's surface, and gasses of all types escaped into the atmosphere. There were volcanic eruptions everywhere. Between the greenhouse effect created by the volcanic ash blown into the atmosphere, the poisonous gases, cyclonic winds, tidal waves, earthquakes, and massive flooding, it was impossible for the aliens to predict the damage that was about to take place. They were facing the death and destruction of almost all life on the planet.

The aliens, aware of what was going to happen when the collision took place, began to make the necessary preparation to salvage at least a segment of mankind along with some of the more desirable animals. In the Hebrew culture Noah and his family were the ones selected to be the nucleus of the new generation of mankind. To them God gave aid and assistance in the design and construction of a boat called an ark. Into this ark, built to survive the flood, the winds, and poison gaseous of the atmosphere, the gods, the alien commanders around the world, placed their property, both man and beasts.

In South America it was the Uros who survived on an island of reeds. In Africa it was Noah. With each race of people that survived the flood there is in their myths and legends a story of their own particular Noah.

When the collision did occur, the expected catastrophe, feared by the aliens, was not as wide spread as they had expected. If it had, than animals such as the komodo lizard, koala bear, kangaroo, and a few of the other more exotic animals located in the more remote and isolated places around the world would now be extinct.

When the collisions occurred, the earth wobbled to such an extent, that it was thrown off it's axis. Gigantic winds ripped up forests, killed animals instantly, and the shift in the earth's mantle caused an instant freeze. Such a freeze can be verified by the existence of animals found in North America, frozen solid with green vegetation, food, still in their mouths. They were apparently killed instantly. Many of the animals found had stakes, slivers of tree trunks, driven through their bodies. Tropical vegetation was found along with the frozen bodies of the animals. This has been found in the frozen north and reported in National Geographic.

There are some discrepancies noted in scripture as to who else might have survived the flood besides Noah and his family. It appears that not every one died as a result of the catastrophe. The scriptures indicate that both Abraham and his father were at least two individuals that are said to have been "on the other side of the flood" along with Noah and his family.

Noah and his family are of particular interest to the history of the Jewish people because Noah is the focal point from which their history and their religion begins. Noah was the patriarchs of three diverse groups of nations. Except for the descendants of Noah through Shem all of the other nations, even those that were related, became the "heathens" and "idolaters" despised by the Jewish God Jehovah, and therefore the Jewish people who descended from not from Abraham but from Jehovah, Isaac and Jacob.

Jehovah was not a god. He said that he would be a god to the Hebrew people but only if they agreed to obey his commands, worship and follow him. He was a governing official given his authority by the original commander of the alien expedition, the Lord God when that commander return to his home world.

Adam, Eve, and the original first humans were genetically engineered, laboratory produced individuals, clones of the aliens. They were not created nor born by natural childbirth. Natural childbirth began with Cain, Abel and the children born to man and the aliens who cavorted with earth women. The conception and birth of these children was made possible between man and alien, our gods, because both of our species were and are biologically compatible. We are therefore "kissing cousins" to the aliens who created us.

Adam was cloned from the genetic material of the unit commander, an individual with the title of God or Lord God. Eve was cloned from the red blood cells taken from the bone marrow of the rib taken from Adam.

The workers, men created after Adam, were created from the genetic DNA material taken from the individual members of the crew of the Lord God. These members, as the immediate supervisors and instructors of the people under their control, became the gods later worshipped by the people after the flood.

Adam is considered to have been the first human created. He is also believed by the Jewish people to have been the son of the Lord God. As their heritage goes back to Adam it is easy to understand why they believe themselves to be the chosen people of God himself. But their ancestry was not possible until the creation of Eve and the birth of her son Seth. Cain is not considered as a part of their heritage because he is believed to have been the son of either Lilith or of Satan and Eve and not Adam.

Once Eve was created and found to be functional, it was her DNA which was used to create the women who were created after her to be the helpmates and reproductive companions of the existing male workers. These new women were all based upon the design of Eve and were cloned from her DNA cells.

These women and the men previously created, began to biologically produce the children which became the replacements of the existing workers as the first Adams began to die of disease, accidents and old age.

Except for Cain and the workers which lived at the mines and away from the presence of the Most High God, the first humans lived, worked and served the gods in a place somewhere close to what is identified in the Bible as the "Garden of Eden." It was a place where the aliens grew their food, which according to Genesis, was *every tree that is pleasant to the sight, and good for food; the tree of life also in the midst of the garden, and the tree of knowledge of good and evil.* (Gen. 2:9)

There were a number of things unique about this garden. First, it was a place designed for beauty. It was a source of food good to eat. It had a special food considered necessary by the gods for their longevity. There was also one plant, the one they prized above all others, which when digested expanded their minds in a manner which they described as either good or evil. It was a garden planed and cultivated. It was not an act of nature conductive to the act of the Universal Creator.

I have no idea as to what plant the gods used or considered necessary for their longevity. It may have been a plant used as food or one from which they extracted certain chemicals and used in a mixture as a medical stimulant. But the plant which they called the tree of the knowledge of good and evil, I believe, was a narcotic, the coca tree, a plant from which we obtain the drug cocaine.

When Adam and Eve sampled this drug it expanded their minds and thus began man's long and turbulent journey to freedom.

I also believe that there were many gardens of Eden scattered around the world. They were the home bases of each of the different mining companies working the globe.

The Nazca lines or symbols, found in some of the most remote areas of the globe, were not only the landing sites which belonged to those companies but were also the particular design or logo of that company and identified their particular territory.

The aliens mated with the slave women under their control. This mating produced children said to be the mighty men of old; children born of sturdy earth women but with the capabilities and intelligence of their fathers, the gods. These individuals, half alien and half man, became the blue-blooded aristocracy, the rulers and kings of early times. They ruled by right, power and authority of the gods.

The kings and queens of Europe and the Emperors of Japan are among the last remaining monarchs on earth ruling by such religious edicts.

After the flood the gods appeared to be no longer interested in man and his affairs. There were no mines to operate and very few individuals left alive to govern. Because of this many of the old original gods faded into oblivion.

Later, as man increased in numbers, and began to utilize his intelligence and skills, did the gods again take notice of man. When they did they took man and began to scattered him across the face of the globe.

I think we can also assume that once man was scattered across the face of the globe his contact with the old gods diminished. As he began to adjusted to his new environment he began to create new gods appropriate to his new status and his new environment.

As he began to multiply, so too did his imagination and his sexual appetite. With this increase in his sexual appetite came an increase in the social acceptance of bizarre sexual behaviour, decadence and moral decay. These traits became an excepted facet of everyday life and eventually worked their way into the religious and sacrificial rites of the people. When these rites became too decadent, as were the rites and rituals of Sodom and Gomorrah, Jehovah decided that it was about time to again make his presence known. He appeared to Abraham and to Sarah. At that meeting, a reference is made to Isaac, a future son of Abraham.

Since Sarah was approximately ninety years old at this time and long past the age when she could conceive, then it is biologically impossible for Isaac to have been conceived in a normal male/female relationship with Abraham.

Isaac was the son of Jehovah and Sarah, rather than a son of Abraham. Jacob was the grandson of Jehovah and this gives us an explanation as to why Jehovah was given to Jacob as an inherence by the Lord God. (Deu. chapter 32.) It also helps to explain why Jehovah was said to love Jacob and recorded that they travelled to the far places together.

Deu. 32 also offers us an explanation as to why the Hebrew people, the descendants of Jacob, in bondage in Egypt, are chosen to be the vassals of Jehovah. They were his property. This chapter also explains how the Hebrews, later the Jewish nation, came to be punished for the acts of Jacob.

While Jehovah was said to have loved his grandson, Jacob ridiculed his grandfather and thereby set in motion the pain, suffering, and torment that the Jewish people have endured down through the ages as the full extent of the retribution of their god.

During a time of famine and drought Jacob and his sons moved to Egypt. For 400 years they suffering in bondage without the aid of their god. But when that god decided to become a deity worthy of notice, a god with priests, temples, servants and sacrifices, it became necessary for him to intervene in the lives of the Hebrews people.

While scriptures state that the Hebrews were freed from the yoke of Pharaoh they were not freed from the curse of their god. The punishment of Jacob's descendants began almost immediately after they had left Egypt and came under the complete control of Jehovah.

By the complete destruction of the army of Pharaoh, Jehovah guaranteed that the Hebrews would not return to Egypt. He established his control by threats, bribes and fear. To maintain that control he selected the most feared family of the twelve tribes, the family of Levi, to be his immediate servants. They became the priesthood, a body of enforcers, that had no qualms about killing, or of carrying out the laws and commandments of their new God.

Rules, laws, rituals and sacrificial procedures were laid down. Specific instructions were given. All of the above was designed to give to Jehovah the status of a god, for without these things he was merely a name mentioned in passing.

As a god without priests, temples, servants and sacrifices, he had no status. The Hebrews, the descendants of Jacob, aware of his name, were a perfect choice for the type of servitude he had in mind.

For almost 400 years the twelve tribes had observed and most likely participated in the worship service and sacrificed to some if not all of the gods of Egypt. They were at least familiar with the calf cult or they would not have demanded that Aaron create a golden calf for them to worship.

In order to obtain the allegiance worship and sacrifices of the people Jehovah had to offer them something. He offered them freedom from their bondage, a land of their own, health, long life and prosperity. In return for these promises he demanded abject obedience to all of his demands, laws and commandments. Jehovah, like Genghis Khan, began his dynasty upon the blood, death and destruction of not only the Egyptians but his own people as well. As such he became the first Godfather.

The term worship is a misnomer. It implies love and devotion. These are not terms indicated in the relationship between the Hebrews and God. Quite the opposite is true. The people were servants to the extent that they were slaves, not in physical but in mental bondage. The people gave to God and the priests according to the law, a tenth of all that they possessed. This tribute included their gold, silver, fine fabrics, animals, slaves and labour. He also demanded the very finest in food, in drink and in exotic fragrances. He demanded to be fed on plates of gold and his sanctuary covered with the finest fabrics. He even demanded that firstborn of all life was to be given or dedicated to him. Those he chose not to except were to be bought back at a price or were to be killed.

These laws became the foundation upon which the Christians base their rituals of worship, sacrifices and religious tithing.

Jehovah ruled the Hebrew nation with an iron hand. He lived the good life. To ensure the continuation of that style of living, and to ensure that the people did not rebel against him he killed his dissenters without mercy. He ruled by a fear that was so great that no one dared question his authority.

As ruthless as his authority was, his leadership of the people, through men like Moses and Joshua, did mold a nomadic people into the Jewish nation it is today.

In their march into history, those nomads, on the orders of God, slaughtered thousands of men, women, children and animals. The one exception to this edict appears to have been young girls and women who were considered virgins. They were either kept by their captors, given to the priests, or sold into slavery.

A tenth of everything that was of any worth, captured from the destroyed nations went into the coffers of God, the priests and the men who killed, and died for God.

The religious organizations of the Jewish and Christian faiths have become rich because of the tithes and tribute given by the disciples of the various faiths. These disciples justify their every action as the will of God and they have no choice but to obey his commands. That is the only way that they feel they can escape his wrath.

God promised many things to the Jewish people in return for their servitude but history relates that basically, until recently, none of those promises have ever been realized. Whatever the Jewish people have achieved they owe to their own strength of will, determination and self sacrifice. They have achieved their status as a nation not by the benevolent of God but by their own merit. In fact if the events of history are called upon to be the judge it would be found that Jehovah, true to form has tried his level best to erect one barricade after another in trying to maintain the Jewish people in a condition of servitude.

It is true that the Jewish people down through the ages have suffered greatly, but so have the people of every culture, race and nationality. They were not an exception. Their suffering was the result of their religious beliefs and the manner in which they appear to have isolated themselves within a community. Because of their unique religious beliefs and the manner in which they maintained their family and community integrity they were and are feared by those who do not understand this devotion to their god, their family and their community.

If the Jewish people feel put upon, they merely have to review their history and their relationships with their neighbours in order to understand the fear and distrust associated with their name and their religion.

In their march to Canaan, no one was more ruthless. They were without mercy.

They have inflicted as much pain and suffering on others as they them selves have received. The wheel of life and justice turns slowly but it does turn and eventually one reaps what one sows.

In all of their achievements, conflict and suffering, there is to be found the hand of God. As such, it can be argued that the concentration camps of World War II was merely another example of God's punishment of his chosen people. It was a punishment inflicted upon them for their failure to rigidly adhere to his commands.

What we are and what we become is not controlled by a god. It is what we as a person, a people, a nation and a world do that will determine the future of mankind. It seems ironic that the more the religions of the world expand, the deeper man falls into the pits of slime and degradation.

Today we have achieved the status of gods. We can duplicate life through the process of cloning. We are no longer bound to the process of natural birth for the continuation of our or any species. We have reached the stars. We have developed energies far beyond anything ever imagined by man before. We have the medical technology to replace living organs, regenerate destroyed living tissue, and we are on the verge of scientific discoveries limited only by our imagination. None of which has had anything to do with god, religion, priests, worship or sacrifices.

Once we realize that religion is nothing more than a mental crutch, an ancient relic, created out of fear, by ignorant and superstitious people, then and only then will we ever find that peace of mind and spirit that will allow us to be truly free.

Jesus said, render unto Caesar that which is Caesars' and unto God that which is God's. This, a person can do if they remember to separate the material from the spiritual.

To Caesar you obey the laws, pay your taxes, respect the rights of others and you meet your family, community and worldly obligations.

You render to God, the universal creator, that which is his, every time you find peace and harmony within yourself. Your reality is your mental state of mind which was given to mankind as a part of his creation. It came from the Creator of the universe and not from the creator of man.

We must realize that there is only one true GOD. It is an entity beyond our imagination. It rules and controls the heavenly cosmos. It is not the individuals identified in religious writings as god. To them we owe nothing except our existence. They did give us as a part of our creation some idea as to who they were.

We received a moral and civil code. It is a way by which we humans can live in peace and in harmony. It is a shame that we have forgotten how.

The servants of God strive to store for themselves treasures in heaven. Why is this supposed to be necessary when their religion teaches them that God has promised to feed, clothe and shelter all who put their faith in his promises?

The church teaches that to help a deprived person is to do the will of God. Then it is not God that is helping, but man helping man. Man therefore does not need a God if he is required to do the work of that God. When a people depend on their religion to feed, clothe and comfort themselves they become lazy, shiftless and unreliable. When the Christian speaks of God feeding the birds, what he fails to say is that the birds would starve if they did not go out and find their own food. If a man does not work in order to provide for himself and his family, then that family will stave without the charity of others.

No matter how hard a person prays, fasts, or the degree of their faith and belief in a god, without work they will suffer the hardships of the deprived.

Even hard work and obedience does not necessarily guarantee a good life.

When the children of Israel were hungry and asked their heavenly father for meat, he fed them dead and poisoned quails. He fed them death. When the Israelites were tired, hungry, thirsty, and complained to Moses and God, they were fed the bites of fiery serpents for their efforts. That was the righteousness not of a just and loving God, but an example of a very powerful and inhuman Godfather.

In time, the people Jewish people strayed from the teachings of Moses and they suffered, he sold them into slavery.

Jesus, the supposed son of God and saviour of the world, came, not to bring peace and harmony to this world, but to try and bring the people back into slavery.

Matt. 10: 34-36. *Think not that I came to send peace on earth: I came not to send peace, but a sword. For I am come to set a man at variance against his father, and the daughter against her mother, and the daughter-in-law against her mother-in- law. And a man's foes shall be they of his own household.*

Jesus merely used a different approach to obtain the desired result for Jehovah, the return of man into the condition of slavery and service to him.

The scriptures state that the children of Israel were the only families known to God. He was therefore going to punish them for their iniquities. Since the Lord God Jehovah himself stated that he has not known any families except the Israelites, then he will not seek to punish us for what we do. It also stands to reason that if Jehovah has never known anyone else but the Israelites, he cannot be the Lord God of creation, nor the God of man. He was a god to the Jewish people and to no one else. Therefore, he was not and is not a god. His religion is without substance; his priests are super salesmen, and there is no such thing as sin.

I brought you out of Egypt and out of bondage, therefore you owe me. If you do not obey me I will punish and destroy you.

Bring me your tithes and your offerings and I will reward you many fold. This is a promise that to some has never been fulfilled.

How many times have people given to the church in the belief that it was the will of God? How many times have the heavens opened up with any blessing much less one that was more than a person could bear?

The blessing was in the lesson. Do not be naive. How can you bargain with a god that does not know that you exist?

How many stupid and ridiculous things have been done in the name of God?

There were the hermits who lived in isolation. There were those who tortured and mutilated themselves in an effort to pay for sins and guilt which they had never committed. There were those who faced starvation, torture and death all in the name of God, all seeking a place in Paradise. How many people today are trying to follow the teachings of Jesus and are confusing his parables with real life and reality?

Man prays to God for help and guidance. Man prays for the healing power of Jesus, but it is man that heals man, not the God Jehovah.

The healing power in man is the power of healing given to him by the Universal Creator. It is a power that man has had since his creation.

When we were created as clones, duplicates or replicas of the Lord God, our Creator, an alien life form, we were endowed with this power. It did not come from the Lord God, nor Jehovah, but from the Universal Creator itself. It is the same with all living things up to a point.

When we cut ourselves, the cut heals itself. If we break a bone, the bone put back into place mends itself. When we eat and drink, our bodies break down the food, convert it into the fuel and materials which are absorbed, converted into energy and the building materials which are necessary for the repair and the functions of our every operation. All of this is accomplished on a subconscious level without our conscious interference. This is not the result of some mythical god. It is our will and our power. We are the gods that control our own destiny. We are what we eat and what we believe.

But, what are we?

We are really insignificant creatures in the cosmic order of things. Yet we have been led to believe that the creator of the universe, vast beyond our abilities to imagine, requires that mankind atone for the disobedience of one woman. To achieve this end, God offered up his own son as a blood sacrifice so that we might be able to purify ourselves and return to his service. Jesus is said to have been the blood sacrifice required for this marvelous event to take place. It mankind sinned why was a blood sacrifice required?

How can any man love, respect and consider worthy of worship, a being who would willing give up his son for crucifixion? If Jehovah were a true god could he not find some other way of appeasing his anger and his ego, other than watching his son be crucified? It he is willing to give up his son so easily how much faster will he be willing to sacrifice man to appease his anger and ego?

To demand a blood sacrifice, the killing of an innocent life, just to see a demonstration of a willingness to obey, serve and worship, is the very height of evil megalomania. It is a clear example of the maniacal thinking of Jehovah, the God followed by the Jews and Christians.

There appears to be very little difference between the sacrificial rituals specified in scripture and demanded by the God of the Jews, with those of the Satanic rites cults. They both demand bloody sacrifices. Under both rituals, the sacrifices are given to appease a God, to obtain power, forgiveness and to control the worshippers in attendance. The only difference that I can perceive between the two rituals is the rationale behind the practice. One group claims to offer their dead to a god of good and the other to a god of evil.

The killing, according to scripture, must be done in a prescribed manner in order to demonstrate a devotion of faith and belief in that particular god.

The religions of the world are the organizations in which the forces of good and evil gather together the forces which each believe will be required to do battle in the last days before the end of the world as we perceive it to be.

The disciples of both armies believe that their god will deliver them into a promised land of paradise somewhere in heaven. There, their every dream will be fulfilled. There will be power and glory, no suffering, tears, and pain. There will be only everlasting joy and peace. Only their religious text clearly states that the kingdom of this mythical god will be right here on this earth, and it will not last forever. It has been predicted that one day the sun will burn out, and the everlasting kingdom of god will cease to exist.

Religious disciples are slaves who delight in declaring their love and devotion to their master. For their proclamations of love and devotion they expect a place in paradise. This is to be their reward for the sacrifices and suffering which they experienced here on earth. For those who do not believe, proclaim and serve, they are doomed to suffer the wrath of their God. They are to be given to the god of evil to do with as he pleases.

Satan in his wrath for having been defeated by Jehovah will make all who enter into his kingdom suffer the pain and torment of the fires of hell and damnation for all eternity.

Those individuals which will be alive in the last days, whenever that occurs, will be those who will fight the final conflict for the possession of the earth, Revelation gives us a clue as to what they can expect from their gods, Jehovah and Satan.

If Revelation is a true prediction, there will be nothing but blood, destruction, pain and suffering until there is a winner. No matter which god is victorious, man will be the ultimate loser. He will once again be a slave, waiting for the beck and call of his lord and master. Revelation need not come true. There is an alternative for man, but it is only possible if and when man realizes that the control of his own destiny lies with his actions and not with the spiritual aspirations of religion.

Only when man comes to realizes his own god-like potential and becomes a god himself will he take his first step towards true freedom. To do this he must rid himself of the idea that he cannot exist without a god. Even then he may not be strong enough to withstand the forces of mental indoctrination implanted into his mind for thousands of years through the repetitious   religious practices and beliefs. But man must at least try.

It has been said that rain fall equally on both the good and evil, the rich and poor like. Blessings are given to both. Pain, suffering and death comes to all men. Where is the reward or the punishment for obedience or for disobedience?

If there is a god and he deals equally with all men, how can there be a salvation, a heaven or a hell? If a man is believed evil, it is said that he has sold his soul to Satan for an earthly reward. But, if a man sells his soul to God for a promise of heavenly paradise he knows nothing about he is said to be a saint.

If a man sell his soul to either god it is the same no matter who the buyer might be. The seller is hoping to gain some reward in exchange for his soul and his freedom.

In the olden days prophets and disciples were rewarded for their beliefs and dedication to God with prison, persecution and death. Today our electronic servants of God have vast empires. They live in the lap of luxury, reaping the rewards previously reserved for ruler, kings and High Priests.

Once I came to believe that there was, in reality, no god except the Universal Creator, I came to see religion as a hoax and the servants of God as super salesmen trying to sell me an insurance policy to a heavenly paradise which no one has ever seen and cannot be verified.

For the first time in my life I felt that I could do something or nothing without a feeling of guilt or remorse. There was no need for me to feel guilty for failing to feed, clothe and suffer along with the poor, needy and the deprived just because I had obtained what they denied themselves by passing up the opportunities to be the best that they could be.

I became my own high priest. I could talk to my own God. I could forgive my own sins and I came to know peace within myself. No man can ask for anymore out of life. I have reached a point in my journey of life beyond which I no longer care or need to go. I have found my inner peace. My heaven has opened up and I have received my blessings. I hope that the reader shall someday find and receive theirs.

"Jehovah, The First Godfather," was written in order to put into proper perspective the religious similarities of the people of this world; a perspective that may someday reduce much of the violence, killing and destruction of men, women and children of all faiths due to the differences in their religious beliefs. In time, the realizations of the beginning of man, the reality of God and the subterfuge of religious beliefs, may one day manifest itself into changes in the customs, political, religious beliefs, and practices of people everywhere. When this happens, the shedding of innocent blood, because of misplaced religious beliefs, will end.

The religions of the world are based on false and misleading premises. The primary premise being that man was created by an almighty entity to be the supreme life form within the universe. Second that man was so important to that supreme creator that he or it abandoned the glories of the universe in order to reside with man upon this planet.

I present my theory so the reader, of whatever religious, or political philosophy based on religious principals, so that they might be given an alternative point of view; a new perspective upon which they might base their future lives, religious hopes and material dreams.

The reader has every right to believe or not to believe what is written here. That, of course, is their prerogative. But, while the reader may not choose to believe the interpretations and explanations which I have given, the words of the bible speak for themselves. The reader need only review what is said from the church pulpit in the light of the above perspective to realize that the words of the Bible leave much to be desired. If the doctrines preached by the various religions are true, than our souls were a part of the beginning creation; as such, we can never die. We shall exist until the end of time whether we believe in a god or not. It does not matter.

Like all matter (dust or elements) we never cease to exist but merely change from one form to another. Whether we will do this in a conscious form or not is the big question. If we no longer have a consciousness, there is no reality. If there is no reality there is no way to ever determine if there ever was a heavenly kingdom and/or a godly salvation.

Medical science has indicated that every cell of the human body is a hologram of the entire DNA of an individual. It is a complete record of every thought, action, feeling and learning experience up to that moment when a single cell is removed from its host.

Every cell in our bodies is a micro recording device. It is believed that somehow every bit of the above information, past and present is stored in the DNA molecule waiting to be recalled. This information also includes all of the information passed down to us from our ancestors from one generation to the next. Each of us as individuals are the sum total of all of our ancestors, from both our father and mother who have gone before us. We in turn pass this heritage to our children who will pass it on to their until the line runs out or time ceases to exist.

Our DNA is a recording and only time and technology will determine if medical science will ever devise a machine/ computer that will be able to decipher or decode the information stored within our cells and DNA codes. We are living computers.

If I am a culmination of all those who have gone before me, then by the same token I shall also be a part of all of my descendants who shall come after me. My immortality comes not from God but from my children, their children and their children down through time, until they cease to exist. As long as my children continue to reproduce offspring I shall continue to exist. I will be for all practical purposes immortal. I will not realize this of course but I at least know it now.

Science may alter the DNA of a human cell in order to create a new individual designed to meet certain specifications for tomorrow. But the basic traits characterises, thoughts, feelings and emotions will still be encoded somewhere with the new creation. This was the flaw overlooked by the gods when they cloned Adam, Eve, and early man. It was a flaw which allowed Eve to bypass her initial programming and to disobey the Lord God her master. Even this is not necessarily true. Satan was a god to Eve. If she were given a command by him or he expressed a desire for her to eat from the tree of knowledge she did not disobey the orders of the Lord God. The Lord God erred when he failed to instruct her in which gods she was or was not to obey.

The desire for knowledge, was a part of the cell structure of the Lord God, therefore it was also a part of the need and physical makeup of all the humans cloned by the Lord God.

As scientists continue to splice, mold and alter the genetic structure of a living cell, there will undoubtably be some valuable aspects of that particular species which will be lost in the transition. But there is also the very real possibility that the essence of a species will continue to exist.

As man evolves and moves forward into the future, science will one day discover the mental block, decoding device placed within the mind of man which shall remove the "flaming sword which turns every way, to keep the way of the tree of life." It will be a time when man shall be able to understand and utilize, not just a small portion of his brain and mental abilities, but enjoy, realize, and utilize his full mental potential. Then nothing shall be beyond his abilities. Man will truly become a god.

The bible says that the sins of the parents are passed down to their children even to the seventh generation. How is all of this possible if it is not accomplished through the genetic makeup of each child as it is conceived?

An alcoholic or drug addicted parent will produce an alcoholic or drug addicted child. A parent which has contacted a disease whether through promiscuity or by accident, will instill in their descendants either the disease or the effects of that disease.

Happiness is a state of mind. Peace within oneself is a state of mind. Both can be achieved without a god.

A man at peace within himself has no need of a God or a Godfather. It is important that the reader ask himself several questions in light of the hypothesis outlined in this book.

Why is it that man continues to believe that everything that is wrong with man here on earth will be made perfect in heaven?

How does a man who finds the daily routine of life here on earth dull and monotonous come to believe that the exact opposite will be true in heaven?

How does a man come to believe that everything he hates or despises on earth will change and bring him joy and happiness once he reaches heaven?

Religions teach man that all of the hate, prejudice, and bigotry he encounters on earth will disappear and is not allowed in heaven. There every man will love his brother. Every wrong will be made right. All will be forgiven and each man will be able to embrace those he is killing today. All will be forgiven and we, like the lion and the lamb, will lay down together.

That will be true because we will all be slaves, programmed and conditioned to wait upon and serve the gods. As robots we will not be allowed to do anything else except obey the commands of God in order to continue to exist in what we are told will be paradise.

Heaven has been made to sound like a paradise. It may look and sound good coming from the church pulpit but the nature of the creation which is all around us tells a different story.

If I am wrong and there is a heaven, what will the saved do with the treasures they believe are stored there? Who are they going to compare their riches with? And what will a person do with one room full of precious gems compared to someone who has two rooms? How will a person use those precious stones if everybody has everything that they will ever need or want? Will these treasures bring joy and pleasure, buy what one does not have or will it entice someone with less into corruption so that they might acquire more?

If some are going to have more than others, what are they going to do with it? Lord it over the poor and the have me nots? Is heaven going to be another earth? According to Revelation, the answer is yes.

According to Revelation mankind and the earth will be ruled by a race of beings old before mankind existed. These are the gods of man made even more powerful by religion. They are flesh and blood beings with the same needs, wants and lusts as man, the people which they have created and want to control.

Mankind has been duped into believing in religion and gods because of the lies, half truths, myths and legends, generated by the priests and followers of these created gods.

Mankind in his efforts to reach the stars has indicated his desire to return to the heavens from which our creators and our ancestors came. We yearn for the glory, adventure, excitement and the riches that was once reserved for the gods.

As we begin our exploration of the stars we might do well to review the laws and the commandments given to us by those same gods, our ancestors. Those laws, rules and regulations may well apply, and observed by all intelligent life throughout the galaxies. We would do well to remember that life is life wherever it may be found and the punishment for violating its laws and regulation may well be permanent annihilation.

Most people acquaint the "Ten Commandments" with the laws of God, Moses and the Hebrew people. But those laws may be universal and apply to intelligent life throughout the inhabited planets. To break any one of them would in most cases be considered a criminal act and a violation of the law against society and the civil code of a community.

To observe or to break those laws in space may carry a far greater responsibility and penalty.

The "Ten Commandments" along with the other laws found in the first five books of the bible were given to the Jewish people only and not to the Gentiles. It must also be remembered that those same laws had their roots in the laws of Hammurabi, given to the people, many decades before the Hebrews ever left Egypt. These laws appear to be universal in their concept.

Jehovah gave the Hebrews a set of civil laws and moral codes. The Hebrews included those laws and codes into their religion and their worship of their god. For them to commit a trespass against any one of those laws is considered a sin because it is a religious edict.

But if there is no god then there is no divine law. If there is no divine law to break then there is no sin for breaking what does not exist. If a man does not sin then there is no guilt. If there is no guilt then a man does not have to worry about saving his soul from hell fire and damnation which also does not exist. If there is no hell and damnation, then sacrifices made in the name of a god and the worship of a god which does not exist is an effort in futility.

Man is in his embryonic state. He is a god in his infancy. In time, as he grows to maturity, he will master the stars looking for other worlds to conquer. He will bring with him his technology, medical and mechanical devices. He will conquer and colonize new worlds. It is possible that on some of those worlds where life might be difficult for man to survive, he might clone genetic duplicates of himself to seed that world. The new beings, cloned from man, will be genetically designed and adapted to survive on this new world. These clones will be made in the image of their God now called man.

In all of life we are only what we make of ourselves. We need no gods, priests or religions on which to lay the blame for our failures and our short comings.

When each and every person is taught that the greatest good for the greatest number is achieved when each and every person strives to help the other to advance and to reach their greatest potential, then and only then will mankind begin to realize his true potential.

Jehovah and the biblical Satan rely on fear, superstitions and promises which cater to the greed and lust of man.

They are not gods in the sense that they are endowed with divine power. They are flesh and blood beings with limited power and control. We obey their laws, belong to their religious organization, follow their priest, and believe in their divinity out of the fear of death and eternal punishment.

We are and have been conditioned to these facets of life because of our beginning as slaves to the gods. They need this control in order for man to serve their needs and to accomplish their desires.

Is Jehovah, the Jewish God of the Torah, a reality or a figment of the past?

He is a god today only because the Jewish people still choose to believe that he exists.

The reality of the existence of any god, Jehovah for instance, is only as strong as the beliefs of the next generation. Should they choose to believe in or to follow a different god than the belief in Jehovah will begin to fade and in time cease to exist.

The Christian believer, said to follow the teachings of Christ, place their utmost trust in the teachings and letters of an apostle named Paul. He was a butcher and a man possessed until he is said to have been converted by a flash of blinding light, a sunstroke, on the road to Damascus. By his conversion and by his efforts as a super salesman and publicity agent for a man called Jesus, a cult became a full fledged religion. A Jesus cult was born. As a result of their influence around the world the whole of mankind has suffered and endured an enormous amount of bloodshed, sweat, tears, heartbreak and misery.

The suffering and misery of man will not go away as long as he continues to believe in mythical gods and follow religions based on the imagination and superstitions of man.

In the book of Jeremiah God is said to have told the people that there would come a day when he would write a new covenant, forgive the iniquity of man and remember his sins no more. If this is true, why does the religious disciple still believe that there is a book of life recording all that he does in order for him to be judged? If the sins of man who believes in the reality of Jehovah, has been forgiven and forgotten for what is he to be judged, and by whom?

Also the true believer is told to lay up the words of God within his heart, and bind them upon his hand and fix them as an emblem on his forehead. Mark your hands and your forehead. The Biblical God required the same signs as those required by the beast of Revelation. Are these two one and the same?

Those who bear the mark of Jehovah in their hands and on their forehead, are they the servants of the God Jehovah or the image of the beast, the God Satan? Is the beast Satan or is he the Lord God?

According to the scriptures of Revelation and the teachings of the church, the God Jehovah, is by his own words, the beast.

Both the Jews and the Christians have for the past two thousand years been worshipping evil. This helps to explain the reason for all of the bloodshed, death, murder, corruption and suffering that is so vital a part of the worship of this deity and the result of his worship.

Rev. 13:18. *Here is wisdom. Let him that hath understanding count the number of the beast: for it is the number of a man; and his number is Six hundred threescore and six."*

If this is the number of man and man is a clone of God, then it is also the number of God.

When God says that he will make a new covenant with the house of Israel and of Judah, how many more covenants will he make before the time of retribution? And what will happen to those who have lived, served and died under the old?

"Jehovah, The First Godfather", is not only about the evil and falseness of the biblical god, his religion and his servants, it is also a positive denial of his divinity. It is an expose of religion, and a realistic look at those who serve the church in the name of God.

The God Jehovah was no different than the Godfathers of today.

Both control by fear and the power of greed.

Nowhere is there anything more than a sketchy record of evidence that indicates that God ever kept any promise that he ever made. There is no evidence that his followers every lived in peace and in harmony. In fact the very opposite seems to be true.

The Jewish people have been persecuted in wars and tormented by political, mental and physical slavery for almost all of their history. They have followed Jehovah. But where is the joy, the happiness, the health, peace and prosperity so often promised them by their God?

To follow God in the manner in which he demands is to be a slave in one form or the other throughout one's life.

In the beginning of creation there was the divine creator. It was not the Gods Jehovah and Satan. They are what man has become, bloodthirsty, greedy and paranoid.

In order for man to advance as a species we must forget the worship of idols and false gods. We must look to ourselves and our own humanity. We must overcome the godlike traits of lust and power and rise above the levels that we call the plateau of the gods. It is only then that we will assure for ourselves and our children a home among the stars.

Man does not need the gods to exist but the gods need man if they are to be gods. Without man and his worship the gods are nothing more than mortal beings. They take on the crowns of power and glory only when they are worshipped by men.

Mankind worships the gods because he fear them and because he fears himself.

We were created to be complete within ourselves. We reproduce our own species and we are basically no different than the animals around us who have no god. Like the animals, we survive by our own efforts. If we fail to work we starve. If we do not find shelter from the weather we die from exposure, either from rain, the heat or the cold. When we die we both return to dust. Is there really any difference between us? Man needs nothing beyond food, air, water and shelter to survive. He does not need the gods as much as the gods need man.

Gods are for our imagination. They protect us from the storms of life. They are the strength that we use to ward off the fears of the night and the days of sufferings which we do not understand. Gods are the source we use to declare our success and the object of our curses for the reasons of our failures.

Gods like Jehovah and Satan are our imagination. They are not our reality.

Jehovah and his band of angels were our blessing, our curses, our ancestors and our past. They were not and are not our present and our future.

We owe to the race of the Lord God our gratitude only because they created us, for without them we would not exist. But in our gratitude we must also remember under what conditions and circumstances that our creation occurred.

Our gods walked among us. They ate, drank and ruled with an iron hand. They gave us our laws, began our culture and our industries.

They put us onto the long evolutionary road to the stars, where someday we shall meet.

How we will react to that encounter will depend upon our frame of mind at the time of that meeting. Will we be servants or a race willing to stand before a race of beings old before we were born and say we are no longer children.

We will be like the prodigal son, we will have returned to the cosmos to claim our right to exist among the stars. We are the gods of the future. We shall bring forth new worlds and new creations. They will meet our needs and our desires among the stars.

I believe in the universal creator, it is my God. It has no name nor any organized religion. It requires no worship, no sacrifices and no rituals. It is sufficient unto itself. It is that power and intelligence that is responsible for the action, reaction and inner action of all that exists. I worship my God whenever I am at peace within myself and at harmony with all that exists around me.

Whenever I am in harmony within myself, my family, and my surroundings, I know an inner glow, a peace that comes with an understanding that brings meaning into my existence. I am one with the universe and therefore one with my God.

It is at those time that I honour my creator. And it is at those times that I find I am the most blessed.

May this book and the ideas contained within be the beginning, the first step towards inner peace.

It is a step upon a path which I believe will, in time, help each reader to find their own creator as I was able to find mine. If they are as fortunate it will help to reduce or eliminate at least some of the mental guilt and anguish which has been generated down through the years by false and misleading religious ideas, dogma and doctrine. With the removal of religious guilt the reader is sure to find their own peace of mind and universal harmony.

It is hoped that the lives of all of mankind may someday be rich in the spirit from which all blessings flow. That is the goal of the author and the purpose of this book.

Amen.